Ernest Griset

Little Wide Awake

An illustrated magazine for good children

Ernest Griset

Little Wide Awake
An illustrated magazine for good children

ISBN/EAN: 9783744657303

Printed in Europe, USA, Canada, Australia, Japan

Cover: Foto ©Suzi / pixelio.de

More available books at **www.hansebooks.com**

LITTLE MISS PATTY.

FROM A DRAWING BY KATE GREENAWAY.

AN ILLUSTRATED MAGAZINE FOR GOOD CHILDREN

EDITED BY

MRS. SALE BARKER

ILLUSTRATED BY
HARRISON WEIR, ELLEN STAPLES, M. KERNS, A. T. ELWES, FRANK DADD,
AND OTHERS.

LONDON
GEORGE ROUTLEDGE AND SONS
BROADWAY, LUDGATE HILL
NEW YORK: 416 BROOME STREET
1880

MONTHLY MAGAZINES FOR
THE HOUSEHOLD.

London: R. Clay, Sons, and Taylor, Printers.

CONTENTS

iii

Contents.

LITTLE MISS PATTY.

BY THE EDITOR.

A GREAT big bonnet, a large white frill,
A little round face just the bonnet to fill.
    Little Miss Patty!

Blue solemn eyes, looking now very grave,
With a clear bright gaze in them, honest and brave.
    Little Miss Patty!

Strange wee woman, from whence do you come?
What time did you live in, where is your home?
    Queer little Patty!

Your little black bag, and your very long clothes,
Hanging down in straight lines, just escaping your toes,
    Prim little Patty!

All tell a tale of a long time ago—
A time when our grandmothers all were dressed so.
    Ancient Miss Patty!

Ah, can it be true that your hair has turned white,
That the bright days of childhood have changed into night?
    Poor little Patty!

Your dress tells a tale that your life is all done,
Your sweet rosy face says 'tis only begun.
    Fair little Patty!

I'd rather by far believe it the last;
Look into the future, not dream of the past.
    Dear little Patty!

Bright days are coming, they're not left behind:
That you've work in the world, I'm sure you will find.
    Brave little Patty!

'Tis the dress that's untrue, not the sweet little face,
The child now exists, full of life and wild grace.
    Not a stiff little Patty!

You've put on that dress, and straightened your limbs,
For the sake of the picture and artistic whims.
    Pretty small Patty!

Yet we'll not call it whim, but fancy, or taste;
I just wrote the word down rather in haste.
    Forgive me, dear Patty!

'Tis a quaint pretty picture, we all must agree,
Of a dear little model, whoever she be.
    Little Miss Patty!

1

HOODIE.

By Mrs. MOLESWORTH, *Author of " The Cuckoo Clock," &c.*

" What makes the lamb love Mary so ? "
The little children cry.
" Why, Mary loves the lamb, you know,"
The teacher did reply.

CHAPTER I.—AT WAR WITH THE WORLD.

" Who would think so small a thing
Could make so great a pother ? "

PRETTY, cheerful nursery—a nursery in which surely children could not but be happy—with pictures on the walls and toys in the glass-doored cupboard, and rocking - horse and doll-house, and everything a child's heart could wish for. Spring sunshine faint but clear, like the first pale primrose, peeping in at the window, a merry fire crackling away in the tidy hearth. And just in front of it, for it is early spring only, a group of children pleasant to see. A soft-haired, quiet-eyed little girl, a book open on her knee, and at each side, nestling in beside her, a cherub-faced dot of a boy, listening to the story she was reading aloud.

Such a peaceful, pretty picture ! Ah yes—what a pity to disturb it. But I must show you the whole of it. Into this pretty nursery flies another child—a tiny fairy of a girl, tiny even for her years which are but five—in she flies, down the long passage which leads to the children's quarters, in at the nursery door, which, in spite of her hurry she carefully closes, and seeing that the other door is open closes it too, then, flying back to the centre of the room, deliberately sets to work to—children can you guess ?—to *scream !*

She sheds no tears, there is no grief, only wrath, great and furious, in the little face which should have been so pretty, in the big blue eyes which should have been so sweet. She shakes herself till her fair, fluffy hair is all

in a " touzle," she dances with rage till her neck and arms are crimson, from time to time in the middle of her screams calling out at the pitch of her voice,

" I don't love *any* body. I don't want *any* sing. I don't like *any* sing. Go away ugly everybody. I don't love Prince. Go away ugly Prince."

The girl by the fire looked up for a moment. " Prince isn't here," she said. " Oh Hoodie, she went on wearily, " how *can* you—how can you be so naughty ? "

Hoodie turned towards her sister.

" I don't love *you*, Maudie. Naughty, ugly Maudie. Prince *sall* be here. Naughty Maudie. I *sall* be naughty. I don't love *any* body."

" Nebber mind, Maudie dear, nebber mind naughty Hoodie. Hoodie's always naughty. Please go on Maudie," said one of the two little boys.

Magdalen tried to go on. But in the midst of such a din, it was very difficult to make herself heard, and at last she gave up in despair.

" It's no good, Hec," she said, " I can't go on. Hoodie spoils everything when she gets like that."

The little fellows' faces lengthened.

" Hoodie 'poils oberysing," they murmured.

Just then the door opened.

" Miss Hoodie," said the maid who came in, " Miss Hoodie again ! And Sunday morning too —the day you should be extra good."

" She's nearly always extra naughty," said Magdalen, with the superiority of eight years old. " It's no good speaking to her, Martin. She's going to go on—she shut the doors first."

Martin seated herself composedly beside the three children.

" I never did see such a child," she said ; " no, never. You would think, Miss Maudie, she might stop if she liked, seeing how she

2

can keep it in like, as long as she's afraid of her Mamma hearing. If she can keep it in till she shuts the doors, she might keep it in altogether, you would think."

"Stop! of course she can stop if she likes," said Magdalen. "What was it set her off, Martin, do you know?"

"Something about Prince," replied Martin. "Thomas said she was trying to get him to come up stairs with her, and he whistled to him, not knowing, and Prince ran away from her."

"Hoodie's keeped all her biscuits for Prince, for a treat for him for Sunday," said little Hec, with some evident sympathy for Hoodie.

"She shouldn't be so silly then," said Maudie. "What do dogs know about its being Sunday, and treats? I know Hoodie always spoils *our* Sundays, and we're better than dogs."

"I don't love you, naughty Maudie. I don't love *any* body," screamed Hoodie.

"It certainly doesn't look as if you did, and very soon nobody will love you, Miss Hoodie, if you go on so," said Martin, virtuously.

"I wish," said Duke, the second twin, "I wish papa would build anoder *gate* big house and put Hoodie to live there all alone, don't you Maudie? A gate big house where not nobody could hear her scaiming."

Great applause followed this brilliant idea—but the laughter only increased Hoodie's fury. Duke was the next she turned upon.

"I don't love you, naughty, ugly Duke," she screamed. "I don't love *any* body. Go away evybody, go away, go *away*, go AWAY."

Such was Hoodie—poor Hoodie—at five years old!

What had made her so naughty? That was the question that puzzled everybody concerned—not forgetting Hoodie herself.

"I didn't make myself. 'Tisn't my fault. God should have made Hoodie gooder," she would say defiantly.

And was it not a puzzle? There was Maudie, just as nice and good a little girl as one would wish to see, and Hec and Duke, both comfortable, good-natured little fellows—all three, children to whom things came right, and whose presence in the world seemed as natural and pleasant a thing as that of birds in the trees or daisies in the grass. Why should not Hoodie

3

be like them? She was born in July—one bright sunny day when all the world was rejoicing—and little Maudie had been so pleased to have a baby sister, and her godmother had begged that she might be called "Julian" and everybody had, for a time, made much of her. But alas, as the years went on, they told a different tale—governesses and nurses, sister and brothers, it was the same story with all—Hoodie's temper was the strangest and the worst that ever a child had made herself and other people miserable by.

"I could really fancy," said Maudie one day, "I could really fancy, if there *were* such things as fairies, you know—that one of them had been offended at not being asked to Hoodie's christening."

And when Hoodie grew old enough to hear fairy tales, this speech of Maudie's came back to her mind and she wondered, with the strange unexpressed bewilderment of a child, if indeed there were some mystery about her naughtiness—some spell cast upon her which it was hopeless to try to break. For she knew she was naughty, very naughty—she never thought of denying it. Only deep down *somewhere* in her—where, she could not have told—there was a feeling that she did not *want* to be naughty—she did not *like* being naughty—there was a mistake about her somehow or somewhere, which nobody could understand or ever would, and which it never entered her head to try to explain to any one.

The screaming went on steadily—agreeably for Hoodie herself, it is to be hoped, for it certainly was anything but pleasant for other people. Suddenly there came a lull—a step was heard coming along the passage, and light as it was, Hoodie's quick ears were the first to hear it. It was mother!

Hoodie's power of self-control was really very great—her screams ceased entirely, only, as her fury had this time been *very* great even for her, it had naturally arrived at tears and sobs, and in consequence she was not able all at once to stifle the sobs that shook her, or even by scrubbing at her poor eyes with all her might, with a rather grimy little ball which she called her "pocket-hankerwich," could she succeed in destroying all traces of the storm.

She ran over to the window and stood with her back to the door, staring, or pretending to stare, down at the pretty garden beds, gay with crocuses and snowdrops. But mother's eyes were not to be so easily deceived. One glance at the peaceful, though subdued group round the fireplace, one anxious look at the little figure standing solitary by the window, its fat dimpled shoulders convulsively heaving every moment or two, its face resolutely turned away, and mother knew all.

"What is wrong with Miss Julian?" she asked.

"Really ma'am I can't quite say. I was down stairs and when I came back she was in one of her ways, and you know, ma'am, it is no use speaking to her while she's like that. It was just some trifle about Prince, but if it wasn't that it would be something else."

Martin's tone was slightly querulous, but Mrs. Caryll could not resent it. Martin as a rule was so good and patient with the children, and with the other three—Maudie and the boys—there was never a shadow of trouble. Even to Hoodie she was really kind, and though sometimes it did seem as if she did not take what is called "quite the right way with her," it would hardly have been fair to blame her for that, seeing that this mysterious right way in Hoodie's case, was quite as great a puzzle as the passage round the North Pole! So great a puzzle indeed that its very existence had come to be doubted, for hitherto one thing only about it was certain—no one had ever succeeded in finding it.

On the whole, mother herself managed Hoodie better than any one else, but that, I fear, is not saying much. For whenever, after a long talk and many tears, Mrs. Caryll left the nursery with a somewhat lightened heart, thinking that for some time to come at least there was going to be peace, she was almost *sure* to be disappointed. Generally these very times were followed by the worst outbreaks, and in despair Mrs. Caryll would leave off talks and gentle measures and simply lock the aggravating little girl into her bedroom, whence in a few hours, the fit having at last worked itself off, Hoodie would emerge. silent indeed but *so* cross, so unbearably irritable, that no

4

one in the nursery dared look at her, much less speak to her, till a night's rest had to some extent soothed her down.

It really seemed as if, as Martin said, there was nothing to do but leave her to herself, and it was with a terror of making things worse that Hoodie's mother now stood and looked at her, asking herself what *would* be best to do.

"Perhaps it would have been better," she said to herself, "if I had taken no notice of anything wrong," for she believed that Hoodie's intense mortification at *mother's* knowing of her naughtiness was what gave her more influence over her than any one else. But it was not quite the kind of influence she most cared to have—mortification, to my thinking, never does any one any good, but only fosters the evil *roots* from whence all these troubles spring. "If Hoodie cared about my knowing for fear of it grieving me, I would understand better how to manage her," thought Mrs. Caryll. "But if it were so she would show her sorrow in a different way. It is her pride, not her love that is concerned."

She was right, but wrong too. Hoodie was proud, but also intensely loving. She did grieve in her own wild, unreasonable way, at distressing her mother, but most of all she grieved that *she* should be the cause of it. It would have made her sorry for mother to be grieved by Maudie or the boys, but still that would have been different. It was the misery of believing herself to be always the cause of the unhappiness that seemed to come back and back upon her, making the very time at which she was "sorriest," the time at which it was hardest to be good.

Hoodie's mother stood and considered. Then she crossed the room and touched her little girl on the neck. The bare white dumpling of a shoulder just "shruggled itself up" a little higher, but Hoodie gave no other sign of having felt anything.

"Hoodie," said her mother.

No reply.

"*Hoodie*," a little louder.

Hoodie *had* to look round. What a face! Red eyes, tangled hair, frowning forehead, tight shut lips. No, the good angels had not yet 'found their way back to Hoodie's heart—the little black dog was still curled up on her back, scowling at every one that came near.

"Hoodie," said her mother very quietly, "come with me to my room."

Hoodie did not resist. She allowed her mother to take her hand and lead her away. As the door closed after them Maudie gave a sigh of relief.

"Let's go on with our reading as long as we can," she said. "Hoodie will be worse than

ever after she comes back. As soon as ever mother has gone down again and she thinks she won't hear, she'll begin again. Won't she, Martin?"

"She often is like that," said Martin, "but perhaps she'll be better to-day. Go on reading,

5

Miss Maudie, and take no notice of her when she comes in."

In about ten minutes the door opened and Hoodie appeared. She marched in with a half defiant air—evidently "humble-pie" had at present no attraction for her. No one took any notice of her. This did not suit Hoodie. She dragged her little chair across the room and placed it beside her sister's.

"Doin' to be dood," she announced.

"I'm glad to hear it, Miss Hoodie," said Martin.

"Doin' to be dood. Maudie, litsen," said Hoodie impatiently, giving Magdalen's chair a jerk, "doin' to be *dood.*"

"Very well, Hoodie, only please don't pull my chair," said Maudie, in some fear and trembling.

"You're not to read, you're to litsen when I speak," said Hoodie, "and I will pull your chair, if I like. I love mother, don't love *you*, Maudie, ugly sing that you is."

Maudie did not answer. She glanced up at Martin for advice.

"Well, Miss Maudie," said Martin cheerfully, "aren't you going on with your story?"

"It's done, Martin, you forget," said Maudie.

Martin gave her a glance which Maudie understood. "Say something to take off her attention," was the interpretation of it.

"I'll look for another. Don't run away, Hec and Duke," said the elder sister quickly. "I am afraid there is nothing in this book but what we have read lots of times," she added, after turning over the leaves for a minute or two. "I wish it was somebody's birthday soon, and then we'd get some new stories."

"My birthday next," observed Hoodie, complacently.

"No Hoodie, 'tisn't," exclaimed both the boys, "'tisn't your birthday nextest. 'Tis ours. Aren't it now, Martin? You told us."

"Yes, dears, it is yours next. In June, Miss Hoodie dear, is theirs, you know, and yours won't be till July."

Martin made the statement gingerly. She was uncommonly afraid of what she might be drawing on herself by her venturing to disagree with the small autocrat of the nursery. To her surprise Hoodie took the information philosophically, relieving her feelings only by a piece of biting satire.

"That's acos the months is wrong. When *I* make the months they will come 'July, June,' not 'June, July,'" she said.

Hec and Duke thought this so original that they began laughing. A doubtful expression crept over Hoodie's face. Should she resent it, or laugh with them? Martin took the bull by the horns.

"Shall I tell you a story, my dears?" she said, "of what I once did on one of my birthdays when I was little? It came into my mind the other day, and I wonder I never told it you before, for it's something like the story of 'Little Red Riding Hood,' that Miss Hoodie got her name from."

"No, no, Martin. Hoodie didn't get her name from that," said Maudie eagerly. "It was this way. Mother got her a little hood *like* Red Riding Hood's in our picture—only it was pink and not scarlet, and Hoodie liked it so, she screamed when they took it off, and once she was ill and she screamed so for it that they had to put it on her even in bed, and she had it on three days running."

"Zee days zunning," repeated Hoodie, nodding her head with great satisfaction. She was evidently very proud of this legend of her infancy.

"Dear me!" said Martin, "that was a funny fancy, to be sure. But the hood wouldn't be so pretty after that."

"No of course," said Maudie. "It was all crumpled up and spoilt. And mamma got her a new one, but Hoodie wouldn't have it on, and so after that she didn't have hoods any more, only she was always called Hoodie."

"Always called Hoodie," reiterated the heroine of this remarkable anecdote, quite restored to good humour by finding herself looked upon as a historical character.

"And now, Martin, what did you do on your birthday?" said Magdalen.

"It was when I was eight," said Martin. "We lived in the country and we had a nice little farm. My father managed the farm and my mother had the dairy. And my old grandmother lived about three miles off in a little cottage near a wood—that was one thing that made me say it was like Red Riding Hood. I was very fond of going to see my grandmother, and I always counted it one of my treats. So the day before my birthday mother said to me, 'Janie, you shall go to your grandmother's to-morrow, if you like, as it is your birthday, and

I'll pack a little basket for you to take to her, with some fresh eggs and butter. And I'll make a little cake for you to take too, and you shall stay to tea with her and have the cake to eat.'"

"Had it pums in?" said Hec.

"And laisins?" added Duke.

"Silly boy," said Hoodie from the elevation of her five years, "pums *is* laisins."

"Oh," said Duke submissively.

"Do on, Martin, do on, kick, kick, Martin," said Hoodie "gee-up-ping" on her footstool as if Martin was a lazy horse she was trying to make go faster.

"Well," continued Martin, "I was pleased to go as you can fancy, and the next afternoon off I set. It was such a nice day. The flowers were just at their best—I stopped more than once to gather honeysuckle and twist it round the handle of the basket, it looked so pretty, and when I got to the little wood near which stood grandmother's cottage, I could hardly get on for stopping to look at the flowers that peeped out at the edge that skirted the road. And then I thought to myself how beautiful it must be further in the wood and what a lovely bunch of cowslips I might gather. There was a little stile just where I was standing—I climbed over it and put the basket down on the ground, as I could not run with it in my hand, and then off I set, down a little path between the trees, glancing at every side as I ran, for the flowers I wanted. But I was disappointed —in the wood the flowers were not near so pretty as at the edge, and after picking a few, I threw them away again and turned back to the stile, where I had left my basket. But fancy my trouble when I found it was not there! I had been away such a short time, I could not believe it was really gone. I searched and I searched—all in vain—it was really *gone* —so at last I sat down and cried. I cried till I was tired of crying and then I got up and walked slowly on to grandmother's. She was so kind I knew she would not scold me but still

she would be sorry and disappointed. And I really felt as if I would be too ashamed ever to go home and tell mother. When I got to grandmother's and walked up the little path to the cottage door—she had a nice little garden with roses and stocks and gilly-flowers and sweet-williams and lots of other nice old flowers—I was surprised to see it closed. It was not often grandmother was out of an afternoon and besides, being my birthday she might have known I would likely be coming to see her.

"Everything's gone wrong with me to-day," I said to myself, and vexed to think of the lost basket and the long hot walk back in the sun. I sat down on the little bench at the door and began to cry again. It seemed too bad that my birthday should be spoilt like that. I had cried so much that my eyes were sore and I leant my head against the back of the bench— it stood in a sort of little arbour—and closed them. I was not sleepy, I was only tired and stupid-like, but you can't fancy how startled I was when suddenly I felt something lick my hand, which was hanging down at my side. I opened my eyes and jumped up. There stood beside me a great big dog—a dog I had never seen before, looking up at me with his gentle, soft eyes, while on the ground at my feet was my lost basket! I was so delighted that I couldn't feel frightened, besides who could have been frightened of such a dear, kind-looking dog? I threw my arms round his neck and hugged him and told him he was a darling to have found my basket, and for a minute or two I really thought to myself he must be a sort of fairy—he seemed to have come so wonderful-like, all of a sudden. Just then I heard voices coming along the road. I ran to the gate to see who it was, and there, to my joy, was grandmother and beside her a neighbour of hers, a gamekeeper I had seen now and then. I had my basket on my arm and the big doggie stood beside me."

(To be continued.)

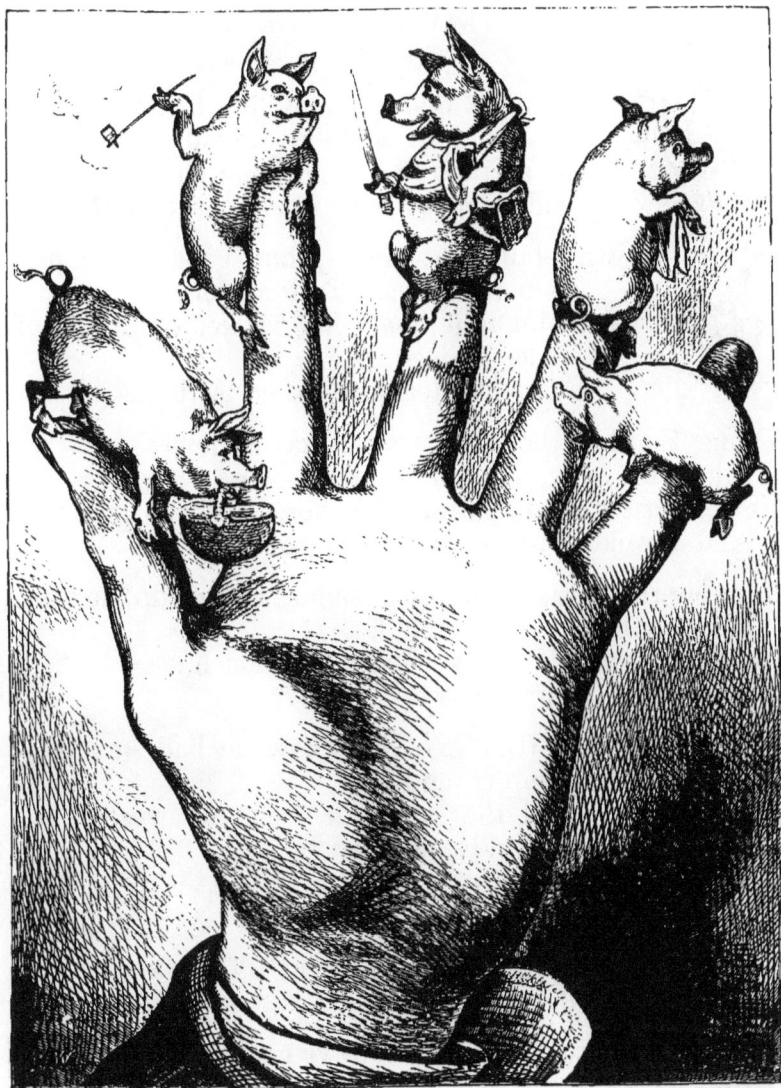

FIVE LITTLE PIGS.

8

FIVE LITTLE PIGS.

FIVE lit-tle fin-gers, and five lit-tle pigs!
  Of each I've a sto-ry to tell.
Look at their faces and fun-ny curl-ed tails,
  And hear what to each one be-fell.

Ring-tail, that stead-y and good lit-tle pig,
  To mar-ket set off at a trot;
And brought home his bas-ket quite full of
    nice things,
  Con-tent-ed and pleas-ed with his lot.

Young Smi-ler, the next, was a stay-at-home pig,
  Liked his pipe, and to sit at his ease;
He fell fast a-sleep, burned his nose with his pipe,
  And a-woke with a ve-ry loud sneeze.

Num-ber three was young Long-snout, who ate up the beef,
  He was both greedy and fat,
He made him-self ill by eat-ing too much,
  And then he was sor-ry for that.

And poor lit-tle Grunt-er—you know he had none—
  A pig-gy so hun-gry and sad;
He si-lent-ly wiped the salt tears from his eyes,
  I think it was real-ly too bad.

Young Squeak-er cried, "Wee, wee, wee!" all the way
  A pig-gy so fret-ful was he.   [home;
He had a good whip-ping, was sent off to bed;
  And de-served it, I think you must see.

Oh, these five lit-tle pigs, how they've made child-ren laugh
  In ages and ages now past!
And they'll be quite as fun-ny in years yet to come,
  While small toes and small fin-gers last.   EDITOR.

9

NEW YEARS DAY

TALKS ABOUT THE MONTHS.

JANUARY.

By Mrs. GEORGE CUPPLES.

" Pondering that Time to-night will pass
The threshold of another year."

ARK to the bells "ringing out a festive peal from every church tower in every corner of the land ;

'A tuneful offering for the weal
Of happy millions lulled to sleep.' "

If the old year has been a happy one we are sorry to let it go; but as it is courteous to speed the parting guest when we cannot induce him to stay any longer, so we ring out the old year as merrily as we ring in the new. Of course the New Year's chimes have a meaning, reminding us that we might have done more good during the past year than we really did,

10

but they cheer us on too, and keep telling us that now is the time for making a fresh start, and with God's help to try to make this a good New Year in every sense of the word. It does seem strange to find ourselves at New Year's Eve once more, but that being the case, we should like to have a little talk about it and the month we are entering, while the bells are so busy.

The name January means "the open gate of the year," for now that the shortest day is past, the days begin to lengthen, and Nature prepares to waken up out of its long sleep. This month was named after Janus, one of the Roman deities who was said to have two faces, and who presided or ruled over time. One face was said to be old, wrinkled, and weather-beaten, looking backwards, while the other, looking forwards, was young and fresh; implying that he stood between the Old and the New Year. It has been a custom among northern nations to see the Old Year out, and the New Year in, with all sorts of festivities and social merriments. In England, few fail to sit up on the last night of the year, listening for the bells, and ready when twelve o'clock strikes to jump up and wish each other a Happy New Year. The merry-makings of New Year's Eve and New Year's Day used to be celebrated long before the Saxon times, by the drinking of spiced ale out of a bowl comically called "lambs-wool," and afterwards the Saxons called it "The wassail bowl," which means "To your health." Do any of the children in your neighbourhood come to your door with a bowl gaily decked with bright ribbons, as they used to do long ago, singing,

"Here we come a wassailing
Among the leaves so green"?

After all, in spite of this being the coldest month of the year, we manage to have "a very good time," on the principle of making up for the outside bleakness by the glow within. Everybody has a holiday, and there is an up-gush and an out-flow of old association, caused by the return of this annual reminder that we are all of one family, from one source, bound for one great home. First come all the wonderfully-made toys, delicious bon-bons, lovely bound story-books, and all sorts of pretty things besides; then as many of our

relations and friends as possible dine together because of their good-feeling towards each other, and we are as merry and happy as crickets. Could we see up in a balloon and take a voyage round the world in a few minutes, we should be certain to find in almost every portion of the globe, that people were "keeping" the New Year in some merry way or other. In France, and in the United States, they give much more importance to the New Year's Day than is generally done here in England, and it is likewise the case in Scotland, and in general in the Colonies, indeed wherever the great stress laid upon Christmas festivities does not tend to throw New Year's Day somewhat into the shade. When people have been keeping it up for some days on end, there is apt to be less liveliness left for attending to this day with spirit. Perhaps there is more enjoyment to be got out of New Year's Day, especially for children, going out with their parents on some sight-seeing or visiting expedition; when everybody seems to be out too on the same errand, so that the streets are astir, and the public show-places are open, and the toy bazaars and the confectioners look all the more tempting just because the others are shut, and all is so bracing and happy under the frosty sunshine, with the powder of the snow under foot, and the whiteness of it above on the houses. Ah, how we remember it all ever after, and it does us good all our life long thenceforward—

"A thing of beauty, and a joy for ever!"

At this very time, if we were to look out for a moment from our balloon we should see our friends in Australia and in New Zealand, though keeping New Year's Day as gaily as we are, suffering even more from the heat than we are doing from the cold. However, they have delicious strawberries and cream for dessert, and lovely summer flowers in all the vases instead of the red holly berries.

"Janiveer—
Freeze the pot upon the feir,"

so says the old saw, but would not the Canadians laugh at us were we to complain of the cold? When they have the frost three feet down, and the thermometer twenty to thirty degrees below zero! They manage to keep themselves warmer than we do, however, for their houses are so delightfully heated with the great stoves, and the hot pipes ; then they wrap up very carefully when out of doors, for were they to expose their ears for a moment to the bitter blast, John Frost would nip them, causing them great pain. But in their warm fur cloaks and caps, off they go in their sledges over the snow, with the bells jingling merrily. Even in the direction of the Netherlands, and where the Rhine branches out into long canals, we should find all the inhabitants were having a happy time of it as well. They have put on their skates, and are setting out to market or to visit a friend some ten miles off, perhaps with a heavy load on their heads. In Scotland, if the frost is strong enough, the curlers will be out, hallooing at the top of their voices, and sweeping away the snow lest the stones be prevented from reaching the desired point. Ah, the curlers look out quite as anxiously as the boys do for signs of frost on New Year's Day, and when it does not come they shake their heads and say—

" If January Calends be summerly gay,
'Twill be winterly weather till the Calends of May."

We cannot say that the festivities of New Year season are over till the sixth of January, when Twelfth-day comes. It is a festival of the Church, in commemoration of the appearance of Christ to the Gentiles, especially to the three wise men from the East. It is not held in such pomp and splendour as it used to be in this country, but no doubt, in many homes still, there will be "the Twelfth-night" party, the large cake, and the drawing for king and queen amidst a great deal of fun. In Rome the Carnival or "farewell to flesh" begins, and oh, such a merry-making ! Men in all sorts of queer dresses, in carriages and on foot, the ladies in the balconies pelting the masqueraders with sugar-plums and bouquets, and they in turn pelting the company at the windows. It would take pages to tell you of all the gay doings there, in Paris, and elsewhere at this season. But St. Distaff's Day and Plough Monday are waiting to turn all the merriment into work once more.

12

" Partly work and partly play, you must on St. Distaff's Day :
Give St. Distaff all the right ; then give Christmas sport good-night,
And next morrow every one to his own vocation."

But before letting the happy and good feelings pass away which a New Year brings up in the heart, we must consider that there are many in every nation who cannot enter into these gay doings. This is often a sad time of the year to the poor, for many are thrown out of work, and so they cannot buy coals to warm them, nor proper food to eat, and though there are now soup kitchens and free dinners in almost every town, still there are always some left out who would be all the better of a kindly help. Then there are our friends the birds to be thought of ; we must save all the crumbs, for there are many hungry sparrows, blackbirds, and thrushes, who would be thankful for them, not to speak of Robin Red-breast and his friend Jenny Wren with her large small family. It is pleasant to think that the little dormouse, who will be giving herself a shake now in her snug nest, will have a good store beside her this year after such a bountiful harvest, and you may have a peep at her at the foot of some tree when you are out gathering lichens, for of course you know they are to be had in perfection this month, making up to us for the want of any wild flowers.

And as we return from the evening parties, we must not forget to turn our attention to the skies, for the clear frosty air of this month will give us an opportunity of seeing some of the principal stars and planets. As the shapes of the Constellations sparkle out, we can but wonder at them ; whilst the Planets excite a livelier interest, so strangely akin to our own world do they seem, moving on their way round the sun. We enter this month into what is called the Zodiacal sign of Aquarius, the water-bearer, the mark which was used in old almanacs to let people know, when they looked up to the skies, that January had come. It is most delightful to get some one of the party to point out the names of the stars and the planets, and if the Aurora Borealis, or northern lights, are seen, that walk home is often the best time of the whole festive season.

And though the cold may be strengthening, with the lengthening of the day, still it is a delightful season in which to take a brisk walk. We come upon many strange water-fowl among the reeds, beside the deep ponds and rapid currents in our neighbourhood; herons, wild ducks, coots, and others, may be seen wading and swimming wherever they can find water. Our rivers, shores, and creeks are crowded with migratory waterfowl all the way from Norway and elsewhere, who have been driven from their homes by the severe cold, and now crowd our shores till the weather begins to get a little warmer, when away they fly. Towards the end of the month some signs of vegetation may be observed. Wolfs-bane, a tall sombre-looking poisonous plant, is getting into flower, and in southern aspects, when well sheltered, the red dead-nettle, groundsel, and dandelion, look green and vigorous. Here and there a snow-drop may be seen, and the blossom of the mezereon and the catkins of the hazel are on the point of blowing.

Whenever we first see these catkins waving in the cold air of January, let us stop and examine one of them, and admire how curiously our bountiful Creator has preserved it from the weather. The stamens are those on which the future fruit depends, and these are placed in clusters from one end to the other of the blossom, looking like a succession of little flowers. Every cluster is protected, and thus ranged, tier above tier, the stamens lie in their snug retreats, not a drop of rain or a flake of snow ever reaching them. The whole catkin hangs like a graceful pendant, and is so pliant, that it yields to the breeze and is preserved from injury amidst the storms of this inclement period. Trees and shrubs which are exposed to the action of the cold and blasts of winter, have their new and soft parts shut up in buds. The coverings of these buds are so beautifully overwrapped, and so firmly knit together, that the frost rarely gets into them.

Winter is the grand season for social amusements, ushered in by old Father Christmas himself, which while away the long winter nights, and make us forget the pitiless cold, and the bare and barren face of nature. These social and domestic assemblies, when temperately conducted, enlarge our affections, call our best and most ennobling feelings into play, and make us love our fellow-creatures. Let us then be careful to mingle a little instruction with all our sports and amusements, and thus make ourselves wiser and better, and A Happy New Year will be the result.

" There is in souls a sympathy with sounds,
And as the mind is pitch'd the ear is pleased.
*   *   *   *   *

How soft the music of those village bells,
Falling at intervals upon the ear
In cadence sweet—now dying all away,
Now pealing loud again, and louder still,
Clear and sonorous, as the gale comes on !
With easy force, it opens all the cells
Where mem'ry slept.'

STORM AND HIS MASTER.

STORM AND HIS MASTER.

BY THE EDITOR.

"CAN'T do nothing with him; can't indeed, Sir; " said William the coachman to my father, who was inquiring about a new hunter he had lately bought.

My father and I had just got out of the carriage, and stood on the doorstep while he spoke to the coachman. I remember it was a frosty day in January, and I stood shivering there, with my little cold hand clasped in my father's large warm one, while listening to the conversation about the horse. The name of the new purchase was—Storm, and you may judge from the name what kind of horse he was. My father had already hunted him two or three times, and found him as much as he could possibly manage, bold and clever rider as he was. Still he liked the horse: Storm was an excellent fencer, handsome, well-bred and strong, just suited, indeed, to carry a heavy weight across country.

Unluckily about a fortnight before the day when we stood on the doorstep, a hard frost had set in, and if Storm was barely manageable when he had plenty of work to do, he became unbearable, furious, and mad, when he had no longer any hunting to carry off his surplus energy. Indeed, he drove both our worthy coachman and Young, the groom, almost to despair.

William went on with his complaints of Storm :—"I do assure you, Sir, he ain't safe. This morning it took us an hour to get the bit into his mouth, and to get him outside the stable for a little exercise. Then as soon as I give Young a leg up, and afore he was hardly in his saddle, why, the horse had him over his head. The beast kicks, and bucks, and rears: anything so vicious I never see. Last night he rammed Young up agin the side of his stall, till he a'most knocked the breath out of his body. Young's a good rider, but he won't never back him again, he says; and don't seem to like to have anything to do with the horse. You see, sir, he have a wife and two children."

My father looked grave at this description of Storm's behaviour, and murmured, "If this frost would only break up, I'd soon take it out of him." Then turning to William, he said, "Well, I'll step round to the stable, and have a look at the horse."

"Do let me come, father," I pleaded.

"Very well, little woman : but we must look at this terrible beast from a respectful distance, you know. No going up to him with cake or sugar, as you do to Brown Bob or Mousie."

Reaching the stable, my father raised the latch and opened the door; but, at the door, we stood motionless with astonishment. We beheld this ferocious animal, whose terrible doings we had just heard described, standing quite still in his stall, with a little child about three years old sitting on the ground close to one of his formidable hind feet, and busily engaged clipping away the hair on his fetlock with a large pair of scissors. The little fellow, quite unconscious of danger, held on to Storm's hock with his left hand, and was so taken up with his work that he never heard us come into the stable.

Storm was standing stock still, all four legs planted firmly on the ground, with his head just turned to one side, and his ears rather back. He seemed to be eying with more curiosity than anger the impudent little person who dared to take such a liberty with him. As he looked at the little helpless creature, that he could have struck dead in an instant with his iron-shod hoof, his savage nature seemed to soften, and I am sure that he kept so still on purpose that he might not hurt the child. I lost my own fear of Storm from that moment.

Just then up came Mrs. Young, in great alarm, searching for her little boy, who jumped up and ran to her directly she called him ; and you may imagine how glad we were to see him safe in his mother's arms. But from the day that Master Freddy showed himself so entirely without fear of the great horse, Storm seemed to acknowledge him as his master; and in his most stormy moods would become mild and gentle whenever the child went near him.

JEREMY SPICE.

BY THE AUTHOR OF "AUNT EFFIE'S RHYMES," Etc.

JEREMY SPICE in the cinnamon tree,
A comical four-handed monkey is he;
With a hideous face, and a curious pair
Of eyes that peep out from his grizzly hair,
Of eyes that can twinkle and glitter and stare.

Jeremy Spice has a wife like himself,
And a small monkey baby—a queer little elf
That clings to its mother with hands and with tail,
Clings with a grip that never can fail,
And cries like a child with a piteous wail.

Cousins and sisters and brothers has he,
A right merry company up in the tree,
And they jabber and chatter and yelp and shout,
Hanging by tails and swinging about,
Or racing and chasing—a noisy rout.

16

What squealing, what peeling, what husking of roots,
What munching and crunching and gnawing of fruits,
What grinning, grimacing, and knitting of brows,
What breaking of branches and bending of boughs,
What biting and fighting and making of rows.

Where are they? the monkeys? Oh, quicker than light
They are off to the forest and far out of sight.
When neither a fountain nor rivulet flows,
No one so well as old Jeremy knows
Where to find water to cool his nose.

There, by the water-hole, down on the ground
There's where the grim little mischiefs are found,
Crawling and sprawling and squabbling there,
Sunning themselves in the sultry air
Combing each other and dressing their hair.

Oh, what if some terrible Jamrach or Cross,
Soft footed, should stealthily spread on the moss
His snares ; and the poor little monkeys should find
They have no longer freedom for body or mind !

Shut up in the Zoo
That children like you
Should go and peep through
At the monkeys behind.

BLACK ROLF OF ROOKSTONE.

By the Right Hon. E. H. KNATCHBULL-HUGESSEN, M.P., *Author of "Uncle Joe's Stories," &c.*

HE Baron Fitzuron had gone to his lordly couch. It was late, very late. He had sat deep into the night, alone in the circular tower, deeply engrossed in his own thoughts.

It was cold; bitterly cold. Although there was no wind outside the castle walls, the Baron's room was draughty, and the heavy, dark curtains waved to and fro around his bed. It was a ghostly room, and ever and anon the dead stillness of night was broken by sharp, sudden, unaccountable creakings of the ancient chests and cumbrous chairs with which the apartment was filled.

It was late, I say, very late, and the Baron was weary in body and mind. Yet no sleep came to close his heavy eyelids in the repose he so much needed. Restlessly he tossed upon his pillow. With fingers stiffened by cold he strove to pull the scanty covering higher and higher over his chest. No fire smouldered upon the hearth. That hearth had known no fire for all the years during which the Baron had slept in the tower, and when at home he had occupied the same room every night of his life.

He was getting to be an old man now, and the end of that life could not be far distant. He might as well have made himself warm and comfortable for his few remaining years. But it was not cold that kept sleep from those aged eyelids. It was not suffering. It was not sorrow. It was joy. A joy so strange and so unusual to his bosom that he could not feel at home with it. He could not rest. All his life long had been spent in the steady, unwavering, determined pursuit of one object. After many years of doubt and difficulty, of anticipation of success and intense bitterness of failure, that object had been at last attained.

In the days long gone by, when the Baron Fitzuron was very young, a babe too young, one would have thought, to have understood such things, he first was told that a title should by rights have been his, and that the name by which he was then known was but the family name of the ancient Barons Fitzuron. By dark deeds of treason against the reigning king, an ancestor had forfeited the name and rank which had come down to him through long centuries, come down to him from those who had won and kept both name and rank with their own true hearts and sharp swords. Nor was this all. The greater part of the vast estates belonging to that ancient family had been confiscated, and the infant Rolf inherited but a few barren acres beyond the castle walls.

He was but a child indeed when this was told him, but he was no common child. There was more of force and stern resolve in that tiny heart, more determination expressed in these sharply chiselled baby lips, more thought beneath that infant brow, than many a grown man has possessed through life. In his childish heart he registered two solemn vows. One that he would recover every inch of land that had formerly belonged to his family; the other, that he would regain the old title, and once more should the representative of his ancient house take place among the nobility of his native land. Cost what it might this vow should be kept. From that time he began to save and to scheme, to plot and to work for the accomplishment of these two purposes.

It has been said that the boy's inheritance had been small, yet before he had reached middle age, little by little he had regained every rood of land which had been owned by the Barons Fitzuron in the old times. Strange to say, these lands had all come for sale within that time, and he had never failed to obtain them. He had done even more; much more. He had greatly added to the former possessions of his race. Far and wide he could gaze from the battlements of his castle upon high mountains and pleasant valleys, and feel with internal satisfaction that all was his own, his very own.

He could have taken his place with the richest of the land. But he did no such thing. He

18

lived in utter solitude in his mountain fastness, and still he saved and saved, ground down his vassals, and screwed the last farthing out of the poor tenants of his domain. The gold he had accumulated was said to be of fabulous amount. No man knew how he could have gathered such treasures together, although of course the proceeds of his estates were vast as the latter increased in extent. But other means of gaining wealth were attributed to him by common report, and some such he must certainly have employed. Men spoke of his hardness and cruelty as equalling his avarice and parsimony. Even in days when lawlessness was the rule rather than the exception, and when dark deeds too often disgraced the land, people stood aghast at the tales of terror which were rumoured concerning Black Rolf of Rookstone.

Many a poor and ruined family had been driven from their humble homes to seek refuge where they could, in order to make way for men better able to pay the extortionate demands of the lord of the land. Nay, there were even whispers of wickedness still greater. It was said that people had been missing—people who were in debt to the Baron—and that their fate was still worse than that of the outcasts I have named, for that they had been sold as slaves in foreign lands. It was muttered in fearful but angry tones that the dark dungeons beneath the rocks on which the castle stood could have told fearful tales of anguish and despair.

It was known that a secret communication existed between these horrible places and the sea, and that twice or thrice in the year strange vessels were seen hovering about that coast. At these times dark, rough men of foreign appearance were noticed about the castle. They spoke in a strange tongue, and none but the master of the castle could hold converse with them, but it was strongly suspected that it was by their agency that refractory vassals were disposed of, and the coffers of Black Rolf more rapidly filled than would otherwise have been the case.

But whatever reports were set afloat respecting him, the master of Rookstone, even if he heard of them, cared not one jot. With unaltered resolution and with untiring energy he followed out the second great design of his

19

life. As yet the title was not his, but his it should be, and nothing should turn him from his purpose. Saving, penury and cruelty had become such habits of his existence that he continued to practise them long after the need to do so had ceased to exist. As time progressed he even increased the care with which he constantly added to his hoarded wealth. Old retainers died; their places were not filled up and so the expense of their maintenance was spared. Anything like new furniture or new curtains or carpets had long been unknown in the old castle, and for some years before the accomplishment of the second part of Rolf's cherished design, he had lived with but a very scanty establishment around him, at the head of which presided his old nurse, Elfrida, who had ever been deeply attached to him and to his fortunes.

Years and years had passed away before the fulfilment of his second wish, and his rugged temper had not been softened by the delay. His hope had ever been that the rank and title of his forefathers would have been bestowed upon him, either on account of his great wealth and power, or by the judicious employment of that wealth at some time when the king, perchance in distress for money wherewith to pursue his pleasures or prosecute his wars, might be willing to grant an empty title in exchange for solid gold.

At last the thing really had come to pass. From the day he had come of age, and had taken possession of the property which he had afterwards so greatly increased, the young man had never ceased to importune his sovereign for the boon he so eagerly craved. By every conceivable method he had petitioned and implored; every possible influence had been set to work in his behalf, but hitherto always in vain. With a wise and righteous king Rolf's character had of itself been a fatal bar to his success. But now a young, needy and thoughtless monarch had ascended the throne, and the request having been urged at a fortunate moment, the bauble of an empty title was flung, not unwillingly, to the eager applicant in exchange for a portion—"alack," thought he, "a large portion" of his hoarded gold.

Had the young king known how boundless

was the wealth from which that portion was drawn, he would surely have required more. As it was, he was pleased and satisfied with the price paid, and laughed with his courtiers at the folly of the old man who had been willing to pay so much for a mere title, remarking that after all, the Black Rook of Rookstone had employed his gold better in giving it to his sovereign than if he had kept it buried and hidden away in his mountain home.

Black Rolf was well content that the king should believe that he had drawn heavily upon his resources, for he desired that men should think him less wealthy than he really was. But, in reality, he would have paid a far higher price sooner than have failed in the great object which he had so long desired, and he chuckled within himself as he thought of the mighty treasures he still possessed. He chuckled, deeply and grimly, as he lay that night upon his sleepless couch—that night which followed the day on which the formal deeds which confirmed him in his new title had come down by a special messenger from his royal master: that night of the day on which his retainers had called him "my lord" for the first time, every such appellation reminding him of the success of his life-long struggle. Still he tossed restlessly upon his bed. Would that night never end? Would it never be day, when he might sally forth to hear again the new title which tickled his ears so mightily, and feel that he really occupied the position which he had so long coveted?

Ha! what sound is that? Day cannot be far distant now, for he can faintly hear the low, regular, continued caw of the rooks in the old rookery close to the tower. He knows that sound well: he has known it all his life: it has been the accompaniment to many a meditation of dark and evil deeds; to many a bitter hour of disappointed hopes in his eager pursuit of that which he had won at last, to many an anxious thought about the future of the house whose power he had so ardently laboured to restore. He chuckled again to himself as he recognised that familiar sound, and at last he dozed off in an uneasy sleep.

Those rooks had long been considered as household birds by the family of which Baron Fitzuron was now the head. If the old legends which tradition had handed down were to be believed, and if the records in the pages of the great red velvet book, with massive iron clasps, which lay in the old oak-pannelled library, deserved any credit, it was these birds who had been the cause of the building of Rookstone Castle and from whom its name was taken.

It was told in that book that in the far past the fair heiress of the broad lands of Fitzuron used to meet her favoured lover, in spite of her father's disapproval of his suit. He was a foreigner, dark, handsome, accomplished, but with neither wealth nor lineage to recommend him. His ship was moored off the shore near the Fitzuron lands, and it was by the hands of his followers that the passage beneath the rocks was made. By this passage the lover was wont to come to the rookery, where the fair damsel met him, and more than once they interchanged their vows. One day, said the legend, they were surprised by her father, who had received notice from a traitor of their meeting, and fully intended to put a summary end to his daughter's engagement by destroying her lover. But the rooks, flying down in large numbers, not only warned the foreigners to stand on the defence, but so flurried and annoyed the attacking party with beak and wing that in the end they were routed, and the cruel father himself perished in the brawl. Afterwards when the heiress married her affianced suitor, they built a castle on the site of the present building, and named it Rookstone in honour of their brave and friendly birds.

Since that time there had always been an appointed hour in each day when golden grain was spread in the great court of the castle for the rooks, and oftentimes the lady of the house, and sometimes the Baron himself, had attended the repast. But Black Rolf would have none of this folly. The grain was costly, and the expense must be stopped. So stopped it was.

The Baron slept: but it was not for long. The cawing grew louder and louder, until at last it became a volume of sound which startled the owner of the castle from his coveted rest. What was it? Where was he? In vain he strove to collect his scattered thoughts; for several seconds he could remember nothing, and all reasoning power seemed to have left him. Then, by a mighty effort of the mind, he brought himself to know who, what and where he was; the mists cleared away from his mental perception and he recognised again that he was the Baron Fitzuron, and in the tower bedchamber of his own mansion.

But he was no longer alone. There was a Presence with him in the room—a Something which seemed to oppress his senses and to make him doubt the reality of the scene that was

passing before his eyes. He seemed to see a mass of black, glossy, shining feathers, as if he were gazing upon a vast concourse of rooks with their breasts all towards him, whilst at the same time their loud, angry cawing rent the very drums of his ears with its sound. It was as if the castle walls were opened and the rooks advancing in battle array against him. Then, gradually, the cawing grew fainter and fainter, until at last it ceased entirely; the wall seemed to have closed again, and returned to its natural condition, the windows were still

21

fastened and the door locked, and there was no visible way in which an intruder could have entered, unless he had tumbled down the chimney, the passage by which, moreover, was rendered more than commonly difficult by huge bars of iron which traversed it from side to side with but narrow space between.

Still, the Presence was there, and as soon as he was thoroughly awake and found himself able to collect his senses and try to realise the situation, the Baron perceived that upon the wooden framework which passed from bedpost to bedpost at the foot of his old-fashioned bed, there was seated no less an intruder than a rook. Yes, an undoubted rook; a large rook; an enormous rook; a glossy rook; a particularly glossy rook; an old, nay a venerable rook, and doubtless also a respectable, influential, perhaps even a generally meritorious rook, but for all that, to the best of the Baron's understanding, only a rook after all, and that, too, seated in a position which no bird had, in his opinion, the slightest right to occupy.

"Halloo!" cried the Baron, as soon as he had sufficiently recovered from his surprise to speak.

"Halloo!" retorted the rook in a perfectly natural voice, and without in the smallest degree shifting his position.

"What! you speak man's language, bird?" asked the astonished Baron.

"Certainly, when necessary," responded the other, and then after giving vent to a sound which partook partly of the nature of a caw and partly of a cough, but which was evidently intended as a clearing of the throat before he commenced his speech, thus addressed the owner of Rookstone Towers:—

" For years you have laboured, Black Baron Fitzuron,
  Your title to gain and your seat to sit sure on.
But now that your ends you've accomplished and carried,
  I'll tell you some news ; 'tis for this I have tarried.
Before to this site the house-builders e'er took stone
  The rooks were established as owners of Rookstone ;
They lov'd it ; and thought it the dearest of places ;
And men who the same thought stood high in their graces ;
Your ancestors, Rolf, the rooks lov'd and respected :
By you the same birds have been foully neglected,
And therefore, altho' 'tis an issue distressing,

23

Their curse is upon you, instead of their blessing.
To what I now tell you attentively listen
'Twill make your heart stop, blood run cold, and eyes glisten
With tears which you'll shed when you see that it's true in
My words 'twill be told your unspeakable ruin.
Don't doubt what I say, for the proof is quite handy :
Your mother had twins—but the eldest was bandy—
And therefore your sire said, " Away with this baby !
His better-shaped brother my eldest thus may be."
He spoke : no one thought of his word disobeying,
For what he'd have done if they had, there's no saying !
But they threw the poor baby as food to the fishes,
And told him they'd fully accomplish'd his wishes.
The " better-shaped brother" was you, you old tyrant,
(In badness you very unlike your old sire 'ant)
And thenceforth all trouble, they fancied, surmounted,
As eldest and heir you were always accounted.
But now comes the wonderful part of the story
Related to me by a worthy John Dorey,
From whom, Baron Rolf, you need never expect lie ;
He will tell the truth—should you boil him directly !
That baby was scarce the deep waters thrown then in
When by came a boat with a number of men in,
Who, seeing the child, whilst all up and down bobbing,
Secured him at once, tho' the fish they were robbing.
They went not ashore, for they didn't require to,
And no one was ever desired by your sire to,
And so he ne'er knew what had chanced on that morning,
And you never knew till this same hour of warning.
The child was conveyed to a land at a distance,
Too young, had he wished, to make any resistance.
He grew up—got married—had daughters and sons too,
And died—but now, Rolf, you may see what this runs to,
Your brother's first son, a lad full of ambition,
Has lately been told of his father's position.
He ne'er would have known he'd been shamefully cheated,
Had you treated rooks as they ought to be treated,
Your conduct, as that of your fathers the same a'nt
And therefore we rooks have gone in for the Claimant.
Till fortune and title were safe we have waited,
But now, to lose both you are certainly fated.
Our grain you denied us. So now, Rolf, you may know
Your fate—and may trust what I say—not cum grano,
But fully, entirely. The warning pray book it—
Your nephew's at hand, and you'll soon have to "hook it ! "

Whilst the rook repeated the above statement in calm, slow, and measured accents, the Baron lay still and listened as if bound by some mighty spell. The story was of course entirely new to him. He had, it is true, been told that he once had a brother who died in early childhood, but, with all his cares and hopes concentrated on the future, wherein lay the task which he had projected for himself, the past had but little interest for him, and he had scarce remembered the fact. As the words of the rook, however, fell upon his ears, he could not but feel the possibility of their truth, and that very possibility, remote though it might be, chilled his heart with horror.

What! was it then possible that his life-long toil should have been in vain! Much, indeed, of the land which he had acquired could hardly be wrested from him, but the title, having been restored to him as the rightful heir of the old family, and not given as a new creation, of which he had made, in his blindness as he thought now, a particular point, would probably, nay, certainly, have to be relinquished, whilst beyond all doubt the castle itself and its immediate surroundings, would pass from him into the hands of the legitimate heir. What he would have left would be but the wreck ; that which he might save from the bulk which he now possessed, and even that might be sadly diminished if the men of the law were once called in upon the business. All these thoughts passed through the Baron's brain whilst the rook sat solemnly at the foot of his bed, reciting his unpleasant communication, and doing it, moreover, as if he rather liked it than not.

By the time he had finished, however, rage and indignation had conquered every other feeling in the mind of his hearer : rage, that such a statement should be made to him at all: indignation that the creature, whoever or whatever he might be when at home, should coolly force himself into a man's own bedroom in order to tell him, with infinite glee, of his coming ruin. So the rook had scarcely concluded his narrative before the Baron hurled the pillow at his head, with all his force, accompanying it with an exclamation couched in somewhat strong language, and following it up, at excessively short intervals, with one of

his slippers and the bootjack, which happened to be at the side of his bed, and within reach. This action, however, produced no other result than, in the case of the last-mentioned article, to knock a china-cup, which the Baron rather valued, off the mantelpiece and break it into a thousand pieces. As far as the rook was concerned, he took not the slightest notice whatever of the incident, but merely shook his feathers after the manner of rooks, ruffling them all up with one tremulous motion of his body, and smoothing them all down by another, and having done this, he put his head slyly on one side, winked knowingly at the irate Baron, and remarking in a somewhat comical tone, " We shall see, old fellow, we shall see," flew, apparently straight through the wall as if there had been no wall at all, and in another moment had entirely vanished from the sight and hearing of the perturbed owner of Rookstone.

For a time Baron Fitzuron lay as one bereft of sense and reason, so stupefied was he by the extraordinary nature of the vision which he had just seen. He had fallen back upon his bed utterly amazed and bewildered at seeing the various objects which he had hurled at his visitor apparently pass through him as if he was air, without affecting his composure in the slightest degree. There lay the Baron, I repeat, for a time, and there ran through his body a tremor of a cold and shivering character, such as might seize upon a man who had been greatly alarmed and terrified.

But fear was a sensation which had no abiding-place in the bosom of Black Rolf of Rookstone. Presently with a mighty effort he recovered himself, and sat upright in his bed, gazing before him at the wall through which his uninvited guest had come and gone. It presented no unusual appearance to his keen eye ; everything was the same as it ever was, and he could have fancied the whole scene a dream, if he had not been perfectly well aware that it was a frightful reality.

(To be continued.)

MONKEYS or CHILDREN.

ONCE up-on a time a la-dy went to see the Mon-keys at the Zoo-lo-gi-cal Gar-dens.

"Pret-ty lit-tle dears," said the la-dy, who had no child-ren, but had, in-stead, a cat and a dog, three par-rots, four squir-rels, some dor-mice, and a great ma-ny more pets. "Just like child-ren," she went on, "on-ly pret-tier, and bet-ter be-haved. I real-ly think I must buy a Mon-key; I'll look at them well, and see what kind I should like."

24

So say-ing the la-dy went a lit-tle near-er to the Mon-key cage, when sud-den-ly a long arm was thrust out of the cage, and the veil on her bon-net was seized; next, the bon-net it-self was torn off her head and drag-ged into the cage, and with it un-for-tu-nate-ly her wig went too, for the poor la-dy had no hair of her own.

The Mon-key tried on wig and bon-net, in which he looked ve-ry fun-ny, ex-cept to the poor la-dy. Then the bon-net and wig were snatched away by o-ther Mon-keys in the cage, and tried on by one af-ter a-nother a-mid most dread-ful yells and shrieks. The Mon-keys bit, and tore, and scratched, and near-ly pulled each o-ther's tails off, to get at the la-dy's wig and bon-net. At last they tore them up, and ate the rem-nants both of bon-net and wig.

The poor la-dy went home bald and ve-ry sad, with a bad cold in her head and a hand-ker-chief tied over it. I won-der which she liked best af-ter this—Mon-keys or Child-ren.

HIDDEN IN THE SNOW.

HIDDEN IN THE SNOW.

BY THE EDITOR.

HE winters in Germany are much more severe than in England, and the story I am going to tell happened some time ago during a winter of unusual severity in that country. I spent the greater part of that winter living on an island in the river Rhine.

The island is called Ober-werth. It has the city of Coblenz near it on one bank of the river, while, on the other, the heights are crowned by the grand old castle of Ehrenbreitstein. The only habitations on the little island are one large house and three or four cottages. At the house lived a German lady, who owned the island, and with whom I was staying at the time I speak of. The principal cottage was occupied by a ferryman, who ferried people to and fro between the island and the shore: the others were inhabited by the families of labourers employed in the cultivation of the island.

In summer Oberwerth itself, and all the surrounding scenery, are most picturesque and lovely: even during that cold winter there was beauty of a certain kind. Huge blocks of ice came floating down with the stream on one side of the island; while on the other side, where the river is narrowest, the water was completely frozen over, and there was skating going on.

However, it is not with the river that my story has to do, but with some children that lived upon the island. They were the son and daughter of Bernard the ferryman. I should say one was about six, the other seven years of age; and their names were Herman and Anna. One bitter morning in January I met them—a joyous little couple—trudging merrily through the fast-falling snow to school: they could cross to the mainland on the ice then. Such a little man and woman they looked! laden with their books and slates; and Herman,

27

besides, carrying the large umbrella, which sheltered them both from the blinding flakes of snow. I asked them where they were going.

"To school," they answered both together with a merry laugh.

"You seem very cheerful about it," I said.

"Oh, but we are so happy," cried Anna, "because to-day we have a half-holiday, and the Grafine has told us we may ask some of our schoolfellows on to the island, if it leaves off snowing. And we are to have games, and play at snow-balling, and run about, and get as warm as we can; and afterwards we are all to have supper in the great kitchen at the House."

"Well, I hope it will leave off snowing," said I, and so we parted.

In the afternoon sure enough the snow ceased, and the sun came out. Sitting in the house, I could hear the merry shouts of my little friends, and other children, romping and playing in the grounds outside. Afterwards I went, with my hostess, into the great kitchen, and saw them feasting; as merry a set of children as were ever seen. Supper over, they went out into the garden once more, to have a game at hide and seek among the trees and bushes before it became quite dark.

The night was just closing in, and snow was falling heavily again, when Bernard, the ferryman, came up to the house asking eagerly for help to search for his children. The poor man knew the interest which both the lady of the house and I took in his little boy and girl, and he at once hurriedly told us that neither of them could be found.

"My foolish little ones," said the poor father, "must needs have a game at hide and seek in the snow. Ah, mein Gott!" here he began wringing his hands, "there are places in the island where the snow lies five and six feet deep; they may sink into one of these drifts and be frozen to death before we can find them; and now it is getting dark."

He told us how the two children had gone off together out of the warm kitchen to hide, bidding their schoolfellows follow and search for them. This they did ; searching the garden, which was near the house, thoroughly : but they searched in vain. Then they became frightened : it was growing dusk, snow was beginning to fall, and they dared not extend their search beyond the garden. One of them ran to the cottage of Bernard, and brought him out. He said he had looked about, calling his children by name, hallooing, and using his whistle, whose sound they knew so well, but no answering cry had come, and he was in despair.

The mistress of the island immediately ordered all the men about the house to go out with lanterns and torches, and she and I joined in the search. We divided into two parties, each taking half the island. It is not large; only about a mile in length, and much less in width ; and in a short time we had searched it thoroughly. The children were not found.

Then all in a moment an idea struck me, which I am surprised did not occur to me before. Most of you, my little readers, have heard of the Mount St. Bernard dogs, who search for and find poor travellers, who have been lost in the snow on the Alps. Now, though I had no St. Bernard dog, I had a Scotch Shepherd's dog—what is called a Colley —with me at Oberwerth. This dog had belonged to my brother, who was so fond

of him that for some time he made him the companion of his travels, but on going on from the Rhine into Italy, he left Kelpie with me at Oberwerth.

I immediately called Kelpie to me, and leading him through the garden to the ground beyond, pointed forwards, saying : " Seek, Kelpie, seek ! " My doggie seemed to understand exactly : he put his wise old muzzle near the ground, and went sniffing about in all directions. In a very few minutes he stopped at the foot of a large tree, on one side of which the snow had drifted into a heap. Here, lifting up his head, he gave a loud deep bark, and scratched away at the snow. The good dog's instinct had done more than all our knowledge, experience and intellect could do. He had found, and—thank God !—saved, the children. They were lying in each other's arms, buried in the snow.

The simple little ones had hidden behind the tree, and at last, getting tired, but not liking to leave their hiding-place, had lain down on the soft snow, and fallen asleep : then the fresh snow falling, quickly covered them up. They were carried into the house, and soon restored to consciousness, nor did they seem much the worse afterwards from sleeping on such a cold bed. As for poor Bernard, I shall never forget his joy, or his gratitude to Kelpie.

Thus, you see, my dear old doggie saved both the children to gladden their father's heart, and my little story is ended.

BILLY HOOD.

Allegretto spiritoso.

I know a boy in our town, whose name was Bil-ly Hood; He had a sword all made of tin, A mus-ket made of wood. His drum would al-ways let you know when Bil-ly Hood was coming; For the neighbours al-ways used to say, "I wish he'd stop that drumming." Row de dow, dow dow! Row, dow, dow! Row de dow de! Row de dow de! Row dow dow!

2.

Now very brave this Billy was,
  At least so Billy thought.
And he was not afraid; not he!
  Of anything that fought.
"With this good sword and gun," said he.
  "I'll fight until I die.
And let man or beast come on : who fears ?
  Not Billy Hood : not I."
       Row de, &c.

3.

But ah ! one day this Billy went
  Where six old geese did stray,
And on his noisy drum began
  Somewhat too loud to play.
An old goose chas'd him from the field,
  And Billy screaming ran
Till he on the kitchen floor sank down :
  That valiant little man !
       Row de, &c.

DOCTOR PILL.

ALICE declared that there never was such a darling child as hers in the whole world; she said the child was simply perfect.

"You see," boasted the little motherkin, "Angelina is not only quite beautiful, but she is as good as she is beautiful. She never cries except when she is pinched, and then I'm sure it isn't to be wondered at; and, as for going to sleep,—why, I have only to lay her down, and she goes off to sleep directly."

Angelina was much loved by her little

mamma, Alice; but Angelina had an aunt, Edith. who was rather blind to the beauty and the merits of the doll-child. Edith had lately been suffering from a slight illness brought on probably by indulging rather too freely in Christmas fare. The doctor had been called in, and Miss Edith had been obliged to swallow certain powders and draughts instead of plum-pudding and mince-pie.

"I don't think Angelina pretty at all," said she, "and I don't like her one bit. I know what I wish! I wish Angelina was ill, and I was the doctor come to see her. Wouldn't I order her plenty of nasty things!"

"Angelina would be better than some naughty girls I know," spoke up the little fond mother-kin; "she would take her nasty medicine, every bit of it, without being bribed by having sixpences given her, and goodies, like somebody I know."

"Very well then," said Edith, growing very red as she answered, "I will play at being the doctor, and ugly Angelina shall be ill. But will you promise to do as I tell you? I mean, will you promise to 'follow my instructions,' as Doctor Thompson says?"

Now Edith became more and more angry as her little mind dwelt upon the remark about bribery. She went on :—

"I think you are very unkind, Alice, to talk about my being *bribed* to take my nasty medicine. You would like to be bribed too; you know you would. Every one likes goodies after nasty things. You are very disagreeable: I don't love you, and I hate Angelina."

Saying this she sat down, and pouted; with her pretty little face flushed, and her lips projecting.

"Don't be so cross, Edie dear," said kind little Alice. "I daresay I should like goodies after meddy too, and you know I'm a year older than you, so it would be worse in me. Come, do be good, darling, and we will have a nice game; we will play that Angelina is very ill, and that I am her poor anxious mamma; then you shall be the doctor. Yes, and I do promise faithfully that I will do everything you order for her, just as if you were a real doctor, and she was really ill."

31

Edith recovered her good humour directly, and went bounding out of the room to make her preparations for playing the part of doctor. But she put her head in again at the door for a moment, with a cunning look upon her little face, to say :—"Mind, you have promised faithfully to do whatever the doctor tells you to the child."

"Oh yes," said Alice, "but do make haste."

Alice prepared to receive the doctor's visit by calling up a sad and troubled expression to her face, and, taking the sick child on her knee, began to rock her gently to and fro. Perhaps she almost fancied for the moment that she really was an anxious mother waiting for the doctor.

Presently a tap was heard at the door: "Oh, there's the doctor at last; I'm so glad!" said Alice, thoroughly acting her part. "Pray come in gently, doctor," she added, "for my dear child has just fallen asleep."

In walked Edith on her tip-toes, with brother Charlie's hat upon her head, and his great coat on her back. Grandmamma's spectacles were on her nose, and a great stick was under her arm, and a large bottle of medicine peeped out of her pocket.

"What's the matter, what's the matter with my little friend here?" said she in a gruff voice.

"Oh, Doctor Thomson!" Alice was beginning, when Edith stopped her with—"Don't call me Doctor Thompson, ma'am, I'm Doctor Pill."

Here Alice very nearly burst out laughing, but she contrived to call back the serious look to her face again, and went on :

"Doctor Pill, my poor child is very ill, very ill indeed; she is dreadfully feverish, and has been quite sick. She suffers, too, from pains in her head and legs and——"

"Ah, ma'am," interrupted Doctor Pill, "I am sure she is greedy : she has such an ugly-coloured face. I believe she squints too; and —gracious me! how her nose turns up!"

"Her nose doesn't turn up, Doctor Pill," cried the indignant mother, "and she doesn't squint, and she hasn't an ugly face, and you are not Doctor Pill at all; you are only stupid Edith to talk like that; no real doctor ever says such things. Doctor Thompson never said such things about you to mamma." And as she spoke, the little girl burst into a flood of tears.

"Well, I wont play if you are so cross," said Edith; "if I'm to be the doctor, I must say what I think best. You know you promised to do whatever I told you, and you don't keep your promise at all."

A great many more reproaches would have followed, but Alice, who was always the first to make up, put her arms round Edith's neck, and said :—"Do, please, go on being Doctor Pill, dear Edie."

Then Edith consented, provided Alice would keep her promise of obeying the doctor's instructions in all things. Alice repeated the promise she had before given, and so the game went on.

"I was telling you, dear Doctor Pill," began Alice, "that my little Angelina is suffering a great deal from pains in her head and in her legs. Pray, dear Doctor, what do your order for her ?"

A look of malice passed over the rosy face of Doctor Pill, as in a gruff and decided voice he pronounced these terrible words :—

"Put her head in boiling water, and cut off both her legs ! "

My little readers may imagine the horror and despair of the unhappy mother.

"I won't do it, Edith. Nonsense ! Of course I won't," cried Alice.

"*But you promised*," was the stern reply of the terrible Doctor Pill.

Alice, who was an honest and truthful child, wrung her hands in dismay.

"Oh, what shall I do ; what shall I do ?" she cried, and the tears began to stream down her face.

Just then the door opened behind the doctor, and brother Charlie's head was popped in. He had heard the last few words, and he said :—

"If you are Doctor Pill, I'm Doctor Powder, and I order you off to Bedlam, and to wear a straight waistcoat, for thinking that a doctor would ever advise such horrible cruelties. I order that Angelina shall be rolled up warm and put to bed ; and you, Doctor Pill, and you, little mother, are both to come down stairs, and have a game at ball with me."

And so Angelina was saved.

KNOCK, KNOCK, NO ANSWER.

HOODIE.

By Mrs. MOLESWORTH, *Author of* "*Hermy*," "*The Cuckoo Clock*," &c.

CHAPTER II.—HOODIE GOES IN SEARCH OF A
GRANDMOTHER.

"I care for nobody, no not I,
And nobody cares for me !"

MARTIN went on with her story :
  "'Janie!' cried grandmother when
  she saw me. 'What a nice picture
they make—my little grand-daughter and
your great dog—don't they ?' she said to the
gamekeeper.

"'And it was *your* basket, little Janie, that
he found at the stile, then,' said the dog's
master, and then he and grandmother explained
that walking along the road—grandmother was
going up with him to see his wife who was ill
—the dog who was following them had suddenly darted to one side and then crept from
under the hedge with the basket in his mouth.
They couldn't think whose it was, for no one
was to be seen about, but when grandmother
started to come home again the dog would

follow her with it still in his mouth, so Roberts, that was the man's name, came along with her to see the end of it. Now wasn't it clever of the dog to know it was mine and bring it to me like that?"

"*Very*," said the children. "But mightn't your grandmother have known it was your mother's basket?" said Magdalen.

"It was a common enough one, but if she had looked inside she'd have known mother's butter and cake, I daresay," said Martin. "But the funny thing was, the dog would let no one touch it but me—he growled at grandmother when she tried to look in, but he stood by and saw me take out the things and just wagged his tail."

"And did zou have nice tea, and cake, Martin?" said Hec.

"Oh yes, dears, very nice. But for all that it cured me of setting down baskets or anything like that when I had to take them anywhere. For you see it isn't every dog that would have had the sense of that one."

"And then he *might* have been a woof," suggested Hoodie. "The picture says a woof."

"Yes," said Maudie. "But this isn't the picture story, Hoodie. This was a real story of Martin herself, you know, for there aren't wolfs now."

"Not none?" said Hoodie.

"No, of course not."

Hoodie nodded her head, but made no further remark, and the nursery party congratulated themselves on the astonishing success of their endeavours to "put her crying fit out of her head."

This happy state of things lasted nearly all day. Hoodie was really most agreeable. She was rather more silent than usual, but, for her, surprisingly amiable.

Martin was delighted.

"Take my word for it, Miss Maudie," she said, "the only way with a child like her, is to take no notice and talk of something else."

"But we can't always do that way, Martin," Maudie was not of a sanguine temperament —"sometimes, you know, she's naughty about things that you *must* go on talking to her about, till you get her to do them."

"I can't help it, Miss Maudie," said Martin.

"Talk or no talk, it's my belief that no power on earth will get Miss Julian to do what she wants not to do. And folks can't live always quarrel—quarrelling. She may improve of herself like, when she gets older, but as she is now, I really think the less notice she gets the better."

Maudie felt rather puzzled. She was only nine years old herself, remember, and Hoodie's queer ways were enough to puzzle much wiser heads than hers.

"I don't think Martin's way would do," she said to herself, "but still I think there must be *some* way that would make her gooder if only we could find it."

The children all went to church in the afternoon. The morning service was too long for them, their mother sensibly thought, but the afternoon hour, or hour and a quarter at most, no one, not even wee Hec and Duke, found too much. And Hoodie was rather fond of going to church. What she thought of, perched up by herself in her own corner of the pew no one ever knew; that she listened, or attempted to listen to what was going on, was doubtful in the extreme. But still, as a rule, church had a soothing effect on her, the quiet and restfulness, the monotony itself, seemed to calm her fidgety querulousness; possibly even the sensation of her Sunday clothes and the admiring glances of the little school-children helped to smooth her down for the time being.

This special Sunday afternoon their mother was not with them. They went and returned under Martin's convoy, and till about half way on their way home again all went satisfactorily. Then unfortunately occurred the first ruffle. Maudie had been walking on in front with little Duke, Hoodie and Hec, each with a hand of Martin, behind, when Maudie stopped.

"Martin," she said, "may Duke walk with you a little? He says he's tired."

"Of course, poor dear," said Martin; "come here Master Duke, and you, Miss Hoodie, go on a little with your sister."

Hoodie let go Martin's hand readily enough.

"Wonders will never cease," thought Martin, but alas, her rejoicing was premature. Hoodie let go her hand, but stood stock still without moving.

"No," she said deliberately, "I won't walk with Maudie. Why can't Hec walk with Maudie and me stay here?"

"Because he's such a little boy, Miss Hoodie dear, and I daresay both he and Master Duke are getting tired. They've had a long walk you know."

Martin was forgetting her own advice to Maudie. He who stopped to reason with Hoodie was lost indeed!

"And so has me had a long walk, and so you might daresay me is tired too," returned Hoodie, standing her ground both actually and figuratively. Two fat little legs apart, two sturdy little feet planted firmly on the ground, there she stood looking up defiantly in Martin's face, armed for the fight.

"Was there ever such a child?" thought poor Martin. Maudie's words had indeed been quickly fulfilled — here already was a case in which the taking-no-notice system was impossible—the child could not be left by herself on the high-road, where according to present appearances it was evidently her intention to stay unless—she got her own way!

"Well, my dear, I daresay you are tired too," said Martin soothingly, "but still not *so* tired as poor little Duke. You're ever so much bigger you know. Think what tiny little feet your brothers have to trot all along the road on."

"Mines is tiny too. I heard you saying them was very tiny to Mamma one day. And them's just as tired as Duke's; 'cos I'm bigger, my feets have more heavy to carry. I *will* have your hand, Martin, and I won't walk with ugly Maudie."

"But you must, Miss Hoodie," said Martin, attempting firmness and decision as a last resource.

"But I mustn't, 'cos I *won't*," said Hoodie.

Martin glanced back along the road despairingly. Several groups of the country people on their way home from church were approaching the little party as they stood on the footpath.

"Do come on, Martin," said Maudie; "it is so horrid for the people to see such a fuss. And then they say all about that we are all naughty. Look, there's farmer Bright and his

35

daughters coming. Do come on—you'll *have* to let Hoodie walk with you, and Hec 'll come with me."

"Miss Hoodie," said Martin once more, "you are to walk on with Miss Maudie, do you hear?"

"Yes," said Hoodie, without moving an inch, "I hear, but I *won't* walk with ugly Maudie."

The Bright family were fast approaching. In despair Martin turned to Hoodie.

"I am obliged to let you walk with me, Miss Julian," she said, solemnly, "because I cannot have everyone in the road see how naughty you are. But when we get home I shall speak to your Mamma and ask her to let you go walks alone. You make us all miserable."

Hoodie took Martin's hand and marched on.

"I should like to go walks alone, werry much," she said, amiably, to which remark Martin did not make any reply.

The Bright family passed them with a friendly word to Martin, saying something in praise of the nice appearance of her little charges. And Hoodie smiled back to Farmer Bright, as if she thought herself the best and sweetest-tempered of little girls. Then when they were out of sight, she suddenly dropped Martin's hand.

"I don't want to walk with you. You're an ugly 'sing too," she said. "I like to walk belone, but I would walk with you if I *said* I would."

And on she marched defiantly, well in front of the whole party. And again poor Martin murmured to herself,—

"Was there *ever* such a child?"

What was Hoodie saying to herself on in front where no one could hear her?

"They don't love me. They like me to be away. Nobody loves poor Hoodie. Hoodie can't be good when nobody loves her. It isn't Hoodie's fault."

And through her babyish brain there ran misty, dreamy ideas of something she would do to make "them" all sorry—she would go away somewhere "far, far," and never come back again. But where? This she could not yet settle about, but fortunately for the peace of the rest of the walk her cogitations kept her quiet till they were all at home again.

Hoodie.

Martin's threat of speaking to Hoodie's mother was not at once carried out. And Martin herself began to think better of it when at tea-time Hoodie behaved herself quite respectably. The naughty mood had passed again for the time, it seemed.

Sitting round the table in the intervals of bread and butter and honey—for it was Sunday evening, "honey evening" the little boys called it—the children chatted together pleasantly. Martin's story had greatly impressed them.

"Weren't you frightened at first when you saw the big, big doggie, Martin?" said Maudie.

"*Might* have been a woof," remarked Duke, whose ideas had a knack of getting so well lodged in his brain that it was often difficult to get them out again.

"But there *are* no wolfs. I told you so before," said Maudie.

"No," said Duke, "you toldened Hoodie so. You didn't tolden me."

"Well, *dear* Duke, what does it matter?" said Magdalen, with a slight touch of impatience in her tone. "You heard me say it, and you do go on and on so about a thing."

Hoodie looked up with a twinkle in her eyes.

"Peoples always calls each other 'dear' whenever they doesn't like each other," she remarked.

Maudie flashed round upon her.

"That isn't true. I do like Duke—don't I Duke? And Hec too—don't I love you dearly, Hec and Duke?"

The two little boys clambered down from their chairs, by slow and ponderous degrees, and a hugging match of the three ensued.

"Children, children," cried Martin, "you know it's against the rules for you to get down from your chairs at tea. Miss Maudie, dear, you shouldn't encourage it."

"But Hoodie said unkind 'sings to Maudie, and we had to kiss dear Maudie," said the little boys. "Naughty Hoodie," and they glanced round indignantly at Hoodie.

A hard look came over Hoodie's face.

"Always naughty Hoodie," she muttered to herself. "Nobody loves Hoodie. Nebber mind. Don't care."

36

"Little boys," said Martin, "you must go back to your seats and finish your tea. And don't call Miss Hoodie naughty for nothing at all but a little joke."

Hoodie gave a quick glance at Martin.

"Martin," she said, gravely, "if there is no woofs now, is there any grandmothers?"

"Any grandmothers, Miss Hoodie?" repeated Martin. "How do you mean, my dear? of course every one has a grandmother, or has had."

"Oh!" said Hoodie; "I didn't know. And is grandmothers always in cottages?"

"Oh, you silly girl," said Maudie, laughing; "of course not. Don't you remember *our* grandmother? She was here two years ago. But I suppose you're too little to remember."

"Don't laugh at her for not understanding, Miss Maudie," said Martin; "besides, don't you remember your grandmother's address is Parkwood Cottage? Very likely she's thinking of that."

"Yes," said Hoodie, "I was 'sinking of zat. I want a grandmother in a cottage. Grandmother in a cottage would be very kind, and there is no woofs."

"Oh no, Miss Hoodie, there are no wolves," said Martin; "all the wolves were sent away long, long ago. Now, dears, you must have your hands washed and your hairs brushed to go down to the drawing-room."

Hoodie was very quiet that evening. Her father noticed it after the children had gone up to bed again, and said to her mother that he was in hopes the child was going to turn over a new leaf. And her mother replied with a smile that she had been speaking to her very seriously that morning, and was glad to see how well the little girl had taken it. So both father and mother felt satisfied and happy about the child, little imagining the queer confused whirl of ideas at that very moment chasing each other round her busy brain.

For Hoodie did not go to sleep till much later than the others, though she lay so still that her wakefulness was unnoticed. Under her pillow, wrapped up firstly in a piece of newspaper, over that in the clean pocket-handkerchief Martin had given her for church, were three biscuits she had got at dessert, two pieces of bread-and-butter and one of bread and honey, which unobserved she had "saved" from tea. What she meant to do with these provisions was by no means clear, even in her own mind. She only knew that the proper thing was to have a basket of eatables of some kind, provided for a voyage of discovery such as that on which she was resolved.

"The little Hoodie-girl in the picture has a bastwick, and Martin had a bastwick when she was a Hoodie-girl," she said to herself dreamily. "I will get more bead-and-butter to-morrow and then I can go. After dinner-time Martin wented when she was a Hoodie-girl. I will go after dinner-time too. The grandmother in the cottage will love Hoodie and there is no woofs. Peoples here doesn't love Hoodie."

And so thinking she fell asleep.

The next morning happened to be rainy. Hoodie ate her breakfast in silence, and what she did *not* eat she quietly added to the contents of the pocket-handkerchief parcel. Martin noticed her fumbling at something, but thankful for the quiet state of the atmosphere—otherwise Hoodie's temper—thought it wiser to make no remarks. For after all it was a very April sort of sunshine; and two or three times before dinner there were signs of possible storms—once in particular, when the little boys had got Prince up into the nursery to play with them and Hoodie insisted on turning him out.

"Him's not to come in here," she said; "Hoodie won't have him in here no more."

"*Really*, Hoodie," said Maudie, "this isn't all your room. Why won't you let poor Prince come in? It was only yesterday you were crying because he wouldn't come."

"'Cos I loved him yesterday and I don't love him to-day," replied Hoodie coolly.

"And how would you like if people spoke that way to you?" said Maudie virtuously. "Suppose we said we wouldn't have you in the nursery 'cos we don't love you to-day."

"Don't care," said Hoodie. "You can't send *me* out of the nursery. I'm not a dog. But if I like I can go of my own self," she added mysteriously. "And if peoples don't love me I *sall* go."

37

Maudie did not catch the sense of the last few words, but Prince, being in his own mind by no means partial to the nursery, where the children's affection expressed itself in clutches and caresses very unsettling to his nerves, had taken advantage of the discussion to go off "of his own self," and in the lamentation over his running away, no more was said, and it was not till afterwards that the elder girl remembered her little sister's threat.

But through dinner-time the hard, half-sullen look stayed on Hoodie's face, and again poor Martin shivered with fear that another storm was coming. Somewhat to her surprise things got no worse—not even when a message came upstairs from "mother," that Maudie was to be ready to go out a drive with her at two, did Hoodie's rather curiously quiet manner desert her.

"I don't care. Nobody loves me," she repeated to herself, but so low that no one heard her.

"It'll be your turn next time, you know, Hoodie dear. Mother never forgets turns," said Magdalen consolingly, as, arrayed in her "best" white alpaca trimmed with blue, and white hat with blue feathers to match, she ran into the nursery to say good-bye to the stayers-at-home.

"And Miss Hoodie will be good and help me with the little boys, won't you Miss Hoodie dear?" said Martin. "There's some ironing I do want to get done for your Mamma this afternoon, if I could leave you three alone for a little."

"Susan may stay with them," said Mrs. Caryll, who just then came into the nursery to see if Maudie was ready. "It is too damp still for the boys to go out, but Hoodie can play in the garden a little. She never catches cold and she will be the better for a run—eh, Hoodie?"

No answer. Mrs. Caryll turned to Martin with a question in her face. "Anything wrong again?" it seemed to say.

Martin shook her head.

"I think not ma'am," she said in a very low voice, "but really there's no saying. But I think she'll be all right once you're started with Miss Magdalen."

Mrs. Caryll said no more. She took Maudie by the hand and left the nursery, only nodding good-bye to the little boys as she passed through the doorway.

"Good-bye darlings," said Maudie. "I'll bring you back something nice for tea."

"Dood-bye, dear Maudie," called out Hec and Duke in return. Then they flew—no, I can hardly use that word with regard to their sturdy little legs' trot across the room—they trotted off to the window to see the carriage as it passed the corner of the drive and to kiss their little hands to Mamma and Maudie. And Hoodie remained determinedly looking out of the other window, from which no drive and no carriage were to be seen.

"Nobody calls me darling. Nobody cares for Hoodie," she said to herself. "Nebber mind. Hoodie will go far, far."

When Martin called to her a few minutes afterwards, to put her hat and jacket on for the run in the garden, which her mother had spoken of, she came at once, and stood quite still while her nurse dressed her. The submission struck Martin as rather suspicious.

"Now Miss Hoodie, my dear," she said, "you'll not go on the grass or where it's wet. Just run about on the nice dry gravel for half an hour or so, and if you see the gardener about, you may ask him to show you the rabbits."

Hoodie looked up in Martin's face with a rather curious expression.

"I won't run in the grass," was all she said. Martin let her go off without any misgiving. For all Hoodie's strange temper she was in some ways a particularly sensible child for her age. She was quite to be trusted to play alone in the garden, for instance—she might have been safely left within reach of the most beautiful flowers in the conservatory without any special warning; not one would have been touched. She was truly, as Martin said, a strange mixture and contradiction.

She had made her way half down the staircase, when she suddenly remembered her basket. "Oh, my bastwick," she exclaimed. "I was nearly forgetting my bastwick," and upstairs again she climbed to the cupboard, in one dark corner of which she had hidden it. Luckily it was still there; no one had touched it, so

feeling herself quite equipped for the journey, Hoodie walked out of the front door, crossed the gravel drive and made her way down a little path with a rustic gate at the end leading straight out on to the high road. When she got there she stood still and looked about her. Which way should she go? It had turned out a beautiful afternoon, though the morning had been so stormy. The road was nearly dry already, the sky overhead was blue, save here and there where little feathery clouds were flying about in some agitation; it might rain again before night, for though not exactly cold, there was no summer glow as yet and the sunshine, though bright, had a very April feeling about it.

Hoodie stood still and looked about her, up and down the road. It was a pretty, peaceful scene—the broad well-kept highway, bordered at one side with beautiful old trees just bursting into bloom, and across, on the other side of the low hedge, the fresh green fields, all the fresher for the morning's rain, in some of which already the tender little lambkins were sporting about or cuddling in by the side of their warm woolly ewe-mothers.

"I wish I was a lamb," thought Hoodie, as her glance fell on them. Then as she looked away beyond the fields to where in the distance the land sloped upwards into softly rising hills, a flight of birds attracted her attention. How prettily they flew, waving, now upwards, now downwards, like one long ribbon against the sky. "Or a little bird," she added. "If I was up there I could see so nicely where to go, and I could fly, fly, till I got to the sun."

But just then the sound of wheels coming near brought her thoughts down to earth again. Which way should she go?

She *must* pass through a wood. That was the only thing that at present she felt sure of, and there was a wood she remembered some way down the road, past Mr. Bright's farm. So down the road Hoodie trotted, her basket firmly clasped in her hand, her little figure the only moving thing to be seen along the queen's highway. For the cart to which the wheels belonged had passed quickly—it was only the grocer from the neighbouring town, so on marched Hoodie undisturbed. A little on this side of Farmer Bright's a lane turned off to the left. This lane, Hoodie decided, must be the way to the wood, so she left the road and went along the lane for about a quarter-of-a-mile, till, to her perplexity, it ended in a sort of little croft with a stile at each side. Hoodie climbed up both stiles in turns and looked about her. The wood was not to be seen from either, but across a field from the second stile she saw the tops of some trees standing on lower ground.

"That must be the wood," thought Hoodie, and down she clambered again to fetch her basket which she had left on the other side. With some difficulty she hoisted it and herself up again, with greater difficulty got it and herself down the steps on the further side, and then set off triumphantly at a run in the direction of the trees she had seen.

So far she was right. These trees were the beginning of a wood—a pretty little wood with a tiny stream running through the middle, and little nests of ferns and mosses in among the stones and tree-stumps on its banks—a very pret y little wood it must be in summer-time with the trees more fully out and the ground dry and crisp, and clear of the last year's leaves which still gave it a desolate appearance. Hoodie's spirits rose. She was getting on famously. Soon she might expect to see the grandmother's cottage, where no doubt the kettle would be boiling on the fire to make tea for her, and the table all nicely spread. For already she was beginning to feel hungry; she had journeyed, it seemed to her, a very long way, and more than once she eyed her basket wistfully, wondering if she might eat just one piece of the bread-and-butter.

"The little Hoodie-girl in the picture didn't, and Martin didn't," she said to herself. "So I 'appose I'd better not. And perhaps if the woofs saw me eating, it would make them come."

The idea made her shiver.

"But Maudie said there was no woofs," she added. "Maudie said there wasn't no woofs. But I *wish* I could see the cottage."

On and on she made her way,—here and there with really great difficulty, for there was no proper path, and sometimes the big tree stumps were almost higher than her fat, rather short legs could either stride across or climb over. More than once she scratched these same bare legs pretty badly, and but for the resolution which was a strong part of her character, the queer little girl would have sat down on the ground and burst into tears. But she struggled on, and at last, to her delight, the trees in front of her cleared suddenly, and she saw before her a little hilly path surmounted by a stile. Hoodie clapped her hands, or would have done so but for the interference of the basket.

"Hoodie's out of the wood," she said joyfully, "and up there perhaps I'll see the cottage."

It happened that she was right. When she reached the stile, there, sure enough, across another little field the cottage, *a* cottage any way, was to be seen. A neat little cottage, something like the description Martin had given of *her* grandmother's cottage, which, jumbled up with the picture of long ago Red Riding Hood the first, on the nursery walls, was in Hoodie's mind as a sort of model of that in quest of which she had set out on her voyage of discovery. This cottage too had a little garden with a path up the middle, and at each side were beds, neatly bordered, which in summer-time no doubt would be gay with simple flowers. Hoodie glanced round the little garden approvingly as she made her way up to the door.

"It's just like Martin's cottage," she thought. "But the Hoodie-girl in the picture was pulling somesing for the door to open and I don't see nosing to pull. I must knock I 'appose. I am so glad there's been none woofs."

Knock—knock—no answer. Knock, knock, *knock*, a little louder this time. Hoodie began to wonder if the grandmother was going to be out, like the one in Martin's story—no—a sound at last of some one coming to open.

(*To be continued.*)

39

MY LITTLE SOLDIER.

MY LITTLE SOLDIER.

BY THE EDITOR..

EARLY this winter's morning I hear a step on the stair:
Is it a ghost or robber? No; a soldier I declare!
A brave and gallant soldier is waiting for me there.

With a braided cap or helmet upon his noble head,
A musket in his strong right hand, a firm and martial tread,
A knapsack on his shoulders broad, a waving flag bright red.

Brave soldier, whom do you seek, thus armed quite ready for war?
I hope you're a friend, oh warrior, standing outside my door;
Or I think I shall fly and hide in bed, as I was before.

How came this valiant soldier to march into our domain?
Has he come to reconnoitre, and will he go home again?
Or perhaps if we ask for mercy, our prayer he'll entertain.

Has he come our house to pillage, ransack our fair old home?
But where has he left his army? why does he come alone?
Perhaps he's a wandering soldier, one who loves to roam.

Perhaps he's bent on murder, and wishes to shoot us dead;
Perhaps he has got some bullets—hard cold bullets of lead:
Perhaps he'll spare our lives, and make us his prisoners instead.

But stay, let me look at this soldier, of whom I have such fear.
I don't think he's so forbidding, when I see his face quite near;
Perhaps I may find that he's some one my heart holds very dear.

I see that his lips are rosy, his eyes large, soft, and bright,
That his pretty fair hair is all curly, his little face pink and white;
I begin to think my soldier a very pleasant sight.

Can it be my own little sonny, my dear little Johnny boy,
My pet, my companion, and darling, my plaything and my toy?
Ah, little rogue I have caught you, my fear is all changed into joy.

And what has the helmet turned into? Why, the teapot's own cosy cap.
And the knapsack? What but the footstool just fastened on with a strap.
Just think what a droll little soldier to rouse me out of my nap.

And then papa's old walking-stick helps to make up a flag,
Just a common walking-stick set off with a bit of rag,
While on the top of the footstool the child has put my bag.

And the wonderful death-dealing musket is Johnny's little toy gun.
So much for the little man's get-up. We think it a great piece of fun.
And now let us go and call father to look at his own soldier-son.

41

HOW PETER LEARNT TO READ.

HOW PETER LEARNT TO READ.

BY THE EDITOR.

WON'T go into that place. I won't learn to read nor to write neither. No, I won't, I tell yer! I hates the beastly old letters, that gets all muddled up together when I looks at them. I shan't go in, I tell yer."
So cried Master Peter Stretton, as he and his elder sister neared the National School-house, which stood not far from the little by-street where these children and their parents lived in Bayswater.

"Come along, Peter, mother'll be angry if you don't, and father'll give you a hiding. You know father's hands are precious evy."

"I shan't," cried the obstinate boy.

"Well, I shall catch it if you ain't in school to-day," added his sister Matty, beginning to get out of temper; "so come along, I tell you!"

She spoke these last words in a loud, angry voice, and, catching hold of her little brother, tried to give effect to her words by force. A regular tussle followed, as you see, little readers, in the picture. Slates and book-bags fell in the mud, and the scuffle ended by both children rolling over together, their clothes being torn and dirtied. This disgraceful scene was acted in the sight of several scholars on their way to the school : the little boys generally laughed at it, but the little girls looked on in dismay. Peter conquered : he won the battle at last by a kick upon his sister's shin; and while she stopped to rub it, he bounded off as fast as his young legs would take him, leaving books and slate upon the ground.

After crying a little, Matty turned and entered the school-house, considerably the worse for her struggle. She was about ten or eleven years old, while Peter was only seven, and, besides being a sharp, sensible girl, she had arrived at an age to understand the advantage of learning. Her father and mother could neither read nor write ; when they were

young education was not so general ; but they had often felt what an inconvenience and drawback this was to them, and were quite as determined as Matty was that Peter should learn as much as he could be made to learn. It was not only a dread of the School Board fines that made them insist upon his going to school ; it was also a sincere desire that, for his own sake, he should acquire knowledge.

Peter rushed away from his sister and the hated school-house, but he did not run home—for a very good reason, he dared not do so. He played in the gutter with other little truant boys, and for a time amused himself very well, making mud pies, or playing hocky, and other little games, on the pavement, to the annoyance of the passers-by. At last Peter began to feel cold—it was the early spring—particularly about his little legs, which were bare from the knee to the ankle. He was reminded also that it was past his dinner time, for he felt exceedingly hungry.

While he was considering what he should do, and feeling in a very troubled state of mind, his attention was attracted by the sound of many feet coming towards him, and of voices shouting. He turned round and saw a number of men and boys running along the street. Patter, patter, came the feet, and louder grew the shouting till he could distinguish the words —Fire ! fire ! fire !

As the crowd rushed past him, Peter joined it and shuffled along as fast as his little, tired, cold legs would carry him. The excitement and the exercise made him forget for the moment both his hunger and the cold. The crowd kept on increasing, and the noise became almost deafening. More than one fire-engine tore past them on its way to the place where the fire was raging. Peter neither knew how far he went, nor in what direction. All sense of fatigue was lost in the half-fearful yet eager curiosity which he felt to see the fire.

Presently Peter could see that the sky was

43

black with smoke above their heads, and in another minute, after turning up one street and down another, he suddenly found himself occupying a foremost place among a crowd of people who stood in a square, almost in front of a large house which was on fire.

There was a frightful roaring noise caused by the fire, which burst out at every opening. The windows had fallen in, and through the vacant spaces angry flames rushed out, and darted upwards toward the sky. While Peter stood there, a part of the roof fell in with a tremendous crash, and the flames rose up higher still, as if in triumph. A larger engine than any that had yet played upon the burning house came up, and volumes of water were sent upon the raging fire, but it seemed impossible to quench it. The long, trailing hose, through which streams of water went spouting forth, was twisted and turned in all directions where the flames burst out, but the only effect seemed to be that the volume of water meeting the volume of fire made a hissing noise and caused a quantity of white steam to mingle with the black smoke. The fire happening in the daytime, the inmates of the house had all left it in time, and the firemen were now exerting themselves, and risking their lives, to save the valuable property the house contained.

But to return to our poor little friend Peter. He was pushed and jostled by the crowd, and began to feel frightened, sick, and faint, but he knew it was impossible to get back through the mass of people behind him. The poor child wished himself anywhere but there, watching the fire : he even wished he was at the hated school-house, puzzling over his lessons. He thought about his home and longed for a sight of his mother's face : he longed to hear her voice, though it might scold him ; and to feel her hand though it might be laid heavily upon his own small person.

Now the burning house, whose front was in a large square, was a corner house, and its side was in a street. In that street the crowd appeared to be much less dense, and Peter at last, in his despair, determined to run across the open space in the front of the house, where the engines were stationed, and which was kept clear by policemen, that so reaching the side

street he might get out of the crowd that way. Off he darted, and was just passing the corner of the burning house when he heard a crash above him, and in a moment all poor little Peter's fears and hopes, his thoughts of home and of his mother, came to an end ; everything was dark to his eyes and mind alike.

A large portion of the side wall of the house had fallen, and some of the bricks had struck down and nearly killed our poor, little, truant boy.

When he recovered consciousness he was lying in a little bed ; one of a row of many such little beds ; most of them being occupied by some pale-faced suffering child like himself. He was in the child's ward of a great hospital, where care and skill and kindness were doing all that was possible for his recovery. The little wounded boy had a terrible cut upon his head, and one of his legs was broken. For two days after he ran away, Peter's father and mother had suffered intense anxiety : they thought he was lost, and wandered about in search of him. At length, through inquiries made of the police, they learnt what had happened, and where he was.

He had been three days in the hospital when, on awaking from a feverish sleep, he saw the sorrowful face of his sister Matty by the side of his bed. His mother was not far off ; and his first words were to beg his mother, in a little weak voice, that she would forgive him, and to tell her that, if he got well, he would never shirk school again. And he kept his promise.

Peter remained at the hospital nearly three months, and my little readers may imagine how he had changed, and what a good boy he had become, when I tell them that during those three months he learnt to read. Matty went to see him very often, and used to bring books with her : she would read to him and give him lessons in reading too. There was a kind nurse also who used to teach him sometimes when Matty was not there, and before he left the hospital he could occupy and amuse himself by reading.

When Peter was well enough to go to school again, he soon gained the character of being a good and clever boy.

44

THE FROG'S PARTY.

The frog who would a woo-ing go Gave a par-ty you must know; And his bride all
dressed in green Looked as fine as an-y queen. Their re-cep-tions number'd some,
Of the best in Frog-gie-dom. Four gay frog-gies played the fiddle, Hands a-cross and
down the mid-dle, Oh! oh! oh! oh! A-way we go! Hopping and jumping a-way we go!

2.

Some stern old croakers there did come,
With white chokers in the room;
Froggie belles with rush-leaf fans,
Froggie beaux in green brogans,
Flirted in the bowers there
Hidden from the ball-room's glare;
Three old froggies tried a reel—
Twist 'em, turn 'em toe and heel: with

Oh! Oh! &c.

3.

One little Miss was asked to sing,
But she had a cold that spring;
Little frogs were sound asleep,
Late hours—bad for them to keep.
Each one wish'd the couple joy;
No bad boys came to annoy;
This next fall—the news is spreading—
They will have a silver wedding;

Oh! Oh! &c.

45

AN HONEST THIEF.

AN HONEST THIEF.

BY THE EDITOR.

DARESAY you children would like me to tell you about the very funniest dog 1 ever knew : indeed, I can scarcely help laughing now when I think of him. He belonged to an Irish footman, who lived in my grandfather's service when I was a child. Joseph was an old servant, and a very worthy and excellent one in most respects, but alas! he was rather too fond of indulging now and then in what he called a "dhrop."

Sometimes he would be sober for weeks and even months together, if no temptation came in his way : but let there be any merry-making, or anything festive going on in the neighbourhood, to which he could obtain leave to go, and Joseph never came home sober. He was looked upon among his friends as extremely good company, and was sought for and welcomed by all party-givers in his class of society. These sprees were overlooked by his kind-hearted old master : but Joseph belonged to another besides his master, and that other was a worthy and most respectable, though not too indulgent, wife.

Joseph lived and slept in my grandfather's house, while Norah, the wife, lived in a cottage close by ; but whenever she heard that he had, what she called, disgraced himself, she would make him feel her anger pretty severely. Not only hard words were showered upon him, but, if report spoke truly, harder blows would sometimes follow. Now one evening Joseph returned from some merry-making more than usually the worse for his "dhrop," and my kind old grandfather was so annoyed that, the next morning, he walked down to the cottage where Joseph's wife lived, to have a talk with her upon the subject.

"He sha'n't have no more outings, Sir William," said the worthy Norah, "I'll take care of that."

And she did take care. Now what do you think she did? I must tell you that Norah, being an industrious woman, increased her income by taking in washing, and she washed for the family at the great house, including her husband. So the next time he wanted to go out—it was to a wedding-party at a farmer's that he was invited—she took a sure means to prevent his going, by simply refusing to let

him have a clean shirt. Joseph tried scolding and persuasion by turns, he even complained to his master, but all to no purpose. "It is not my fault, Joseph," said my grandfather laughing, "I will give you leave to go if you promise to keep sober."

"Sure," said Joseph, "and it's at home I'll have to stay, if the wife won't hear reason."

Now I come at last to the hero of my story. Joseph, among other indulgences, was allowed to keep a pet dog at the house. This dog's name was Paddy : he was a mongrel, of no breed in particular, and certainly was no beauty ; but he made up for the want of that quality by his cleverness, his funny ways, and his affection for his master. Joseph and Paddy would hold long conversations ; the dog answering the man by a low whining ; and, strange to say, they seemed always to understand each other perfectly. Besides this Paddy had many accomplishments, and would learn with wonderful quickness any funny trick his master taught him.

When Joseph was in trouble about a shirt he confided his sorrow to his dog, who seemed to feel it as deeply as his master. On the morning of the wedding-party Joseph determined to make a last appeal to his wife, and walked towards the cottage accompanied by Paddy. As he approached it, he saw some of his own shirts hanging out on a string to dry, and pointing to them, said to Paddy :—"Sure but I wish I had one of thim shirts now." In a moment the dog scampered off, and jumping up, pulled one of the shirts from the line, and brought it in triumph to his master.

Joseph's wish was fulfilled, but it did him no good after all. The shirt was neither starched nor ironed, and was made dirty besides by being dragged over the grass. He was just thinking that he would turn back rather than encounter his wife's anger, when she appeared at the door; so he went on, and made the best excuses for Paddy that he could. Norah was in a good humour that morning : she was struck by the dog's devotion to his master, and sent Joseph back with a nicely got-up shirt under his arm. I regret to say, on his return from the wedding-party he was as usual the worse for a "dhrop."

BEAUTIFUL SNOW.

BY THE AUTHOR OF "AUNT EFFIE'S RHYMES," Etc.

BEAUTIFUL snow, light as a feather,
Where did you go in the sultry weather?
You came from the heavens last winter you know,
And well I remember you, beautiful snow.

Are things up there, in the higher air,
Always unchangeably bright and fair?
You have come to a world where we change our light,
Sometimes for darkness, and always for night.

Beautiful snow, when last you fell
It was evening-tide—I remember it well—
And we were exchanging our wintry light
For the heavier gloom of a moonless night.

I knelt at the window and saw how you came,
Not like the boisterous pattering rain,
But wavering softly, hovering down,
You nestled at last on the wintry brown.

Oh it was wonderful; overhead
The darkness gathered like molten lead.
But up from the ground that you covered below,
Light seemed to come from the fallen snow.

48

Beautiful Snow.

It was time to sleep. and the mother said,
" Tuck up the little ones snugly in bed."
Oh it seemed hard, but I had to go,
Though I cried when I left you, my beautiful snow.

In the land of dreams, where we spend our nights,
There are heavenly sounds and heavenly sights,
And the Angel of Sleep with its loving care,
Dried up my tears and carried me there.

Holding my hand as we passed along
The back of the clouds where the light is strong,
We saw how the great cold drops of rain
Turn into hail and fall down again.

Vapoury mist, like a silvery shroud,
Folded us up in a sunlit cloud,
And we saw it like diamond dust below,
Changing itself into beautiful snow.

I did not awake in the land of dreams,
But just in my bed, and with baby's screams,
And when I looked out on the ground below,
Not a flake was left of you, beautiful snow.

A FUNNY TWIN BROTHER

A FUNNY TWIN BROTHER.

AST sum-mer when we were in the coun-try hav-ing a hap-py ho-li-day, we of-ten went in-to the hay-field, and you lit-tle ones may fan-cy the fun we had. John-ny and Lil-ly rolled in the sweet fresh hay, and were bu-ried and came up a-gain ma-ny and ma-ny a time; and just when we thought there was not a bit of chub-by child to be seen, a round red laugh-ing face would peep out, fol-lowed by a sort of wind-mill of arms and legs.

It was on a bright sum-mer's day in that hay-field that we met Tim and his lit-tle mis-tress. " Who was Tim ? " you say. Well, Tim was a don-key, and such a hap-py pet-ted don-key has sel-dom been seen be-fore. Liz-zy— the lit-tle girl you see in the pic-ture—was the far-mer's daugh-ter, and as she led Tim round her fa-ther's field, she picked up the sweet hay and fed him with it.

When Tim and lit-tle Liz-zy came near us, we all went up to pat the don-key: then the lit-tle girl told us how good and gen-tle her Tim was. " We are very luc-ky to have such a good don-key," said she.

" And I think he is luc-ky to have such a good lit-tle mis-tress," said I.

" Oh, but he be-longs to us all," an-swered the child, " and there are six of us; we all feed and pet him. My father bought him when he was quite lit-tle. He is five years old now; just the same age as my lit-tle bro-ther Willy. So he is his Twin Bro-ther you see," ad-ded Liz-zy grave-ly.

St Valentine's Day

TALKS ABOUT THE MONTHS.

By Mrs. GEORGE CUPPLES.

FEBRUARY.

"February, welcome, though still cold and bitter,
Thou bringest Valentine, Pancake, and Fritter."

"Good-morrow, Valentine,
First 'tis yours, then 'tis mine,
So please give me a Valentine."

JANUARY, with all its New Year's festivities, is over, and February has come full of new life and pleasant bustle. "What?" I hear some one saying, "pleasant bustle!" How can any one use such a word when it is still as cold as winter, and the weather is so uncertain that we cannot begin to trim our gardens or do anything comfortably out of doors? For our own part, we would rather have January out-and-out for thirty-one days more, in spite of its sharp cold. But, come, wrap yourself up extra warmly and take a brisk walk abroad with me, and I shall do my best to prove to you that February, in spite of its disagreeable thaws, and uncertain weather, has its own special enjoyableness. Out in the open country roads what do we hear? It is a sky-lark soaring up towards the clouds. He has taken advantage of a broad burst of sunshine that has streamed from between the clouds, and is piping his joyous song in glad anticipation of the Spring to come. The mellow flute-like voiced blackbird, and the liquid trill of the speckle-breasted thrush, are heard sweet, though low, from among the opening white blossoms of the blackthorn. In the

52

fields, on either side, the rooks are following close upon the heels of the ploughmen, fluttering and cawing along the furrows, and greedily pouncing down upon any unfortunate worm that the plough has turned up. In some sheltered spot we come upon a daring snowdrop, "the herald of the infant Spring,"—the yellow winter aconite, and sometimes an orange-coloured crocus; all apparently anxious to see what the Spring is to be like. If it be mild for the season, probably we may see some early catkins of the hazel opening their buds, as well as the common blue periwinkle, and even, if we have extra sharp eyes, and look carefully in the warmest corner of the woods, we may find an adventurous sweet violet. I think that after the good bracing walk we have had, with all the sights we have seen, and the sounds we have heard, you will now agree with me in thinking February is rather pleasanter than you at first supposed. Before we pass indoors again, if we take a look at the cabbages in the garden, we shall very likely find them beginning to sprout, and this fact led our Saxon forefathers to call the month Sprout-Kele, because the cabbages or coleworts began then to sprout. They afterwards changed it to Sol-Monath, or Sun Month, because the increasing warmth of the sun made plants begin to vegetate, and Pancake Month, because pancakes were then offered to the sun.

It was the Romans who gave this month the name of February, calling it after the goddess Februa, and from the custom of burning atoning sacrifices for their sins. This month was also placed under the especial protection of Neptune, the god of the waters, and had for its sign—in the twelve clusters of stars that represent the months in the circle called the Zodiac—*Pisces*, the Fishes. Into this sign or constellation the sun enters on the 19th of the month, shining for a longer period than he did during January. There is a saying about this, that "as the day lengthens the cold strengthens." Perhaps we feel it the more on account of the longer time of daylight during which we have to brave it, as one is apt to fancy that the dusk and the dark are a kind of covering; not to say how much depends on being beside a good warm fireplace, with the

53

lamps shining round. A frosty moonlight often seems to make the cold thrill to the very marrow of our bones; even still more so the stars of a moonless but bright night during frost; when, as they glitter and twinkle so icily overhead, every one of them is like a special needle-point, piercing between the smallest chink of people's wraps and furs.

On the second of the month, many people will be looking anxiously out of their windows to see what kind of weather we are going to have, hoping to find it *not* sunny and bright—as, no doubt, *you* would like to have it, that you may go comfortably to church (this year)—but wet and windy; for there are many who still believe in the old rhyme :—

If Candlemas day be dry and fair
The half o' winter's to come and mair ;
If Candlemas be wet and foul,
The half of winter's gone at Yule :

In Germany they have two proverbs about it; first, the shepherd would rather see the wolf enter his stable on Candlemas Day than the sun; and second, the badger peeps out of his hole on Candlemas Day, and, when he finds snow, walks abroad—but if he sees the sun shining, he draws back into his sleeping-burrow. Many a young inexperienced long-tailed mouse, and active squirrel, have been sadly put out by finding the beginning of February warm and bright: they shake themselves, and nibble away at the stores that were so carefully hoarded up in autumn, for they think to themselves the winter frost is gone. If they had known that old rhyme they would have been more cautious, and not have made so much haste to be up and out, till the February snow was quite gone.

I think that in spite of the general damp, foggy state of the weather at the beginning of the month, you will find that February is an active, sprightly month. It has its festivities as well as January. First comes Valentine's Day, and you know how anxiously we look for the postman coming along, and how disappointed we are if he does not leave us at least one valentine. But the delight with which Valentine's Day is looked for by boys and girls is nothing compared to the joyous welcome it receives from the birds. The air is full of the sweetest twitterings and warblings, for this is the day when each chooses its mate :

> Hail, Bishop Valentine ! whose day this is ;
> All the air is thy diocese,
> And all the chirping choristers
> And other birds are thy parishioners :
> Thou marryest every year
> The lyric lark, and the grave, whispering dove ;
> The sparrow that neglects his life for love,
> The household bird with the red stomacher ;
> Thou makest the blackbird speed as soon
> As doth the goldfinch or the halcyon—
> This day more cheerfully than ever shine:
> To-day we'll happy be, old Valentine.

Then, on the 25th of the month, this year, comes Shrove Tuesday; and though the old customs connected with it are in many places scarcely remembered, still they are not altogether forgotten, especially in rustic localities. The merriment begins the day before, with what is called "Collop Monday," from the practice of eating "collops"—slices of salted meat—and eggs on that day. The boys keep a bright look-out for Shrovetide treats; up and down the village or streets they go singing,

> "Shrovetide is nigh at hand,
> And I be come a shroving ;
> Pray, dame, something,
> An apple, or a dumpling."

Then when Shrove Tuesday dawns, the bells are set a-ringing, and everybody indulges in a holiday. There is such a stirring about of pancake batter, and such a frizzling of them in the pan everywhere ; for all try who will devour the largest quantity. True, the fatiguing game of football—for every man and boy who can play, joins in that game on that particular day—*must* give them an appetite. It is to be hoped that the day will be calm, for in February very often the wind rises to a perfect hurricane, and then instead of enjoying the game of football, all will be busy, in the country districts, laying on logs or rails, or anything handy and heavy enough to keep the roofs *on*. Old wives are looking anxiously to their pig-styes and hen-roosts, and there is a sound in the bare woods, and in the fir-plantations, like the roaring of the sea. But though it is an anxious time as long as it lasts, it is "an ill wind that blows nobody any good ;" for, after it is over, the old wives will have quite a harvest of decayed

branches to gather and carry home. After all, perhaps, the pancakes will taste all the sweeter after such a stormy day, and when all are snug in-doors round the blazing fire, the warring of the tempest without will only make us enjoy the comforts within all the more. Not if we live close to a seaport or a village harbour, though ; for there are always anxious groups gathered there, keeping as bright a look-out as possible, in case some homeward-bound craft gets into difficulties. Their hearts and their eyes if not their lips, are saying—as we should all do when it is stormy weather—

> "Eternal Father, strong to save,
>   Whose arm hath bound the restless wave—
> Oh, hear us when we cry to Thee
> For those in peril on the sea."

A walk at the end of February will be found to be a very different thing from what it was at the beginning, for now the birds sing joyously, and the rooks are cawing in every direction, as they visit their old homes to see what state these are in. The raven is busy looking out for material for his nest ; and the gander is making a loud quacking, for the goose is now laying her eggs, and he likes to have a large troop of fluffy goslings sailing after him. We do not require to put out so many crumbs now, for many of the birds who lately came to our windows have gone off to the woods, and are busy with their domestic preparations. The wren and the robin are hopping from spray to spray, and the blue tit-mouse and the impudent little tom-tits are darting here, there, and everywhere, piping out a few sweet notes. If the days are mild, and our walk leads along a sheltered hedge-row, we are almost sure to see a swarm of gnats gambolling and sporting in constant motion, and one or two early butterflies flit across our path, enticed out of their hiding-places by the first gleam of warm sunshine. We, too, think the winter is gone, and set to to trim our gardens, for the young leaves are budding and the hedges are showing a faint flush of green. The snow-drop, "fair maid of February," has now come boldly out in the warm borders, and the crocuses and the blue-and-white hepaticas are plentiful everywhere. You will scarcely believe it, but the shepherds are keeping a bright look-out for snow, for even up to the end of February snow may come again, and many sheep in the mountainous districts are lost during this month; still, for all that, we keep singing as a welcome to the coming Spring :—

"Up !—let us to the fields away,
  And breathe the fresh and balmy air :
The bird is building in the tree,
The flower has opened to the bee,
  And health and love and peace are there !"

FORBIDDEN FRUIT.

THERE was an old Boar who said :—"How !
Do you think my small pigs you'll take now ?
  They are not afraid,
  No, indeed not a shade,
So be off, and we won't have a row."

Mr. Wolf, who was but a sneak,
At once became humble and meek,
  Said :—"I'll wish you good-day,
  And be off on my way,
I'm afraid other game I must seek."

FOUR GREEDY BIRDS.

FOR VE-RY LIT-TLE CHILD-REN.

SAID the first lit-tle bird to the second lit-tle bird:—
"Here's a plate, lit-tle bird, here's a plate."

Said the se-cond lit-tle bird to the third lit-tle bird:—
" You'll be late, lit-tle bird, you'll be late."

Said the third lit-tle bird to the fourth lit-tle bird:—
" Here's good stuff, lit-tle bird, here's good stuff."
Said the fourth lit-tle bird to the third lit-tle bird:—
" Not enough, lit-tle bird, not enough."

Said the third lit-tle bird to the fourth lit-tle bird:—
" Then a-way, lit-tle bird, you may hop."
Said the fourth lit-tle bird to the third lit-tle bird:—
" Think I'll stop, lit-tle bird, think I'll stop."

Said an-other lit-tle bird to these four lit-tle birds:—
" Here's one more lit-tle bird, here's one more."
Said the four lit-tle birds to the fifth lit-tle bird:—
" Get a-way, there's but just e-nough for four."

Then cried other lit-tle birds to these four greedy birds:—
" We are hungry, lit-tle birds, and we are cold."
Said the four greedy birds to the other lit-tle birds:—
" Don't be bold, lit-tle birds, don't be bold."

And the poor hungry birds watched the four greedy birds,
  While they ate up the food in a row;
And the poor lit-tle things beg-ged in vain for a share,
  As they shiver-ed and shook in the snow.

The four greedy birds were still busy at the plate,
  When the gar-den-er came walk-ing past that way:
Fright-en-ed, they flew off, with-out fin-ish-ing their feast;
  The hun-gry ones were brave e-nough to stay.

BLACK ROLF OF ROOKSTONE.

By the Right Hon. E. H. KNATCHBULL-HUGESSEN, M.P., *Author of " Uncle Joe's Stories,"* &c.

CHAPTER II.

E, the Lord of Rookstone, the Baron Fitzuron, the richest and most powerful person in the country round, had been bearded in his own bedroom by a common—or rather a most uncommon—rook, and had been denounced to his face as the wrongful possessor of the title and estates which were so dear to him as the reward of a life's work. It was not to be endured for a moment. Gradually, every other sensation which had agitated his breast gave way to rage: deep, dire, grim rage at the rook, at his threats, and at the world in general, for when a man once gives way to his anger, nothing appears pleasant or agreeable, and he feels a disposition to quarrel with everything he sees and every-

58

body he chances to meet. As soon as he had a little recovered his composure and collected his thoughts, the Baron rose and performed a hasty toilet, during which operation he frequently gnashed his teeth and uttered imprecations of a nature more decided than polite.

Since the departure of the foreboder of evil he had formed a portentous resolution, upon the carrying out of which he became more determined every moment. He would destroy the rookery! His mind was quite made up upon the subject. No more should those birds be harboured around the mansion against whose owner they had rebelled. Even supposing that every word uttered by the rook had been true as gospel, there was something to be said upon the other side. True, he had treated the birds somewhat differently from his ancestors, in that he had denied them their daily feast of grain. But what of that? Had he not still permitted them to inhabit the lofty elms and limes which they had so long occupied, and from whence they could swoop down at will and gather food for themselves like other rooks? Why, forsooth, were they to fare better than other birds of their own species? What had they done to maintain the ancient power and prosperity of the House of Rolf? And in what was he beholden to them for his present position? He had achieved it for himself by the might of his own right hand and the work of his own brain. Why had he denied them their old meal of grain? It was because he was bound to practise every economy in order to build up the fortunes of his fallen house. Had the rooks done so for him, economy would have been unnecessary, and they might have eaten grain till they burst for all he cared.

Thus did the Baron argue with himself as he dressed, and soon came to the conclusion that he was a wronged and injured man, that the rooks had behaved infamously to him and his, and that the sooner they were got rid of the better. When, therefore, he left his room and proceeded to the old oak parlour, in which he always ate his morning meal, his first care was to summon the old Elfrida to his presence. She came, surprised indeed at the message, but anxious to know what service she could do to the being she loved best on earth.

In a few curt words the Baron informed her that the woodmen and foresters who still remained attached to the castle must be summoned forthwith, for that he had resolved to cut down the rookery.

On hearing this, the old woman threw up her arms with a despairing cry! "Oh sir— master—my lord," she exclaimed, "surely my ears are deaf with age and I cannot have heard rightly. Destroy the rookery? Goodlack, but I must be mad to think thou saidst such a thing."

The Baron frowned darkly. "Did'st ever know me trifle?" said he sternly. "The rookery falls: every tree, lime and elm, comes down. They have harboured a nest of black feathered traitors, and I will none of either."

Again the old woman wrung her hands in anguish as she renewed her appeal. "Bethink ye, good my lord," she urged in sad but earnest tones; "bethink thee, 'tis easy to destroy, but hard to build again. These trees have seen generations of thy noble family spring, flourish, and pass away. The rooks have ever been accounted friendly unto thine house: to fell the one and banish the other! Can it be right? Can it be prudent? Alas and alack, I fear me terribly there will be evil days if it is to be so!"

Black Rolf struck his fist fiercely upon the table. "Begone, woman!" he cried in a loud voice, "and execute my orders. Had'st thou not carried me on thy knee when I was a puny child I had not brooked to hear so much from thee. Begone, I say!"

Alarmed at his words and threatening manner, old Elfrida withdrew, weeping bitterly, for although she knew that her master must have some hidden reason for what he did, she felt sure that evil would follow, and felt sad at heart for the nursling she had watched from childhood to youth, from youth to middle age, and from middle age until his head had begun to whiten and age to creep slowly on. She was herself very aged, but the feelings of her heart were warm as ever towards the child she had nursed, and bitterly did she grieve over the thought that of a surety misfortune was at hand. Under any circumstances this would not have been a very unnatural thing to suppose, for when a man directs his home rookery to be

cut down he must either be mad, in considerable
difficulty with regard to his money affairs, or
remarkably badly off for timber, in either of
which cases there is a great probability of misfortune being nearer than his friends could
wish.

However, the Baron's orders had been so
peremptory, that Elfrida could do nothing else
than carry them out. Accordingly she gave
directions that all the woodmen and foresters
about the place should be summoned, and
directed to bring axes, hatchets and saws, in
order that the work of destruction might be
begun that very afternoon. There were not
many people to send, and not many people to
be sent for, since the Baron had been constantly
reducing the number of his servants and depen-
dants for many years past. However, some
fourteen or fifteen men were got together by
about two o'clock in the afternoon, and the
Baron was duly informed that they were ready.

Accordingly, he strode forth from his room
and stood upon the sloping lawn in front of
the castle, close by the ancient terrace walk.
Immediately upon his right hand stood an oak of
enormous girth, said to be the largest for many
miles round. It was probably the oldest without doubt, and was hollow within from age,
but still of grand and noble appearance and
likely to see out several more generations of
the House of Rolf. On the Baron's left hand, at
the end of the lawn, stood that noble grove of
elms and limes, part of which formed an avenue
by which the castle was approached on that
side, and which, together, constituted the
rookery which the owner had doomed to
destruction. It was a magnificent sight, and
beautiful also was the view upon which the
Baron gazed as he stood upon his lawn.

At that moment the ancient Elfrida came out
again and threw herself upon her knees before
him. "Oh, good my lord!" she cried, as the
tears coursed down her aged cheeks, and her
whole frame quivered with fear and excitement,
"Think what you do! You may bring a curse
upon the place and upon yourself. Oh, pause
before it be too late, my dear, dear lord!"

But Rolf spurned her roughly from him.
"Up!" he cried in anger. "Up and begone!
This is no place for crones and aged drivellers.

I tell thee, Black Rolf will no more be moved
from his purpose than yon oak from its place!"

Wonder upon wonders! Scarcely had these
words left the lips of the Baron, than the
venerable and gigantic tree to which he had
alluded gave a creak from top to bottom, and
a groan as if struck by heavy wind, altho'
there was not a breath stirring in the heavens:
and then, its mighty roots seemed all at once
to fail it, and without any perceptible cause
it toppled over, and fell with a terrific crash
upon the ground.

With a shriek of terror the ancient dame
fled into the house, and the workmen who were
assembled at the end of the walk nearest the
rookery, stared in horror-struck amazement at
the extraordinary occurrence. But the Baron
was only moved to wrath.

"Fool that I was to speak!" muttered he to
himself, "as if my speech could have had anything to do with the fall of that tree. It was
as old as the hills, and the only wonder is that
it did not fall long before." So saying he turned
his back upon the fallen monarch of the forest,
and approached his men with the intention of
cheering them up by his presence, and encouraging them to begin their work at once.

All this time the rooks, evidently aware of
the measures about to be taken against them,
were wheeling about overhead, describing rapid
circles in the air, which they darkened with
their number as with a cloud, and giving continual vent to a loud and indignant cawing.

This, however, caused the Baron rather satisfaction than otherwise, since he interpreted it
to mean that they recognised his power to
dispossess them of their homes, and did not
like it at all. He grimly smiled, therefore, as
he bade his men approach the rookery and
begin their work upon a large elm that stood
near, which, but for the season of the year,
would have been full of new nests, but as it
was winter, had of course nothing but old ones.
Hardly, however, had the party got within a
few yards of the tree, when the whole aspect of
the heavens changed, and a storm began of which
the like had never been seen or heard within
the memory of man. The peals of thunder
rolled like the roar of twenty thousand cannons
fired all at once, so that every window in the

castle was either broken or cracked by the vibration.

The lightning darted with such vivid and awful flashes that it lighted up the whole country for the moment that it lasted, and made it seem dark as pitch by contrast when it ceased. Large, heavy drops of rain began to fall; the wind rose, and it first wailed mournfully through the tops of the elms and limes as if it was the spirit of the trees moaning and sighing over their approaching downfall. Then all of a sudden it changed its tone, and began to roar. And it *did* roar, louder than wind had ever been heard to roar there before. Out at sea it lashed the waves until they danced about like mad things, and hurled huge white flakes of foam and froth high into the air, and tossed the ships and boats about as if they were so many straws, and then came rushing and dashing against the rocks as if they had made up their minds to sweep them right away once for all.

Yet none of the elms or limes blew down, and the trees around the castle stood firm, although they groaned and bent before the fury of the blast. And then the wind partially lulled, but with no apparent intention of making matters better, for it only did so sufficiently to permit a hailstorm to sweep over the earth without blowing the hailstones away. Such hailstones were never seen. Their average size was that of a blackbird's egg, and they came down with such force and rapidity that nothing could stand against them. This settled the question of the rookery for that afternoon, at least, for as soon as the woodmen and foresters felt the hailstones, they turned to a man and ran away as fast as they could to find shelter.

The Baron left the place last; but he, too, was driven off by the violence of the storm. Still he turned slowly and sullenly round, as a stag driven to bay by hounds, and scarce felt the hailstones as they pattered against him, so consumed was he by the flame of anger which burned within him. Drenched to the skin with hail and rain, dazzled by the lightning and deafened by the thunder and wind, he re-entered the castle a different man from him who had so recently quitted it, so far at least as personal appearance was concerned.

But the proud spirit was still unquelled: the stubborn disposition was unchanged, and the firm determination with which he had set out remained the same as ever. What! the fall of an oak, a clap or two of thunder, a gale of wind and a hailstorm! Were these things to change the purpose of a Rolf of Rookstone?

He was more than ever determined that the Rookery should be destroyed. That night the Baron drank deep, but his nerves were of iron and his constitution too hardy to be affected by a chance carousal. Yet his potations, instead of cheering him, only darkened the cloud which hung over him, intensified his anger and hardened his inflexible purpose. He was later than usual in retiring to rest, and again he tossed upon a sleepless couch. Do what he would, the words of the rook kept ringing in his ears in the most unpleasant manner, especially those concluding lines in which the bird stated that his nephew was near, and intimated, in coarse and vulgar phraseology, that he would shortly be called upon to relinquish his hereditary possessions and quit the castle of his ancestors.

He half expected that his unwelcome visitor would reappear: there was no reason why he should not, for if he could come through a thick wall at one time, the Baron supposed he could do so with equal ease at another. Moreover, he thought that the bird would probably wish to say something disagreeable about his day's expedition, and indulge in a little chaff at his expense in consequence of its failure. But nothing of the sort occurred. After he had lain awake rather longer than he liked, he dropped off to sleep, and slept till morn.

His dreams, to be sure, were not of the most pleasant nature, being composed of a medley of strange things, storms, thunder, trees falling, rooks cawing, and a number of other things wrought into curious, fantastic, and horrible images by the magic power of dreaming. But at last morning came, and Baron Fitznron arose as calmly as if nothing particular had happened, and on looking out of the window, perceived that the day was fine and the sky clear overhead. His first act was to repeat his yesterday's orders, and direct the woodmen and foresters to be summoned as before. Once more did old Elfrida endeavour to restrain him, but he rebuked her more sternly than on the previous day, vowing that but for the peculiar relations in which she stood to him, she should be consigned to the dungeons for daring for the third time to cross the will of a Fitzuron.

Thus silenced, the ancient crone forbore to reply, and abandoned every hope of turning her whilom nursling from his infatuated course. Again he stepped forward on the lawn, called to his people, and approached the Rookery. At

a short distance from the first tree he paused and spoke to the men.

"Now," said he "ye know that I am a man of my word. I will have these foul birds here no more, destroying the whole place, and 'preventing sleep with their abominable and eternal cawing. The only way to drive them hence is to fell the trees which harbour them. I have said it shall be done, and what I say I mean. Go therefore to work with a will, and ye shall have double pay if within six days the last tree falls."

"But when will the first fall?" asked a voice in defiant tones, as the Baron finished his speech.

He looked around, but could see no one. It seemed to come from above his head, but when he looked up he could only see a quantity of rooks flying to and fro, and he preferred not to look up any longer.

"Onward!" he shouted, and the woodmen and foresters, who had not previously appeared very eager to commence the work, advanced with some readiness under the prospect of the double pay to which their master had alluded.

No sooner, however, had the first axe been raised to strike the old elm at the head of the avenue, than a novel and extraordinary scene occurred. From every side the rooks swooped down boldly upon the men, uttering a loud, constant, and fearful cawing, and attacking with beak and claws the would-be destroyers of their homes. The workmen were so taken by surprise that they hardly knew what to do. Accustomed to consider rooks as quiet birds, of a domestic turn of mind and of peaceable habits generally, they were completely astonished to witness the warlike demeanour which was now assumed by their feathered foes, and the pertinacious valour with which they did battle for their hearths and homes, if indeed a rook's nest can by any poetic license be called a hearth. The men struck wildly and blindly at the birds, and speedily knocked over a number of them. But more and more came swooping down, and so many attacked each man at one and the same moment, that defence was almost impossible against such overwhelming odds.

The Baron, who had stood aghast at the sudden and unexpected nature of this new obstacle to the accomplishment of his designs, now thought it high time to interfere. Waving over his head his favourite spud, with which he usually walked about the Park and grounds of the castle, he uttered a loud and indignant shout, and with one blow knocked down half a dozen of the birds who were assailing his dependents in so strange and violent a manner. What effect might have been produced by this active and timely interposition on the Baron's part can hardly be guessed, for at this identical instant the horn which hung at the outer castle gate was sounded loudly, in a manner which showed that some one required admittance who deemed his business important and pressing.

The Baron paused for a moment, unwilling to relinquish the combat, and yet startled by the suddenness and vehemence of the ringing at the bell. But even whilst he paused the ringing recommenced, and it was evident that his presence was necessary to receive the visitor who demanded entrance with so much urgency. Casting a look of fury at the rooks, who appeared to be gathering for another attack upon him, he strode hastily towards the castle, whilst a loud and triumphant cawing told the defeat of his servants, who as soon as his back was turned, dropped axe and hatchet and fled in dismay from the wrath of the furious birds.

Before the owner of the castle could reach the gate, it had been thrown open by the hand of the aged Elfrida, and the clamorous visitor admitted. He proved to be a messenger from the Baron's agent for law matters, who lived in the nearest town, some ten miles distant from the castle. The messenger carried a scroll which, with a lowly obeisance, he presented to the Baron, and said that he was to wait for a reply.

Upon the outside of this scroll was written in large, sprawling characters, "For the hands of the noble Baron Fitzuron of Rookstone Towers. Haste—Post-haste. These with speed. Ride—Ride—Ride."

(To be continued.)

PICTURE PAGE WANTING WORDS.

A Prize of a Guinea Book will be given for the best Short Original Story descriptive of this picture. Competitors to be under fourteen years of age, and the stories to be sent to the "EDITOR OF LITTLE WIDEAWAKE," care of Messrs. GEORGE ROUTLEDGE & SONS, by the 15th February, 1879.

HOODIE.

By Mrs. MOLESWORTH, *Author of* "*Hermy*," "*The Cuckoo Clock*," &c.

CHAPTER III.—LITTLE BABY AND ITS MOTHER.

> "Polly put the kettle on,
> And let's have tea."

HE latch was lifted from the inside, and there stood before Hoodie—not an old woman with either "big" or little eyes, not a "grandmother" with a frilly cap all round her face, such as she had been vaguely expecting, yet certainly not a "woof" either! The person who stood in the doorway smiling down on the little girl was a very pretty and pleasant-looking young woman, with a fresh rosy face and merry eyes, and a sleeping baby in her arms!

For the first moment Hoodie was too surprised to understand what she saw.

At last, "I want my grandmother," she said. "*You* aren't my grandmother. I thought this was her cottage."

Hoodie.

The young woman smiled again. "No Missy, you must have made a mistake. But *your* grandmother doesn't live in a little cottage like this, Missy, I'm sure. You must have quite come out of your road. Whose little lady are you?"

Hoodie shook her head. "I want to live with my grandmother," she replied. "I don't want to be anybody's little lady. I've come such a long way—I know the cottage should be aside a wood, just like this. And I'm *so* tired and firsty."

The quiver in her voice told that the self-control was coming to an end. The young woman's sympathy awoke at once. "Poor dear," she said. "Tired, of course you must be tired. Come in, dearie, and sit you down, and you shall have something to drink and to eat too, if you please. What would you like?" she went on after she had established Hoodie on a funny little arm-chair by the fire—a chair bought last fair-day by her husband in his extreme delight at being the possessor of a fortnight old baby—"what would you like, Missy—a cup of milk—or some tea? Kettle's boiling and 'tis just upon tea-time."

"What a nice little chair," said Hoodie, making the observation that first came into her head before replying to the questions asked her, as was a habit of hers. "What a nice little chair! It just fits me," turning her fat little body—to confess the truth, a rather tight fit—and the chair about together, like a snail congratulating itself on its shell.

"Yes, Missy, and you're the first as has ever sat in it. It's to be for baby, the dear, as soon as she's old enough to sit up in it. But about what you'd like to drink, Missy?"

"I were going to tell you," said Hoodie with a touch of her usual authoritative manner. "I were going to tell you. I'd like tea—proper tea on a table, 'cos I've got my bicsits and 'sings in my bastwick, and we could put them out nicely. And if it's so far away to my grandmother's perhaps I'd better stay here and fancy you're her"—she glanced up in the young woman's face with such a queer, half-puzzled, half comical look in her eyes that her new friend really began to wonder if the child

66

was quite "right" in her head—"it would seem more like it, if we had proper tea on a table. But asides that, I'm so firsty I'd like a cup of milk first—just cold milk belone you know, to take away the firsty. Martin *some-times* gives me a drink of milk *like* that just afore tea when I'm *very* firsty, even though she says it spoils my tea."

"But I don't think it'll spoil your tea to-day, Missy," said the young woman, as she fetched the cup of milk. "You've come a long way, you see," she added, with a view to drawing Hoodie out as to her home and belongings.

"And you'll give me *real* tea, won't you, little baby's mother? Not just milk and pertence?" inquired Hoodie, anxiously, as she watched the preparations for the meal.

"Of course, Missy, you must have real tea, as you've come so far to see me. Which way did you come? I don't think I've ever seen you before, but then we've only been here a few weeks, since Thomas engaged with Farmer Bright.'

"I didn't come to see you, little baby's mother," said Hoodie, "I came to look for a grandmother in a cottage. But you're very nice, only—oh, do let me hold the little baby! she exclaimed, seeing that the still sleeping child was about to be deposited in its cradle, as it was rather in its mother's way when lifting the kettle and so on;—"*do* let me hold it?"

She held out her arms and smoothed a place on her knees for it, all ready. "Little baby's mother" had not the heart to refuse, though somewhat misdoubting but that poor baby would have been better in its cradle. But baby did not seem to think so; she gave one or two funny little yawns, half opened her eyes, and then composed herself to sleep again most philosophically in Hoodie's embrace. She was a nice baby and daintily cared for, even though her home was only a stone-floored cottage. She was number one in the first place, which says a good deal, and she was an extremely healthy and satisfactory baby in herself—and altogether as sweet and fresh and loveable as a wee baby buttercup under a hedge.

The young mother eyed the little couple with great admiration.

"How cleverly she holds it, to be sure!" she said to herself; adding to Hoodie, "You must have a baby at home, Miss, surely?" the remark as she made it reminding her of her anxiety to find out where the "home" of her mysterious little visitor was. "I cannot but give her her tea," she said to herself; "but I hope I sha'n't get into blame for keeping her here, if she's run away from her nurse unbeknown-like."

"No," said Hoodie, with a melancholy tone in her voice. There isn't no baby at home. Only Hec and Duke, and they're too big to be pettened, and they like Maudie better than me."

"Do they really, Missy!" said the young woman. "Well, I'm sure, *I* think you're a very nice young lady, and baby thinks so too, it's plain to see. See, she's waking, the darling."

Hoodie stared solemnly at the baby as if some extraordinary marvel were about to happen. What did happen was this. Baby stretched itself, doubled up its little pink fists, as if to box some one, yawned, half opened its eyes, and then closed them again, having apparently considered the question of waking up and thought better of it—rolled over again, and again yawned, and finally opening its nice, baby blue eyes and gazing up inquiringly into Hoodie's face, slowly and deliberately *smiled* at her—a sweet baby smile, half-patronising, half-mysterious, as if it had been away in some wonderful baby fairy-land which it would have liked to tell her about if it could, and rather pitied her for not having seen for herself. Hoodie gazed, enraptured. A pretty bright smile, a smile, it must be confessed, not too often seen there, broke over her own little face, and at the sight baby's satisfaction expressed itself in a regular chuckle. Hoodie turned to the young woman with a curious triumph.

"Little baby's mother," she said, half awe-struck as it were, "I do believe she *loves* me."

"Of course she does, and why shouldn't she?" replied the young mother heartily, yet feeling conscious of not altogether understanding the little girl. "Why shouldn't she love you, Missy? Little tiny babies like her always does love those as is kind to them. Don't you love your dear mamma, Missy? and your sisters if you have any—and what made you love them first, before you could understand like, if it wasn't that they loved you and were kind to you?"

Hoodie shook her head—her usual refuge in perplexity.

"I don't know," she said. "I like peoples to love me lots—gate lots. I don't 'zink any body loves me lots. If I was always to sit here holding baby so nice, do you think she'd love me lots?"

Baby's mother laughed outright.

"I don't know that, Missy," she said "she'd get very hungry and cry. And you'd be hungry, too. Aren't you hungry now? The tea's all ready, see, Missy, and your bread and butter's laid out. But I'm afraid it's rather hard. Won't you have some of mine instead —its nice and fresh. Has yours been packed up a long time?"

Hoodie's attention being drawn to the bread and butter, she allowed baby's mother to regain possession of her treasure, and clambered up herself to the chair placed for her. When safely installed she eyed the provisions suspiciously.

"I 'zink yours is nicer, little baby's mother," she said graciously, having first bitten a piece of her own rather uninviting bread. " It was only packened up last night—but perhaps it was the taking it to bed. I took it to bed acos I didn't want nobody to see. But the bicsits is nice. Mayn't baby have a bicsit, little baby's mother? If I had got to the grandmother's cottage there'd have been cake. You hasn't none cake, has you?"

"No, Missy. You see I didn't know you were coming. If your mamma would let you come another day and I knew in time, I could bake a nice cake."

"Yes," said Hoodie, "and baby might have some. Does baby like cake!"

"She hasn't no teeth to bite it with yet, Missy dear," said the young woman.

"No teess!" exclaimed Hoodie, "what a funny baby. Did God forget zem?" she added, in a lower voice.

The young woman turned away to hide her

laughter; and just at this moment there came a rap at the door—a well known rap evidently, for up jumped the young woman with a pleased face.

"David!" she exclaimed, as she opened, "I thought you wouldn't be back till late, or I'd have waited tea."

"I came in to say as I've got to go out again," said the man—a good-humoured looking young labourer—"little baby" had every reason to be good-humoured with such pleasant tempered father and mother!—"I've to drive over to Greenoaks to fetch some little pigs, so I mayn't be in till late. But bless us!" he exclaimed as he just then caught sight of Hoodie seated in perfect satisfaction and evidently quite at home, at the tea-table, "who ever's this you've got with you, Liz?"

His surprise was so comical that it set "Liz" off laughing again.

"Bless *me* if I can tell you, David," she said. "She's the most old-fashioned little piece of goods I ever came across. But such a nice little lady too, and that taken with our baby! She won't tell me her name nor nothing," and then she went on to describe to David, Hoodie's arrival and all she had said.

David scratched his head, as, half hidden in the doorway, where Hoodie had not yet caught sight of him, he glanced at the child, still deeply interested in her "tea."

"It's my opinion," he said solemnly, as if what he was about to say was something that could not possibly have struck any one else; "it's my opinion as her nurse or some one has been cross to her and she's runned away."

"But what shall we do?" said Mrs. Liz, a little anxiously. "How shall we find out where she belongs to?"

"Oh, easy enough," said David. "She's but a baby. And even if she wouldn't tell, you may be sure they'll soon be sending after her. I could take her home on my way to Greenoaks if I knew where it was. Can't be far off—may be it's one of the clergyman's children down by Springley."

"They've none so little," said Mrs. David. "But there's Squire Caryll's—I heard say there's a sight o' little ones there. 'Twill be there."

"Likely enough," said David. "But I'd like a cup o' tea, Liz, if the young lady'll excuse my being rather rough like."

Lizzie laughed.

"She's but a baby," she said; and so David came forward and sat down at the table.

Hoodie looked up from her tea and stopped half way through a "bicsit" to take a good stare at the new comer.

"Who is zou, please?" she said at last.

David looked rather awkward. It was somewhat embarrassing to be calmly challenged in this way at his own table, poor man, by a mite of a creature like this! He relieved his feelings by a glance at his wife and a faint whistle.

"Well, to be sure!" he exclaimed.

Lizzie understood the small questioner better.

"Why, Missy," she said, "'Tis David. He's baby's father and this is his house, and he's very pleased to see you here."

Hoodie looked again at David; this time he seemed to find more favour in her eyes.

"At the grandmother's cottage there wouldn't have been no Davids," she remarked. "His hands is rather dirty, isn't they, little baby's mother?"

This was too much for David—he went off into a roar. Hoodie looked up doubtfully—was he laughing at *her?*—in her opinion, an unpardonable crime—but David's funny, good-natured face gained the day, and after a moment's hesitation Hoodie joined in the fun and laughed too, though at what she certainly didn't know.

Friendly feeling thus established, David thought it time to begin his inquiries.

"Hope you've enjoyed your tea, Miss," he said. "You must a been hungry after such a long walk. Round by Springley way was it?"

"*What* did you say?" said Hoodie opening her eyes. David's tone and accent were puzzling to her.

"He says, was it round by Springley way you came, Missy—the way the church is?"

"Oh no, not the church way. I comed srough the wood and past Farmer Bright's. Home is not the church way," said Hoodie unsuspiciously.

David and his wife nodded at each other. "Squire Caryll's," whispered Lizzie.

"I'll be passing that way in the cart," said David. "Would you like a ride, Miss?"

Hoodie shook her head.

"No," she said decidedly, "I want to stay and nurse baby. May I take her now?" she added, preparing to descend from her chair.

David could not help bursting out laughing again.

"What wages is her to get, Liz?" he enquired.

Hoodie turned upon him indignantly.

"Ugly man," she exclaimed; "you'se not to laugh at me. I don't love you. I love baby—*please* give me baby," she said beseechingly to the young woman. "I'm all zeady," for by this time she was again settled in the little chair and had smoothed a place for baby.

Lizzie good humouredly laid baby again in her arms.

"Hold her tight, please Missy," she said, turning towards the door with her husband at a sign from him, and Hoodie sat in perfect content for some minutes till baby's mother returned.

"Has zat ugly man gone?" inquired Hoodie coolly. "I'll stay with you and baby, but I don't like zat man."

"But he's a nice man, Missy," said Mrs. David. "I don't know about his being very pretty, but he's very kind to baby and me, and that's better than being pretty, isn't it, Missy?"

"I don't know," said Hoodie.

After a time, in spite of her devotion, baby's unaccustomed weight made her little arms ache.

"When does baby go to bed?" she asked.

Baby's mother seized the opportunity.

"Now, I think," she said. "I'll put her in her cradle for a bit, and then you and I can talk a little.—Don't you think, Missy?" she went on, when baby was safely deposited and Hoodie was free to stretch her tired little arms, "don't you think your poor mamma will be wondering where you are all this time?"

"She's out d'iving in the calliage with Maudie. She won't know where I'm goned," replied Hoodie.

"But your nurse, Missy—*she'll* have missed you?" said Mrs. David.

"We haven't no nurse. We've only Martin," replied Hoodie, "and Martin loves Hec and Duke and Maudie best. She 'zinks Hoodie's naughty. She *always* says Hoodie's naughty."

"Little baby's mother" did not know very well what to reply to this, so she contented herself with a general reflection.

"All little girls are naughty sometimes," she said.

"Yes," said Hoodie, "but not *always*. I'd like to stay here with you and baby, little baby's mother, 'cos baby loves me, if you wouldn't have zat ugly man here."

"But its his house, Missy. We couldn't turn him out of his own house, could we? And I'm afeared there'd be many things you'd want we couldn't give you? At home you've a nice little room now, all carpeted and curtained, haven't you? And a pretty little bed all for yourself? We've nothing like that— we've only one room besides the kitchen."

Hoodie did not at once reply. She appeared to be thinking things over.

"I'd *like* to stay," she remarked after a while, "but I'd rather be let alone with you and baby. I don't like zat man. But if you haven't a room for me perhaps I'd better go and look for a grandmother's cottage again, and I'll come and see you sometimes, and baby, little baby's mother."

"Yes, that you must, Missy, and bring little brothers too. You won't think of going off to look for your grandmother again just yet. Perhaps it's quite a long way off by the railway she lives. Couldn't you ask your mamma to write her a letter and tell her how much you'd like to see her?"

"But I want to go to her *cottage*," persisted Hoodie. "I know it is a cottage, Martin said so. I shouldn't want her if she wasn't in a cottage. And I saw it in the Hoodie girl picture too."

This was getting beyond poor Mrs. David; and finding herself not understood, added to Hoodie's irritation. She was half-way, more than half-way, fully three-quarters of the way into one of her hopeless crying fits, when fortunately there came an interruption.

Hasty steps were heard coming up the garden path, followed by a hasty knock at the door. And almost before Lizzie could get to open it, two people hurried into the room. They were Martin and Cross the coachman. Hoodie looked up calmly.

"Has you come to fetch me?" she inquired. "I didn't *want* to go home, but little baby's mother hasn't got enough little beds, but I'm going to come back here again. I *will*, whatever you say."

Well as Martin knew the child, this was a degree too much for her. To have spent between two and three hours in really terrible anxiety about the little girl; to have had to bear some amount of reproach for not having sooner discovered Hoodie's escape; to have rushed off to fetch her on receiving the joyful news from the young labourer as he drove past Mr. Caryll's house, her heart full of the tenderest pity for her stray nursling who she never doubted had somehow lost her way,— all this had been trying enough for poor Martin. But to be met in this heartless way by the child — before strangers, too—to be coolly defied beforehand, as it were—it was too much. It was a toss-up between tears and temper. Unfortunately Martin chose the latter.

"Miss Hoodie," she exclaimed, "you're a naughty, ungrateful little girl, a really naughty-hearted little girl—to have upset us all at home so; your poor mamma nearly ill with fright, and then to meet me like that. Speaking about not wanting to come home, and you will and you won't. I never heard anything like it. And to think of all the trouble you must have given to this—this young woman," she added, turning civilly enough, but with some little hesitation in her manner, to Mrs. Lizzie, as if not *quite* sure whether she did not deserve some share of the blame.

Poor Lizzie had stood a little apart, looking rather frightened. In her eyes Martin was a dignified and important person. But now she came forward eagerly.

"Trouble," she repeated, "oh dear no, ma'am. Little Miss hasn't given me one bit of trouble, and nothing but a pleasure 'twould have been,

but for thinking you'd all be put out so about her at home. But you'll let her come again some day when she's passing, to see me and baby. She's been so taken up with the baby, has Missy."

Martin hesitated. She wanted to be civil and kind—Mrs. Caryll had expressly desired her to thank the cottager's wife for taking care of the little truant, and Martin was by nature sensible and gentle, and not the least inclined to give herself airs as if she thought herself better than other people. But Hoodie's behaviour had quite upset her. She did not feel at all ready to reply graciously to Lizzie's meek invitation. So she stood still and hesitated. And seeing her hesitation, naughty Hoodie darted forward and threw her arms round Lizzie's neck, hugging and kissing her.

"I *sall* come to see you, I will, I sall," she cried. "Never mind what that naughty, ugly 'sing says. I *will* come, dear little baby's mother."

Martin was almost speechless with indignation. Poor Lizzie saw that she was angry, yet she had not the heart to put away the child clinging to her so affectionately, and David's words "perhaps her nurse is cross to her at home," came back to her mind. Things might really have become very uncomfortable indeed, but for Cross, the coachman, who unexpectedly came to the rescue. He had been standing by, rather, to tell the truth—now that the anxiety which he as well as the rest of the household had felt, was relieved—enjoying the scene.

"Miss Hoodie's a rare one, to be sure," he said to himself, chuckling quietly. But when he saw that Martin was really taking things seriously, and that the young woman too looked distressed and anxious, he came forward quietly, and before Hoodie knew what he was doing he had lifted her up with a spring on to his shoulder, where she sat perched like a little queen.

"Now, Miss Hoodie," he said, "if you'll be good, perhaps I'll carry you home."

Hoodie, though extremely well pleased with her new and exalted position, was true to her colours.

"*Carry* me home, Coss," she said imperiously; "hasn't you brought the calliage for me?"

"No, indeed I haven't," replied Cross; "little Misses as runs away from home can't expect to be fetched back in a carriage and pair. I think you're very well off as it is. But we must make haste home—just think how frightened your poor mamma has been."

Hoodie tossed her head. Some very naughty imp seemed to have got her in his possession just then.

"Gee-up, gee-who, get along, horsey," she cried, pummelling Cross's shoulders unmercifully with her feet. "Gallop away, old horse Coss, gee-up, gee-up. Good night, little baby's mother, I *sall* come back;" and Cross thankful to get her away on any terms turned to the door, humouring her by pretending to trot and gallop. But half-way down the little garden path Hoodie suddenly pulled him up, literally pulled him up, by clasping him with her two arms so tightly round the throat that he was nearly strangled.

"Stop, stop, horsey," she cried, "I haven't kissed the baby. I must kiss the baby."

Even Cross's good nature was nearly at an end, but he dared not oppose her. He stood still, very red in the face, with some muttered exclamation, while Hoodie screamed to Lizzie to bring out the baby to be kissed, perfectly regardless of Martin's remonstrances.

And in this fashion at last Hoodie was brought home—Martin walking in silent despair alongside. Only when they got close to the lodge gate Hoodie pulled up Cross again, but this time in much gentler fashion.

"Let me down, Coss, please," she said meekly enough, "I'd rather walk now."

And walk in she did, as demurely and comfortably as if she had just returned from an ordinary walk with her nurse.

"Was there ever such a child?" said Martin to herself again.

And poor Cross, as he walked away wiping his forehead, decided in his own mind that he'd rather have the breaking in of twenty young horses than of such a queer specimen as little Miss Hoodie.

(To be continued.)

HAPPY PRISONERS

HAPPY PRISONERS.

BY THE EDITOR.

WO little prisoners, flying gay and free!
A pretty little jailer, gentle as may be!
She says—"Dickies darling, I've made your home so neat,
Fresh water, seed, and sand well spread, a lump of sugar sweet."

One tiny Dickie chirrups, and flutters here and there,
But thinks not of returning to his little jailer fair.
"Ah, no!" he says, "we love you, and think you very kind,
But we'd rather flutter up and down—that is, if you don't mind.

"It seems a grand new world to us, this drawing-room of yours;
We stretch our wings and fly about; 'tis just like out-of-doors.
Why don't you let us live like this, so happy, free, and gay?
We like it better than a cage, whatever they may say.

"There are flowers on the table, leaves painted on the wall;
We like to smell, and feel, and taste, although we are so small.
To us the world is beautiful, a grand great world of joy!
You people can't tell what that is—pure joy without alloy.

"You—even little children—have some sorrow, pain, or fear:
We birds enjoy our glorious life to fly both far and near;
We dream not of the future, we think not of the past,
But revel in our sunshine; we think 'twill always last.

"So, gentle little mistress, but grant us our one prayer,
Do give us but our freedom, all other woes we'll bear;
We'll float, and sing, and revel, content that we are free;
So pray don't ask us to return: we are happy, as you see."

Dear loving little Flory stood uncertain what to do;
She wished her birds quite happy, yet wished to keep them too;
She knew of many dangers undreamt of by her bird;
She knew birds died of hunger, of traps, too, she had heard.

A hope arose within her: but *one* bird spoke his mind;
She trusted that the other bird more sensible she'd find.
"Oh, Dickie dear!" she turned to him, "now tell your thoughts quite pat."
He shut one eye, and turned his head, and chirped the one word—"Cat!"

Then, with a flirt and flutter, he flew from screen on high,
And settled back within his cage, a twinkle in his eye:
He cried, "Oh, brother, quickly come; 'tis better to be safe,
A prisoner, even in a cage, than lost and homeless waif."

TALKS ABOUT THE MONTHS.

MARCH.

By Mrs. GEORGE CUPPLES.

" A bursting into greenness,
   A waking as from sleep,
   A twitter and a warble
      That make the pulses leap ;
   A gush, a flush, a gurgle,
      A wish to shout and sing,
   As filled with hope and gladness
      We hail the vernal spring."

ONG ago, March used to be the first month in the year, in the oldest Calendars, and was named after Mars, the god of war, as it was the month in which wars and expeditions were usually undertaken, both by the Romans and by the Goths. Afterwards it became the third month, and though our Saxon ancestors called it by different names at different times, it still retains its oldest name of March. One of the Saxon names was Lenet Monat, partly because the days begin to lengthen and to exceed the night, and partly because that Lent means Spring. It was called too the rugged or stormy month, for the vernal equinoctial gales blow during this month, so that we must still recollect to be careful to wrap up well when we go out of doors, for though there may be bright sunshine stealing now and then over the landscape, the air is dry and chill. We can

74

certainly walk about with more comfort, for the roads are now firm and dry. March hastens to dry up the sloppy roads of February, even though no sunshine is seen. If the truth must be told, with all the fretting about the wet roads during February, we are almost tempted to wish that some of the moisture could be brought back again, for the dust of March is rather a formidable thing to face. But what says the husbandman about it—"A peck of March dust is worth a King's ransom," he is now able to sow his precious seed, for now that the soil is dry there is no fear of it rotting and perishing. And after all what do we care for the dust compared with the delight of feeling that Spring is here, or at any rate close by, with all its buds, its tinge of verdure, its fresh airs, its building and twittering of birds, and a feeling of hope and gladness to young and old. The early yeaned lambs have now become strong, and are frisking about with one another. The hens in the poultry yard are crooning their song as they peep here, there, and everywhere in search of a quiet corner where they may lay their eggs, while their lords and masters, perched upon the highest rail or ground, crow lustily.

March has its festivities too, though Lent is a time of fasting. There is St. David's Day, the Apostle of Wales, when all true Welshmen keep his festival with great rejoicing—wearing leeks in their hats and decorating their mantelpieces with that useful and wholesome vegetable; throughout the Principality immense specimens too are carried in the processions of the Welsh Friendly Societies on this annual day of their patron Saint, for this custom is said to have arisen from the Welsh having gained a victory over the Saxons, when they wore leeks as a mark of distinction.

Mid-Lent brings Mothering, Sunday, called so because people used to visit their parents, and take little presents, more especially to their mothers. It is a good old custom, and one that should not be allowed to die out, for after leaving the old home of our youth how delightful it is to return to it for a breathing space from the busy, bustling world. No one ever listens like our parents to our plans for the future and sympathises so heartily with our

earnest endeavours to walk honestly in the sight of all men. This is an old rhyme connected with the sweet-cake that was always baked, and used during the season of Lent, and called a Simnel cake :—

> " I'll to thee a Simnel bring,
> 'Gainst thou go a mothering,
> So that when she blesses thee,
> Half that blessing thou'lt give me ! "

It is nice, too, to think how happy the good mothers will be preparing their wheat grain and steeped pease for the Carling pancakes. They will have a great frying of them when the children arrive, who no doubt will repeat their

> " Tid, Mid, and Misera,
> Carling, Palm, Pan-egg day,
> We shall have a week's play,
> And pretty frocks on Easter-day."

You would no doubt like to know why the cakes were called by the strange name of Simnel. Long ago, I think it was in Shropshire, there lived an honest old couple, known by the name of Simon and Nelly. It was their custom at Easter to gather their children together, and thus meet once a year under the old homestead. The fasting season of Lent was just ending, but there was some of the unleavened dough still left over that they had been using for bread during the forty days of fasting. Nelly was a careful housekeeper, and not wishing to waste anything she proposed to turn the dough into a cake. Simon was quite agreeable, nay, thought it an excellent plan, and further advised that the remains of their Christmas pudding should be put in, and chuckled at the thought of the pleasant surprise it would be to the young people when the Lenten crust was cut open. The cake was mixed, but alas ! a quarrel arose as to whether it should be boiled or baked. From words the stupid old bodies came to blows. Nelly was so angry at Sim for interfering with her, that she jumped up and threw the stool she had been sitting on at his head; and as Sim was a man of some spirit he caught hold of a broom and laid it sharply about Nell's shoulders. At last the quarrel came to an end, by Nell proposing to boil the cake first and bake it afterwards. Accordingly the big pot was put on the fire, the stool broken in pieces and put on under it, while the broom furnished fuel for the oven. Some eggs that had been broken in the scuffle were used to give the top a glossy appearance, and this remarkable production became known by the name of Simon and Nell, afterwards Sim Nel, and now being joined together it is called Simnel.

Then March brings St. Patrick's Day, long looked for in many parts of Ireland, when every-one searches for the greenest shamrock leaves to fasten in their hats, or a posey on the breast.

" Brave sons of Hibernia, your shamrocks display,
For ever made sacred on St. Patrick's day,
'Tis a time of religion, the badge of our saint,
And a plant of that soil which no venom can taint;
Both Venus and Mars to that land lay a claim,
Their title is owned and recorded by fame,
But Saint Patrick to Friendship has hallowed the ground,
And made hospitality ever abound."

The shillelaghs, too, are in great request, for an Irishman would feel like a fish out of water without his stick, especially on St. Patrick's Day. All sorts of games are set on foot, for every one must do full justice to the great annual holiday in honour of their patron Saint, who did such good service to Ireland, not only by spreading Christianity, but by driving all the venomous reptiles out of the Island. Many people affirm that for ever after, the Irish soil was rendered so obnoxious to the serpent race, that to touch it causes instant death. Some people who like the beverage called Poteen say it was Saint Patrick who taught his followers how to distil it, and large quantities are drunk between the games and at the fairs. Of course there are others who deny that St. Patrick had anything to do with it, and are justly angry because they say he was far too good a man to introduce such a dangerous article; and besides, it is well known that he would not allow his disciples to drink strong drinks in the daytime, but commanded them to wait until the bell rang for vespers in the evening.

" Long may the shamrock,
The plant that blooms for ever,
With the rose combined,
And the thistle twined,

76

Defy the strength of foes to sever :
Firm be the triple league they form,
Despite all change of weather,
In sunshine, darkness, or in storm,
Still may they fondly grow together."

During our walks we can now pick quite a bouquet of flowers, for the crocuses are in full bloom and the yellow coltsfoot covers entire fields with a mantle of beauty. The pale and delicate primrose appears on warm banks, and the low and sheltered fields are decked with the daffodil. And if we have learned to keep our eyes wide open, and our minds active, we shall see many sweet things around us at this delightful season of the year. Everything is so fresh and so green and looks so happy, that unless we have very hard hearts we cannot help feeling happy too. If we are going to set out on a walking excursion we watch eagerly to see if any bees are flying about, for if so it is a sure sign that the day is going to be fine. At this early time of the year they never venture out of their hives when either heavy rain or storms of wind are likely to happen. The instinct of these little creatures serves them as a safe and unerring guide as to the weather and the season. If we could only be as clever as the bees we might avoid being caught by the chilling north-east blast, that very often comes in the end of March. If one or two bright warm days come we stupidly throw off some of our winter clothing, and then cry out when the cold winds return, about March being a treacherous, fickle month. But these chilling blasts are wisely sent to keep back vegetation, and thus prevent the full blowing of buds and the too early growth of plants. It is a late spring that makes a fruitful year, and a wet March makes a sad August. Then let us be careful, and not be like the silly hogs or two-year-old sheep, who getting wearied of their lowland pasture wander to the hills too soon, for March saw them, and said to April :—

" I see three hoggs upon a hill,
And if you'll lend me dayes three
I'll find a way to make them dree ;
The first o' them was wind and weet,
The second o' them was snow and sleet,
The third o' them was sic a freeze,
It froze the birds' nebs to the trees ;
When the three days were past and gone,
The three silly hoggs came limping home."

A FRIEND IN NEED.

BY THE EDITOR.

"OH, wifie, wifie!" sighed honest John Burns, "the mare must go; our bonny grey mare, our Whinnie, must be sold." Poor Mrs. Burns gave a sad consent. It was almost as great a trial to her to part with Whinnie as to her husband; but times were hard, crops bad, and the little farm no longer answered. They were losing money this year instead of making it, and in the Burns family there were many little hungry mouths to be fed.

"You see," went on John Burns, "I can make shift with the pony to go about the farm, and I must give up my hunting next winter, that's all."

"Sell the pony, John," murmured Mrs. Burns.

"You are but a poor woman of business," answered honest John. "Should I get a quarter the money for Nobby that our handsome Whinnie will fetch? No, no; times are bad, and the mare must go. She is young, strong, good-looking, and as clever a jumper as you will find in the county. I shall take her up to Squire Streatham's this afternoon: he has often asked if I would sell Whinnie, and he'll give me my price for her, I know."

Now Whinnie was the pet of the Burns family. She had arrived a tiny foal among them, had been reared and broken entirely by the worthy farmer, and by her sweet temper and intelligence had won the regard of them all. She had been talked to, played with, and made much of by the children until they considered her—and perhaps she considered herself—quite one of the family. The boys and girls made a loud outcry when they were told to bid good-bye to their favourite: it seemed as if one of themselves was going away. Indeed, a chubby urchin of four years old suggested that one of his brothers should be sold instead. Whinnie's soft muzzle received many kisses,

and not a few tears dropped upon it too. However, Farmer Burns was firm, although very sad, and having made up his mind what to do, lost no time in doing it. As soon as dinner was over, he saddled and bridled the mare, and rode upon his way to Squire Streatham's. It was a fine bright day in Spring: fresh green leaves were on the trees; the grass was getting long; flies and beetles were beginning to creep or fly about in the sunlight; and the sweet birds were singing in their joy to find that grim winter had departed. Tiny flowers studded the banks, and peeped out from the hedges; the sky was clear, the sun shone warm upon the lanes and meadows, and the whole world seemed happy to poor John Burns as he rode slowly along, making his own sadness seem greater by the contrast.

Squire Streatham was a good-hearted man, and a kind landlord. When Farmer Burns brought the mare to him, and in few words explained his errand, the Squire could easily see how matters stood, and with what reluctance the farmer parted with Whinnie. He paid the price without hesitation, and the pair mare changed hands; but he felt sorry for John Burns, and tried to comfort him by promising that, if it was in his power to make Whinnie happy in her new quarters, she should not repent having changed masters. When the groom came to lead Whinnie off to the stables, the Squire gave him particular directions to pet her and treat her gently. Then he said a kind good-bye to Burns, who walked off on his way home, the squire having promised to send the saddle and bridle over to him on the following day. John Burns felt a tear trickling down his nose as he turned away after giving a parting pat to his four-footed friend.

He expected to find grave faces when he reached home, but the poor farmer little anticipated the trouble that awaited him. One of the many olive branches of the Burns

77

A FRIEND IN NEED.

A Friend in Need.

family had just met with a terrible accident. Little Nelly, the youngest but one, had been playing in the washhouse, where she ought not to have been, and had upset a can full of boiling water over her little self. The poor child was in dreadful pain, and appeared to be dangerously hurt.

As John Burns walked slowly up his pretty trim garden, his wife rushed out to meet him with an expression of despair upon her face. She told him in hurried and rather incoherent words of the accident that had happened, imploring him to go off and fetch the doctor instantly. Alas, alas! the doctor lived seven miles off, and John had just parted with his faithful Whinnie, who would have carried him like the wind.

"Take the pony, John," cried his wife.

"The pony!" exclaimed the farmer, "why, the little beast could not carry me so far. No, no, I can walk faster; besides I can take the short cuts across the fields."

So saying he turned back into the lane, and walked briskly for a little distance; then vaulting over a gate, ran across two or three fields as fast as he could run. In his anxiety to get on, he ran till he was out of breath and exhausted. At last, weary, sick at heart, and panting for breath, he was obliged to stop for a moment and lean against the gate of a paddock he had just entered, and in which Whinnie had been accustomed to be turned out; for John was still upon his own farm. He threw off his hat, and burying his face in his hands, rested them on the upper bar of the gate. His brain seemed in a whirl, he felt sick and despairing. It was one of those dark moments which at times come to us all, at least to us grown-up people; you little ones I trust may be very long before you know them.

"Heaven help me!" exclaimed John, aloud though to himself, "what shall I do if I can't get on?"

He had hardly uttered the words when he felt a gentle touch upon his shoulder, and heard a low whinnying sound at his ear. Raising his head quickly, there he beheld Whinnie herself, saddled and bridled as she was when he had parted from her, standing close to him, ready for him to mount. Was it a dream? How did she get there? Astonished though he was, Farmer Burns wasted no time in trying to answer these questions to himself. Scarcely a moment passed ere he was on the mare's back, and away, away across country to fetch the doctor to his sick child.

Now we can answer the questions that puzzled Farmer Burns. The fact is that Whinnie no more relished being made over to a new master than the Burns family relished parting with her. So, instead of allowing herself to be quietly led into Squire Streatham's stables, she watched her opportunity, and broke away suddenly from the groom who was leading her. Once free, she galloped across country in the direction of her old home, and reaching the paddock where she had so often been turned out, stopped there to graze a little, and enjoy her freedom, till she saw her master at the gate, and went up to him, as we have seen.

The end of this little story is quite satisfactory, and soon told. Thanks to Whinnie, John Burns soon brought the doctor to his little girl's bedside. Nelly was badly scalded, but the hurts were not dangerous; and before many days were over she was about again.

The Squire was so struck by the love of the mare for her old master and his family, that he insisted upon Farmer Burns taking her back again. At the same time he offered to lend him the money that had been given for her. He knew he could trust the farmer to repay him as soon as better days should come: and so things were happily settled. I am sure my little readers will be glad to hear that the good days were not long in coming. The squire was soon repaid, and Whinnie lived to a good old age; nor did she ever again leave the home and friends that she loved so well.

John used often to tell the story of her unexpected appearance to him in the paddock after he had sold her; and he always wound up his story with the saying, *a friend in need is a friend indeed.*

GOLDEN FISHES.

BY THE AUTHOR OF "AUNT EFFIE'S RHYMES," Etc.

H the golden fishes,
　How they dart about!
Larger than a minnow,
　Smaller than a trout.
Dressed in gorgeous scarlet,
　Gay at any rate,
Like a flashing varlet,
　Powdered up in state.

Only think how funny;
　Fresh and pleasant air,
Which we breathe so gladly,
　Fishes cannot bear;
Quick as life and agile,
　While they're in the pond,
Gasping, choking, dying,
　In the air beyond.

Golden Fishes.

Oh the golden fishes,
  How they gape and stare,
Gulping up the water,
  As they gulp the air.
Now then let us feed them,
  Tiny crumbs of bread,
Drop them on the water,
  Gently overhead.

Ah, they're off, they're diving
  In the depths below.
Wait a moment—patience—
  They'll come back I know.
"Pretty golden fishes,
  Come up and be fed."
There, I see you coming,
  Brown, and white, and red.

Rising all together,
  Crowding side by side,
All their eyes are staring,
  Mouths all gaping wide.
Riggle, jiggle, riggle,
  Beautifully red.
Oh how nice to see,
  The golden fishes fed.

HORACE'S LIKENESS.

FOR VE-RY LIT-TLE FOLKS.

"MAM-MA! duck-y dar-lin' mud-der! Lil-ly makes me ug-ly: she *will* make me ug-ly," piped lit-tle Ho-race.

"What is it, my lit-tle man-nie?" asked Mo-ther, who was bu-sy wri-ting.

" Li-ly is draw-ing me, and mak-ing me *so* ug-ly. Dar-lin' Mam-ma, *do* make her stop."

Mo-ther smiled, but be-fore she had time to speak, Miss Li-ly had her lit-tle word to put in. " I'm mak-ing his like-ness ; it's just like him, Mam-ma."

At this Mas-ter Ho-race pout-ed, and then sud-den-ly ran out of the room cry-ing out :—" Sha'n't look at me no more."

Li-ly put up her pen-cil with a re-signed grown-up air. She boast-ed of six years of ex-pe-ri-ence and wis-dom, while Ho-race had but four years know-ledge of the world and its trou-bles.

" You must not tease Ho-race, Li-ly dear," said Mam-ma, grave-ly.

" I didn't tease him, Mam-ma," said Li-ly ; " I on-ly want-ed to make his pic-ture, but he does-n't like it, be-cause he is so vain and 'ceit-ed."

Mam-ma went on with her wri-ting ; Li-ly took her lit-tle self off to some o-ther a-muse-ment, and Mas-ter Ho-race was for the mo-ment for-got-ten.

Af-ter some time Mo-ther miss-ed her little man-nie. She called to him o-ver and o-ver a-gain, but there was no re-ply. Then a great search be-gan up-stairs and down-stairs ; but Ho-race was no-where to be found. Mam-ma was in trou-ble : where could he be gone to ? Li-ly be-gan to cry ; but still Ho-race did not ap-pear. Not on-ly Mam-ma and Li-ly but the ser-vants searched high and low :—it was all in vain. Soon af-ter-wards Pa-pa came home ; he add-ed one more to the num-ber of search-ers, and was as anx-ious as Mam-ma or Li-ly.

At last Li-ly thought of call-ing shag-gy old Tip— an old Scotch ter-ri-er—to help them, and he went sniff-ing a-bout as bu-sy as a-ny-bo-dy, search-ing like the rest for the lit-tle lost boy.

Pre-sent-ly they all heard a loud bark-ing go-ing on in the spare bed-room, and run-ning to the spot, found Tip stand-ing in front of a square ot-to-man, near which al-so lay a drum and a fa-vour-ite doll of Mas-ter Ho-race. When Tip stop-ped bark-ing, they could hear a queer sort of chuc-kle com-ing from the ot-to-man. All at once the lid was rais-ed, and a fun-ny lit-tle face peep-ed out. Tip put his head on one side, and prick-ed up his ears, as much as to say—"Pray how did you get there?" But he did not bark a-ny more, for he knew his lit-tle friend Ho-race was found.

Then Pa-pa made this pic-ture of his lit-tle boy look-ing out of the ot-to-man; and Ho-race was pleas-ed, for he thought both he and dol-ly were made ve-ry pret-ty.

HUMPTY DUMPTY.

HUMPTY DUMPTY.

BLACK ROLF OF ROOKSTONE.

By the Right Hon. E. H. KNATCHBULL-HUGESSEN, M.P., *Author of "Uncle Joe's Stories," &c.*

CHAPTER III.

NOW the messenger certainly had ridden with a vengeance, to judge by the appearance of his horse, which was covered with white flakes of foam, whilst the blood upon its sides and flanks showed the frequent application of whip and spur. The Baron took the scroll from the hands of him who bore it, and turned it over and over in his hands. The only thing which prevented him from opening it at once was the unfortunate circumstance of his being unable to read. In those days few save monks and holy clerks, or wily men of law, could either read or write, and the Baron was no exception to the general rule. So he turned the scroll in his hands, held it up to the light, looked at it again and again, and then bade the bearer return whence he came, and take back word that the Lord of Rookstone would send back an answer in due season.

The varlet departed, right glad to be dismissed from the presence of one so feared as Black Rolf, and in spite of his jaded horse, and his own fatigue after so hasty a ride, set off home without delay.

Then the Baron gazed long on the scroll, and for the first time regretted the priest who in old times had his allotted room in the castle, wherein he dwelt, and who could now have expounded the document, which might perchance be of such great importance. But some years before, the holy man had quitted the castle in disgust, partly on account of the general bad character of its owner, and partly because the latter had kicked him down stairs for some trifling cause, and further insulted religion in his person by filling his bed with black beetles. So now, in his hour of need, no priest was at hand to unravel the mystery which might be hidden in the missive of the man of law. Rolf bit his lips, as he pondered thoughtfully over the circumstances in which he was placed. So deeply was he impressed with the probable importance of the contents of the scroll that he entirely forgot for the time his projected destruction of the Rookery, or if he remembered it, put it aside as something which might be postponed for the present.

So the day wore on, and the Baron worried himself a good deal about the matter, without being able to make up his mind what would be the best course to pursue. The shades of night stole over the castle whilst he was yet undetermined, and after another evening during which his potations were again more deep than was his wont, he retired to his bed full of restless and uneasy thoughts. He slept : but the thoughts were only changed to dreams, and after the fitful slumber of scarce an hour, he started up in bed as suddenly as if a pail of water had been thrown in his face, or the gout had given him one of those terrible twinges with which it knows so well the way to rouse its unhappy victims. It was neither cold water, nor the gout, however, which had awakened the Baron, but a visitor still stranger and more unwelcome than either. There, in the old place, sat the detested Rook, as composedly as

if he were a pet dove, or a parrot, or any other well-conducted bird which is frequently admitted to the homes and houses of mankind. It sat there, I say, as happily as possible, and winked knowingly at the Baron as soon as it saw that he had discovered its presence.

Nor did the bird long delay to declare the object of its coming. "Now then !" it called out in a hard, disagreeable tone of voice.

"Now then!" responded the Baron moodily, who had nothing else to say, and knew that it was perfectly useless to be silent and sulky in dealing with a creature against whom slippers and bootjacks were nothing, and who could come and go through thick walls without effort or inconvenience.

The bird then proceeded to elevate his right claw and place it confidentially against his beak, whilst he thus addressed the individual whose privacy he had so unceremoniously invaded :—

" Your conduct, Black Rolf, since I paid my last visit,
Is hardly deserving of pardon—now is it ?
I told you some truths which were possibly ugly,
But Truth in a Well doesn't *always* quite snug lie,
And when it *is* told, unless mad as a hatter,
A person will just make the best of the matter.
You, Rolf, all the rights of our Rookdom invading,
'Gainst old limes and elms have gone wildly crusading,
Because you've been told you've a nephew plotting,
The fact is quite true—there's no plot or contriving,
And you, if you're wise, your bad conduct regretting,
No longer will follow this fuming and fretting,
But search out your nephew—your title abandon
To him, and this bargain I'll give you my hand on,
That if you'll withdraw all your claims—which are rotten,
Your many misdeeds shall be wholly forgotten,
And you, who now frowned on by angels on high are,
Shall wander a while as a mendicant friar,
And then, when your sand to the last grain is driven,
Shall peacefully die with your crimes all forgiven ! "

Whilst the rook chaunted forth these lines in a monotonous tone of voice, the Baron listened somewhat more composedly than he had done upon the first occasion. As the concluding words fell upon his ear, a grim sense of humour crept into his rugged breast, partly at the idea of a rook being selected as a messenger to reclaim the sinner from his evil ways, and partly at the fanciful thought that he, Black Rolf, of Rookstone Towers, could under any circumstances become a priest of any sort or kind. This latter point so tickled him, that for the first and last time in his life he felt stimulated to endeavour to pay back his visitor in his own coin, and answer him in rhyme. So looking the bird steadily in the face, and speaking in a gruff, but withal a somewhat comic voice, he thus addressed him :—

> " Rook ! you are nothing but a daw !
> *You* give your hand ? you mean your claw !
> And tho' you sing so high a note
> Your bargain isn't worth a groat.
> Whoe'er you be, where'er you live,
> *You've* got no warrant to forgive ;
> And all you say, a man of sense
> Will count as sheer impertinence.
> Think you Black Rolf to fright and funk
> Until he turn a canting monk ?
> Before he'd live one hour as such
> He'd rather be a monkey—much.
> So hence, foul bird, you've said your say,
> And now had better go away ! "

A scornful laugh ended Rolf's address to the bird, who now stood upon his other leg, and acted with his left claw in the same manner as he had previously done with his right, whilst he again accosted the Baron. This time, however, he abandoned rhyming, either because his versifying powers failed him, or perhaps because he had had enough of it.

"Fool !" he exclaimed (at which word the Baron started, and hastily stretched out his hand for his bootjack, but recollecting his previous failure, subsided quietly). "Fool ! thou hast had thy chance, and hast rejected it. Now, listen once more. Thou doubtest my power, and perchance thou doubtest my story. I will give thee such proof that thou shalt doubt no longer. In the old chest in the dark recess of the oak library there is a secret place which thou hast never yet found. Open the farthest drawer at either end. At the back of each drawer is a brass knob. Press each at the same moment, and at the same time pull out the middle drawer. Behind the latter the woodwork will then open and disclose a recess which holds the secret. Attempt to destroy it, and the everlasting caw of the Rooks of Rookstone shall sound your doom for ever." So saying the Rook turned round, and flew straight through the wall with the most provoking coolness, leaving the Baron in a state of alarm

and vexation such as it would be difficult to describe.

No more sleep had he that night, and on the morrow he arose gloomy and dejected, with forebodings of evil heavy upon his wicked soul. He determined that he would search the chest named by the rook without any unnecessary delay. At any rate, he might as well know whether there was a secret, and, if so, what it was, for it would be safe in his keeping, especially if the disclosure would in any way affect his own interests. So he dragged one of the heavy, old-fashioned library chairs opposite the chest, and sat down to look more carefully than ever into the same. The drawers were of ebony, black and shining, and without difficulty he pulled out those on the right and left, and at once perceived the brass knob at the back of each. These he pressed as the bird had directed, but as it took both his hands to do so, he found he could not conveniently pull out the middle drawer at the same time.

A third person was required for this process, and his old nurse appeared to be the most suitable member of his establishment to be trusted in the matter. So he summoned Elfrida to his presence, and acquainted her with his desire. Anxious to do anything her beloved nursling wished, the old woman readily undertook to draw out the middle drawer sharply, whilst he pressed the brass knobs on either side. She did so, and sure enough, the woodwork behind opened and out dropped a miniature and a piece of old parchment, yellow and shrivelled with age. The Baron eagerly seized the former, and opening the case, beheld the portrait of a child with dark and unlovely features, but bearing upon them the unmistakeable impress of the Rolf family.

Was this then the baby brother of whom the Rook had spoken ? And what said the parchment ? That, indeed, Rolf could no more discover for himself than he could decipher the contents of the scroll sent by the man of law. He felt, however, that it could be nothing favourable to himself, and the thought crossed his mind that his best plan would be to destroy both miniature and parchment then and there. Seizing the two, therefore, in his hand, he held them in the flaring light of the pine torch which he had brought with him, the better to examine the dark recesses of that ancient chest. Wonder of wonders! they burned not : the flame flared steadily enough, but the fire appeared to have no effect whatever upon either parchment or picture.

Astonished at his action, the old nurse hastily interposed. "What would'st thou, good my lord!" she cried in alarm. "Perchance these contain some rare treasure, or disclose some secret which it were ill to destroy."

"Secret!" returned the Baron, with a sound between a growl and a sneer. "Secret indeed! it is some jugglery of that vile Rook, and nothing else."

"What rook? my dear lord," quoth the old dame, and forthwith in a few words the Baron told her all, though he had meant to have buried the story of the Rook's double visit deep within his own breast.

Elfrida wrung her hands in dire dismay as she heard the tale. "Alas and alack aday, my lord," she said, sobbing bitterly as she spoke, "these are evil tidings. Hast thou never heard the old saying of thine ancient family, darkly spoken ages since?

"He who sees by night the rook
For his sins is brought to book."

"Fool and dotard!" cried the Baron, "prate not of such folly to me! The bird has never yet been hatched that shall frighten Black Rolf of Rookstone. Yet since these things will not be burned, I will e'en place them in safety till I can know more." With these words Baron Fitzuron carefully picked up the miniature and the parchment, looked once again at each, and then left the room, muttering words which I fear me were scarce a blessing.

No interruption of his rest took place that night, and early on the following morning the Baron ordered his favourite black charger, Belial, to be saddled for his use. He had resolved to do that which he had never done since he was quite a boy, namely, to ride over to the famous abbey which stood some five miles from his castle, there to obtain the assistance of some learned monk to unfold to him the contents of the scroll and parchment which had not unnaturally excited his curiosity.

At the appointed time the steed was brought

round, but o'er he mounted old Elfrida sought his chamber, and begged him to observe that since yesterday, not a rook had been seen about the place. An unusual bustle had been observed among the birds during the previous afternoon, after which they seemed all to have taken their departure. "A malison light upon them!" cried the Baron in reply. "I think they have left their cawing behind them, for since the time we stood together by yonder chest, I seem to hear it constantly in mine ears."

The old crone shuddered as her master spoke, for although he had not told her the threat which the Rook had made, if he should attempt to destroy the secret which he should find in the old chest, yet she well remembered another old distich respecting the House of Rolf—

"Whose ears the rooks with ceaseless caw shall greet
Is nigh the time when he his doom must meet,
And when the caw shall cease, the doom's complete!"

As she called these words to mind, the old woman burst into tears, and sobbed bitterly.

But the Baron laughed lightly, and springing into his saddle with an agility which belied his years, galloped off in the direction of the abbey. As his gallant steed carried him quickly over the ground, thoughts ran with even greater rapidity through his brain, and he felt perturbed and unquiet in his mind to a greater degree than had been the case for many a long year. He could not but feel that he bore upon him documents which might exercise a wonderful influence over his future fate, and a burning desire to know their contents raged within his bosom. So the distance was traversed in little more than half the usual time, and the Baron Fitzuron found himself at his destination, and loudly rang the bell which hung at the ancient gateway.

The abbey was a venerable pile of buildings, erected many years before, and bearing a great reputation as a holy place. It was long, indeed, since Black Rolf of Rookstone had been near it, but the monks received him none the less gladly, hoping perchance that he had come to avow his repentance for many bad deeds in the past, and perhaps even to make some atonement for sins against Mother Church by adding somewhat to the endowments of their beloved House.

No such motive, however, had Rolf for his ride, and his intention in coming was made known to the brotherhood with but little delay. One of their number, old Brother Peter, took in hand the scroll of the man of law, and forthwith proceeded to acquaint the Baron with its contents. It told him that he must prepare to defend his claim to house, lands, and title, and that both law and arms might possibly be employed against him. The new claimant had, by hook or by crook (verily, by *rook*, thought the Baron) obtained access to the young king, and by all accounts had interested him in his cause. At all events, said the man of law, the matter is too serious to be neglected. The appearance of the stranger was reported to be in his favour, and to bear a marked resemblance to the family of which he claimed to be a member. He had documents, it was said, and other proofs that he was what he asserted himself to be, and he had avowed a steadfast determination to fight to the last for what he termed his rights. As the Baron heard these words, which the old monk mumbled over with great deliberation, his brow knitted and a fierce look of dogged determination came over his countenance.

He muttered a low but deep oath when the good brother had concluded, and gnashed his teeth in bitterness of spirit. Then he stamped his foot hard upon the ground and spake out his mind more boldly than befitted that holy place. "Beshrew me!" he cried, "but the knaves are malapert! But think they that Black Rolf of Rookstone can be driven from house and home like a vassal who has failed to pay his dues? By the claws of Lucifer they shall learn a different tale ere long!"

"Oh hush, my son!" exclaimed Brother Peter, terrified at the violence of the Baron. "Speak not such evil words, but put thy trust in the Powers on High to guard thee—"

"Hush thyself, prating priest," roughly interrupted the Baron, "thou hast but half performed thy task. I have here another puzzle for thy clerkly skill, and see that it bear better news than the last." With these words he drew from his vest the parchment which he had found in the old chest, and handed it to the trembling monk, again bidding him to make haste, and not to stand there chattering like an old woman.

But Rolf had used at random a word which was literally true, the parchment was a complete puzzle to the old man. He turned it upside down; held it up to the light, first in one hand and then in the other, and finally confessed that he could make neither head nor tail of it. The crooked characters, written in a crabbed handwriting, in ink which had long since turned yellow from age, could be mastered by none save those of knowledge and experience more vast and wondrous than that of Brother Peter. Such a man was to be found, however, in the person of the Lord Abbot, a man whose age was very, very great, so that no one knew the date of his birth, though it was said that the deeds which he could recall as an eye-witness proved that he had long passed his hundredth year.

It was not upon every day, not at every hour that an audience could be had of this venerable man. In the present instance the Baron was forced to wait, and although he ill brooked the delay, he had no remedy but patience. At last he was ushered into the Abbot's room, which was a low, vaulted chamber, thickly strewn with rushes, and hung round with the skins of wild animals on three sides, the fourth having a sable curtain hanging before it, behind which were many holy relics and emblems only to be looked upon by pious eyes.

The Abbot sat in a low chair, nigh to the hearth, on which a large log was smouldering, the dying embers casting a fitful and uncertain light upon the objects around. He half-inclined his head as the Baron bowed before him, overcome for the moment by the appearance of the man and the sanctity of the place. Then he took the parchment from the hands of his visitor, and read every word carefully from beginning to end without uttering a syllable. When his task was completed, he slowly lifted his hoary head and regarded the Baron steadfastly with his filmy eyes. Presently he spoke in the feeble accents of extreme old age.

"What knowest thou, my son, of these documents?" he asked.

"Not a jot," replied the Baron, "seeing that never a word of writing can I read, be it fair as it may. I found the rubbish in the old black chest at Rookstone, Holy Father, and fain would I know the import thereof."

The aged eye wandered from the Baron's face back to the parchment again, and Black Rolf began to fear he had come too late : the intellect was waning. Not so. In another moment a light beamed over the face, wrinkled and seamed by the cares of more than a century, and again the old man spake :

"This is a wondrous page, my son. It carries me back many, many years, even to the time when I played, a white-headed boy, beneath the ancient chestnuts of my father's park. I well remember thy mother, the writer of this scroll, though she must have been dead these sixty years or more. Ah's me, ah's me! she was a winsome lass a while since. It seems but yesterday she was bright, and blithe, and bonnie—ay, and I could hold my own with the best of them then, too! That was before I came here at all. Long ago—yes—long, long ago."

During this discourse, the Baron became half wild with impatience. He had already got over his respect for the presence in which he stood, and nought but his eager and passionate desire to learn the contents of the parchment restrained him from breaking out into some act of violent anger. It was maddening to be kept from the desired knowledge by the garrulity of old age, but inasmuch as that knowledge could only be obtained through the aged man before him, he restrained his impatience by a gigantic effort, and compelled himself to listen whilst the Lord Abbot prated on about a childhood which no living creature but himself could remember, and the details of which had long ceased to interest any one. At last, however, the Baron found an opportunity of interposing a word, and accordingly asked,

"But what of the scroll, Lord Abbot, what of the wondrous page thou hast just read through ? "

"It is indeed a wondrous page," replied the old man in the same tremulous tones, "and thou hast done full well to bring it here, albeit it may not be to thine own worldly advantage. Yet perchance it may be so, it may be so indeed, noble sir, for as I have heard, thou hast no heir

91

to thy title and broad lands, and it were well to yield them to one of thine own blood during life, rather than know that thy race would end with thine own breath."

At these words the Baron gave vent to his feelings in a deep groan, for they seemed to confirm the statement of the foul Rook, and were of evil augury towards himself. The Abbot slowly lifted the parchment in his hand, and as he began to read it, the cawing in the Baron's ears sounded louder and louder, as if the rooks were rejoicing over the news which was about to be told. And thus read the Lord Abbot—

"This is by mee writ. Joan, wife of James, rightful Baron Fitzuron of Rookstone Towers, tho' deprived of the rank which is truly his. This year my eldest soune Egbert, being of such foul shape and small that my Lord and I do judge him unfit to hold after us these lands and castle, was by my Lord doomed to be drowned so that my littel soune Bertram being stronger and better favoured, should inherit. But by trusty hand I procured that the childe should be saved, and carried to the fair land of Provençe. There he dwelleth and will dwell, and there are wrytings with him withal which shall this tale prove true. And further to prevent ill-doing, I have this parchment steeped in distillerys of herbes which shall garde it safe from fire."

"Signed by mee Joan, wife of the said James."

Black Rolf listened to these words in horror-struck rage. Then the bird had spoken true. There could be no doubt of it. It was more than sixty years ago that his mother had died. Supposing his brother to have married abroad, say at the age of thirty, he might well have a surviving son old enough to do manful battle for his rights. If it were so, and if the young man should be able to prove himself the lawful heir, there would be nothing for it but either to yield him peaceful possession, or strive by force of arms to hold the position which he had struggled so long to obtain. It was a terrible alternative, and the very thought of what was before him nearly drove the dark, stern man distracted. Snatching the parchment rudely from the hands of the Lord Abbot, and thereby causing dire amazement to that saintly man, he strode hastily from the apartment. There was no need to tarry longer in the abbey. Little had he sought from the holy men who dwelt there, and little had they had from him during his long life of crime and recklessness. He had this day learned from their chief tidings which boded him no good, and he hastened to leave them and their dwelling behind. So he flung himself quickly on his black steed, and rode off at best pace on his homeward journey. As he rode, he muttered curses loud and deep against the fate which seemed to pursue him, against the claimant who dared to appear against him, ay, even against the mother, whose lingering affection for her puny child had prevented its destruction, and preserved the life which was about to prove so troublesome and dangerous to her second son.

The Baron ground his teeth savagely, and dug the spurs cruelly into the flanks of his faithful steed, as he pressed madly forward towards the home which might haply be his but for a short time longer. And ever and anon, as he rode, there sounded in his ears that fearful, mysterious cawing, now low and faint like the distant noise of the waves rippling on to the beach on a calm summer's evening, now loud and angry, like the sound of the same waves lashed into fury by the wild winds of heaven. In vain he strove to think it was but fancy: it was something more; some dread reality which perforce he must carry about with him, and which even his iron nerves could scarce endure for ever. He neared the ascent to his castle, and as he looked on the strength and position of Rookstone, he smiled proudly in his confidence that the foe, be he who he might, who should dare to attack so fine a fortress, would have a hard nut to crack ere he won his venture. What figure is that ascending the hill and nearing the castle-gate? Figure, nay, there are two—one, his old nurse Elfrida, and the other, one of those prying monks whom he had long since forbade the castle, and for whose canting and praying he had no forbearance. He urged his steed forward still, and shouted for the pair to stop. Yet they glided on from tree to tree, and at first seemed to take no heed of his summons. But as he roared out his commands a second time, being now close upon them, the monk and the woman stayed their upward course, and awaited his approach.

"What dost thou here, Elfrida?" asked the Baron, in angry tone.

"And thou, caitiff, with thy head shaven and shorn, as bare, methinks of hair as thy heart of aught brave and manly. What seekest thou at Rookstone? 'Tis no place for such as thou —hence—begone!"

The monk made no reply, but the old woman faltered out in trembling accents:—

"Oh, good my lord, chide not I pray thee, neither this holy man nor thy poor old servant. It is long since I have had ghostly counsel and comfort, and my age is so great I know not how long I may be able to receive it. So while wandering forth to watch for thy return, when I met this holy man I persuaded him to turn back to the castle, and—"

"Peace, fool!" growled the Baron, "cease thy prating, and let thy holy man take his holiness off without further delay. I like not such cattle, and would have him wait next time until the master sends for him before he visits my castle. Hence, sirrah! Be off, and thank thy stars thou dost so with a whole skin! We have a rough way of treating trespassers here!"

The person thus addressed drew himself up to his full height, and looked the Baron full in the face. As he did so, his eyes seemed to glare from beneath his cowl like live coals, and the Baron felt less easy than he could have imagined possible when confronting a mere lazy priest, such as he imagined the stranger to be. The monk gazed upon the Baron for a moment in silence, and then laughed aloud.

"I go!" he cried, "but, thou man of foul tongue, and heart still more foul, beware thou of our next meeting!"

With these words, before the incensed Baron could either make reply or take such summary steps towards his apprehension as he might possibly have felt inclined to do, the monk stepped hastily into the adjoining thicket and disappeared among the trees. Then the Baron turned to Elfrida, and sternly upbraided her with negligence, if no worse, on having been about to introduce into the castle one who was evidently no friend to its master. The old woman, however, protested her innocence of any evil intention, and vowed that she had only acted from an intense and increasing desire to obtain that spiritual consolation of which she had so long been deprived. Forced to be content with this explanation, the Baron rode moodily into the court-yard, dismounted from his steed and entered the castle. All that evening he brooded gloomily over the events of the last few days, and strove by deep potations to drive away, or at least deaden, the perpetual cawing which sounded in his restless ears. This, however, was beyond his power, and although he obtained some fitful snatches of sleep during the night, the morning found him but little refreshed in body, whilst his soul was filled with gloomy thoughts and melancholy forebodings as to coming events.

The next morning dawned dull and lowering. Black, brooding shadows seemed to rest upon the lawn and shrubberies near the castle, the sky was heavy with leaden clouds, which like a vast sable shroud swept slowly over the face of the heavens, and the sun only relieved the darkness of the day with a fitful, lurid light, as if unable to penetrate through the mists and vapours which wrapped the world in their murky folds. The Baron's mind was a faithful reflection of the outward world. Clouds of doubts, distrust, uncertainty, and uneasiness possessed his soul. A stranger to bodily fear, still a dread feeling, which he could not have defined, stole gradually over him, and he experienced sensations more nearly akin to terror than had ever hitherto fallen upon him during his reckless life. The prescience of coming evil seemed to be with him, and he vainly strove to shake off the heaviness which oppressed him, whilst ever and anon that unearthly cawing continued.

In such a state of mind and body anything was more tolerable than inaction. Something he must do. He roamed over his castle like one distraught, stood gazing from the battlements at one moment, and at the next hurried from room to room, as if in search of something, he knew not what. At last a thought suddenly struck him : he would go forthwith to the man of law and learn from him, face to face, what was likely to be the issue of this affair. No sooner had the idea come into his head than he proceeded to put it into execution, and at once ordered his horse. But was it safe to leave the castle with such few retainers as were still in his service ? Thrift, avarice, and the long years of saving which had passed over his head, had left him with but a scanty garrison in case the castle should be attacked in his absence. True, this might scarce be likely, before other and more peaceful means had been tried by the claimant of his title and estates, but the risk was too great to be run. He sat down in the old library and thought silently for a few moments. Then he started up, having fully determined upon the best course to pursue.

Before proceeding to the town where dwelt the man of law, he would betake him to the Towers of Barnascran, where dwelt that stout old knight, Sir Hugh de Montenoy. Although the Baron had never been intimate with his neighbours, and had indeed but few with whom he could have associated had such been his wish, yet he had always managed to preserve friendly relations with the owner of Barnascran. Perchance this had resulted partly from the fact that the lands of the latter, commencing some ten miles off, ran in a direction so far away from those of the Baron that none of those jealousies had arisen which have at all times been apt to prevail between the owners of neighbouring estates, and partly from the fact that Sir Hugh, being a noted warrior and one who kept a large band of retainers about him, was a person with whom no one was likely to be desirous of picking a quarrel.

(To be continued.)

GOOD NIGHT.

FOR VE-RY LIT-TLE FOLKS.

IT-TLE mer-ry May-bird,
Trot-ting off to bed,
Kiss-es ro-sy fin-gers—
Bows her pret-ty head.

Up the broad oak stair-case,
   Hold-ing Na-na's hand ;
Oh dear ! what a jour-ney
   Up to nurse-ry-land !

Short legs seem quite wea-ry
   Mount-ing up so high ;
May thinks, to-night, her nurse-ry
   Far too near the sky.

Soon the lit-tle maid-en,
   Up-on her nurse's knee,
By the nice bright fire
   Sits co-sy as can be.

Wash-ed, and brush-ed, and com-fy,
   May is rea-dy quite
To kneel down by her bed-side,
   With lit-tle hands clasp-ed tight.

Lit-tle lips now mur-mur
   Child-hood's sim-ple prayer,
Up-ward borne by an-gels
   With all things pure and fair.

The cur-ly head is hea-vy,
   Blue eyes fill with sand,
Soft cheek lies on pil-low—
   May 's in fai-ry-land !

Through the long dark hours
   Of the win-ter's night,
Lit-tle May lies dream-ing
   Of scenes gay and bright.   EDITOR.

PUZZLES.

CHARADES.

1.

My first is found in every house,
My second is used to cover my first,
My whole is used at many meals.

2.

Man could not live without my first,
My second is used to hold my first,
My whole is found in a bedroom.

3.

My first is part of the body,
My second is found in every house,
My whole is a very comfortable second.

4.

My first is used to make a drink,
My second is used to hold my first,
My whole is found in many cupboards.

5.

Oh bright and glorious day!
The truant schoolboy cries,
As, hastening on his way,
My first aloft he spies.

With tender care a little girl
Nurses and pets my second,
For in the heart of London here
A treasure it is reckoned.

My whole a large majestic plant,
'Tis of a brilliant hue;
If you are brilliant too, my friend,
This will not puzzle you.

6.

My first is a preposition,
My second is an adverb,
My third is a stronghold,
And my whole a noted ship.

7.

The setting sun may be seen in my first,
Contentment never wishes for my second,
Sailors are generally glad to see my third,
My whole is a part of our country.

DECAPITATION.

Behead a part, and you will see
An animal it then will be;
If you again cut off its head,
Part of a verb you'll have instead.

BURIED BIRDS.

1.

Roll in nets, and if you see a fish with a gold fin, chase it.

2.

Clasp arrows in your hand; her robe is black; capture her.

4.

Yes, nip each of them.

BURIED TREES.

1.

Get a pin, Eva, and fasten your sash.

2.

Bring me a helmet, a lance, darts, and arrows.

3.

A bee chased a wasp, ending by overtaking it.

ENIGMA.

I'm found in seaside places,
I'm found upon the beach,
I'm found far out at sea,
And found in Corney Reach.
I'm found among the bathers
In the middle of the day.
Without me you can't travel,
For I'm always in the way.

HOODIE.

BY MRS. MOLESWORTH, *Author of "Hermy," "The Cuckoo Clock," &c.*

CHAPTER IV.—MAUDIE'S GODMOTHER.

"If you'd have children safe abroad,
Just keep them safe at home."

HEY were all standing at the door—
Maudie, Hec and Duke, that is to
say, and mother in the background,
and farther back still, half the

servants of the household. But Hoodie marched
in demurely by Martin's side—nay, more, she
had taken hold of Martin's hand. And when
Mrs. Caryll came forward hurriedly to meet
them, of the two, Martin looked much the more
upset and uncomfortable.

"You have brought her back safe and sound,
Martin!" exclaimed Hoodie's mother. "Oh

97

Hoodie, what a fright you have given us! What was she doing? How was it, Martin?"

Martin hesitated.

"If you please, ma'am," she said, "I think I'd rather tell you all about it afterwards. It's not late, but Miss Hoodie *must* be tired. Won't it be as well, ma'am, for her to go to bed at once?"

Mrs. Caryll understood Martin's manner.

"Yes," she said. "I think it will. Say good-night to me, Hoodie, and to Maudie and your brothers. And to-morrow morning you must come early to my room. I want to talk to you."

Hoodie looked up curiously in her mother's face. Was she vexed, or sorry, or what? Hoodie could not decide.

"Good-night, mother," she said, quietly. "Good-night, Hec and Duke and Maudie," and she coolly turned away, and followed Martin up stairs.

The three other children crept round their mother. She looked pale and troubled.

"Mamma," said one of the little boys, "has Hoodie been *naughty?* Aren't you glad she's come home?"

Mrs. Caryll stroked his head.

"Yes, dear," she said. "Of course I'm glad, *very* glad. But it wasn't good of her to frighten us all so, and I must make her understand that."

"*Of course,*" said Maudie, virtuously. "You don't understand, Hec."

"But if we had all kissened Hoodie, she'd have known we were glad she had comed back," said Hec, still with a tone of being only half satisfied.

A shadow crossed Mrs. Caryll's face. Was her little son's instinct right?

"Shall us all go and kissen her now?" suggested Duke in a whisper to Maudie.

"No, of course not," replied Magdalen. "You're too little to understand, and you're teasing poor mamma. Come with me and we'll play at something in the study till Martin comes for you. Don't be unhappy, dear mamma," she added, turning to kiss her mother. "I am sure Hoodie didn't mean to vex you, only she is so strange."

98

That was just it—Hoodie was so strange, so self-willed and yet babyish, so heartless, and yet so impressionable. A sharp word or tone even would make her cry, and she was sensitive to even less than that, yet seemingly quite careless of the trouble and distress she caused to others.

"My good little Maudie," said Mrs. Caryll, "why should not Hoodie too be a good and understandable little girl?" she added to herself.

And what were the thoughts in Hoodie's queer little brain; what were the feelings in her queer little heart, when Martin had safely tucked her into her own nice little cot, and, rather shortly, bidden her lie quite still and not disturb her brothers when they came up to bed?

"I wish I had stayed with little baby's mother," she said to herself. "Nobody was glad for me to come home. They is all ugly 'sings. Nobody kissened me. If it wasn't for zat ugly man I'd go back there, I would, whatever Martin said."

* * * *

"I really think sometimes that there's something wanting in her nature," said Hoodie's mother, sadly, that same evening. She had been listening to Martin's account of the meeting at the cottage, and was now telling over the whole affair in the drawing-room, for Mr. Caryll had only returned home late that evening, as he had been some way by train to meet a visitor who was coming to stay for a time at his house. This was a cousin of his wife's, a young lady, named Magdalen King, who occupied the important position of Maudie's godmother. It was some years since Cousin Magdalen had seen the children, but she had so often received descriptions of them from their mother that she seemed to know them quite well. She listened with great interest to the account of Hoodie's escapade.

"She must be a strange little girl," she remarked, quietly.

"Yes," said Mrs. Caryll, "so strange that, as I said, I really think sometimes there is something wanting in her nature."

"Or unawakened," said Magdalen, "I don't pretend to understand children well—you know

I was an only child—but still, a little child's nature cannot be very easy to understand at the best of times. It must be so folded up, as it were, like a little half-opened bud. And then children's power of expressing themselves is so small—they must often feel themselves misunderstood and yet not know how to say even that. And oh, dear, what a puzzle life and the world and everything must seem to them!"

"Not to them only, my dear Magdalen," said Mr. Caryll, drily.

"And," said Mrs. Caryll, "it really isn't always the case that children are difficult to understand. None of ours are but Hoodie. There's Maudie now—she has always been a delicious child, and the little boys are very nice, except when Hoodie upsets them. But for her, as she is constantly told, there never would be the least ruffle in the nursery."

"But does it do any good to tell her so?" said Miss King.

Hoodie's mother smiled.

"My dear Magdalen," she said, "wait till you see her. What *would* do her any good no one as yet has found out. She is just the most contradictory, queer-tempered, troublesome child that ever was known."

"Poor little girl," said Maudie's godmother, thinking to herself that a little dog with such a *very* bad name as Hoodie was really not to be envied. She loved her own god-daughter Maudie dearly, and she knew it to be true that she was a very nice child, but her heart was sore for poor cantankerous Hoodie. You see her patience had not yet been tried by her as had been the patience of all those about the little girl, so after all she could not consider herself a fair judge.

And her first introduction to the small black sheep of the nursery did not, it must be confessed, tend to prove that Hoodie's doings and misdoings were exaggerated.

This was how it happened.

Maudie's godmother was generally an early riser, but this first morning she somehow—tired perhaps with her journey—slept later than usual. She was not quite dressed, at least her pretty curly brown hair was still hanging about her shoulders, when a knock—

a lot of little knocks, and then one rather firmer and more decided—came to the door, and in answer to her "Come in," appeared Martin, an old acquaintance of hers, beaming with pleasure, and ushering in her little people, all spick and span from their morning toilet, looking not unlike four rather shy little sheep under the charge of a faithful "colly."

But when Martin caught sight of the young lady in her white dressing gown and unarranged hair, she drew back.

"Oh, ma'am I beg your pardon," she said. "My mistress said I might bring them in to see you first thing, as you were always dressed so early, but I can take them back to the nursery till you are ready. They've been worrying to come to you for ever so long."

"And you were quite right to bring them," said Cousin Magdalen, heartily. "Come now, darlings, and let us make friends. I can tell Maudie and Hoodie in a moment of course, but I'm quite in a puzzle as to which is Hec and which Duke."

"I'm Hec," and "I'm Duke," said the two little boys shily, nestling up to their new friend as they spoke. She kissed them fondly.

"Dear little fellows!" she said.

"Yes, Cousin Magdalen, aren't they dear little boys? And will you please kiss me too?" said Maudie in her pretty soft voice.

Magdalen put her arm round her as she did so.

"And Hoodie?" she said. "I must have a kiss from Hoodie too, mustn't I?"

Hoodie stood stock still.

"Come now, Miss Hoodie," whispered poor Martin. All the time she had been dressing the child she had been telling her how good she was to be to Cousin Magdalen, and hinting that perhaps if she behaved *very* nicely it would help to make them all forget the trouble she had caused the day before. But alas, with what result?

Hoodie stood stock still!

Magdalen put out her hand and tried to draw the child to her.

"You have plenty of kisses on that rosy mouth of yours, Hoodie," she said. "Won't you spare me one?"

Hoodie screwed up her lips tighter than before; that was the only sign she gave of hearing what was said to her.

"*Oh*, Hoodie," said Maudie, reproachfully. Hoodie turned upon her with a glance of supreme contempt.

"*You* can kissen her," she said; "she's yours, she's not mine. *I* don't want to kissen her."

Cousin Magdalen looked at Maudie for explanation.

"What does she mean?" she said.

Maudie and Martin looked greatly distressed.

"Oh," said Maudie, "it's only about your being my godmother and not hers. We were speaking about it in the nursery, and she said nobody ever gave her anything—like me having you, you know Cousin Magdalen—and she was vexed, you know," she added in a lower voice, "because she couldn't find our grandmother's cottage yesterday."

"Yes," said Cousin Magdalen, "I know. But Hoodie dear, you *have* a godmother and a very nice one, as well as a grandmother."

"They're none use having," muttered Hoodie. "I never see them."

"But some day you will. And besides even though I'm Maudie's godmother, can't I love you too?"

"No," said Hoodie bluntly.

"And won't you kiss me?"

"No," said Hoodie again. "I don't like you. I don't like your hairs. They is ugly, hanging down like that. I don't want to kiss you."

And she turned her back on Cousin Magdalen, and marched quietly to the door.

Martin began some apologies, but Miss King stopped her.

"Never mind, Martin," she said. "It really doesn't matter. She will get to know me better in a little."

But all the same, Cousin Magdalen, being, though very amiable and sensible, only human, *did* feel hurt by the little girl's rude repulse. It is never pleasant to be repulsed by any one; it is, I think, to even right-feeling people, particularly hurting to be repulsed by a *child*. And then Magdalen had been thinking a great

100

deal about this poor little Hoodie that nobody seemed able to manage, and planning to herself various little ways by which she hoped to win her confidence, and thus perhaps be of real service to the child, and through her to her mother.

"And now," she said to herself, "she has evidently taken a prejudice to me at first sight. What a pity! Yet," she added, as she brushed out and arranged the long thick brown hair which Hoodie had objected to, "she is only a baby. Perhaps she will like me better when my hair is fastened up. I must try her again."

The other three children had stayed in their cousin's room—Martin having flown after Hoodie, whom she was now afraid to trust for a moment out of her sight—and while she finished dressing they chattered away in their own fashion.

"Poor mamma's dot one headache zis morning," said Hec.

"Yes," said Duke, "papa comed to the nursley to say Hoodie wasn't to go to be talkened to, 'cos it would make poor mamma's headache worser."

"Won't nobody talken to Hoodie zen?" said Hec.

"Don't be silly; Hec dear," said Maudie, "of course mamma mustn't talk to her when her head's bad. Papa said to Martin that she must not let Hoodie out of her sight, but that he couldn't have mamma bothered about it any more, and that it would be better to drop the subject. What does it mean to 'drop the subject,' Cousin Magdalen? I thought perhaps it meant to put down the lowest bar on the gate at the end of the garden, where Hoodie sometimes creeps through to the cocky field. Could it be that?"

"No," said Magdalen, turning away so as to hide her face, "it just means not to say any more about Hoodie's running away yesterday, because it has troubled your mother so much."

"Of course," said Maudie. "It is all that that has given her a headache. It is nearly always Hoodie that gives her headaches. I wonder how she *can*."

"But Maudie dear," said her godmother very

gently, "do you think it is quite kind of you
to speak so? It is right to be sorry when
Hoodie is naughty, but remember how much
younger she is than you. And she does not
want to make your mother ill—when she is
naughty she just forgets all but the feelings
she has herself, but that is different from
wishing to hurt her mother."

Maudie grew very red.

"Yes," she said in a low voice, "I see how
you mean, Cousin Magdalen. I don't want to
say unkind things of Hoodie."

"No dear. I don't think you do," said her
godmother. "Tell me why do you call that
field "the cocky field?""

Maudie laughed.

"Oh it's because in one corner of it there's
the little house papa's made for the bantam
cocks. Oh, Cousin Magdalen, they are *such*
ducks."

"*Such* ducks," echoed Hec and Duke. "And
they lay such lovely eggs."

"What remarkable creatures they must be,"
said Miss King. "But I must own I don't
quite see how they can be *ducks* if they're
cocks and hens."

All the children laughed.

"They isn't really ducks," explained matter-
of-fact Duke, condescendingly. "But you
see we calls zem ducks 'cos zey is so nice and
pretty."

"Ah yes, I see," said Cousin Magdalen,
gravely. "So perhaps when you know me
better if you think me *very* nice, you'll call me
a duck. Will you, Duke? Even though
really, you know, I'm an old woman."

"Yes," said Duke, "p'raps I will. But I
didn't know zou was a *old* woman."

"Didn't you, you dear old man?" said his
cousin, laughing. "Never mind, you may call
me 'a old duck,' if you like. And after breakfast will you take me to see these wonderful
bantams—that's to say if you're allowed to go
there."

"Oh yes," said Maudie. "We may go
whenever we like. They're so tame—indeed,
they're too tame papa says, and that was why
he made them a place further away from the
house than they used to be. They used to come
and hop about all the rooms, and once they laid

101

an egg on one of the library armchairs, and
another time in papa's paper basket. They
thought that was a lovely nest."

"And are they better behaved now?" said
Miss King.

"Oh yes, only sometimes they lay astray.
So papa gives us a penny if we find any of
their eggs about the field or in the hedges
anywhere," said Maudie. "That's what makes
Hoodie so fond of going in the cocky field.
She's far the cleverest at finding eggs. You
should see her—and she's got such a way with
the cocks. She can cluck, cluck them close up
to her, and often she catches them. They're
not a bit afraid of her."

"How funny," said Magdalen, not sorry to
see Maudie's childish attempt at saying something in praise of her little sister. "I must
certainly go with you to see the bantams after
breakfast."

"Timmediate after breakfast!" said Hec.
"Will you come timmediate? For after zen
Maudie has lessons."

"Yes," said Maudie. "I have lessons.
Miss Meade comes from Springley to give
me lessons."

"And doesn't Hoodie have any?"

"Sometimes," replied Maudie. "When she's
in a good humour. When she's not, its no use
trying. I heard Miss Meade say so one day,
and so now Hoodie very often says she's in a
bad humour whether she is or not, 'cos she
doesn't like lessons."

"She *says* she's in a bad humour," repeated
Magdalen, astonished.

"Oh yes, she just calls out to Miss Meade,
'oh one's come, one's come,' that means a bad
humour's come, and once she says that, *nothing's*
any good. She sometimes puts her fingers in her
ears if Miss Meade tries to speak to her. So
mamma settled it was no good doing anything; it did so interrumpt *my* lessons, and
I'm getting big you know. But please, Cousin
Magdalen, will you come with us just the very
minute after breakfast, and then there'll be
time?"

"Very well," said Magdalen. "I'll be ready
'timmediate,' I promise you."

Whether or no Miss King knew much about
children, she knew enough to understand that

to them, a promise, even about a small matter, is a very sacred thing. And she took care not to forfeit their confidence. No sooner did the four little figures appear on the lawn just outside the dining-room window than she started up from the table where, though breakfast was finished, she was loitering a little in pleasant talk with her friends.

"Why, where are you off to, in such a hurry?" said Mrs. Caryll.

"I beg your pardon," said Magdalen, laughing. "I promised the children to go with them before their governess comes, to—"

"Excuse my interrupting you," said Mr. Caryll, "but I would just like to see if I can't finish the sentence for you. I am certain they are going to take you to see the bantams, now aren't they? They have all four, Hoodie especially, got bantams on the brain."

He opened the glass-door as he spoke, and Miss King passed through. Three of the children ran forward joyously to meet her, the fourth followed more slowly, and from her way of moving, Cousin Magdalen strongly suspected that either "one" had just come, or that "one" had not yet gone. There was a decidedly black-doggy look about her fat little shoulders.

But Miss King took no notice, and slowly, very slowly, the fourth little figure drew nearer to the others. Still she did not speak—the boys chattered merrily and Maudie joined in, being sensible enough to understand that just now, at any rate, the taking no notice plan was the most likely to bring Hoodie round again.

And by the time they reached "the cocky field," it was crowned with success. Hoodie forgot all her troubles in the pleasure of showing off her pets, and greatly distinguished herself by the cleverness with which she caught them and brought them up, one after the other, to be admired.

"Isn't they *sweet?*" she said, ecstatically; "when I'm big, I'll have a house with lots and lots of cocks and hens."

"I thought you were going to live in a cottage, like Red Riding Hood's grandmother, when you're big?" said Maudie, thoughtlessly.

Hoodie turned upon her with a frown, and Cousin Magdalen felt really grieved to see how in one instant her pretty, round rosy face lost its childlike expression, and grew hard and fierce.

"You's not to laugh at me," she said. "I won't have nobody laugh at me."

Maudie looked up penitently in Cousin Magdalen's face.

"I'm so sorry. I *didn't* mean to set her off. Truly I didn't," she whispered.

Cousin Magdalen felt that she knew and understood too little to attempt the interference she would have liked to use. More than interference indeed. For the moment she felt so provoked with Hoodie's naughty, silly bad temper, that she really felt ready to give her a severe scolding. She was too wise to do so however, and certainly it would have done no good. More for Maudie's sake than for Hoodie's, she tried to turn the conversation in a pleasant way.

"It is very queer," she said, "that people almost never do when they are grown up what they plan as children. When I was little I always planned that I should do nothing but travel, and after all, very few people have travelled less than I. I have been very stay-at-home."

"I like travelling a little way," said Maudie; "but when it is a long way, it is so tiring."

"Wouldn't you like the magic carpet that flew with you wherever you wished to be?" said Cousin Magdalen.

"Was it in a fairy story?" said Maudie; and though Hoodie said nothing, she came slowly nearer and stood staring up in Miss King's face with her queer baby blue eyes that could look so sweet, and could, alas, look so cross and angry.

"Yes," said Cousin Magdalen, in reply to Maudie's question, "in a very old fairy story. Are you fond of fairy stories?"

"*I* is," said a voice that was certainly not Maudie's.

Magdalen turned to her quietly.

"Are you, dear?" she said, as if not the least surprised at her joining in the conversation. "And you too, Maudie? And Hec and Duke?"

"Oh yes, very," said Maudie. "Of course Hec and Duke don't like difficult ones—there's some kinds that keeps meaning something else all the time, and they are rather difficult, aren't they?"

"Yes," said Magdalen, smiling. "I like the old-fashioned ones that don't mean anything else. I must try to think of some for you."

Maudie clapped her hands, and Hoodie's face grew very bright. Suddenly she gave a little spring, as if a new idea had struck her.

"I've zought of somesing," she cried, and turning to Miss King,

"Does you like eggs?" she inquired.

"Very much," said her cousin.

"Zen, if you'll tell us stories, I'll get you eggs. Kite, kite fresh. Doesn't you like them *kite* fresh?"

"Yes, quite fresh; they can't be too fresh," said Magdalen.

"Can't be too fresh," repeated Hoodie. "Zat means just the moment minute they'se laid. Oh, that'll be lovely. And when'll you tell us some stories, please?"

"Let's see," said Cousin Magdalen. "I'll have to think, and thinking takes a good long while."

"Nebber mind," said Hoodie. "You'll zink as soon as you can, won't you, dear?"

And for the rest of the morning's walk she was perfectly angelic, in consequence of which Cousin Magdalen felt more completely puzzled by her than ever.

The day passed over pretty smoothly. Late in the afternoon, just as the children were preparing for a run in the garden before tea, an excitement got up in the nursery by the absence of Hoodie's basket, which she insisted on taking out with her.

"My bastwick; oh my bastwick," she cried. "I must have my bastwick."

"What do you want it for, Miss Hoodie?" said Martin. "There'll be no time for picking flowers, and we're not going up the lanes."

"Oh, but I must have my bastwick," repeated Hoodie.

Martin, fearful of an outbreak, stood still to consider.

"When did you have it last?" she said. "Now I do believe it was yesterday at that cottage, and I brought it home for you. Yes, and I put it down in the back hall where your

hoops are. Now, Miss Hoodie, if you'll promise to be very good all the time you're out, you may run and fetch it. I'll be after you with the little boys in five minutes."

Hoodie was off like a shot, but the five minutes grew into ten before Martin and the boys followed her; an ill-behaved button dropping off Hec's boot while the careful nurse was fastening it.

"And if there's one thing I can't abide to see, it's children's boots wanting buttons," she said, "so run down Miss Maudie, there's a dear, and take care of your sister till I come."

Maudie ran down, but as she did not return Martin felt no misgivings, and she was greatly surprised and disappointed when, on going down stairs she was met by the child with an anxious face.

"I couldn't find Hoodie in the back hall or anywhere about there," she said, "and I ran out a little way into the garden, because I knew you'd be so frightened, but I can't see her."

"Oh dear, dear," said poor Martin, "wherever will she have gone to now? Take the boys into the study, Miss Maudie dear, for a few minutes, and I'll run round by the lodge, and ask if they've seen her pass. If she's gone up the wood to that cottage again they must have seen her. Dear me, dear me, I might have thought of it when she teased so about her basket."

Off rushed Martin, and Maudie, faithful to her charge, kept watch over the little boys. They were not kept waiting very long, however. In two minutes Martin put in her head again.

"Is she with you, Miss Maudie?" she said, quite breathless with running so fast. "No? Oh dear, where *can* she be? The woman at the lodge says she saw her running back to the house a few minutes ago. She is sure she did."

"Perhaps she's gone up to the nursery again," said Maudie.

"Oh no," said Martin, "she'd never go there, once she thinks she's escaped again. She's got something new in her head, I'm sure. I'll just ask in the servants' hall if any of them have seen her."

She left the room to do so, but as she passed by the foot of the stairs she heard a step. There, calmly coming down, was Hoodie! Hoodie without her basket, however. But that, in her delight at recovering her truant, Martin did not notice.

"Miss Hoodie, Miss Hoodie," she cried, "where *have* you been? You've given me such a fright again. Where *have* you been?"

"Up in the nursley," said Hoodie, coolly. "I wented out a little, and then up stairs to the nursley.

And with this account of her doings Martin was obliged to be content.

(To be continued.)

A DANCING BEAR.

FOR VE-RY LIT-TLE FOLKS.

OOK at the pic-ture on the op-po-site page, and tell me which of the par-ty you think the fun-ni-est —the bear, the bear-lead-er, the trum-pet-man, or Mr. Mon-key? I think them all ve-ry ug-ly, but I like the poor bear the best; I pi-ty him so much. Poor fel-low! how-e-ver sa-vage he may have been once, they have at all e-vents tamed him now. Who knows what he went through be-fore he be-came so tame, and learned to per-form so ma-ny cle-ver tricks? I fear it has all been done by beat-ing and starv-ing him. And e-ven now, you see, they are half a-fraid of him, for they keep a muz-zle on his mouth.

Ma-ny years a-go, danc-ing bears were some-times seen in the streets of Lon-don. They used to stand on their hind-legs, turn-ing round and round slow-ly and awk-ward-ly in a sort of dance, and per-form-ing other cu-ri-ous an-tics, but ac-ci-dents some-times hap-pened on their ac-count: hor-ses were of-ten fright-ened, and some-times peo-ple too. So the poor danc-ing bears were for-bid-den to per-form in the streets, and if they made their

Frank Grieil.

ap-pear-ance were ta-ken up with their mas-ters, and
popped in-to pri-son.   Ra-ther a fun-ny pri-so-ner Mr.
Bear must have been for the po-lice, I think.

In In-di-a I have seen the na-tives bring round
per-form-ing bears; and they are not con-tent with
mak-ing them dance, but they have sham fights with
them, which now and then be-come real fights.   The
In-di-an bears are small and black, while those that
used to per-form in Eng-land are large brown ones.
They are found in some moun-tain-ous parts of Europe.

EARLY SPRING.

BY THE EDITOR.

SWEET are the sounds, and sweet the smell,
    Of the first glad days of Spring;
When violets peep, primroses shine,
    And the birds are on the wing.

A happy time for children now
  To wander away, away,
Within the wood they love so well,
  And gather the flowers gay.

See, hawthorn blossoms peeping out
  From their hoods of emerald green;
And blue-bells, with their nodding heads,
  May here and there be seen.

The celandine gleams all golden,
  Like the sunshine on the ground;
And the rooks in the trees above us
  Make a chattering pleasant sound.

They are busy and eager at work now,
  Each pair with their cosy nest;
They chat of the good time coming,
  When the leaves are all out, and they'll rest.

Though the dickies are never idle,
  They always have plenty to do,
They've to hatch their eggs, and rear their young,
  And educate them too.

For you know that the dear little dickies
  Must learn to chirp and sing,
To hop, and feed, and flutter,
  And how to use the wing.

You know too that even birdies
  Must be taught what not to do—
Not to quarrel, fight, or bicker:
  And this is told to you.

Oh, you happy country children,
  That can wander about at will,
By the banks of the murmuring river,
  In the wood, or on the hill,

In the years that come so quickly
  Bringing thought, and work, and care,
You'll recall these early spring days,
  When all the world seems fair.

TALKS ABOUT THE MONTHS.

APRIL.

By Mrs. GEORGE CUPPLES.

" Capricious month of smiles and tears,
   There's beauty in thy varied reign!
Emblem of being's hopes and fears,
   Its hours of joy and days of pain.

" Yet there is gladness in thy hours,
   Frail courier of a brighter scene,
Thou fragrant guide to buds and flowers,
   To meadows fresh and pastures green."

APRIL, the month of smiles and tears, of showers and sunshine, clear and cloudy skies, greenness and barrenness, heavy hail and blooming blossoms, we welcome thee! April is the only month in the year that has had a name given to it expressive of the appearance of nature, the name being derived from the Latin word *aperire*, to open, in allusion to the opening of the buds in spring; the other months are all called after heathen deities, or Roman emperors, or according to their place in the Calendar. The Romans however dedicated it to Venus the goddess of beauty. The Saxons called it *Oster-Monat*, or *Easter-Monat*, some say, because their goddess Eostre was particularly worshipped at this time; and others because it was the month during which East winds prevailed; but our present term Easter, whatever was its origin, has been retained with reference to the rising of our Lord from the grave.

"Cuckoo! Cuckoo!" it is the well-known note of the messenger of spring; let us get on our hats and jackets and hasten out, for there are many children scattered about playing merry games or gathering flowers. There they go, chasing one another like butterflies, tumbling and rolling about in the sunshine, and squealing and shouting at the top of their voices, simply because they cannot help it. It is an expression of pure gladness of heart. The birds sing, the fish seem to be dancing for joy, at any rate they keep jumping up out of the water, and the bees, how they do hum! and the butterflies keep dipping and bathing in the warm sunshine, and how can any one expect the children to be still and quiet in the midst of such sweet and such stirring scenes?

Opening a little old-fashioned book given by an old grandmother we find this pretty description of April. "The youth of the country make ready for the morris-dance, and the merry milk-maid supplies them with ribbands. The little fishes lie nibbling at the bait, and the porpoise plays in the pride of the tide. The shepherds entertain the princess of Arcadia with pleasant roundelays. The aged feel a kind of youth, and youth hath a spirit full of life and activity; the aged hairs refreshen, and the youthful cheeks are as red as a cherry. The lark and the lamb look at the sun, and the labourer is abroad by the dawning of the day. It were a work to set down the worth of this month; for it is Heaven's blessing and the earth's comfort. It is the messenger of many pleasures, the courtier's progress, and the farmer's profit, the labourer's Harvest, and the beggar's pilgrimage, and to sum up, it is the jewel of time, and the joy of nature."

The first of April, of all days in the year, enjoys a character of its own, in as far as it,

and it alone, is consecrated to practical joking. It is known amongst us as "All Fools' Day," and has been observed from very early times, nearly in the same way in many parts of the world. It is great fun for the children to try to pin pieces of paper to the coat-tail of some unsuspecting passer-by, or to send a message for some absurd thing such as the "History of Eve's Grandmother," at the booksellers, or to the chemists for an ounce of "strap-oil." Sometimes the opportunity is taken to play off a public practical joke, for we read that in 1860 a number of people received through the post, a card having the following inscription, with a seal marked by an inverted sixpence at one of the corners making it appear quite an official looking document: "Tower of London. —Admit the Bearer and Friend to view the annual ceremony of washing the White Lions, on *Sunday the 1st of April*, 1860. Admitted only at the White Gate. It is particularly requested that no gratuities be given to the Warders or their Assistants." The trick is said to have been highly successful. Cabs were rattling about Tower Hill all that Sunday morning, vainly endeavouring to find the White Gate.

April has its festivities too, but these are more closely connected with the church. First comes Palm Sunday, when the ceremonies of Easter begin, and Rome especially will be full of people to witness these rites. In some parts of England even at this day children will be going out on the Saturday "a-palming," that is, they will be setting out to the woods for slips of willow, which is in England taken as a substitute for the palm. They return with slips in their hats and in their buttonholes, and in their mouths too, while their hands are full of branches to give to the friends who have had to stay at home. The old custom of decorating the churches on this day is almost done away with, but in some out-of-the-way corners, slips of the willow, with its velvety buds are still stuck up in the rural churches, and in some too the people carry a piece in their hands or fastened in their breast.

Then we have Maundy Thursday, a long looked-for day by many poor old people who are in the habit of receiving gifts from kind friends. It used to be a very great day indeed for distributing charity and for practising acts of humility, for we read of the Kings of England, the high church dignitaries and noblemen, who used to have as many old people brought before them as they were years old, and in the chapels these great men washed the feet of their poor pensioners and presented them with money, meat, and clothes. Queen Elizabeth when in her thirty-ninth year performed this ceremony at Greenwich, on which occasion she was attended by thirty-nine ladies and gentlemen. This strange ceremonial, in which the highest of the land was for the moment brought beneath the lowest, was last performed in its full extent by James II.

At Rome on the evening of this day, the shops of the sausage-makers, candle-makers, and pork-dealers are decorated and illuminated in a fantastic way. Festoons of flowers and evergreens are stuck about, and there is a profusion of patches of various colours on the pork, candles, and other articles on the shelf. These decorations draw immense crowds of strangers and others to witness them, and of course the sausages are sold in large quantities. But the day we know best about is Good Friday. This day has been held as a festival by the Church from the earliest times. All business is suspended, and though the religious ceremonies are not performed in England with the same pomp as in Catholic countries, the services are very solemn. Even in the more northern parts of Great Britain, though, the people do not go to church, and there are no religious ceremonies whatever, the children look forward to it as a holiday, and enjoy the hot cross buns as much as the children in the south do. Though buns are not sold in the streets there as in many of the English towns, they know quite well about the cry of these street vendors—

"One a penny, buns,
Two a penny, buns,
One a penny, two a penny,
Hot-cross buns."

How eagerly the poor children gather round the shops where the buns are spread out so temptingly, and what shouts and screams of

delight when some kind lady taking compassion on the little crowd of gazers, suddenly goes in and returns with one for each. At no time does any one feel so happy as when doing a kindness for the little city Arabs who have so few pleasures in their hard life. Of course at this season one feels softened in heart, for we think of Christ and what He did for us, and especially of His kindness to the poor and how He left them as a legacy to the rich, "The poor ye have always with you." That reminds us of the many poor there must be amongst us this year. The winter has been so severe for all sorts of workpeople, and the spring must be bearing on its back, as it were, many suffering people still. It is to be hoped that the little readers of this Magazine are keeping their eyes wide awake to watch if they can help any poor neighbours, or if they happen to have no poor neighbours, but would like to help somebody, no doubt some one will tell them where a penny would be as acceptable as a pound would be somewhere else, where broken toys if mended up would find a hearty welcome, and where little fingers, especially those who find the time hanging heavy, could make pretty scrap-books and balls to be sent to any of the sick children's hospitals, or the day-homes for infants and little children, called crèches. If we try to help on the little children of the poor, we shall have Lents and a Good Friday in every sense of the word, and our hot cross buns will taste, oh so nice and sweet, and on Easter Sunday, it will be a "Sunday of joy" for we will remember that Christ has said, "Forasmuch as ye have done it to the least of these, my little ones, ye have done it unto me."

And now we must not forget to mention St. George's Day, the patron saint of England. We know very little of his history, as the legends which are told of him are not worthy of much credit. But we all know the picture of him on his beautiful prancing horse, and how he is represented with a spear in his hand, killing a dragon. St. George is also the patron of the Order of the Garter, the most ancient and distinguished of our orders of knighthood. St. George was cruelly tortured and beheaded by the emperor Diocletian for refusing to desert the faith of Christianity, on the 23rd of April, and on that account the festivals and installations of the Order of the Garter are still held on the 23rd of that month.

And now does any one object to take an umbrella with them during their walks, but fancies that because the day looks sunny there is no need to be burdened with such an article? why don't you know that the farmer is looking anxiously out for the sudden heavy showers, for he knows that April showers bring May flowers, and that when April blows his horn, it's good for both hay and corn, and that a cold April the barn will fill? Oh yes, we can enjoy the warm sunshine, but we must prepare for the fitful showers. Still, with this drawback, we love April. There is no month in the year that seems to have delighted our great old poets more. How sweetly sang Chaucer in his quaint verse—

> "Whame that April, with his showres sote,
> The droughte of March hath pierced to the rote,
>   *   *   *   *
> And small foules maken melodie
> That slepen alle night with an open eye,
> So priketh hem nature in her corages,
> Than longen folk to gon on pilgrimage."

That is as good as a puzzle to you to make out, but it will be worth trying to do it; and Shakspeare, speaking of the affections of the soul, says—

> "Oh, how this spring of love resembleth
> The uncertain glory of an April day."

But we must not forget the daffodils; are there any sweeter flowers of spring?

> "Fair daffodils, we weep to see
>   You haste away so soon;
> As yet the early-rising sun
>   Has not attained his noon.
>   Stay, stay,
> Until the lasting day
>   Has run
> But to the even-song;
> And having prayed together, we
> Will go with you along.
>   *   *
> Symbol is of nature's power,
>   Beauty always to us bringing,
> And of an Almighty care
> Spreading blessings everywhere."

The last of April may be said to have in it a tint of the coming May. The boys and girls, wisely provident of what is to be required to-morrow, are all preparing to set out to seek for trees from which they may obtain a plentiful supply of the May blossom. As one of the old poets says—

> "Waked, as her custom was, before the day,
> To do th' observance due to sprightly May,
> For sprightly May commands our youth to keep
> The vigils of her night, and breaks their rugged sleep."

111

CLEVER MASTER JACK.

CLEVER MASTER JACK.

BY THE EDITOR.

ACK was a remarkably sharp boy. He was a rosy handsome little lad of about ten years old at the time of my story. His father and mother had been obliged to go to India when he was a very little fellow, and Jack had been left in the care of his grandmother in England. Now grandmamma was very fond of the child, and spoiled him dreadfully, letting him have his own way in everything. His uncle David, seeing this, strongly advised grandmamma to send the little lad to school.

"My dear mother," said Uncle David to Lady Gordon, "you let him have his own way too much : indeed you do. He orders the servants about, he gets into all manner of mischief, and he is such a sharp little fellow that he can generally persuade you all he does is right."

Grandmamma sighed as she thought of losing her little companion. "Well, my dear," said she to Uncle David, "I will think about it : I cannot make up my mind to send him from me just yet."

However, on the very day after this conversation Master Jack managed to get into more mischief than usual. He jumped out from behind the dining-room door with a loud shout just as the butler was bringing in a tray for lunch ; the poor man was so startled that he dropped the tray, and both glass and china were broken. Then a little later in the afternoon, finding grandmamma's pet cat and her Skye terrier sleeping side by side on the rug, Jack contrived to tie their tails together with a piece of string without waking them ; and you may imagine, when they *did* wake, what a spluttering, and barking, and hissing there was.

It was this last piece of mischief which decided grandmamma upon sending him to school at last, for, as she rightly said, there was more cruelty than fun in it ; and Uncle David was commissioned to find out a school at once. This he soon did, and Master Jack started off for Birchley Academy after a tender and tearful parting from his dear grandmamma.

At school Jack was rather liked than otherwise both by his schoolfellows and the master. The boys liked him because he was full of fun and up to all sorts of pranks, while he pleased the master by his cleverness and quickness in learning. On his return to his grandmamma for the holidays, it soon appeared that he was not less sharp for having been to school, and that he had learnt to turn his sharpness to good account, as you will see by the little story I am going to tell you.

The first evening of his holidays Jack was amusing himself by building a house of cards, while grandmamma sat by the fire working. He was building up his house rather carelessly, and as fast as it rose to two or three stories down it toppled. At last he said suddenly :

"Grandmamma dear, will you give me a sixpence if I build my house six stories high ?"

"Yes, my dear."

"But will you double the sixpence if I build seven stories, and go on doubling for every extra story that I build ?"

"Yes, my dear, I will," said grandmamma rather sleepily, for she was just going to indulge in a nap, and little dreamt of the trap she was falling into.

Having obtained this promise, Jack set to work carefully, almost breathlessly, to build his house, and in a few minutes grandmamma's slumber was disturbed by hearing him say : "Six stories : that's sixpence, grandmamma !" Then in another minute : "Seven stories : a shilling !" Here he paused to get a chair to stand upon, for the house had grown so high. "Eight stories : two shillings !—Nine stories : four shillings !—Ten stories ! eight shillings !" And so he went on, building up and doubling the money, till at the thirteenth story down fell the house. My little readers can calculate what a large sum by that time the sixpence had grown into, and they may imagine grandmamma's astonishment.

TOM TIT'S WEDDING DAY.

By the AUTHOR of "AUNT EFFIE'S RHYMES," Etc.

TWO little Tom Tits,
  Sitting on a tree,
Suddenly bethought themselves
  How pleasant it would be,
If instead of living all their lives,
  As sister and as brother,
They billed and cooed like other birds,
  And married one another.

When somebody is bridegroom,
  And somebody is bride,
Of course the proper thing to do,
  Is fly away and hide.
So they crept beneath a tuft of leaves,
  And cottoned close together,
And talked about their little selves,
  The sunshine and the weather.

A busy happy little thing
  Was Sukie Tit the bride;
She did not care to sit up there,
  And did not wish to hide,
And much to do had little Su,
  For saint or bird or sinner
Must have a breakfast every day,
  And, if he can, a dinner.

Tom Tit's Wedding Day.

So like an arrow from the bow,
    From out the shade they darted,
And one went up and one below,
    But never widely parted.
From branch to branch, from spray to spray,
    About the tree they flitted,
One minute they were side by side,
    The next were off and quitted.

As neither of the Tits could sing,
    Each kept a little bell,
Its tone was sweet and musical,
    And answered quite as well
Tommy rang his music out,
    "Jingle, jingle, jingle,"
Sukie told her whereabout,
    "Tingle, tingle, tingle."

Deftly, nimbly, peep, and pry,
    Searching crack and hollow,
Anywhere a grub can lie,
    Slender beaks can follow.
"Tingle, tingle," down below,
    Changing sides and places,
"Jingle, jingle," better so :
    See each other's faces.

One is clinging to the bough,
    One is hanging under,
Topsy turvy, any how,
    Never far asunder.
What a merry wedding day,
    Tingle, tingle, Tom Tit,
Always on the first of May,
    Mind that you remember it.

BLACK ROLF OF ROOKSTONE.

By the Right Hon. E. H. KNATCHBULL-HUGESSEN, M.P., *Author of "Uncle Joe's Stories," &c.*

CHAPTER IV.

FROM whatever cause, however, the Baron had acted, it is certain that during all his career of reckless profligacy and crime he had never been otherwise than friendly with the old knight, and to him he now turned in the hour

116

of his distress. He rode forthwith to the Towers of Barnascran, and, having been at once admitted to the presence of their owner, lost no time in making known his request.

"I am harassed, good neighbour," said the wily Baron, "with evil reports, the which, whilst they were yet but reports, I cast aside, as idle fables unworthy the attention of a man

Black Rolf of Rookstone.

and a warrior. But I can treat them so no longer, since from safe channels I learn that there is a false knave abroad pretending to have descended from an elder branch of my family, and to have a claim upon my lands and title."

Sir Hugh smiled grimly. "Methinks, neighbour," said he, "it must be a bold man indeed, and foolishly reckless withal, who shall think to oust Black Rolf of Rookstone from his ancient halls. But hath the knave thy blood in his veins?"

"Not a drop hath he," promptly returned the Baron, "but hath somehow or other got possession of some old legend of our family, out of which he has coined a tale to win over idle fools, and hath thus gotten to himself friends by whose aid he threateneth to despoil me of mine own."

"Beshrew the knave!" returned the good knight. "It grieveth me deeply that such men should exist. But say, neighbour mine, how can I serve thee in this matter, and by my halidome it shall be done. No DeMontenoy will see a friend and neighbour wronged an he have power to shield him."

"Thanks, kind and true friend," replied the Baron: "thou canst mightily aid me, since thou art so well inclined. Thou knowest full well that, for one cause or another, I have disbanded the followers who once filled my halls, and the Towers of Rookstone are now but feebly defended. I must needs go to the town to seek from my man at law certain deeds, and to hear more certainly the doings and plottings of this evil foe. It may be one day, two, or even three that I shall be away. Should the enemy hear of my absence, he may take that moment to fall upon my castle, and, with so small a force as I have to defend it, mischief may follow. But if thou wouldst take some small portion of thy followers, and occupy the castle until I return, the danger would be avoided, and I should speedily be with thee again to pledge thee in red wine and drink confusion to all who war against thee and me."

Sir Hugh de Montenoy willingly listened to the proposal of the Black Rook of Rookstone, and readily agreed to ride forthwith to Rook-

117

stone with five-and-twenty men, and hold the place in safety during the absence of its owner. His preparations were not long to make, and that same evening the Baron returned with his friend and his friend's followers, and confided them all to the care of old Elfrida, who was somewhat astonished at the number of visitors, and the change which appeared to have come over her master, who for so long a time had scarcely admitted a single stranger within his walls.

Being now well satisfied of the security of his castle against a surprise, Black Rolf mounted his horse betimes next morning and set off for the town, determined to find out all that could be discovered about the person of whom the man of law had written. He rode moodily on, still accompanied by the ceaseless cawing which would have driven an ordinary man mad, but which merely had the effect of making the Baron more savage than usual. Still he rode not with the headlong haste which had marked his ride to the abbey. The intense excitement he had then felt seemed to have passed away, and to have given place to a deep, sullen feeling of resentment, and a sense of injury which was none the less keen because it was hardly justified by the circumstances. In truth it was the new claimant to his property who had been really injured, and cruelly injured, in the past. but this mattered little to the Baron. He had been in possession of the old castle so long, and had (though by means which would not bear inquiry) so added to the family estates and position, that the bare thought of being dispossessed was like gall and wormwood to his haughty soul.

He could not—he would not—believe the tale of his brother's wrongs. Yet there was it written in black and white: there could be no doubt that the ancient Abbot had rightly read the scroll and interpreted its meaning, and the disbelief, real or pretended, of the person whose property was affected by its contents would weigh but little with others who might be made acquainted with the same. The evidence was strong—too strong—and if the brotherhood at the abbey should make the facts known, and give their endorsement to them, it is certain that many would accept these facts as true, and the new claimant would find a host of friends among those to whom the name of Black Rolf was already sufficiently obnoxious to render it certain that they would gladly join his foes. All these thoughts passed through the Baron's mind, and did not tend to lessen the gloom which overshadowed him. He gnashed his teeth savagely as he rode onward, and muttered low, but deep, imprecations upon the head of his enemy, as he deemed the stripling to be who had come to claim his own from the hand of him who had so long withheld it from its rightful owner. The sun was high in the heavens when the Baron Fitzuron rode into the town and followed the twistings and turnings of the narrow streets which led to the abode of him whom he sought. The man of law dwelt in an ancient house, in a quiet part of the town, away from the main thoroughfare, the noise and bustle of which might have interfered with the work which doubtless fell to his lot in the study of old deeds, the disentangling of matters clogged by the intricacies of the law, and the settlement of questions which people might have settled for themselves less expensively but less securely than by his legal craft. He was a man well advanced in years, one who had long followed his profession in that place, and who bore withal a name respected among his fellow-men. From him the Baron felt sure that he should obtain a just and true opinion upon the matter which lay so near his heart, and, whatever that opinion might be as far as the merits of the case were concerned, he trusted that the man of law, who had served him so long, would do so still, and would by his subtle craft postpone, even if he could not altogether avert, the evil with which he was threatened.

As he neared the door of the abode he sought, he perceived a horse standing near it, held by a boy. It was a magnificent roan, fit for a prince to ride, and perfect in shape and strength, as the Baron could tell at a glance. He had, however, neither time nor inclination to gaze long upon the animal, for he was in haste about the business which caused him so much anxiety. So he hastily sprang from his own horse and sounded so loud a peal upon the bell, that there was little delay before his summons was

answered. To the page who opened the door he carelessly flung his rein, scarcely asking whether his master was at home as he strode rudely into the house. .

"My lord, my lord!" called the youth, who had seen the baron before and knew him at once, "my master cannot see thee at this moment. He is engaged in converse with a gentleman—he will see no other now—and I was bid to deny admittance to all."

But the lad might as well have spoken to the winds, for Black Rolf merely swore a deep oath, and strode forward to the office-room, which he knew full well. Without knock or call, or warning of any kind, he opened the door, and burst roughly and suddenly into the room, to the great apparent surprise and discomfiture of two persons who were seated therein and who instantly arose at the same moment rose from their seats. The one was the man of law ; the Baron knew him well and recognised at a glance the old-fashioned office-table at which he sat, with deeds and papers scattered all around, doubtless containing the secret records of many an ancient and noble family. But who was the person with whom the man of law had been closeted ? Tall and dark, a goodly and well-proportioned frame, sinewy limbs, finely-cut features, and hair of the raven hue, he was a man of mark beyond all doubt, and of this the man who beheld him was well assured at the first glance. But there was something more. That face brought back memories to the proud Baron which had long slumbered in his brain, or if they had ever arisen had been speedily stifled or banished : that eagle look, that keen, flashing eye, those lineaments that so vividly recalled the features of the dead—all told Black Rolf a tale which he doubted not for an instant, and it required not the words of a witness to convince him that he stood in the presence of one of his own race and blood.

Forthwith the man of law interposed with trembling accents, stammering in his haste and fear, and scarce knowing how to excuse himself to his old patron and employer for the circumstance of being found in consultation with his relative and rival.

"My lord," he said, "this is sudden—this is

unexpected—this honour—your lordship's visit —had I but known—your lordship's goodness will understand—'twere difficult to have refused the interview I hold with this noble gentleman —your lordship will believe me—I know not— I fear me I may not rightly explain—your lordship's nephew—"

During this somewhat unconnected harangue the Baron had stood still, gazing with lowering brow from one to the other of his two companions and biting his lip as if to control some intense feeling : but at this point he broke out with a furious oath.

"Treacherous hound!" he yelled, rather than shouted, "art thou also in league with mine enemies ? Nephew, sayest thou, thou plotting rascal—what knowest thou of nephews, thou foul quill-driver ? And how darest thou prate thus to me whom thou hast betrayed ?"

The Baron's rage prevented his further speech, and the man at law, overwhelmed with mingled fear, anger, and confusion, could only stammer forth in trembling accents—

"My lord, my lord—I cannot—I do not—I did not—I could not—" and then broke down entirely and stood speechless. But the third person present at this strange interview now took up the conversation. One step forward he took and laid his hand firmly upon the desk of the man at law as he thus gave utterance to his feelings :—

"The man hath done no wrong," he said in a calm, clear tone of voice, which seemed to strike like a chill upon the heart of him who listened ; "he hath but heard what he could scarce avoid hearing—a tale of woe and wrong —of woe suffered and of wrong to be redressed. And thou be'st mine uncle, noble sir, I would have thee listen too, and deem him not thine enemy who seek but mine own. I am the son of thine elder brother, as I can verily and surely prove, and I come to claim the name and inheritance which neither force nor fraud shall withhold from me. But I seek no family quarrel, nor would I willingly injure my father's brother. Yield the place which by right belongeth to thine elder brother's son, and all may ye be well. Thou hast wealth enough beside, men say, and why shouldst thou grudge thy kinsman that which is his own ?"

119

Tho Baron ground his teeth savagely at these words. " Kinsman!" he shouted, " No kinsman thou of mine. Bastard ! Caitiff ! Pretender ! I own thee not—I know thee not. Thou hast neither part nor lot with the Rolfs of Rookstone ; " and he glared furiously at the other as he spoke.

It was a strange sight to see the two men at this moment. The elder, mad with rage, every muscle in his aged frame quivering with excitement, regarded his disowned kinsman with a withering glance of concentrated wrath and hatred, which the young man returned with equal pride and indignation. And, in that instant, any one who had looked upon the twain must have been struck by their wondrous resemblance in form, figure, and features, ay, even to the keen, dark, wild eyes from which flashed those hostile glances from one to the other. Incensed beyond measure at the last words of the Baron, the other laid his hand upon his sword, and was about to stride hastily and angrily forward, when the man of law, having somewhat recovered his courage, interposed his venerable form between the two.

"Stay, noble sirs, stay, I pray you, by the holy rood," he cried in trembling and anxious tones. " Break not the peace, nor brawl in any unseemly fashion as drunken churls might do ; such conduct beseemeth not noble persons, nor is there any occasion for this outbreak. The law will see right done if nothing else can settle matters between ye. Noble lord, I pray you stand back—brave youth, raise not thine hand against thy father's brother."

" What ! " thundered the Baron, on hearing the last word. " Sayest thou this to my face ? Art thou no traitor, who ownest this false knave before my very eyes ? The foul fiend seize thee and him together, for thou art assuredly in league with him, and shalt feel my vengeance accordingly. This is no place for honest men who wish to keep the estates they have fairly won with their own right arms. I go, ye thieving villains, but beware ye of the wrath of Black Rolf of Rookstone ! "

So saying the Baron turned upon his heel without another word, and left the room in a state of mind bordering upon frenzy. He passed down the passage to the door at which he had left his steed, which was still held by the servant of the man of law, on whom he scarcely bestowed a glance, as he sprang hastily into the saddle and rushed down the street, hardly knowing which road he took, so vehemently did the wrathful tempest rage in his soul.

Down the streets his horse's hoofs clattered anon, through the market-place and past the outskirts of the town into the open country beyond. Away, away over the open downs he sped, the fresh breeze of heaven scarcely cooling his heated brow, his teeth clenched with rage and his whole frame quivering with excitement. Away, away! and still there sounded in his ears that ceaseless cawing, now low, now loud, but ever the same wearisome, dull, continuous sound that marked but too surely that Black Rolf of Rookstone was under the ban of the sacred birds he had so boldly defied. Away, and still away, and in his frenzy he spared neither whip nor spur, but goaded on his already weary horse, as if in the pursuit of some object still far off, and only to be reached by frantic haste.

Away! Off the downs and into the great ravine, and over the ford and through the wood, all at the same headlong speed, though his brave horse was well nigh spent, and his flanks were covered with blood and foam, and he laboured heavily over the soft ground of the valley, as they came nearer the sea-shore, and the castle stood but a short two miles before them.

The day was wearing fast, and the Baron spurred on, making but little of his steed's distress. and consumed by the force of his own internal fury. Onward, still onward; but the two miles are all too long for the brave horse. Poor Belial! He had carried his master well through many a long day's ride, and borne him safely out of many a fray when brave and strong men had been left behind: nay, save the old Elfrida, there was perhaps no living thing that loved the Baron more than his faithful charger; he would start round and neigh at the sound of his voice, would prick up his ears and come to meet him in the paddock, and by arched neck and stately step showed the pride with which he carried the master whom

he had served so long. But neither his love nor his length of service availed him aught to-day. Forgetful alike of one and the other the Baron had urged the noble animal on beyond his strength, until the chords of the brave heart snapped asunder in the struggle. The black steed stumbled—once—twice—blundered forward upon his head, rolled over, and with one convulsive sob which quivered through his whole frame, lay dying at his master's feet.

The Baron, an expert horseman, quickly extricated himself as the horse fell, and stood still for an instant, calmed and sobered by the occurrence. The filmy eyes of his faithful steed seemed for one instant to be turned upon him with looks of reproachful anguish—the next they were glazed in death. It was done. No more would that pleasant neigh welcome his approach to stable or paddock—no more would those strong limbs bear him abroad or that high courage support his own in the battle. It was over; and he had lost a trusty servant —ay, a friend. For one moment softness came over that hard heart, and remorse entered that stubborn breast.

Not long, however, did such unwonted guests remain. The Baron swore a deep oath and stamped savagely on the ground. The castle was still near half a mile off—curses on the ill-luck that had followed him of late—curses on the fate that had robbed him of his best horse when the latter would have had rest and food within five minutes—double, treble curses upon the foul birds who had worked him all this evil. He turned from the carcase of poor Black Belial and strode forward towards the castle. All was as it should be. The rays of the setting sun fell full upon the old tower, upon which floated the banner of Sir Hugh de Montenoy, side by side with his own. The brave old knight sat carousing in his neighbour's hall, and Rolf heard the sound of laughter and revelry as he entered by the postern gate. He ground his teeth savagely : for such sounds ill suited with his humour at that moment, and turning into a side passage sought the private way into the oak library. There he threw himself into a huge old-fashioned arm-chair that seemed as if it had been made in the age of giants, to suit the requirements of their mighty frames, and for a while remained there, wrapt in thought. Then again starting from his seat and striding hastily to the hall, he joined Sir Hugh, who received him with a loud greeting of welcome. For a short time the Baron shared with his guest in his carousal, but ere long he pleaded fatigue, and quitting the hall again, once more betook himself to the oak library, and summoned old Elfrida to his presence. She obeyed, though not without some misgiving, for she feared that the prospect of losing that for which he had worked so long might have tempted her master to plot some dark and deadly deed against him whom she somehow knew to be the rightful owner.

Black Rolf, however, said nothing of such matters, he did but require her assistance to obtain again from the chest in which he had replaced them after his visit to the abbey, the scroll and miniature which had caused him so much trouble. He had a project in his mind, upon the accomplishment of which he was now entirely bent. The secret way communicating with the passage which led from the castle to the sea-shore was known to few—to no one, as Rolf believed, but to Elfrida and himself, nor, indeed, to her in any such practical way as that in which he knew and had long known it. For the old dame, though she knew the existence of the secret way and the entrance thereto, had never had occasion to explore it.

The Baron had long turned it to account as a hiding-place for his treasures, and the thought which was now in his mind was neither more nor less than the getting rid of the chief evidence against his title to Rookstone by placing the miniature and scroll in some inner recess of the rocks through which wound the passage, where in all human probability the eye of mortal would never see them. Thus secured he thought he could defy his adversary in spite of all the rooks that had ever cawed. With this intention he claimed the assistance of old Elfrida, and having obtained the articles he desired, dismissed her again from his presence, answering with rough words her earnest prayers that he would not attempt to sin against the unseen powers by destroying those things which were forbidden to be destroyed. He bade her

begone in a manner which showed her that further entreaty would be useless, and as soon as she had left the room threw himself once more into the same arm-chair and pondered deeply. The fiends take that cawing ! How it bothered him ! He could not collect his thoughts—that dull, heavy, monotonous, wearisome sound was beginning to wear out his patience and to prevent the free exercise of his thinking powers. Presently he arose and passed out of the oak library into the passage, from which a small spiral staircase led to some of the upper chambers of the castle. This he ascended, and passing through several large rooms, almost wholly empty of furniture, and bearing the desolate appearance which characterised the greater part of the interior of his dwelling, he paused for a moment before an old and curiously carved door at the far end of one of these chambers.

For a little while he stood silent as if doubtful of his purpose, and then, as if his mind was finally made up, he seized the handle of the door with a sudden grasp, and entered that which was known as the tapestried room. It was hung all round with very ancient tapestry, mouldy and moth-eaten in many places from age and want of care, but still presenting an imposing appearance as it hung heavily upon the walls, imparting a dark and sombre aspect to the room. Towards the corner to his left the Baron directed his steps, and drawing aside the tapestry, was about to stoop down to a panel in the wall, when a low sigh suddenly arrested his attention.

He started and turned round. "Whom have we here ?" he angrily asked, but there was no reply. Muttering an oath, he stood for a moment irresolute, and then, striding to the other side of the room, from whence the sound had appeared to come, hastily tore away the tapestry, and disclosed the form of the old Elfrida cowering in a recess.

"Old beldame !" he shouted, "what dost thou here, and how darest thou play the spy upon thy master's doings?" With these words he seized the aged woman by the shoulder and shook her roughly.

In trembling accents she endeavoured to excuse herself. "Oh, my lord, my dear lord," she cried, whilst sobs and fear almost choked her voice, "what is it that thou seekest to do? Thou wouldst enter that awesome place. I pray thee hold back. The power thou defiest is too strong for thee—it is for thee I fear—" Black Rolf swore a fearful oath. Her words showed that she had not forgotten, as he had hoped, the secret ways of the castle, known only to her besides himself, and this knowledge on her part, coupled with her evident fear of, if not friendship for, those who were opposed to him, betokened evil to his cause.

"Thou besotted old harridan!" he shouted, "thou pratest of that of which thou knowest nought. What place? What power? Hence at once, or it will be the worse for thee!" As he spake, he stamped violently on the ground, whilst the cawing in his ears became so loud and harsh that he was nearly driven wild.

"Oh, my lord," responded the terrified old woman, "I meant not thy mortal enemies, though they, Heaven knows, are mighty enough. But mightier still is the curse of the ancient rook, and much I fear me thou art lost if thou strive not to avert it. Oh, think whilst yet there is time, my nursling! Submit to the doom, yield thy goods to save thy precious life, forsake thine evil life, give up thy present plan of wrong, and make friends with thy nephew before—"

She spoke no more—incensed beyond measure at her words, Black Rolf seized her by the throat with another fearful imprecation, and drawing the dagger which ever hung by his side, would in another second have plunged it into her heart, when a hand, laid heavily upon his shoulder, caused him to drop the senseless frame of the old woman, and start hastily upon one side.

There, boldly confronting him, stood the monk whom he had angrily dismissed but two days before. His eyes flashed fiercely beneath his cowl, and his hand was still upraised in menace against the Lord of Rookstone. For an instant the latter was paralysed between rage, shame, and surprise, and staggered back uncertain whether to believe the eyes which beheld a stranger and evidently an enemy, in one of the most secret parts of his castle.

But during that instant something occurred to excite still more strongly his surprise and

wrath. Stooping down, the monk lifted the form of Elfrida as if it had been that of a child, and stepping back to the opposite side of the room, lifted the tapestry; at the same moment, in a low, stern voice he addressed the astounded Baron.

"Doomed wretch!" he exclaimed. "Go to thy fate unpitied and unwept. I bid thee beware of our next meeting—we meet no more." And with these words he passed rapidly behind the tapestry with his burden, and disappeared from the eyes of the person he addressed.

The latter could scarcely yet recover himself from his astonishment, but as soon as he did so, he rushed furiously to the spot where the monk had stood, lifted the tapestry, and, dagger in hand, sought everywhere for his enemy. In vain. The monk had apparently vanished into thin air, and his disappearance opened up a new source of anxiety to the perplexed Baron. One secret passage from that apartment he knew well. To prevent its existence coming to the knowledge of others, he had been ready to slay even the old servant who had served him so long and loved him so well. But could there be another outlet, and unknown to him? The thought was indeed alarming, and such as would at another time have induced him to postpone or abandon the work on hand until he had carefully sought out the truth of the matter.

But his nerves were at this moment in a state of tension which forbade calm consideration, and the still increasing sound in his ears almost maddened him by its continuance. Only for a few seconds he sought, and then, doubtful whether he had not seen a vision, and the old woman had not been bodily carried off by the powers of darkness, he returned to the corner to which he had first advanced upon entering the room. Stooping down, he touched a spring, and at the same time pushing against a panel in the wainscoting, it flew back and revealed a door in the wall behind. This the Baron opened and passed through, carefully closing it behind him. He now stood in a small vestibule, at the further side of which was a flight of stone steps. It was near the outside wall of the castle, and the only light in the vestibule proceeded from a slit in the massive stonework above, which however, was sufficient to enable the owner of the castle to find his way to the stairs, which he forthwith descended. The way, indeed, was well known to him, for the staircase led, by a long descent, to secret vaults and rooms below, in which he had from time to time stored such portions of his accumulated treasures as could not be readily converted into money. The first of these was entered by means of a massive iron door, of which Rolf carried the ponderous key in his girdle.

Before, however, he attempted to open it, he turned to a deep recess in the wall, wherein stood a silver lamp with a glass cover, and by its side an appliance for lighting it. He carefully struck a light, adjusted the glass firmly upon the lamp, and then, having opened the door, entered the first vault. Within it, scattered here and there around, lay a varied and considerable treasure, rich bales of merchandise, the produce of piratical expeditions upon the coast, costly suits of armour, bars of gold, jewelry, garments of rich texture; all mixed together and thrown carelessly upon the floor, as from time to time the robber Baron had found it convenient to bring them to his secret hiding-place. Amid these he passed with cautious steps, and opened a door, somewhat similar to the first, in which lay gold and silver coin in no trifling quantity. Those were not

the days of banks, and Black Rolf's coined treasure being too vast for ordinary money chests to contain, he kept much of it in these secret vaults.

In this second chamber, he paused, doubtful for a moment whether a safe place could be found in which to deposit the miniature and the parchment. Little did he know how much depended upon his decision. Why should he not hide them there? No human eye was likely to penetrate to the place where he stood, no stranger hand to drag forth the fatal things he bore from a hiding-place in the earth of the vault. Yet it might be that if ill-health fell upon him, or increased age forced him, however unwillingly, to trust the secrets of the castle to others, that the necessity of employing some of his treasure might, one day or another, oblige him to send some one to that place. However trustworthy that some one might be, better that a secret the discovery of which would be fraught with such alarming consequences, should be beyond the possibility of falling into his hands. Yes, assuredly it would be better to make matters safe once for all, and to hide the things he carried in a place still more secure and inaccessible. Of all men living, Black Rolf of Rookstone, as he believed, was the only one who knew the secrets of that place.

(To be continued.)

PUGGIE IN DISGRACE.

124

PUGGIE IN DISGRACE.

FOR VE-RY LIT-TLE FOLKS.

HILD-REN, just look at this queer little Pug,
His small wrin-kled nose, his little black mug!
I fear he's been naugh-ty at les-sons to-day;
And, like naugh-ty child-ren, he's pun-ished this way.

He sits on the stool of re-pent-ance, you see;
Poor Pug-gie is gen-tle and meek as can be;
But when at his les-sons he just took a nap,
And that is the rea-son he wears the Fool's cap.

His neck has an or-na-ment, not like his head,
But a beau-ti-ful lock-et and rib-bon in-stead;
So you see that to some one the dog-gie is dear,
Al-though they all tease him I very much fear.

From Ho-race, the eld-est, to lit-tle Miss May,
All in-sist that Poor Pug-gie should join in their play;
Some-times they pet him, and some-times they tease,
But he bears it all pa-tient-ly, eager to please.

He rolls his big eyes, or just heaves a sigh,
And thinks they'll make up for it all by and by.
For Pug-gie is greed-y, and bears a great deal
For the sake of some cakes or a good heart-y meal.

But though he *is* greed-y, his faults are but few,
He is lov-ing and hon-est, de-vo-ted and true.
If our two-foot-ed friends were as faith-ful as he
Ve-ry for-tu-nate peo-ple I think we should be.

125

TWO LITTLE DOGS.

Moderato.

mf Two lit - tle dogs were bask - ing in the cin - ders, Two lit - tle cats were play - ing in the win-dows, Two lit - tle mice popp'd out of a hole, And up to a fine piece of cheese they stole. The two lit - tle dogs said, Cheese is nice, But the two lit - tle cats jump'd down in a trice, And crush'd the bones of the two lit - tle mice.

2.

Two little lambs were frisking in the meadows,
Two woolly dams were watching in the shadows,
Two little dogs came by with a man,
And over the meadows they barking ran;
The two woolly ewes cried out "Bah, bah!"
And then each little lamb skipt back to its Ma,
And faced the dogs with a merry Ha! Ha!

PICTURE PAGE WANTING WORDS.

A Prize of a Guinea Book will be given for the best short Original Story descriptive of this Picture. Competitors to be under fourteen years of age, and the Stories to be sent to the "EDITOR OF LITTLE WIDE AWAKE," care of Messrs. GEORGE ROUTLEDGE & SONS, by the 12th April, 1879.

PUZZLES.

CHARADES.

1.

My first is of a wheel a part ;
Some wheels do not possess it.
My second's oft a work of art,
Not always I confess it ;

It's also of my whole two-thirds,
And used by all except the birds.
My whole for learning is renowned,
No wonder !—scholars there abound.

2.

My first a lady's name should be ;
My next can draw fish from the sea,
My whole attracts a needle.

3.

My first is made of cork,
My second is an article,
My third is an adjective,
My whole an Indian house.

4.

My first is a bed of stone or mineral,
My second is a precious stone,
My whole is an artifice.

5.

With a scream of defiance I rush on my course,
Strong as an elephant, fleet as a horse.
My first's an interjection small,
My next is a company reckoned by all.
If you have but my third in finding me out,
Twill sharpen your wits I haven't a doubt.

6.

Beneath the shadow of my first
A youth stood listening to a burst
Of melody which stirred his soul :
He knew the singer was my whole.

If you're o'ertaken by my third,
You'll lose your hat, now mark my word ;
And cannot be in safety reckoned,
Until a house you're with—my second.

DECAPITATION.

Rubbish, rubbish, just behead,
Precipitate you'll have instead ;
Behead again and you will see
You'll have at once a well-known tree.

ENIGMA.

I'm expected by the ladies,
I am watched for by the maid,
When the master's late for breakfast,
Upon his plate I'm laid.

I travel far, I travel wide,
I'm stamped upon and broken,
Of love, and faith, and friendship,
I'm the truest, surest token.

Answers to Puzzles on Page 96.

CHARADES.

1. Table-cloth.
2. Water-jug.
3. Arm-chair.
4. Tea-caddy.
5. Sunflower.
6. The Bywell Castle.
7. Westmorland.

DECAPITATION.

Share, hare, are.

BURIED BIRDS.

1. Linnet, Goldfinch.
2. Sparrow, Blackcap.
3. Snipe.

BURIED TREES.

1. Pine, Ash.
2. Elm, Cedar.
3. Beech, Aspen.

ENIGMA.

The Letter A.

HOODIE.

By Mrs. MOLESWORTH, *Author of "Herney," "The Cock-& Clock," &c.*

CHAPTER V.—STORIES TELLING.

"This is the cock that crowed in the morn."

LATE that night, no, very early the next morning, just as dawn was breaking, the peacefully sleeping inhabitants of Mr. Caryll's house were awakened by strange and alarming sounds which seemed to come from the direction of the nursery. The children's mother was one of the first to wake, and yet the sounds which had roused her having been heard indistinctly through her sleep, she was not able to say what they were.

"It must be one of the children with croup —I am sure it sounded like what I have heard croup described, or like that dreadful illness they call the crowing cough," she said to Mr.

129

Caryll, as she rushed out of the room in a fright.

She had only got to the end of the long passage leading to the children's rooms when she ran against Miss King, closely followed by her maid and one, two, three, other servants all pale and alarmed.

"What can it be?" each said to the other.

"Martin, Martin," cried Mrs. Caryll, "are you there? What *is* the matter?"

But before any Martin was to be seen, again the sounds shrilled through the house.

"Kurroo — kurallarrallo-oo-*ook!* " with a queer sudden sort of pull-up at the end, it seemed to sound.

, They all turned to look at each other.

"It must be a real cock," said Miss King, looking less frightened.

"It certainly doesn't sound like croup," said Mrs. Caryll.

"It's just one of them mischievous bantams, ma'am," said the cook, a countrywoman who had made a study of cocks and hens. "They always give that sort of catchy croak at the end of their crows. But, to be sure, what a fright it's gave us all! And where can the creature be?"

As she spoke, Martin appeared at the end of the passage, a basket in her arms, her face pale, leading by the hand a small figure in a white night-gown, a figure that pulled and pushed and kicked valiantly in its extreme reluctance to come any further.

"I won't be takened to Mamma. I won't, I won't. I'm not naughty. It's zou that's ugly and naughty," it screamed.

Mrs. Caryll gave a despairing glance at her cousin.

"Hoodie again!" she said.

Martin hastened forward as fast as she could, considering the difficulties in her way.

"Oh, ma'am," she exclaimed, looking nearly ready to cry, "I am so sorry, so sorry and ashamed to have such an upset in the house at this time of the night, or morning, I should say. It really must seem with all these troubles as if I wasn't fit to manage the children. And just as Miss King has come, too. But oh dear, ma'am, I don't know *what* to do with Miss Hoodie and her queer ways."

130

"But what *is* it, Martin? What has Hoodie been doing?" said Mrs. Caryll, rather impatiently. "Stop crying, Hoodie. You *must*," she added sternly, turning to the little girl, who was now regularly set agoing on one of her roars.

Hoodie took not the slightest notice, but roared on. Her mother turned again to Martin, shaking her head.

"No, ma'am," said Martin, "it's not the least use speaking to her. She has wakened all the others, of course—first with that nasty creature and then with her screaming."

"What nasty creature? For goodness' sake explain yourself, Martin."

"The cock, ma'am — the bantam cock," replied Martin, seeming quite astonished that Mrs. Caryll did not know all about it by instinct. "Miss Hoodie fetched it in in her basket, unbeknown to me, last night, and had it hidden under her bed. The creature was quite quiet all night, as is its nature, I suppose, and very likely frightened and not knowing where it was. But this morning all of a sudden it started the most awful screeching; it really sounded much worse than common crowing, or else it was hearing it half in one's sleep like. I thought to be sure one of those dear boys had got some awful fit. And to think it was nothing but Miss ᴗHoodie's naughtiness — real mischievous naughtiness."

Martin stopped, quite out of breath, and Hoodie's roars increased in violence.

"Had she really no reason for it but mischief?" said Miss King.

Martin hesitated.

"She did begin some nonsense, ma'am, about having brought it in to lay an egg, or something like that."

"Hoodie," said Magdalen, "can't you leave off screaming and tell us about it?"

"No," said Hoodie, stopping at once and with perfect ease, "I can't leave off sc'eaming and I won't. But I'll tell zou, 'cos it was for zou. I brought the little cock in to lay a egg for zour breakfast, 'cos zou said zou likened zem kite fresh, and now Martin's spoilt it all. Of course it c'owed to tell me it was going to lay the egg, and now it won't. It's all spoilt, and I *must* sc'eam."

True to her determination she set to work again and roared so that it was almost impossible to hear one's voice.

"What *shall* we do with her?" said her mother.

"May I take her to my room?" said Cousin Magdalen. "It is further away from the other children, so she can't disturb them even if she screams all day."

Hoodie stopped again as suddenly as before.

"I won't go to zour room," she said. "I don't like zou now—not one bit."

Magdalen glanced at Mrs. Caryll.

"May I take my own way with her!" her glance seemed to say. Mrs. Caryll nodded her head, and notwithstanding Martin's whispered warning, "Oh, Miss King, you don't *know* what a work you'll have with her," Magdalen turned to Hoodie, and before the child in the least understood what she was about, she had picked her up in her strong young arms and was half way down the passage before Hoodie's surprise had given her breath to begin her roars again.

She was opening her mouth to do so, when her cousin stopped for a moment.

"Now, Hoodie," she said, "*listen*. It was kind of you to want to get me a quite fresh egg for my breakfast, but it isn't kind of you at all to make that disagreeable noise, and to kick and fight so because I want to take you to my room."

"I don't care," said Hoodie, "I don't like zou and I will cry if I like. I don't like any people."

"I am very sorry to find you are so silly," said Cousin Magdalen. "If you were older and understood better you would not talk like that."

"I would if I liked," persisted Hoodie. "Big peoples can do whatever zey likes, and if I was big I could too."

"Big people *can't* do whatever they like," said Miss King, "and nice big people never like to do things that other people don't like too."

"Don't zey?" said Hoodie meditatively.

By this time they were safely shut into Miss King's room and Hoodie was plumped down into the middle of her cousin's bed—"Don't

131

zey? Zen I don't want to be a nice big people. I want to be the kind that does whatever zey likes zerselves."

Miss King gave a slight sigh—half of amusement, half of despair. She was beginning to understand that Hoodie's reformation was indeed no easy matter.

"Very well, then. You had better go on screaming if you like it so much," she said, sitting down on the side of the bed and wondering to herself what would become of the world, if all the children in it were as tiresome to manage as Hoodie. In at the window the daylight was creeping timidly; all kinds of pretty colours were to be seen in the sky, and the birds were beginning their cheerful chatter. Still it was very early, and poor cousin Magdalen was sleepy. Was there *anything* that could make Hoodie go to sleep for an hour or two?

"The little birds in the nests are kind to each other. They don't wake each other up in the night and scream so that there is no peace. I wonder why children can't be good too," she said.

"I'm *not* sc'eaming," said Hoodie indignantly. "I've stoppened."

"I'm glad to hear it. But if I get into bed and lie down and try to go to sleep, perhaps you'll begin again, as you don't care for what other people like."

Hoodie was silent for a minute.

"Does you want to go to sleep?"

"Yes," said Magdalen. "I'm very tired."

"Zen I won't sc'eam."

Her cousin felt inclined to clap her hands, but wisely forbore.

"Thank you," she said quietly, as she lay down.

Hoodie wriggled.

"No, zou isn't to say zank zou," she said. "I don't like zou. I don't like any people, 'cos they stopped my getting zat nice fresh egg. I won't get zou eggs no more. I don't like zou."

"Very well," said her cousin.

Some minutes' quiet followed. Then Hoodie's voice again.

"When will zou tell us that story?" she inquired coolly.

"What story?"

"Zat story about oldwashion fairies, or somesing like zat."

"Oh, I said I'd try to think of a story for you," said Miss King, sleepily. "Well, I won't forget."

"Zou must get it ready quick," said Hoodie. "Zou must tell it me, zou know, 'cos I've been so good about not sc'eaming."

"But not now. You don't want me to tell you stories *now*," said her cousin in alarm.

"No, zou may go to sleep now," replied Hoodie, condescendingly, adding after a moment's pause. "*I* can tell stories, lovely stories."

"Can you? well, you had better think of one, and have it all ready," said Magdalen in fresh alarm.

"Mine's is always zeady, but zou may go to sleep now," was the reply, to her great relief, the truth being that Hoodie herself was as sleepy as she could be, for in two minutes her soft even breathing told that for a while her fidgety little spirit was at rest.

Magdalen lay awake some time longer. In a half-dreamy way she was thinking over in her own mind the old fairy tales she had loved as a little girl—with them there mingled in her fancy the scenes and memories of her own childhood. She was glad to find Hoodie so eager for stories, it might be one way of winning the strange-tempered little creature's confidence, and she tried to call to mind some of the tales most likely to interest her. And somehow, "between sleeping and waking," there came back to her mind the shadow of a fanciful little story she had either read or heard or imagined long ago, and as she fell asleep she said to herself, "Yes, that will do. I will tell them the story of 'The Chintz Curtains.'"

When Magdalen awoke again that morning it was, as might have been expected, a good deal later than usual. Hoodie was still sleeping soundly. Magdalen got up and dressed quietly. She was nearly quite ready when Hoodie awoke. A little movement in the bed caught Miss King's notice : she turned round. There was Hoodie, staring at her with wide-open eyes.

"Well, Hoodie," she said. "How are you this morning ?"

Hoodie did not reply, but continued staring, so her cousin went on fastening up her hair. In a minute or two there came a remark, or question rather.

"Has zou had a nice sleep ?"

"Yes, thank you."

"Has zou thinkened of a story ?"

"Yes," said Magdalen. "I almost think I have."

"*I* has too," said Hoodie with a queer twinkle in her eyes.

"Have you," said her cousin, "that's very clever of you."

"Yes," replied the little girl, "zou didn't know Hoodie was so c'ever, did zou ?"

"You'd better tell me the story first, and then I'll say what I think of it," said Magdalen.

"Now ?" inquired Hoodie, "sall I tell it now ? It isn't a long one."

"If you like," replied Magdalen, "you can tell it me while I finish doing my hair."

"Well," began Hoodie, solemnly, "just a long time ago—oh no, that's a mistake, it should be just '*onst*—' "

"Or 'once,' " corrected her cousin, " ' once ' is a proper word, and ' onst ' isn't."

"I don't care," said Hoodie, frowning. "I like to say ' onst.' If zou don't zink my words pretty you'll make one come, and if one comes I can't tell you stories."

"Very well," said Magdalen, remembering Maudie's explanation of the mysterious phrase, "very well. I won't interrupt you. You may say any words you like."

"Well then," began Hoodie again. "*Onst* there was a little girl. She was called—no, I won't tell zou what she was called—she had a papa and mamma and bruvvers and a sister, but zey didn't like her much."

She stopped.

"Dear me," said Magdalen, finding she was expected to say something, "that was very sad."

"Yes," said Hoodie, "vezy sad."

"Why didn't they like her ! "

" 'Cos zey thoughtened· she was naughty. Zey was alvays saying she was naughty."

"Perhaps she was," said Magdalen.

"Nebber mind," said Hoodie. "I want to

go on. One day a lady comed what wasn't *hern* godmozer, so she didn't like her and she toldened her she was ugly. But zen—oh zen she founded out that she wasn't ugly, but she was pretty, vezy, vezy pretty—oh she was so nice, and the little girl liked her vezy much—wasn't zat a nice story ?"

"Beautiful," said Miss King. "All except the part about her papa and mamma and sister and brothers not liking her. I don't like that part."

"Nebber mind," replied Hoodie again. "Nebber mind about zat part zen. Doesn't zou like about the lady ? Can zou guess who it was ? "

"Let me see," said Magdalen, solemnly. "I must think. A lady came that wasn't *her* godmother—dear me, who could it be ? "

"It was zou; it was zou," cried Hoodie, jumping up in bed and rushing at her cousin. "And the little girl was Hoodie, 'cos I do like zou now. I do, I do, and I'll be vezy good all day, to please you."

"That's my dear little girl," said Cousin Magdalen, really gratified. "But won't you try to be good to please your papa and mamma too—and most of all, Hoodie dear, to please God."

She lowered her voice a little, and Hoodie looked at her gravely.

"I don't know," she said. "I couldn't try such a long time and zey *always* says I'm naughty. No, I'll just please zou; nobody else, and if zou aren't pleased, I'll sc'eam. I can sc'eam in a minute."

Magdalen grew alarmed.

"Please don't," she said. "I'll be very pleased if you don't. And when you see how nice it is to please me, perhaps you'll go on trying to please everybody."

Hoodie shook her head.

"Zey *always* says I'm naughty," she repeated.

Just then there came a knock at the door, and Martin put her head in.

"Is Miss Hoodie awake yet, ma'am ? " she inquired. "And I do hope she's let you have some sleep ? "

"Oh, yes indeed, thank you, Martin," said Miss King, cheerfully. "We have got on *very* well, haven't we, Hoodie ? And I think you

are going to have a very good little girl in the nursery to-day."

"I hope so, I'm sure, ma'am," said Martin rather dolefully. Her tone did not sound as if her hopes were very high, and Hoodie's next remark did not make them higher.

"Yes," she said, "I is going to be good—vezy, vezy good, *too* good. But it isn't to please zou, Martin. It's all to please *her*," pointing to Miss King, "and not zou, one bit. 'Cos I like her ; she didn't scold me about the cock—she zanked me, and she's going to tell me a story."

"Hoodie," said Magdalen gravely, "I don't call it beginning to be good to tell Martin you don't care to please her one bit."

"Can't please ev'ybody," said Hoodie with a toss of her shaggy head ; "takes such a long time."

"But speaking that way to Martin doesn't please *me*," persisted Magdalen.

"Very well zen, I won't," said Hoodie with unusual amiability. "I'll give Martin a kiss if you like. Only you must have the story ready the minute moment Maudie's done her letsons —will zou ? "

"Yes," said Magdalen, "it'll be quite ready."

So Hoodie went off triumphantly in Martin's arms, things looking so promising that by the time they reached the nursery, the two were the best of friends.

And, "what a nice little young lady you might be, Miss Hoodie," said Martin, encouragingly, "if you was always good."

*　　*　　*　　*

Magdalen was ready for the children as she had promised. It was such a mild beautiful day, though only April, that she got leave to take them out-of-doors for the story-telling, and in a favourite corner, sunny yet sheltered, they settled their little camp-stools in a circle round her and prepared to listen.

"Only," said wise Maudie, "if Hec and Duke get very tired they may run about a little, mayn't they, Cousin Magdalen ? "

"If even they get a *little* tired they may run about," said her godmother. "But I don't think they will. It is a sort of nonsense story, not clever enough to tire any of you."

"What's it called, please?" said Maudie. "I'm not sure that it has a name," said Magdalen, "but if you'd rather it had one, we'll call it ' The Chintz Curtains.'"

" Please begin then, and say it in very little words for Hec and Duke to understand, won't you?"

Magdalen nodded her head, and began.

" Once," she said, " once there was a little girl."

" That's how my story began," said Hoodie, with the funny twinkle in her eyes again.

"Never mind, *don't* interrumpt," said Maudie.

" Well," Magdalen went on, "this little girl had no brothers or sisters, and though her father and mother were very kind to her she was sometimes rather lonely. And she often wished for other children to play with her. It happened one winter that she got ill—I am not sure what the illness was—measles, or something like that, it wasn't anything very, very bad, but still she was ill enough to be several days quite in bed, and several more partly in bed, and even after that a good many more before she could get up early to breakfast as usual, and do her lessons and run about in the garden and play like *well* children. She didn't much mind being ill, not as much as you would, I don't think. For, you see, except just for the few days that she felt weak and giddy and really ill, staying in bed didn't seem to make very much difference to her, indeed in some ways it was rather nicer. She had lots of story-books to read—several of her friends sent her presents of new ones—and certainly more dainty things to eat than when she was well—"

" Delly?" said Hec. " Duke and me had delly when we was ill."

" Yes," said Maudie, " last winter Hec and Duke had the independent fever, and they had to have jelly and beef-tea and things like that to make them strong again."

" Yes," said Magdalen, "that was why Lena —I forgot to tell you that that was the little girl's name—that was why they gave all those nice things to little Lena. But the worst of it was she didn't like them nearly as much as when she was well, and she often wished they would give her just common things, bread and butter and rice pudding, you know, when she was ill,

134

and keep all the very nice things for a treat when she was well and could enjoy them. She was getting well, of course ; by the time it comes to thinking about what you have to eat, children generally are getting well; but she was rather slow about it, and even when she was up and about again as usual, she didn't *feel* or look a bit like usual. She was thin and white, and whatever she did tired her. Something queer seemed to have come over all her dolls and toys ; they had all grown stupid in some tiresome way, and when she tried to sew, which she was generally rather clever at, all her fingers seemed to have turned into thumbs."

"How dedful," said Hoodie, stretching out her two chubby hands and gravely gazing at them. "All zumbs wouldn't look pretty at all. I hope mine won't never be like that if I get ill."

" My dear Hoodie," said Magdalen as soon as she could speak for laughing. " I didn't mean it that way. Not *really*. I just meant that her fingers had got clumsy, you know, with her being weak and ill. It is just a way of speaking."

" Oh !" said Hoodie, rather mystified still, " I'm glad them wasn't *really* all zumbs."

" Only, Hoodie, I *do* wish "—began Maudie, but Magdalen went on before she had time to finish her sentence.

" And as the days went on and she didn't seem to be getting back to be like herself, her mother grew rather anxious about her.

" ' We must do something about Lena,' she said to her father, ' she is not getting strong again. The doctor says she should have a change of air, but I don't see how to manage it. I cannot leave home while my mother is so ill,' —for Lena's grandmother lived with them and was rather an old and delicate lady—' and you, of course, cannot.'

" Lena's father was always very busy. It was seldom he could leave home, not very often, indeed, that he had time to see much of his little girl, even at home. But he was very fond of her, and anxious to do everything for her good. So he and her mother talked it well over together, and at last they thought of a good plan, and when it was all settled her mother told Lena about it.

"She called her to her one day when the little girl was sitting rather sadly trying to amuse herself with her dolls. But her head ached, and all her ideas seemed to have gone out of her mind. She could not think of any new plays for them, and she began to fancy their faces looked stupid.

"'I almost think I'm getting too big for dolls,' she was saying to herself, when she heard her mother's voice calling her. And she slowly got down from her chair and went up stairs to the drawing-room, where her mother was sitting writing.

"'Are you very tired, dear?' she said kindly.

"'Yes, mamma, I think so,' said Lena, as if she didn't much care whether she was tired or not.

"'You seem often tired now, my poor little girl,' said her mother. 'I think it is that you have not got properly strong since you were ill. The doctor says a change of air would be the best thing for you, but just now neither your father nor I can leave home. Would you mind very much going away for a little without us?'

"'Would it be very far, mamma?' said Lena. She liked the idea of going away, she had not often left home, and she had a great fancy for travelling, but still you can understand to go quite away without either her father or mother seemed rather lonely."

"Hadn't she a nice nurse?" asked Maudie.

"No, she hadn't a nurse quite all for herself. She was the only child, you know, and her father and mother were not very rich people, so the maid who waited on her had other work to do too. Her mother went on to explain to her that it was not to any very far-away place they thought of her going. It was to a pretty little sheltered village near the sea, where in an old-fashioned farmhouse there lived a very kind old woman who had been her mother's nurse long before Lena was born. Lena had seen her two or three times and liked her very much, and Mrs. Denny, that was the old nurse's name, had often told her about her pretty home where she lived with her son, who had never married, and for many years had taken care of this farm for the gentleman it belonged to. Mrs Denny had promised Lena that if she came to see her she should have as much new milk as she could drink, and plenty of quite fresh eggs and all sorts of nice country things. She had also promised her a particular bedroom all to herself—and Lena had forgotten none of these things, so that when her mother told her that it was to Rockrose Farm they were thinking of sending her, Lena, in her quiet way, felt quite pleased. She was not a little girl that made a fuss about things—she had lived too much alone to be anything but quiet—and just now she felt too tired to seem very eager. But her mother was pleased to see the bright look that came into her eyes, and to hear the cheerful sound in her voice when she replied, 'Oh, if it is to Mrs. Denny's, mamma, I should like to go *very* much. And I wonder if she will let me sleep in the room where the bed has such beautiful chintz curtains, all covered with pictures, mamma?'

"Her mother smiled.

"'I daresay she will, dear,' she said. 'I'm just writing to nurse now, and if you like I'll ask her to be sure to let you have the bedroom —with——'

(To be continued.)

SMALL MRS. BAT.

BY THE AUTHOR OF "AUNT EFFIE'S RHYMES," ETC.

I WONDER if you know
You're hanging upside down?
A way that no one stands
In city or in town.
Madam, it is not nice
Or right to hang like that;
Unhook yourself, I pray,
Eccentric Mrs. Bat.

Upon the gravel walk
'Twas Pussy-cat who spoke;
Spoke to small Mrs. Bat
Hung high up in the oak;
It was the usual way
She took her wonted rest.
(Of course our own own way
Appears to us the best.)

Said she, "Town ladies walk
With many foolish airs,
Such affectation suits
Those shallow minds of theirs;

Small Mrs. Bat.

Some trip, some mince along,
Some wriggle in their gait,
And some, like bold young men,
Are swaggering of late.

" My own peculiar flight,
With its soft little flutter,
Bearing me through the air
Like swiftest yacht or cutter,
And my peculiar mode
Of hanging upside down,
They are superior far
To fashions from the town."

The cat's four paws were licked
As white as driven snow:
His ten sharp claws like pearls
Stood in an even row;
He slightly curled his tail
And turned his head aside,
Said Pussy to himself,
" What pride, what silly pride!"

GUY'S RABBITS.

GUY'S RABBITS.

HAVE a lit-tle ne-phew named Guy, who lives all the year round in the fresh, qui-et, hap-py coun-try. He has a po-ny of his own, a dog, and some pet rab-bits, of which he is ve-ry fond. The last time I went to stay at Guy's home, I had not been in the house half-an-hour be-fore he took me to look at his rab-bits; pret-ty lit-tle white, long-haired crea-tures; Hi-ma-la-ya rab-bits they were called, he said. They were ve-ry tame, and had been ac-cus-tomed to run a-bout the house, but they did so much mis-chief to the fur-ni-ture, that at last Guy's mam-ma made him keep them in a hutch in the sta-ble-yard.

One morn-ing Guy ap-peared at break-fast with a ve-ry sad face. He told us that one of his rab-bits—his lit-tle pet, his fa-vour-ite a-mong them all, whom he called Beau-ty—had es-caped from the hutch. She was searched for e-ve-ry-where, in the house, in the sta-bles, in the gar-den, but the day passed, and she had not been found.

The next day I was go-ing out for a drive with Guy's mam-ma, and thought I would put on my best bon-net, which was in a bon-net-box that had been placed un-der the dress-ing ta-ble. Look-ing at the box, I was sur-prised to find the lid ly-ing on the ground by the side of it; and when I drew the box out, what do you think I saw? In-side my love-ly bon-net I saw a fluf-fy white mass, which, on look-ing clos-er, I found to be Mrs. Beau-ty her-self with three lit-tle ones a-bout a day old.

Guy was de-light-ed, but I was not quite so pleased: I thought of my best bon-net.

139

TALKS ABOUT THE MONTHS.

MAY.

By Mrs. GEORGE CUPPLES.

"May, thou month of rosy beauty,
Month when pleasure is a duty,
Month of birds and month of flowers,
Month of blossom-laden bowers,
Month that maketh Spring complete :
May ! thy very name is sweet."

AY ! charming May ! thou invitest us to be "up and through the woods a-maying," for now thou art gay in all thy beauty, with the health, wealth, joyfulness, and youth of the year. The flowers are abundant on every side, the air is full with the fresh fragrance of hawthorn-blossom and the song of the nightingale. The dazzling white of the daisies, the glittering gold of the buttercups, the fragrant lily of the valley, the sweet woodruff, the wild geraniums, all charm the eye. As we walk along the

140

green lanes or across the meadows we hear the plaintive cooing of the ring-doves in the adjoining woods, and when they cease for a moment, out from the chorus of sweet singing of various birds comes the clear bell-like note of the cuckoo high above all, followed by the shriek of the beautifully-marked jay, until it is drowned in the louder cry of the woodpecker.

> " May brings flocks of pretty lambs,
> Skipping by their fleecy dams."

In the rich green pastures there are the sounds of pleasant life, the bleating of sheep and the lowing of the cows. No wonder our Saxon ancestors called May *Tu Milchi*, for even to this day, on account of the rich growth of young grass being so nourishing, the cows give milk now three times a day. May is said by some authorities to have received the name in honour of Maia, the mother of the god Hermes, or Mercury, but others state that the name was assigned to it by Romulus, the founder of Rome, in honour of his nobles or senators, who were called *Majores* or *Maiores*. One thing at any rate we are certain of, that May was called by our ancestors and our old poets the *Merry Month*, as being practically suitable for out-door amusements. And a merry time they had of it in the old days.

May games have come down to us from old heathen celebrations, and are relics of the Roman Floralia, or games in honour of Flora, the goddess of flowers. Let us look at some of the old customs, and then see what is left remaining of them.

In the sixteenth century it was still customary, we are told, for the middle and humbler classes to go forth at an early hour of the morning in order to gather flowers and hawthorn branches, which they brought home about sunrise, with all possible signs of joy and merriment. With these spoils they would decorate every door and window in the village. They called this ceremony " the bringing home the May," and the expedition of going to the woods was called going a-maying. The fairest maid of the village was crowned with flowers, as the Queen of the May.

At an earlier age, ladies and gentlemen were accustomed to join in the Maying festivities,

even the King and Queen condescending to mingle on this occasion with their subjects. We know that in the reign of Henry VIII. the heads of the Corporation of London went out into the high grounds of Kent to gather the May, the King and his Queen coming from their palace to join them, with all the Court, on Shooter's Hill.

> " Then to the greenwood they speeden them all,
> To fetchen home May with their musical ;
> And home they bring him in a royal throne
> Crowned as king ; and his queen attone
> Was Lady Flora, on whom did attend
> A fair flock of fairies, and a fresh bend
> Of lovely nymphs—O that I were there
> To helpen the ladies their May-bush to bear ! "

But the garlanding of their brows, doors, and windows was not all. In every village and district of a town was hoisted a high pole decked with flowers, called the May-pole, round which they danced in rings pretty nearly the whole day. Then there was the custom of having a May Queen or Queen of the May. Poor Queen, hers was by no means a comfortable position. She did not join in the revelries of her subjects, all she had to do was to sit in a sort of bower or arbour covered with flowers near the May-pole and look pretty—rather a dull occupation, you will agree in thinking, for you would greatly prefer to be among the merry dancers. Beauty is a recommendation, but it has its drawbacks too.

If we wish to see a remnant of this custom we must go to France, where it still survives to some small extent ; all that is left of it in this country is to be found among the children of a few outlying places, who on May-day go about among the richer neighbours carrying large bunches of hawthorn-blossom and a finely-dressed doll, and little hand poles wreathed with flowers. They expect a few halfpence to spend on sweets, and when all nature seems so happy and so gay, who can refuse to comply with their modest request, as they sing—

> " A branch of May we have brought you,
> And at your door it stands,
> It is but a sprout,
> But it's well budded out,
> By the work of our good Lord's hands."

In London there are, and have long been, a few forms of May-day festivity quite peculiar. The day is still marked by a celebration in which the chimney-sweeps play the sole part. What is usually seen is a small band composed of two or three men in fantastic dresses, one smartly dressed as a female, glittering with spangles. There is a strange figure, too, called Jack-in-the-green, being a man concealed within a tall frame of branches and flowers decorated with a flag at the top. All of these figures stop in the course of their rounds here and there, and along with a few boys, who cut funny capers and flourish their brushes, dance to the music of a fife and drum. They too expect to get some halfpence from the on-lookers and the passers-by. It is a poor show at best, but many who have still a love for the old customs, or the memory of them rather, and recollect what a grimy, uninteresting employment the poor sweep has, can never see the little troop without a feeling of interest. Only the very crossest old gentleman would ever dream of passing on without " remembering the Mayers," by dropping a sixpence into the hands of the little fellows with the black faces and the pleasant smiles that show their gleaming white teeth.

In a few places the woods and meadows still resound with mirth and laughter in the early morning, for young people have been early astir, their object being to dip their faces in the May dew, in the fond belief that it will keep their cheeks fresh and rosy all the year; and so it will if they only rise every morning before the sun, or with him. Of course every one must return home with a piece of hawthorn blossom to show that they have been abroad " before the lark had left his dewy nest."

Though all the old customs, or nearly all, connected with May Day have disappeared, the season as it was centuries ago is just the same. The outburst into beauty excites as joyful and as admiring a feeling in the human breast as it did then. There is just as great an inclination to go abroad and enjoy the sight of the profusion of flowers, and hearken to the glad singing of the birds, and the humming of the bees, never louder than during this month, for they are preparing for the great event of

142

" hiving off" some day very soon. And above all, there is mingled with it a grateful sense of the Divine goodness, which makes the promise of seasons so stable and sure.

> " Oh, evil day ! if I were sullen,
> While the earth herself is adorning
> This sweet May morning,
> And the children are pulling
> On every side,
> In a thousand valleys far and wide,
> Fresh flowers."

There used to be other festivities connected with May, some more particularly belonging to the Church, and others to the State. These were the Rogation Days devoted to prayers, or beseeching, and the ' Gauge Days," from the Saxon word *gaugen*, to go; so called from the ancient custom of perambulating the boundaries of the parish, when all sorts of ceremonies were performed, and the merry troop rambled through all sorts of odd places. To secure the bounds being kept, if a house had been built or a canal dug across the boundary line since the last walking of the bounds, the procession had to enter the house, often by the door, and go out at a window at the opposite side. It was a merry time for the boys who followed in the track, a sort of hunt-the-hare game, for the canal had often to be swum across, or a high wall climbed, or the thickest part of the wood crossed. Refreshments were served out at different parts of the round, paid for by certain sums of money left as annuities. Of course there used to be a great deal of fun during these marches. A curious scene is recorded as having occurred in London about the beginning of the present century. As the procession of churchwardens and parish officers, followed by a lot of riff-raff, were perambulating the parish of St. George's, Hanover Square, they came to the part of a street where a nobleman's coach was standing just across the boundary line. The carriage was empty, waiting for the owner, who was in the opposite house. The coachman was requested to move on, but this he refused to do, when the leader in the procession immediately opened the carriage door, passed through the carriage by the opposite one, followed by the whole procession, "rag-tag and bob-tail."

Then there is Whit Monday, and a great day it used to be long ago, especially with the Londoners, who set out at an early hour for "Greenwich Fair." There they enjoyed themselves to their hearts' content among the shows and booths, or walking about the grand old park, or running down the green slopes between the high and the low levels of the park, when a great deal of merriment was caused by the tumbling headlong of many of the racers before they were at the bottom. Now all these merry-makings are at an end, but the holiday is kept in many places, and many a party of pleasure sets out for some well-known spot beyond sight of the busy town, where the birds can be heard singing, and the wild flowers can be plucked, and the butterflies can be chased as they take their wavering flight from flower to flower. As they journey along, the cottage gardens seem to be perfect paradises, with their lilacs, peonies, wallflowers, tulips, and anemones. And once out in the fields, how do the city children enjoy the freedom? They bound about in the flowery meadows like young fawns; they gather all they come near; they collect heaps, they sit among them and sort them, till they too frequently perish in their grasp. We see them coming wearily home again with their pinafores full, and with posies half as large as themselves, or with branches of the horse-chestnut, the mountain-ash, the laburnum, hawthorn-flower, and the wayfaring-tree.

" Wayfaring-tree ! what ancient claim
    Hast thou to that right pleasant name ?
Was it that some faint pilgrim came
        Unhopedly to thee,
And there, as 'neath thy shade he lay,
        Blest the wayfaring-tree ?
Or is it that thou lovest to show
Thy coronels of fragrant snow
        In paths by thousands beat ?
A name given in those olden days,
When, mid the wild wood's vernal sprays,
The merle and mavis pour'd their lays
        In the lone listener's ear."

" Hawthorn-blossoms bright and fair,
    Summer sun and scented air !
Through the verdure flowerets come,
    In the shade the insects hum,
Song-birds singing on the spray :
Welcome, gladly welcome, May ! "

PLAIN, OR PRETTY?

PLAIN, OR PRETTY?

BY THE EDITOR.

TRUDGING through the fields so early,
    Whither going, little maid,
With your basket so well laden,
    Walking with a step so staid?

Come now, just look round a moment,
    I so long to see your face;
The crown alone of your straw bonnet
    Should not always take its place.

Stop one minute, pluck a flower,
    Drop your umbrella, pray:
It is wearying thus to follow
    Just a back the livelong day.

I am sure your face is lovely,
    Lilies, roses there combine,
That your eyes are very handsome:
    Do just turn and look at mine!

Or perhaps you are too hideous—
    Fear that you should frighten me:
I have heard of pig-faced ladies,
    And one I should like to see.

I'd like to make you drop your basket,
    Bo at you and make you start:
You are so tiresome and provoking,
    I think you've neither face nor heart.

That stiff strait bow that ties your pigtail,
    So neat and nice and wondrous trim,—
I'd like to tweak it, make it crooked,
    I don't like people when they're prim.

Come, now, do not think me spiteful;
    If you would but turn your head,
I would ask you to forgive me
    For the nasty things I've said.

But the little village maiden
    Calmly trudges on her way,
Heedless both of prayers and scolding,
    Caring naught for what I say.

DAN AND DOBBIN.

DAN AND DOBBIN.

BY THE EDITOR.

OU little people have a fancy, I know, for hearing everything from the very beginning, so I suppose I must tell how Dobbin first came into my father's possession, and how our Dan became the friend and companion of us young people.

Well, you must know that Dobbin was bought by my father when he was but a little slim long-legged colt, and a very few days afterwards one of my cousins—a big boy who came to spend the Easter holidays with us—brought us a little darling fluffy Newfoundland puppy, who in time grew into Dan.

My father, who was not fond of dogs, desired that the young Newfoundland should be kept strictly in the stable-yard. "Mind now, children," said he, looking severely at us over his spectacles, "I won't have this animal brought into the house." Dan, who was standing close to my father when he gave this stern order, looked up at him wistfully with his little sensible-looking eyes, lolled out his red tongue and wagged his tail, as if making a promise of future good behaviour.

Notwithstanding this order I must confess that Dan did now and then find his way not only into the drawing-room, but into the bedrooms too: and in spite of all we children could do to conceal Dan's disobedience, my father more than once discovered the mark of a dirty paw on the carpets.

Dobbin, the pretty colt, soon grew into a handsome horse. My father had him broken in, and had hunted him a couple of seasons when the events happened which I am going to tell you about.

One cold evening late in the season, my father came home from hunting tired out, and, as we soon discovered, feeling very unwell. He complained of shivering and a sore throat,

and went up to bed very early. Now I must tell you that both my brothers were very fond of Dan, even more so, I think, than the rest of us, and one or the other of them often managed to smuggle the great dog—for a great dog he had become by this time—up into his bed-room at night, letting him sleep upon the bed.

On this particular evening Master Dan had unfortunately taken it into his head that he should like to have a snooze on a comfortable bed, but he mistook the room, and when my father went up stairs intending to get into his warm bed as soon as possible, you may imagine his annoyance and disgust at finding a great shaggy head upon his pillow, and a great hairy body stretched out upon the bed. To make matters worse, Dan did not seem to know his mistake, and would not understand our father's wrath and indignation, but kept on wagging his tail, and whining a gentle remonstrance to his master's abuse. It required very strong measures to make Master Dan move from his comfortable quarters, and my father took a positive hatred to the dog from that time, until by one act of sagacity the dear old beastie won his master's heart completely, turning his hatred into love.

Now you must know that the puppy Dan and the foal Dobbin had from the very first shown a great affection for each other, and as they grew up this affection increased so much that they seemed always happier when together. The groom said it made a wonderful difference, when cleaning the horse, whether Dan was near him or not.

"Why, he's a hangel when the dog's there," said Robert, "but as wicious as hanything if he isn't."

Dan would lick Dobbin's nose and fawn upon him lovingly, while the horse showed plainly that he liked these caresses and returned them, in his own rough fashion.

One day, towards the close of the hunting season, my father was brought home, to our great alarm, in the carriage of one of our neighbours. He had had a spill, he said, laughing, and was a little shaken, but not much hurt. It seemed that the accident had happened near the house of some kind friends of ours, who had had out the carriage to send him home. My father evidently was not seriously hurt, and he seemed less anxious about himself than about his horse. He told us that the last he saw of Dobbin was when he first recovered from the stunning effect of his tumble. Then the horse had already jumped a hedge and was in the next field, where he was galloping along after the hunt, shaking his head, and seeming to enjoy the sport all the more for finding himself riderless.

This was pretty early in the day, but hour after hour passed and no one brought back Dobbin. Then it was discovered that Dan was missing too. We all said at once that Dan·had gone off in search of his lost friend,

but nobody was prepared for what really happened.

It was late in the afternoon when the two friends made their appearance together in a curious fashion : Dobbin trotted quietly up to the lodge gate, with Dan leading him, and holding the reins in his mouth. Having passed through the gate, Dan did not let go of his prisoner, but brought him straight up to our front door, and there sat down with an air of triumph, still holding the reins in his mouth, as you see in the picture. I must add that Dobbin looked rather ashamed of himself the while.

Where Dan had found the horse, how far he had gone before he met with him, or how long he had been leading him, a willing prisoner, along the road—we never knew. But Dan's exploit had at least one excellent result. From that day my father became as fond of the poor old dog as he had before disliked him.

BA, BA, BLACK SHEEP!

Ba, ba, black sheep, have you any wool? Yes, master, that I have, three bags full; One for the mas - ter, one for the dame, And one for the lit-tle boy who cries in the lane.

148

FOR
~~R~~
~~STER~~ ME

FOR
THE LITTLE
BOY

BA, BA, BLACK SHEEP!

BLACK ROLF OF ROOKSTONE.

By the Right Hon. E. H. KNATCHBULL-HUGESSEN, M.P., *Author of "Uncle Joe's Stories," &c.*

CHAPTER V.

FROM the vault in which he stood, a secret passage led to the sea-shore —that passage by which, in his earlier days of wickedness, he had held communication with those pirate voyagers who had aided him to amass his wealth. For years past the passage had been disused, and as its outlet to the sea was carefully concealed, few persons knew of its existence and none could have found it from the sea-side. At the end of the second vault were three stone steps, at the bottom of which was a low door. Here Rolf stooped once more and drew from his girdle a small case, containing several wing-feathers of a rook. Carefully passing his hand over the surface of the door, and holding his lamp close, he perceived a small hole, into which he softly and cautiously thrust one of the feathers which he had taken from his case. By this means a spring was touched which held the door—one push—and it swung heavily open. By three more steps the Baron descended, pushing the door to behind him, and he now found himself in a room so low that he could hardly stand upright. It was rather a small room of irregular shape, and its walls on either side were formed entirely of the rough rock out of which it had been cut, and upon which the castle was built. At its further extremity was another low door which led directly into the passage to the sea, and upon the floor of the room were more bags of coin, and sundry precious jewels fit for titled and court-bred dames, but lying there rusty and unused. It was Rolf's intention to secrete the miniature and the parchment in some crevice of the rock within that room, where he felt certain they would remain undiscovered until the end of the world. These once destroyed, he feared no legal proof that his nephew—if such really was his opponent—could bring in support of his claim, and old as he was, he was determined to do battle to the last for the possessions which he had gained by the toil, the arts, the wickedness of a life.

Full of these ideas, he advanced to the middle of the room and stood for an instant peering round to discover the best place for concealment of the objects he bore. At that moment the cawing in his ears seemed to get more violent and furious than ever. It even seemed to shape itself into words : dire, fierce, threatening words, and presently there seemed to ring through his very brain this fearful sentence—

" Ne'er shalt thou quit this fatal room,
Black Rolf ! the rook decrees thy doom ! "

So vividly, so clearly, so loudly did the notes ring through his head, that in spite of all his fortitude, the Baron started violently. It was indeed enough to carry terror to the stoutest heart. Save for the light of his own lamp, all was dark as night around him, and such words, spoken in a tone so strangely un-

natural, between the voice of a man and the caw of a bird, chilled his blood and sent to his heart a sensation as near to fear as he had ever experienced. The doom foretold was an awsome doom indeed, and the prophecy, like some others, aided to fulfil itself. For in the violent start which the Baron gave, he struck his foot against a loose fragment of rock which lay upon the floor, involuntarily stretched forth his hand to recover himself, failed to do so, and in another instant tumbled forward and fell upon the ground, fell too, terrible to tell, upon his lamp, which was extinguished and crushed beneath his body. A thrill of despair ran through the heart of the unhappy man as, in an instant, he realised his position. He raised himself to his knees and clasped one hand over his forehead, whilst the other still grasped the miniature and parchment which he thrust into his breast as he staggered to his feet.

Stay ! there was yet hope : the door by which he had entered was but half closed ; could he regain it the appliance for lighting the lamp would not be hard to find, and but little light would be needful to retrace his steps, if he could once regain the larger, upper vaults in which his treasure lay. At that moment he would have given half that treasure for one inch of lighted candle ! Slowly he rose to his feet and tremblingly felt his way back, his knees knocking together, and his teeth chattering with the real, the dreadful fear which was now upon him. Is he going straight to the door ? He had never before known how difficult it was to walk straight in entire darkness. Yet it *must* be done—he *must* find his way : those nerves, once of iron, *must* be firmly set once more, and the egress from his self-made prison *must* be secured.

But, low and deep, constant, hoarse, awful in its depth and intensity, ever there rang in his ears and through his brain that terrible cawing, paralysing his brain, and adding in a wonderful degree to the terrors of the darkness, and tho confusion of his ideas. And now it seemed to speak to the luckless victim of its wrath, and again it shaped itself into words, and it seemed like the tolling of the passing-bell, and to clang out in harsh and discordant sounds the dreadful words—" Never—never—hence thou passest never." The sound was maddening, but with a mighty effort the Baron girded himself to the task before him, and advancing to the wall, stifled every feeling of doubt or fear whilst he felt steadily along it until he found the steps. An involuntary cry of joy escaped from his lips as he raised himself upon them, and eagerly put forward his hand to find the handle of the door. At that moment the cawing seemed to be redoubled, and in his confusion and hurry he miscalculated the distance, his hand came against the door, whilst he thought he was yet several inches from it, and that so sharply that the door closed with a spring and a snap, and Black Rolf of Rookstone had shut himself into his living tomb with his own hand. With one loud frantic yell of despair he fell down upon the stone steps and lay there as on dead. Presently he rose again to his feet and dashed himself against the door. It was in vain : the massive work could have resisted the strength of a hundred men, and he sank again, with hands torn and bleeding, upon the steps, and gave vent to such a groan as only the agony of despair could have wrung from his soul.

Then occurred a strange and wondrous thing. The cawing which had tormented him incessantly for so long a time ceased completely and at once. He heard again as clearly and well as ever. Alas! what was there to hear ? No human voice might ever sound upon his ears again—no music of birds, no noise of martial array, no, nor even the dull, heavy sound of the waves beating against the rocks as he knew they must be doing not fifty yards from where he lay. No such sounds could reach him, for the thickness of his rocky prison shut them all out, and when he listened with an intensity of nervousness of which he would have thought himself incapable a few minutes before, he could hear nothing but the slow, steady, continuous dripping of water from the roof at one corner of the dungeon. Why had the cawing ceased? Horrible thought! it was the old prophecy of which Elfrida had told him—"And when the caw shall cease, the Doom's complete."

His doom then was at hand. What doom ? He had fought in many a desperate fight, hand to hand with brave foes, and risked

his life full oft in many a daring deed—it had sometimes been his thought that thus it behoved a soldier to die,' and had fancied that he would meet his fate, when it came, as bravely as any of the puling monks over there at the Monastery. But to die like a trapped wolf left to starve in a pit, or worse, for the wolf would have light from above, but to him all was darkness—to die *thus* was a fate too awful to realise ; in his own castle, too, almost within hail of his own people— almost! curses on it, that "almost" would kill him—why not *quite?* Oh! the curses of a dying man upon those who had made such an infernal dungeon and those who had not destroyed it as unfit to be a part of a noble's castle—stay! whom was he cursing? Himself!—yes! had he lived an honest life, he had wanted no secret vaults and passages, and had done away with them long since. Oh, the horrible folly of which he had been guilty? What was all his treasure to him *now?* of what good was his castle — his lands — his long-coveted and hardly-earned title ?

Such thoughts as these coursed through his brain, one after another, and then came an almost worse state of mind. Bright and clear and vivid arose the memory of many a dark and evil deed, done during his wicked life, and never yet repented of until repentance was too late, atonement impossible. The smaller sins of his life, such as he had never recognised as sins, came crowding together upon him, bearing to his awakened mind a different and darker appearance than they had ever done before, while the deeper crimes of which he had cast away the remembrance whenever it arose, came back now with terrible, probing memories, and flung down his guilty soul into the lowest depths of despair.

Once more he raised himself and staggered towards one side of his prison : again he stopped and listened, but there was nought to hear : he peered into the darkness with eyeballs starting from his head : there was nothing to see ! Shut out alike from light—from fresh air— from hope itself—the full consciousness of his position came with crushing force upon the unhappy baron, and with one more yell of mingled agony, fury, and despair, he fell prone among the treasures which seemed to mock him as he touched them, and felt how useless they were to aid him in his hour of need.

Elfrida, Elfrida, where art thou now? thy nursling for whom thou hast sinned and suffered, whom thou lovest as if he were thine own child—thy nursling, whose life thou hast watched over so long, needs thee sorely now. Wilt thou not come to his aid? Can none help him? Ah me! what is the strength of man, of what avail his treasure, his skill, his wrath? In his own castle—near his own people—the mighty Baron raves out his soul in cries useless, impotent, unheard.

When Sir Hugh de Montenoy arose next morning, he marvelled what had become of his host, and was at first disposed to resent his absence from the morning meal. But, remembering the cares and anxieties of the Baron's present position, and being himself of a good-natured and easy disposition, he betook himself to his breakfast without troubling himself greatly about the matter, and doubted not that Black Rolf would show himself at his own time.

An hour or so had rolled away, and the Knight of Barnascon might have thought more of the strange proceedings of the Baron, had not his attention been called to other and more pressing considerations. The sentinels upon the walls announced the approach of a large body of men, advancing with intentions evidently hostile to those who held the castle. As soon as this seemed to have been ascertained, Sir Hugh ordered every preparation for defence to be immediately made. The drawbridge was drawn up, the great gates of the court-yard closed, every weak point strengthened, and cross-bow men posted at every loop-hole whence they might annoy the enemy. About a quarter of a mile from the Castle, the advancing force halted, and presently there rode out a horse-man bearing a spear with a white handkerchief tied thereupon, in token that he demanded a parley. The old Knight of Montenoy forthwith proceeded to the postern gate and sallied forth with two retainers to meet the herald. He halted at a short distance, and lowering his

spear, saluted the Lord of Barnascon as became his dignity. Sir Hugh returned the salutation, and proceeded to demand the errand of the other and the meaning of the appearance of the body of men from whom he had come.

"These," quoth the herald, "be the men-at-arms of Rolf of Rookstone, the rightful owner of this castle and domain, and the lawful claimant to the ancient Barony of Fitzurse. By fraud and violence he hath been despoiled of his due inheritance, and by the strength of his right arm and the edge of his good sword he cometh to win back his own. Wherefore I summon this castle on his behalf. I summon thee, noble Sir, to surrender the castle to its rightful owner, and to quit it, thou and thine, peacefully and of good will."

Sir Hugh de Montenoy drew himself up proudly as these words were spoken, and then made reply forthwith. "Go back to those who sent thee," he said sternly, "and tell them that De Montenoy yields not at the first blast of the trumpet nor to the summons of those he knows not. All the world knows that Black Rolf of Rookstone — I would say the noble Baron Fitzurse — is the Lord of Rookstone Towers and the fair lands around. I know no other lord save mine old friend and neighbour, and until he bids me surrender, I may not quit my trust."

The herald bowed low as he heard these words, and then raising his voice, aloud exclaimed, "Take notice all whom it may concern, that I summon this castle, and demand its surrender to its rightful owner, my worshipful master, Egbert Rolf of Rookstone, by his right and due Baron Fitzurse! Resist him at your peril!"

With these words he turned his steed and forthwith galloped back to his master's host. There was a pause for some minutes after the herald had returned to his friends and the Lord of Barnascon had re-entered the castle. He inquired at once whether the Baron Fitzurse had yet made his appearance, and marvelled much at receiving a reply in the negative.

There was, however, no time for further inquiry or search : the enemy were advancing, and seemed to have at least four or five hundred men, whilst scarce one hundred and twenty, all told, were within the castle walls. Yet such was the natural strength of the fortress, that Sir Hugh felt certain of being able to hold his own, so long as the supply of food lasted and no treachery was at work. His own flag swung proudly upon the towers, side-by-side with that of Fitzurse, and never yet had that flag swung over men unwilling or fearful to defend it. On came the foe, and presently a shower of stones and arrows, from slings and bows in skilled hands, rained upon the walls so fast and thick that scarce a man could show himself with safety. Under cover of this shower the men advanced to whom had been confided the task of scaling the walls, and whilst the archers and slingers took advantage of every tree and bush, and poured forth their volleys with unceasing energy, these advanced with ladders, quickly and stealthily, and drew gradually nearer and nearer the castle. Every now and then came an arrow from the latter, aimed with good aim at the scaling party, several of whom were wounded in their advance, but the main body pressed on, and presently arose a loud shout as they dashed themselves against the wall which surrounded the court-yard, and under cover of which they were protected from shots aimed from the main building.

"A Rolf! a Rolf!" they shouted, whilst some cried "An Egbert, an Egbert," and from the castle came back, in deep stern tones, "A Fitzurse, a Fitzurse," and still more loudly and cheerily (for the Barnascon men much outnumbered their allies), "Montenoy, Montenoy!"

Against the gates of the courtyard a resolute attack was made, headed by a tall figure in black armour, who was evidently in authority, and who fought with a courage and vigour which betokened him a brave warrior. He animated his followers by loud shouts, and with a ponderous battle-axe struck such blows against the gates as before long told with great effect, and at last with a crash they gave way, and the assailants of the castle rushed forward with renewed ardour. But they were now more exposed than before to the aim of the defenders of the fortress, and several more were struck down as they pressed on, whilst at

154

the same time a deep voice from the walls shouted loudly,

"Stand firm, men, and yield not an inch on your lives. Strike for Montenoy!"

The issue of the day might indeed have been doubtful, so great was the courage and determination of either side, when an incident occurred which had a visible effect upon the combatants. Suddenly, and without any previous warning, the air became black with rooks, whose loud cawing filled the air and, even at that moment of excitement, attracted general attention. They wheeled in circles over the heads of the attacking force, apparently encouraging them to fresh exertions, and anon flew with evidently hostile screams right into the faces of the garrison.

Both sides paused as if by mutual consent, and presently the knight in black armour stepped boldly forward and raised his voice, the accents of which were scarcely heard, when the rooks ceased cawing as if by magic, and a dead silence ensued, which enabled every word to be distinctly heard.

"A parley!" he cried. "I crave a parley, and speech with him who commands the garrison." Forth stood the old Knight of Barnascon at once.

"Here I stand," answered he, "Sir Hugh de Montenoy, who never yet turned his back upon friend or foe. I hold this castle for mine ancient neighbour, and yield it not till summoned by one of better right than he."

The Knight bowed with stately courtesy. "Sir Hugh," said he, "none can doubt the skill and valour of which you have given fresh proof to-day. But where is mine uncle, Black Rolf? He was not wont to shun the fray. Let him stand forth and deny me for his nephew if he dare?" As he spoke, the young man unclosed his visor, and displayed features which bore so startling a resemblance to those of the Baron Fitzurse that the Knight of Barnascon stepped back in amazement.

"Sir Knight," he exclaimed after the pause of a few seconds—"thy face doth wonderfully confirm thy tale—but for thine uncle, if uncle he be, I have not seen him since yesterday, and know not why he is not here to speak for himself. But my word is plighted to hold the castle for him, and of a surety he will not be long away."

At this speech the leader of the attacking party seemed somewhat surprised. "By my faith!" he cried. "This is passing strange. We know that mine uncle returned hither yesterday and he could scarce have gone hence, save by sea, without some of our people having seen him, since they have been out on all sides. But was there ever such a thing heard of as a neighbour keeping a castle for one who cares not to hold it for himself? If my uncle be within, let him come and face the matter out. But if, as I begin to think, he has fled secretly by sea, knowing my claim to be just, why should De Montenoy fight with one against whom he has no quarrel? Why should innocent men be killing each other for a cause which does not exist, and for a man who has already confessed himself wrong by his flight?"

"Boy!" returned the grim old warrior whom he addressed, "thou reasonest well, but yet I cannot yield the castle till I know more of the cause of my neighbour's absence. My word has been given to defend it, and so I will."

"But," resumed the other, "does such a pledge last for ever? Hear me for a moment. I will draw off my men for four-and-twenty hours, and during that time, no man shalt lift a hand or shoot a bolt against the castle. If he who calls himself Baron Fitzurse shall appear before that time, thou shalt hear my statement and his answer, and judge whether thou wilt longer defend him : if he appear not, thou shalt withdraw to thine own place, and leave me to hold the towers of my ancestors until a better claimant show himself." Sir Hugh de Montenoy listened attentively to this proposal. He could not imagine what had become of the Baron, whose room was empty, and his bed evidently had not been slept in during the previous night, and who really seemed to have vanished altogether. It seemed an absurd thing to fight for a man who did not seem inclined to fight for himself, and moreover it certainly appeared unreasonable to expose his own followers to the assaults of an enemy against whom neither they nor their master had any cause of complaint. Truly he had undertaken to defend Rookstone Towers if it

should be attacked during the absence of the Baron, but the Baron had certainly returned, and in any case such a pledge could not be interpreted to bind one for ever, nor to prevent the acceptance of any proposal so reasonable as that to which he had just listened, by which the new claimant of the castle offered to submit in a manner to his judgment upon the merits of his case.

Still, so leal and loyal was the old Knight, that he would not run the risk of being accused of treating his pledge lightly. So after a pause of several seconds, he thus replied to the proposal of the knight in black armour.

"Sir Knight, be thou Black Rolf's kinsman or not, thou speakest fairly, nor do I care to adventure more than my word binds me to do in a quarrel which may be doubtful. But twenty-four hours is too short a space. My old neighbour may have been suddenly called away, or even may have been captured by some enemy. But double the time thou namest, and I agree to thine offer. If he be not here when forty-eight hours have passed, I will quit the castle with my men, and leave thee to hold it an thou list, for no man can be bound to fight in another's quarrel for ever, nor did I ever engage to do so."

Thus spoke Sir Hugh de Montenoy, and the person whom he addressed promptly accepted his proposition.

"For," said he, "thou and I may hereafter be friends, and my cause is too good to be injured by the few hours' delay which, for thy friend's sake, thou seekest."

Accordingly the retreat was at once sounded, and the attacking force withdrew to a distance from the castle, where they set about preparing their encampment. The garrison were by no means sorry for this arrangement, and, having posted his sentinels to guard against any possible surprise (though he apprehended no real attempt) the Knight of Barnascon proceeded to make further search for his host. All, however, was in vain, and he had to take his solitary meal, enlivened by the presence of such of his retainers as he chose to summon, and the night once more closed in upon Rookstone Towers. The next day passed away in a listless, easy manner, the garrison quietly keeping their places, and the force which had lately attacked them making no attempt to approach the castle. Another night came and went, and the appointed forty-eight hours passed without any news of the Baron Fitzurse. Then the Knight of Barnascon ordered the two flags to be lowered from the tower in token that he surrendered the castle, and rode out to meet him who was about to become the Rolf of Rookstone. The latter shook him warmly by the hand, and they congratulated each other upon the peaceful termination of that which might have ended in a far more disastrous manner. Egbert Rolf, for so he dubbed himself, declared that, since he was now going to take possession of his ancestral towers, his neighbour and friend, he hoped, that would be, must not leave them without tasting his hospitality.

Provision there was in larder and in the camp of his people, and the castle wine should be broached, in order that his accession to the home of his forefathers should at once be celebrated, and the soldiers who had so lately met face to face in battle should now sit side by side in joyful feastings and council. This proposal suited with the temper of the Knight and the humour of the times, and so it fell out that those who had recently been foes, now became to each other good fellows and boon companions, and the late strife was succeeded by words of revelry and mirth which lasted throughout the evening. Whilst the feast was yet in progress, and the wine-cup and ale-flagon quickly passing round, a loud knocking at the doors arrested the attention of the revellers, and presently a new-comer was ushered into the presence of Sir Hugh de Montenoy and his host, who sat side at the head of the table. It was a monk from the neighbouring monastery, who forthwith explained his errand. Two nights before, he said, a brother who had been accustomed to visit the castle to afford spiritual aid to such of its inmates as were desirous to avail themselves of his services, had returned, bearing with him, more dead than alive, an ancient domestic of the House of Rolf. In consequence of the hostility which Black Rolf of Rookstone entertained towards the priests, the visits of this brother had always

156

been made stealthily, and without the Baron's knowledge. Latterly his ministrations had been specially sought by the domestic in question, whose name was Elfrida, and in order that he might come and go safely, she had revealed to him a secret way, unknown to the Baron himself, which led from the tapestry chamber to the postern gate of the Castle. By this way he had often passed, and on the occasion of his last visit, had been able thereby to preserve old Elfrida and to convey her to the monastery upon the mule which had brought him to the castle. Once safe within the sacred walls, the old woman had rallied sufficiently to open her whole soul in that confession of past misdeeds which she trusted would procure her the consolations of the Church and forgiveness for an ill-spent life.

She had told of much evil done by Black Rolf, to which she had been privy, and which weighed deeply upon her guilty soul. But, freed at last from the trammels in which she had been doubly bound both by her feudal feeling towards her lord and her affection for her nursling — freed because she felt her end was nigh, and that in the eternity before her no such feeling could avail her aught if she left behind her unrevealed wickedness, she had confessed other matters which had greatly moved the holy men at the Monastery.

She had fully confirmed the testimony in the parchment read by the Abbot to Baron Fitzurse, and had added sundry particulars which left no doubt on the minds of those who heard her that every word of the story was true, and that he who called himself Egbert Rolf had a full right to that name, and was the lawful nephew of Black Rolf of Rookstone.

Only on the morning of that day old Elfrida had breathed her last. Her confession had been, at her own request, duly written down and attested by witnesses. Then came the question, what should be done with it? After a short consultation, it occurred to the good monks that, as rumours had reached them that an attack was even then being made upon Rookstone Towers by him whom they were now assured was the rightful owner, the sooner that their newly-acquired knowledge was made known to the combatants, the better chance would there be of putting an end to strife and bloodshed.

Therefore the monk had been sent off to Rookstone, and had arrived to find the strife indeed over, but his tidings nevertheless welcome to those to whom he brought them. They did not stop the feasting and merriment, which continued all that night and so far into the next morning that it was thought well that the visitors should stay one more day before leaving the Castle, in order to recruit their energies and perhaps cement their new alliance by a final carouse. But the course of events was ordered in such a manner as to prevent the latter occurrence.

It had been observed that the rooks had not again departed from the grounds of the castle. As soon as the terms of surrender had been settled, they had apparently ceased to care about the matter, and had occupied themselves, with loud and satisfied cawings, in taking possession of their former habitations. About mid-day, however, of the following day, there was visible uneasiness among them : they flew round and round, cawing hoarsely, and evidently fearful of some impending misfortune. At the same time the sky grew unnaturally dark, the wind rose and moaned from the sea in a melancholy and portentous manner, the waves roared as if excited by some unseen cause, and everything seemed to presage a coming storm. And as the evening closed in, the storm came— a storm never forgotten upon that coast. The wind blew with a vehemence which was perfectly horrific, tearing up large trees by the roots as if they were small sticks, whirling haystacks, cottages, and even animals along with it in its fury, and suffering nothing to stand which was not well and firmly built. The thunder rolled terribly, vivid flashes of lightning illuminated the night, torrents of rain succeeded the wind, and the sea roared against the rocks as the din of constant and heavy artillery. Moreover the earth heaved as if with an earthquake, walls fell, houses rocked, women fled shrieking into safe corners, and men crossed themselves with fear and doubt lest the end of the world had come upon them all unprepared. The inmates of the castle had no thought of carousing that night. The stoutest heart quailed, and the proudest

spirit owned that there was a power in creation beyond that of mortal man.

The omnipotence of Heaven was recognised and the voice of God heard in the crash of the elements. The night passed away at last, and morning dawned, so brightly and peacefully, that it was difficult to believe that so short a time had gone by since the storm had raged so furiously. Sir Hugh de Montenoy and the young Egbert walked forth together to look at the desolation which had been wrought. It was great indeed. The rookery had been much damaged, and there was a plaintive sadness in the cawing of the birds as they busily employed themselves in repairing the mischief which had fallen upon their homes. The two men strolled onward towards the sea, and found that here, too, the ruin had been great. The rocks upon which the castle stood had been rent asunder in places, and huge boulders of stone, displaced from their former position, lay upon the shore.

As they approached, their attention was attracted to a group of children playing in the rocks, and even as they drew near, they perceived some of the children calling the others and pointing at some object in the rocks.

"It moves ! it moves ! " they cried. " It is a ghost coming after us ! " and fled shrieking away. Sir Hugh called the biggest boy back, and walked with his companion to see what it was that had scared the party. He looked at first in vain, until the boy pointed to a hole in the rock, recently rent by the convulsions of nature in the storm. He knelt down and peered in, at first he could see nothing but something white which seemed to wave to and fro, presently he started back : that something was waved by a human hand—what could it be ? what could it mean ?

Forthwith they sent for workmen and tools, the hole was hewn open wider, and a sight presented itself which filled them all with horror. The hole opened into a vaulted chamber, low and long, the door from which to the sea could now be discovered, but the passage therefrom to the castle had been completely blocked by the fallen masses of rock. Upon that floor lay scattered gold and jewels and precious stones—but there lay something more.

Flat upon his back, with eyes wide open and

staring hideously, with his under lip bitten through by his own teeth in his agony, and his knees gathered up, stiff, stark, and stone dead lay Black Rolf, the Baron Fitzurse. His left arm was beneath his body, his right, outstretched to its full length, still held in its death-grasp the miniature and parchment, and it was the fluttering of the latter in the current of air through the cleft rocks that had attracted the attention of the children and had appeared as if waved by the dead man. Yes : dead—and dead in the very midst of those treasures for the sake of which he had wrought so much evil against his fellow-men and against his own soul. Dead—and gone where those treasures could not be taken with him, and where the title for which he had laboured so long and so hard would be his no more. *That* must fall to the nephew whom he had striven to keep from his inheritance, and all the labours of his long life had but served to amass riches for the son of the brother who had been so cruelly wronged. Ay, well, he was dead—and with that word ends all that this world can tell of any of us. They lifted him up—gently and reverently—though the bearers shuddered to look upon his ghastly and distorted face—and as they bore him away until he should be laid in the resting-place of his race, large flocks of rooks came eddying round their heads, and cawed in solemn tones the requiem of the Baron Fitzurse.

The rooks are cawing peacefully enough to-day around the ruins of the old castle, whilome known as Rookstone Towers. I wandered out into the old churchyard hard by, and sat me down on the low wall, and bethought me of the old legend. Close to me was a new grave, wherein had lately been laid a little maiden, but fourteen years of age, to whom the world could hardly have begun to be wearisome. I wondered if she, too, knew of the legend, and had ever heard of the Bad Baron and his wicked deeds in the ancient time. They say his spirit still haunts the place. But I wot the little maiden will sleep none the less soundly in her quiet nook in the old churchyard, and nought of evil will come nigh the resting-place of the young and pure. Then I wondered if there were many who wept for her and mourned that she should have been taken so early, and then again I thought how they might be consoled by comparing her short fourteen years with the long life of the old Baron, how the length of time that each passed on earth was as nothing in the unreckoned ages of eternity; and the shortness of time here in the one case was also the shortness of trial and the safeguard of innocence to the soul, while the length of years in the other had been but more and more opportunity for evil, so that it had been better, far better, for the aged sinner to have died in his childhood. And so I went on my way still deeply pondering on these matters, and feeling more than ever that the ways of Heaven are marvellous, and beyond the searching out of man.

(*Concluded.*)

PICTURE PAGE WANTING WORDS. (FOR PRIZE STORY.)

PUZZLES.

CHARADES.

1.

My first is the season when kind nature yields
The bright tinted fruits of her orchards and
  fields,
And enriches mankind with her store.
My second who is there who does not revere,
And in memory cherish that one spot so dear,
Tho' perchance he may ne'er see it more?
And think, while a sadness steals over his soul,
Of the days when he shared in the joys of my
  whole.

2.

My first is a sportive and timorous thing,
Which bounds through the coverts with joy in
  its spring,
Darting off at the fall of a leaf.
My second's oft heard in the day's busy round,
Striking full on the ear with its echoing sound,
And proclaiming now joy and now grief.
My whole may be seen in the meadows and
  glades,
Where it brightens the earth with its hue ere
  it fades.

3.

In many a rural landscape green,
O'er the tree tops rising my first is seen ;
The villagers dwell neath its guardian shade,
Near the sacred spot where their sires are laid.
My second oft causes the heart to leap
When seen to rush by in its headlong sweep,
And the breast upheaves with the thoughts
  that roll
O'er my mind like the pell-mell of my whole.

4.

Whilst passing a shop in the city one day
I looked through my second and there did see
An elderly lady who stood by my first,
And purchased my whole, pray what may it be?

ENIGMAS.

1.

To you I name a useful thing
Of varied shape and size,
Just find me out and you will count
One more towards a prize.

'Tis true that I possess no legs,
And yet on feet I'm seen,
'Tis true that I possess no arms,
And yet on hands I've been.

I sometimes have a head of brass
And sometimes one of gold,
But oftener my form is cast
Within a common mould.

To keep me clean and beautiful,
Is what some persons love,
And oftentimes I may be found
Within a lady's glove.

I'm part of every yard,
I'm seen fixed in a door,
And on my form you often tread
When walking on the floor.

2.

Wealth and power immense I give,
No feeling have and yet I live,
Before mankind the earth had trod
I held possession of the sod.
Now in the tomb of ages sought,
Again to earth's fair surface brought,
A proof of the eternal's plan
I have so much to do with man,
Enliven all his chequered lot,
I cheer the palace and the cot,
And raise for mortals every hour
A spirit of tremendous power,
Though short my life, yet I supply
A thousand blessings ere I die.

Answers to Puzzles on Page 128.

Answers to Puzzles on Page 128.

CHARADES.

1. Cam-bridge   4. Stratagem.
2. Mag-net.   5. Lo-co-motive.
3. Bungalow.   6. Nightingale.

DECAPITATION.

Trash, rash, ash.

ENIGMA.

The letter A.

HOODIE.

By Mrs. MOLESWORTH, *Author of* "*Hermy,*" "*The Cuckoo Clock,*" &c.

CHAPTER VI.—"THE CHINTZ CURTAINS."

"O lovely land of fairies,
You are so bright and fair."

THE chintz curtains."

Cousin Magdalen stopped for a minute.

"Are you getting tired, dears, any of you?" she said.

All the four heads were shaken at once.

"Oh dear no," said Maudie.

"In course not," said Hoodie.

And " It's a vezy pretty story," said Hec; while Duke faintly echoed, "Vezy pretty."

So Magdalen, thus encouraged, went on.

"You begin to understand now why I said you might call the story 'the chintz curtains,'" she said. "We're now got like to the real beginning. At least I needn't explain and more about Lena—you must just fancy her

M

arriving one afternoon at Rockrose Farm. It was a nice bright afternoon, though the winter was scarcely over, and little Lena already began to feel stronger and better when she ran out into the garden at one side of the house for a breath of fresh air after the long drive from the railway. Her father had brought her to the station, and there Mrs. Denny had met her, so that he might go straight back by the next train without losing any time.

" ' Oh how nice it is,' she said to Mrs. Denny, as she stood in the middle of the little grass-plot beside the old sun-dial, and felt the sweet fresh air blowing softly over her face. ' How pretty the garden must be in summer.'

" ' Yes, my dear,' said Mrs. Denny. ' The flowers are very sweet. It seems to me there never were such sweet ones. But do you hear that sort of soft roar, Miss Lena? Do you know what that is?'

" Lena stood quite still to listen, and a pleased look came over her face.

" ' Yes,' she said, ' I believe it is the sea. It is like far-away organs, isn't it?'

" ' And sometimes in stormy weather it is like great cannons booming,' said Mrs. Denny.

" But just then it was difficult to think of storms or cannons, or anything so unpeaceful. Nothing could seem more perfectly calm and at rest than that dear old garden the first time Lena ever saw it. I don't think anything—any place perhaps I should say—can be more delicious than a little nest of a place like Rockrose, sheltered from the high winds by beautiful old trees, and yet open enough for the sea breezes to creep and flutter about it, and sometimes even to give what Lena called ' a salty taste,' to the air, if you stood with your mouth open and got a good drink of it. But I mustn't go on talking so much about the outside of the house, or I never shall get to the inside, shall I?

" Well, after Lena had admired the garden and promised herself many nice runs in it, Mrs. Denny took her into the house again. They passed through the kitchen, which had a little parlour out of it, where already tea was set out—it was such a delicious old kitchen, the paved floor as white and clean as constant scrubbing could make it, and the old cupboards

and settles of dark wood shining like mirrors —they passed through the kitchen and across a little stone hall with whitewashed walls, out of which opened the best parlour, only used on very grand occasions, and up two flights of stone steps ending in a wide short passage running right across the house. At one end of this passage Mrs. Denny opened a door, which led into a sort of little anteroom, and here another, rather low door being opened, Lena followed Mrs. Denny into the bedroom which was to be hers. It was not a very little room —there were two windows, one at each side— one of them looked out on to the garden, the other had a lovely view far away over the downs, to where one knew the sea *was*, though one could not see it. But fond as Lena was of pretty views, she did not run to the window to look out. She stood still for a moment and then ran forward eagerly to the end of the room, where the bed was placed, crying out with delight,

" ' Oh that's the bed—that's the very bed you told me about, dear Mrs. Denny—the bed I did so want to sleep in. Thank you so much for remembering about it. Oh how *beautiful* it is—I shouldn't mind being ill if I was in that bed.'

" It really was a rather wonderful bed. It was a regular four-poster, if you know what that is—a bed with wooden posts at each corner, and curtains running all round, so that once you were inside it, you could if you liked draw them so close that it was like being in a tent."

" I know," said Maudie, " I've seen beds like that. But I don't think Hoodie and the boys have—let me see ; oh yes, I can tell them what it's like. It's like the bed in our *best* doll-house—the one with pink curtains trimmed with white. You know?"

" Yes," said Hoodie, " the one where Miss Victoria has been so ill in, since she's got too ugly to sit in the drawing-room. I know."

" But it's such a weeny bed," said Hec, " was zour little girl no bigger than zat little dolly. Cousin Magdalen?"

" *Of course*," said Maudie, hastily. " How stupid you are, Hec."

" Maudie," said her godmother, and Maudie

got very red. "Maudie meant it was the same *shape* as that, but much bigger, Hec dear. Just the same as the piano in the study is the same shape as the one in the doll-house, only much bigger."

"Oh zes," said Hec.

"A great deal bigger than any of the beds people have now," continued Magdalen. "It was really big enough to have held six little Lenas instead of one. But it was the curtains that made it so particularly wonderful. They were very old, but the colours were still quite bright, they had been washed so carefully. And the pattern was something I really could not describe if I tried — it was the most delicious muddle of flowers, and trailing leaves and birds, and here and there a sort of little basket-work pattern that looked like a summer-house or the entrance to a grotto.

"Lena stood feasting her eyes upon these marvellous curtains.

"'I never did see anything so nice,' she said. 'Can I see the pictures when I'm *in* the bed,' Mrs. Denny?'

"'Oh yes, my dear, they're double—the same inside as out,' said Mrs. Denny, turning them as she spoke.

"'How nice!' said Lena; 'well, if I'm late for breakfast, Mrs. Denny, you'll know that it'll be with looking at the curtains.'

"'I'm not afraid but that you'll sleep well in this bed, Miss Lena,' said the old nurse. 'There's something very lucky about it. Many a one has told me they never had such sweet sleep or such pretty dreams as in our old bed. It's maybe that the room is a very pleasant one, never either too hot or too cold, and there's a beautiful scent of lavender, Miss Lena, all through the bed, as you'll find.'

"Lena poked her little nose into the pillows on the spot.

"'Oh yes,' she said, 'it's *beautiful.*'

"'But you must be, or any way you should be, hungry, my dear,' said nurse. 'And tea's all ready. Come away down stairs, and then you must go to bed early, you know. I must take great care of you, so that you'll look quite a different little girl when you go home again.'

"Lena did justice to the tea, I assure you.

163

She thought she had never enjoyed anything so much before as the nice things Mrs. Denny had got ready for her. And after tea there was her little box to unpack and her things to arrange neatly in the old-fashioned bureau and on the shelves of the large light closet, opening out of the room. And by the time all this was done Lena began to feel both sleepy and tired, and was not at all sorry when Mrs. Denny told her that she thought it was quite time for her to go to bed.

"And oh how very comfortable she felt when she was fairly settled in the dear old bed! It was *so* snug—just soft enough, but not too soft — not the kind of suffocatingly soft feather-bed in which you get down into a hole and never get out of it all night. It was springy as well as soft, and though the linen was not perhaps so fine as what Lena was accustomed to at home, it was real homespun for all that—and through everything there was the delicious wild thymy sort of scent of lavender which Mrs. Denny had promised her. Lena went to sleep really burrowing her nose, which was rather a snub one to begin with unfortunately, into the pillow, and the last words she thought to herself were, 'I could really fancy myself in a sort of fairy-land. And oh how nice it will be in the morning to lie awake and look at those lovely curtains.'

"There was not so very much lying awake however the first morning as she had expected. It was so late when she awoke that the sun was quite a good way up in the sky, and Mrs. Denny was standing by the bed smiling at her little visitor, and wondering if she would have to make fresh bread and milk for her, as the bowlful that was ready would be quite spoilt with waiting so long. Up jumped Lena.

"'Oh dear Mrs. Denny,' she said, 'I have had such a beautiful, lovely sleep. And you don't know what funny dreams I had. I dreamt that there were fairies hidden in all the little crinks of the curtains, and I heard them talking about me and telling each other that it was the first time I had slept there, and they wondered if I was a good little girl. And then I thought I heard one say "if she is good we can please her well." *Wasn't* it funny, Mrs. Denny?'

"'Very funny,' said Mrs. Denny, smiling.

M 2

'But you know, Miss Lena, I told you you'd have beautiful sleeps and dreams here, didn't I?'

"'Yes,' said Lena, 'and I'm *so* hungry, you don't know how hungry I am.'

"So she jumped up and washed and dressed and said her prayers, and came down to the kitchen as fresh and bright as a little girl could look. And Farmer Denny declared, if the roses in the garden had been in bloom, he could have thought she had been stealing some for her cheeks—for already there was certainly more colour in them than when she had arrived. So the time passed very happily, and Lena did not feel the least dull either by day or by night.

"It had not been the time of the full moon when she first came, but a few days later it happened to be so, and as the weather was beautifully fine just then there were almost no clouds in the sky, and the moon had it all her own pretty way. One night Lena woke up suddenly—it seemed to her that she had been asleep a long, long time, and she didn't feel the least heavy or confused, but quite fresh and brisk as if she had had all the sleep she needed. And the shining moonlight came pouring in at the windows in a sort of wide band of light falling right across the bed and showing out most beautifully the colours and patterns on the old-fashioned curtains. They looked even brighter than by daylight, and as Lena lay and looked at them, she saw wonderful new pictures that she had never noticed before — the sort of pathway between the green branches and foliage that seemed to lead up to one of the little bowers or grottos grew more distinct, and as Lena tried to trace it out with her eyes, she suddenly saw a little figure moving along the path she was looking at. She rubbed her eyes and looked again—the figure had disappeared, but instead she saw clearly in the moonlight two butterflies flitting about the same path, darting first backwards, then forwards, as if inviting her to follow them.

"'If only I were a fly and could walk straight up a wall,' thought Lena, 'I'd really step up that curtain and see if I couldn't make my way into that grotto,' and then she laughed to her

self at the fancy—'as if any one *could* walk into a picture!' she said.

"And then it seemed to her that the butterflies melted into the leaves—and there was no movement at all on the curtains.

"'It must have been the trembling of the moonlight that made me fancy it,' Lena said to herself. And the next morning when she awoke she stood up on tiptoe to examine the particular spot where she had seen those curious things. It looked just the same as the other parts of the curtains—only half hidden among the bushy leaves near the rustic doorway that Lena called the arbour, she found out a queer brown little face that she had not seen before. It seemed to her to peep out at her suddenly, and she fancied that it was the face of the figure she had watched moving along the path in the moonlight.

"'How funny that I never noticed it before,' she said, for when she looked at the same place on the pattern in other parts of the curtains she noticed the same queer little brown face, just like a monkey peeping from among the branches.

"She was so surprised that she thought she would ask Mrs. Denny if *she* had ever noticed 'the monkeys,' but somehow it went quite out of her head. It was not till the next night that she remembered anything more about them.

"For the next night, strange to say, she wakened again in the same sudden way. And again the moonlight was shining right on the curtains, and this time Lena felt more sure than the night before, that something was moving about among the leaves and flowers and branches that seemed to stand out so brightly.

"'Oh dear,' she thought to herself, 'I *do* wish I could creep up quite quietly and see if it is one of those monkeys that has got loose. Oh please, Mr. Monkey, if you are a fairy *do* come down and fetch me,' she added, laughing.

"But her laughter stopped suddenly. Almost as she said the words the most curious sound reached her ears—at first it seemed like the buzzing of lots and lots of flies, bluebottles, midges, bees, cockchafers — every sort of creature of the kind, so that Lena started up in a fright. But no—no flies of any sort were

164

to be seen, but nearer and nearer, louder and louder came the sound, till at last it grew into a sort of chant, as if a great number of little feet were stepping along together, and a great number of little buzzing voices singing in time to them. And glancing up at the curtains Lena plainly saw a whole quantity of tiny brown figures stepping—you couldn't call it sliding, they moved too regularly—downwards in the direction of her face. And if she had looked closer, she would have seen that every place in the pattern where the wee brown faces peeped out was empty! The monkeys had come to fetch her! Where to?

* * * *

"That I must try to tell you—but as to how she got there, that is a different matter. She never knew it herself, so how could any one else know it? All I can tell you is this—she found herself standing in front of a little house—a pretty little house something like the carved Swiss cottages that your mamma has in the library—there was a garden all round it, thick trees and bushes at the sides, and as Lena suddenly, as it were, seemed to awake to find herself there, she heard at the same moment a sort of scuttling all about her, just as if a lot of hares or rabbits had taken flight. And when she quickly turned round to look, she saw disappearing among the shrubs ever so many—*quantities* of pairs of little brown legs and feet—the bodies and heads belonging to them being already hidden in the green.

"'It must be the monkeys,' thought Lena, and as this came into her mind it struck her too that this place where she found herself was the very place where she had wished to be. Till this moment she had somehow forgotten about it, but now she looked about her with great interest—yes—this cottage must be the very place she had called an arbour, for the fence in front of it was of rustic work like dried branches twisted together, and there at the side was one of the trees with the thick leaves where the monkey's face had peeped out —and at the other side were the plants with the big bobbing red flowers, and the other ones with the hanging yellow lilies—all the things she had noticed so often. Lena had really got her wish. She was *in* the chintz

165

curtains. Only there were no birds, no butterflies, nothing moving at all—no monkeys' faces peeping at her from among the leaves. Everything was perfectly still.

"'What shall I do?' thought Lena. 'Shall I go into the house and look about me? I wonder if it would be rude.'

"It didn't seem so, for the door was left open —wide open, as if on purpose; so after knocking once or twice and no one's coming Lena walked in. Such a pretty, but such a queer little house it was. It was more like a nest than a house. There was a little kitchen with cupboards all round, with open lattice-work doors through which you could see what was in them. They were filled with all sorts of queer provisions, nuts, acorns, apples of different kinds, and some fruits that Lena had never seen before. Then in the parlour the carpet was the prettiest you could imagine. Lena could not think what it was till she stooped down and felt it with her hands, and then she found it was moss, real live growing moss, so bright and green, and so soft and springy. And the sofa and chairs were all made of growing plants, twisted and trained so that the roots made the seat and the branches the back. Each was different. Lena sat down in one or two and could not tell which was the most comfortable, they were all so nice, and so pretty. For each was ornamented with a different flower that seemed to grow in a wreath on purpose round the back and down the arms. There was no fireplace in the room, but there were some nice furry-looking rugs lying about, and when Lena looked at them closely she saw they were made of moss too—moss of a different kind, browner than the other, plaited together in some wonderful way with the soft flowery tufts kept outside. Lena lay down on the sofa and covered herself up with one of these rugs.

"'How comfortable it is! What an awfully nice little house this is!' she said to herself. 'But how I do wish some one would come to speak to me. It feels rather like Silverhair in the Three Bears. Mr. Monkey, if this is your house, please come and speak to me.'

"No sooner had she said this than there stood before her a wee brown figure—brown all over, face, hands, feet and all—only his eyes, which sparkled brightly like beads, were black. He was dressed in a short scarlet jacket, and on his head was a scarlet cap with a long, very long tassel. He took off the cap and bowed low—very low at Lena's feet—the top of his head when he stood upright reached about to her knees, and he bowed so low that his nose nearly touched her toes. Lena felt rather uncomfortable—she was not used to such very great respect, and she felt a little startled to think that she had called out to the little man, as 'Mr. Monkey.' No doubt he was rather like a monkey, but still—

"She stood to think of something nice and civil to say, but she could not, try as she might, think of anything better than 'Thank you, sir.'

"It did quite well—the little man seemed quite pleased, for he bowed again as low as before, and in a clear silvery voice like a little bell he spoke to Lena.

" 'What are your biddings, little lady?'

" 'Oh,' said Lena, 'I do so want to see all this funny place. It was very kind of you to bring me up here, but I would like to see it all. May I walk all about your garden, Mr. Mon—oh I beg your pardon,' she added in a hurry.

" 'Never mind,' said the little man. 'One name is as good as another. My brothers and I have been watching you and we wish you well. If you will come with me I will show you all I can.'

" 'Oh, thank you,' said Lena, jumping up in a moment.

"The little man walked out of his house, and standing in front of it he gave a long shrill whistle. Immediately from every direction whole quantities of other little brown men appeared—they seemed to tumble out of every branch of the trees, to peep up out of the ground almost at Lena's feet—till at last she felt like Gulliver among the Lilliputians.

" 'Fetch the carpet,' said the first little man, who seemed a sort of commander, and before Lena had time to see where it came from a beautifully bright blue sheet was stretched out before her, held all round by the dozens and dozens of little brown men, as if they were going to shake it.

" 'Step on to it, little lady,' said her friend.

166

"Lena did so, and no sooner had her feet touched it than she felt it rise, rise up into the air, up, up, till she wondered where she was going to. Then suddenly, as suddenly as it had begun to move, it stopped.

" 'Where are we?' she said, just then noticing for the first time that her own particular little brown man was sitting at her feet.

" 'At the top;' said the little man, 'it would have taken you a long time to climb up here, and we did not want to tire you. Now you shall see our gardens.'

"He jumped off the carpet, and Lena followed him. All the other little men had disappeared, but she hardly noticed it, she was so delighted with what she saw. Before her were beautiful flower paths—paths edged with tall growing flowers of every colour indeed, for they never stayed the same for half a moment, but kept . changing like rainbows — melting from one shade into another in the loveliest way, like the coloured lights at the pantomime.

" 'Oh how lovely!' said Lena. 'May I gather some, please?'

"The little man shook his head.

" 'You cannot,' he said, walking on before her.

"After a while he turned down another path.

" 'These are our birds,' he said; and Lena, glancing more closely at what she had thought were still flowers, saw that they were trees with numberless branches, on each of which sat or perched a bird. They were a contrast to the many-coloured flowers, for each bird was of one colour only, and all the birds on each tree were the same. There was a tree perfectly covered with pure white ones, another with all red, a third all blue, and so on. And the birds swayed gently backwards and forwards on the branches, in time; though there was no sound, it seemed to Lena like hearing beautiful music. And somehow she did not feel inclined to speak or to ask any questions. She just quietly followed the little man, feeling happier and more pleased than she had ever felt in her life. And soon there came another change. Looking up, Lena saw that all the birds and flowers were left behind, and she was walking through a sort of thicket of leafless bushes. She wondered why they were so bare, when everything else in the brownies' country was so rich and bright.

"These are our orchards,' said her guide. 'But we keep the fruit packed up till it is wanted. It keeps it fresher. See now!' As he spoke he touched a bush.

"'Grow,' he said, and in an instant there came a sort of flutter over the tree, and then at once there sprouted out all over the branches the most tempting-looking clusters of fruit. They were something like beautiful purple grapes, but richer and more luscious-looking than any grapes Lena had ever seen. And while she was admiring them the little man touched another, and instantly oranges, golden and gleaming like no oranges she had ever seen before, glistened out all over the branches. And the little man stepped on in front, touching the trees as he went, till the whole path was a perfect glow of fruits of every colour and shape. So beautiful were they to look at, that Lena somehow felt no wish to eat them.

"On went the brownie, touching as he went, till suddenly the path came to an end, and Lena saw in front of her a high wall of bright green grass, with steps cut in it.

"'Up here,' said her little friend, 'are our fish-ponds. Would you like to see them?'

"Lena nodded her head. She was getting quite used to wonderful things, but the more she saw the more she wanted to see. She followed the little man up the steps, and when she got to the top she stood silent with surprise and delight. Of all the pretty wonders he had shown her, what she now saw was the prettiest. Six tiny lakes lay before her, and in each a fountain rose sparkling and dancing. And the fish that were in each lake rose up with the waters of the fountain and glided down them again as if almost they had wings. In each pond the fish were of different colours. There were, let me see, six ponds, did I not say? Yes—well in the first the fish were gold, in the second silver, in the third bronze; and in the three others even prettier, for in them the fish were ruby, emerald, and topaz. I mean they were of those colours, and in the water they gleamed as if they were made of the precious stones themselves. Lena gazed at them in perfect delight, and held out her hands so that

the spray from the fountains fell on them, half hoping that by chance some of the fish might drop into her fingers by mistake.

"The little man looked at her and smiled, but shook his head.

"'No,' he said, as if he knew what she was thinking, 'no, you cannot catch them, just as you could not have gathered the flowers.'

"Lena looked disappointed.

"'I would so like to take some of them home,' she said, gently.

"'It cannot be, child,' said the little man. 'They would have neither life nor colour out of their own waters. There are many, many more things to show you, but I fear the time is over. I must take you home before the moon sets.'

"'But mayn't I come again?' said Lena. She had not time to hear the little man's answer, for again there came the quick rushing sound of the quantities and quantities of little feet, and again a sort of cloudy feeling came over Lena. She tried to speak again to the brownie, but her voice seemed to have no sound, and all she heard was his shrill whistle. It grew shriller and shriller till at last it got to sound not a whistle at all, but more like a cock's crow. And just then Lena opened her eyes, which she did not know were closed, and what do you think she saw? The morning sun peeping in at the lattice-window of her bedroom, and lighting up in its turn as the moon had done a few hours before, the queer quaint patterns on the old chintz curtains. And down below in the yard Farmer Denny's young cock was busy telling all its companions, and little Lena as well, if she chose to listen, that it was time to be up and about."

Magdalen stopped.

"Is that all?" said Maudie.

Hoodie said nothing, but stared up for her answer.

"I don't know," said their cousin.

"You don't know?" said Maudie. "Cousin Magdalen, you're joking."

"No, indeed I'm not. I really don't know. I daresay there's lots more if I had time to tell it you. The little man told her there were lots and lots more things to show her."

"Did her ever go back again?" asked Hoodie gravely.

"I hope so—I think so," said Magdalen. "But I don't think she ever went back quite the same way."

Hoodie stared harder. Maudie looked up with a puzzled face.

"Cousin Magdalen," she said, "I believe after all you've been taking us in. There is something in the story that means something else. How do you mean that Lena went back again to the brownies' country?"

"I mean," said Magdalen, "that it was the country of fancy-land—a country we may all go to, if——"

"If what, please?"

"If we keep good and kind and sweet and pretty feelings in our hearts," said Magdalen slowly, and a little gravely. "But if we let ugly things in—crossness, idleness, and selfishness, and ugly creatures like that—the pretty fairies will never come near us to fetch us away to see their treasures. The brownies would not let untidy or ill-tempered children into their neat little nests of houses. And even if such children *did* get into fairyland or fancy-land—whichever you like to call it, where there are such numberless beautiful and strange things—it would not be fairyland to them, because their poor little eyes would be blind, and their poor little ears deaf."

"I think I understand," said Maudie, "and some day perhaps Cousin Magdalen, you'll tell us some more about Lena."

"Perhaps," said Magdalen, smiling.

But Hoodie said nothing, only stared harder up in her cousin's face with her big blue eyes.

And Hec and Duke, who had been amusing themselves since the story was over and the talking had begun, by sticking daisies on to a thorn, trotted up to Cousin Magdalen to kiss her and say, "Zank zou for the pitty story."

(To be continued.)

LITTLE JOE'S SECRET.

By the AUTHOR OF "AUNT EFFIE'S RHYMES," Etc.

LD Mrs. Dipem, muffled up in blue,
  I have got a secret, but it's not for you;
If you want to know if I can keep it well,
  Ask me what it is and see if I will tell.

"Old Mrs. Dipem, little brother Joe
  When he made the secret, said you should not know.
It was Sunday morning when we were in bed,
  But I shall not tell you what it was he said.

"Old Mrs. Dipem, don't you think the sea
  Far too rough to-day for little Joe and me?
How the waves are rolling, crested up with foam,
  Don't you think that nurse had better take us home?

"When the great machine goes rumbling down the stones,
  How it shakes my head and my poor little bones,
How my teeth do chatter! oh if you could see
  When we're stript and naked, little Joe and me.

169

"And when at last it stops, and nurse unbolts the door,
And shows the chilly water spreading out before,
I wonder how you'd like it and what *you* would do
If some great wet old woman took and cuddled you."

The bathing-woman laughed, and merrily she said,
"I wonder how such thoughts should come into your head;
To make you grow up strong and vigorous," said she,
"There's nothing half so good as bathing in the sea.

"When you're a grown-up man and muscular in limb,
I'll warrant you you'll like to splash about and swim;
And as for feeling cold, there's nothing like a storm
To make the sea feel nice and comfortably warm."

"But I am not a man, I'm only five," said he,
And little brother Joe is only half-past three.
And neither of us like that you or your wet daughter,
Should take us in your arms and plump us in the water,

"At home, when we're in town, and driving in the line,
The carriage sometimes goes close by the Serpentine,
And happy little boys that do just what they choose,
Are wading in the brink with stockings off and shoes."

"Indeed," said Mrs. Dipem, "should you like to be
A little ragamuffin wading in the sea ?
Out at knees and elbows, often short of food,
Such a homeless life is anything but good.".

"Yes, me would like to wade," said bright-eyed little Joe,
"But dipping over head, oh no, oh no, oh no ;
And when I am a man and strong enough to fight,
I'll dip you in the sea and put you out of sight."

"There now the secret's out. You silly little elf,
I said you could not keep the secret to yourself."
"The thing we mean to do is this, and now I ll tell,
To drown the big machine, the horse, and you as well."

"Indeed," said Mrs. Dipem, "now I know my fate,
But there, the tide is coming and it's getting late."
"Nursie, dearest nursie, take us home," said Joe,
"For the tide is coming, and we want to go."

TALKS ABOUT THE MONTHS.

JUNE.

By Mrs. GEORGE CUPPLES.

" 'Tis June, 'tis merry, smiling June,
'Tis blushing Summer now ;
The rose is red, the bloom is dead,
The fruit is on the bough."

*   *   *   *

" June brings tulips, lilies, roses,
Fills the children's hands with posies."

OW quickly the months come and go ! It seems almost like yesterday since we were examining the closed buds and looking for the snowdrops and the crocuses, and now here is June, and in twenty-four days we shall have reached Mid-summer Day, and in a few days after that, we shall notice the days gradually shortening and the nights lengthening. At present we have nothing to do with that however ; we think no such gloomy thoughts at the opening of June. It is joyous summer time, with the whole earth full of beauty and gleaming flowers, and glancing wings, and the sky bright and blue. Adieu to Spring! welcome Summer! Everything is full of life, greenness, vigour, the young birds are now hatched and give their parents a busy life of it till they can pick for themselves, more especially the tenants of the poultry yard.

The Saxons named this month *Weyd-Monat,* or meadow month. As their chief wealth consisted of herds and flocks, we find that many of the names of the seasons amongst them took their origin from something connected with the land. Thus *Weyd-Monat* arose, we are told, because "the beasts did then *weyd* or feed in the meadows." Afterwards its name was changed to *Sere-Monat* or dry month, a very fitting name, as June is the least variable of all our months. It is supposed by some that June took its name from Juno, the wife of Jupiter, in honour of whom a festival was held at the beginning of the month.

In June the pastures are covered with clover in full flower, which fills the air with a delightful perfume; and the bees and other honey sipping insects are busy in all directions keeping up a delicious humming, as we lie in some sheltered spot and close our eyes so that we may hear all the sounds of Nature the better.

In no other country in the world has summer more charms than in our own, and in no other country are they so well seen. With us the flowers are unmixed with the rank growth of weeds which in hot climates mingle with the sweetest flowers, if they do not hide them altogether. Neither have we anything to fear in seeking our summer flowers, as few are injurious; and we have neither poisonous snake nor venomous insect to check our curiosity and delight. There are, however, some plants now in flower which though very beautiful, are poisonous. It is well to learn to know them as soon as possible, lest, tempted to eat of their inviting berries, we may be injured or even killed.

These plants are termed Nightshade, although there is a great difference in their appearance. The best known of these is the Woody Nightshade or Bitter-sweet, a shrubby plant, with dark purple star-shaped flowers with a yellow centre, and bears large clusters of red berries

173

not unlike red currants in appearance. Then there is the poisonous Deadly Nightshade, a large plant with dark green leaves and dark purple bell-shaped flower, and after, a black berry as large as a small cherry. The Garden Nightshade is a smaller plant with white flowers and a small black berry, and though less hurtful than the others ought never to be allowed to grow in a garden.

The honeysuckle, and the various coloured wild roses, make ample amends for the loss of the hawthorn, which has already shed its flowers. They cover our hedgerows, and are often connected by garlands of the great bind-weed, with its snow-white flowers.

Hay harvest has commenced, and, in some southern counties, if the weather be favourable is completed; but next month may be considered as the general season of haymaking. Haymaking is a cheerful and pleasant labour, but its success greatly depends upon the weather. If the weather is fine, the farmer sees, with a glad and thankful heart, 'the swathes' of grass falling before the mowers, as they advance with their scythes. Then follows a merry troop of both sexes and all ages, who shake abroad the hay that it may be speedily dried by the wind and the sun. The children consider it all sport for them together, as they toss it about, throwing it over one another with bursts of merry laughter, but even in their play they are doing good, for hay cannot be shaken too much, and it must be thoroughly dry before it is taken home else it will spoil, or, as is often the case, it may take fire by its own heat if stacked too soon. As hay is often spoiled by fickle weather you may be sure everybody who is going to have anything to do with the hay-fields watches earnestly the appearance of the weather. The rising and the setting sun are considered great marks of a fine or a wet day.

" An evening red, a morning grey,
Will set the traveller on his way ;
But an evening grey, and a morning red,
Will pour down rain on the haymaker's head."

The wind, the various appearances of the moon, and the actions of animals and insects are no unimportant signs. Before rain, it is said, cattle stretch out their necks, and snuff the air with open nostrils; pigs show great uneasiness; ducks, geese, turkeys and peacocks, gabble and scream; hens roll themselves in the dust; bees take short flights; spiders disappear; gnats collect under trees; and swallows skim along the ground. If cattle are heard lowing more than usual, we may calculate on rain, and if the ass bray frequently in the morning. This has given rise to the couplet,—

> "'Tis time to stack your hay and corn
> When the old donkey blows his horn."

If we meet only one magpie abroad during the hatching season we may look for rain; but if we meet two, it is likely to be fine, for both birds have left their nest—a thing they never do if rain is about to fall. The opening and shutting of flowers is another guide. If the chickweed be quite open no rain will fall, so that hay may be safely spread. What a delicious smell of new mown hay there will be in every room of the old farmhouses for days after the stacks are finished; we almost long to take up our lodging there for the sake of the fragrance.

The sun is now moving on to his highest point in the sky, so that during these delightful haymaking days we can stay out of doors till ever so late and still go to bed without using a candle. Long ago the 11th of June was the day of the "summer solstice," or longest day, called in England, Barnaby's Day, hence the old proverb—

> "Barnaby bright,
> The longest day and the shortest night."

But now the longest day is the 21st, when the sun appears to stand still; and from the 11th of the month to the 2nd of July there is no real night, the twilight extending from sunset to sunrise. How strange this long twilight appeared to two little boys who came from New Zealand, for at their home they have no real twilight, dark comes very quickly, and at some other parts of the world, such as in the Island of Mauritius, "when the sun's ray dips, at one stride comes the dark."

What a glad day the 15th of June is for the Egyptians, for then the Nile rises, or is

expected to rise. It is such an important day that it is marked by many religious and festive ceremonies, and we do not wonder at it, when we remember that the Egyptians are depending on the river overflowing its banks for water for their crops and all other necessary purposes.

Midsummer Day happens on the 24th of June. It was formerly a custom to make Midsummer Eve a time for merry-making and rude revelry, both old and young meeting round large bonfires in the open air. It was customary too to keep a watch walking about during Midsummer Night. Every citizen either went himself or sent a substitute. They paraded the town in parties during the night, every person wearing a garland of flowers upon his head. In London, during the middle ages, this watch, consisting of not less than two thousand men, paraded the streets with lighted torches. The great came to witness this marching watch, even the King and Queen joined in it on one occasion, for we read—

> " The goodly buildings that till then did hide
> Their rich array, open'd their windows wide,
> Where kings, great peers, and many a noble dame,
> Of the nights burning lights, did sit to see
> How every senator in his degree
> Their guard attending, through the streets did ride."

As we walk through the woods towards the end of the month we are very much struck with the silence. Last month there was such a loud "musical din," every bird seeming to be trying who would sing the loudest, but now, all is silent or nearly so; what has become of the birds? The cuckoo, after getting hoarser and hoarser, ceases to repeat his call, and with the exception of the lark and the blackbird singing in the early morning, there is scarcely a note to be heard. What is the cause of it, do you ask? Well, the little birds are too busy. There is a time for everything under the sun, even for the singing of the birds; and now there are so many hungry little bills to be fed that it takes their mother and father all the day to satisfy them. The moment there is a faint streak of light the little mouths gape open and the chirp-chirping begins, never ceasing till long after the sun has gone down. Have you ever sat in a corner and watched a pair of little birds feeding their young, or tried to count the number of times they flew in and out? How cleverly they drop the grub or fly into the gaping mouth, and into the right one too, never seeming to make a mistake about which one had it the last time. One may chirp louder than the others, but his mother pays no attention to that. He got his share last time, and he must just wait his turn till the other four or five have theirs.

Have you watched the barn-owls during the month of June? They appear at dusk gliding along the hedgerows and near the barns ready to pounce upon a mouse. They are as industrious as the birds, for it is said that they return to their nests with a mouse every five minutes while they are on the wing.

June is the happiest season of the year, free of the intense heat of July, fine, clear, and glowing. Many of the sweetest flowers have vanished from our path, but they have slid away so quietly, and their places have been occupied by so many fragrant and beautiful successors, that we have scarcely been sensible of their departure.

> " On the fragrant mead,
> Among the new-mown hay,
> We see the daisies tall
> That bloomed but yesterday
> Now withering with the grass—
> Their transient glory gone,
> And in their lesson see
> The fate of every one."

JACK AND GILL.

BY THE EDITOR.

ONE evening in summer, long, long ago, when I was a little child, we were all playing out in the paddock, where hay had been made during the day. The sun was just setting, the air was turning cool, and we children ran, jumped, and tumbled about in the sweet fresh perfumed hay.

The elders of the family were yet in the dining-room; but presently we saw appear at the open window a tall slight figure, which we soon recognised as that of our cousin Peter. He was staying with us, but had just got his commission, and was going away in a day or two to join his regiment in Canada. The garden alone separated the paddock from the house, and we little ones rejoiced as we saw him step out at the dining-room window, and walk across the lawn on his way towards us. Still more did we rejoice when, at a whistle from him, his familiar spirit, Jack his dog, rushed out from some hidden corner to join him, and the two

together came bounding over the thin iron fence, which divided the garden from the paddock, to join in our frolic in the hay-field.

Surely there never was such a dog as Jack, and surely there never was such a boy, or man, as Jack's master; looked at, that is to say, in a romping point of view. I was no judge at that time of men's manners, nor much indeed of anything beyond a good game at play; but certainly for anything in that way Peter and Jack were great acquisitions. I scarcely know which I liked best, the dog or his master.

After Peter had pelted us with hay and almost buried us in it, we all paused to take breath; then he said, "Now children tell the truth, are you sorry I am going away?"

Three pairs of eyes all at once grew grave and sad, and our three little faces lengthened.

"Oh, indeed, we are sorry, Peter," murmured one and all; for who played with us as he did, who contrived so many treats for us, or got us out of so many scrapes?

"Well," said Peter, "will the shock of my

175

JACK AND GILL.

departure he broken to you, when you know that I shall leave Jack behind me?"

Our joy was so great at this news that I fear Jack's master must have seen how much it lessened the grief we felt at his own departure.

"Lulu," said Peter, turning to me, for that was the name I went by, though I was christened Lucy; "in *your* charge will I leave Jack, and I shall expect to find him in good condition when I return from foreign parts. All the love you would bestow upon me were I here, I expect you will show to Jack in my absence."

Jack was of no value in himself on account of breed or beauty, but his intellectual qualities were certainly wonderful, and this little wiry terrier was one of the most affectionate doggies in the world.

Now I have told you how I became possessed of Jack, and I will next give you an account of one of his exploits.

Soon after my cousin Peter's departure, some one gave me a very handsome tabby kitten, who soon grew up into an equally handsome cat. Jack took to her so kindly, and looked after her, and protected her so prettily, that I gave my pussy the name of Gill. Jack and Gill were inseparable companions: it was quite curious to see the two creatures trotting about together. At last an event occurred that showed not only Jack's devotion to his friend, but also his extraordinary intelligence.

It so happened that my pretty little Gill had some kittens, and cook called me into the kitchen one morning to look at them. There they were, four as sweet little things as were ever seen, curled up in a basket. I think I was as proud of them as Gill herself, and Jack's interest in his friend's little family was unbounded. One day, when the kittens were a few weeks old, Pussy went out for a walk, leaving them in their basket. Then the cook called in the coachman, and, with him, took up from the basket, and admired and examined

the kittens one by one. I believe the worthy pair were settling the different destinations of the four kittens.

Now, for a wonder, Jack happened to have stayed at home when Gill went out. Perhaps he had remained on purpose to look after his friend's little ones. The cook and the coachman were quite unconscious, while they were examining the kittens, that Jack was watching them, his ears pricked up, and his whole attention given to what they were saying or doing. His quick brain and anxious heart feared some danger threatening his friend's children. No sooner were the kittens replaced in the basket, and the cook's back turned, than quietly and stealthily Jack took up the kittens, one by one, in his mouth, carrying them quite as gently as their mother would have done, and bearing them off into his own private dog-box in the yard. There he placed them upon straw, and did his best to make them warm and comfortable.

Cook, returning to the kitchen, soon missed the kittens, and suspecting something of the kind that had really happened, determined to watch Jack as he had watched her. She saw he was evidently waiting for the return of Gill, in order to explain to her what he had done, and save her from anxiety on missing her little ones. Presently Gill made her appearance trotting into the kitchen, and she and Jack went together up to the empty basket. Then somehow he managed to explain to her where her kittens were, for in a minute they trotted off side by side to the dog-box in the yard. There Mrs. Gill received a warm welcome from her family, and she at once made herself perfectly at home in her friend's house.

Now how did Jack make the cat understand what had become of her kittens? Yet he not only did that, but he evidently satisfied her that he had acted kindly in removing them, for after this Jack and Gill were better friends than ever. It is a puzzle to me.

UNDER THE HEDGE.

178

UNDER THE HEDGE.

THE leafy hedge a shadow makes
　　Where sits a maiden fair —
A little maid, who sits and plucks
　　The gay wild flow'rets there.

The buttercup shining like gold,
　　The daisy with silver ray,
The white and the red tufted clover,
　　Each blossom that comes in her way.

These wild flowers seem such jewels
　　To a dear little maiden of nine;
They seem but weeds—scarce flowers—
　　To world-worn eyes like mine.

Yet I too love the wild flowers
　　For the sake of a time that is past,
When the world seemed far more happy,
　　And sorrow seemed never to last.

Ah, children, enjoy the bright present!
　　Rejoice in these glad summer days,
When the plants, and the trees, and the blossoms,
　　All brighten beneath the sun's rays:

When you wake with the opening morning,
　　With the song of the birds in the air,
And your hearts give an echoing murmur.
　　To all the glad sounds that are there.

Winter comes, with its frost and its snow;
　　No more joy then in sunshine or shade:
So age, with its sorrows and cares,
　　Brings the sadness those sorrows have made.

I think, when I look at this maiden,
　　Sitting under the hedge in the shade,
Of the time when I gathered wild flowers,
　　And dreamt not such pleasures would fade.

179

THE RHINE CASTLE.

By the Right Hon. E. H. KNATCHBULL-HUGESSEN, M.P., *Author of "Uncle Joe's Stories," &c.*

CHAPTER I.

IT was a very old castle on the banks of the Rhine, and of course it was haunted. Indeed, on that noble river nobody thinks anything of castles which are *not* haunted. In most of them there is a good, old-fashioned, respectable family ghost, with which is connected some wondrous legend of the past, the recital of which in the dusk of a winter's evening, when a party of relations are sitting round the smouldering embers of a wood fire, sends most of them to bed in a remarkably nervous frame of mind. This castle was not a whit behind others in the antiquity and respectability of its ghost, although the legend attaching to the worthy spirit was less tragic and terrible than was sometimes the case.

The castle stood on the very banks of the river, and from its terraces a shrubbery, or rather a wood, stretched down to the very edge of the water. Formerly (so ran the tale), the owner of this territory had a beautiful daughter, who (as is occasionally the case with rich people), had numerous lovers among whom she found it difficult to make a choice. The lover whom she secretly preferred and who on his part was entirely devoted to her, received at her hands no very civil treatment, and at length, being probably somewhat badly off for common sense, he gave way to despair. Having done this for a sufficiently long time, he proceeded to drown himself, which was a useless and ridiculous, not to say wicked, course of proceeding; and having satisfactorily accomplished his absurd object, his body floated down the stream and greeted the eyes of the young lady as she was standing in the wood close to the edge of the river, having just been indulging in her favourite pastime of playing on her harp, which stood by her side as she pensively mused, leaning her head on her hand and gazing down upon the water.

The effect upon her nerves was, as might have been expected, the reverse of soothing. She screamed, tried to drown herself with her lover, and having been prevented from doing so by attendants who were fortunately near at hand, went mad as soon as she conveniently could, died shortly afterwards, and ever after, harp in hand, haunted the spot at which she had thus encountered the body of her unhappy lover.

It was rather a convenient legend, this, for lovers who happened to have the run of the castle woods, for every one took them for the ghosts of the aforesaid legend, and they were thus secure from the interruption of mortal intruders.

At the time of which I speak, the castle was inhabited by an individual of strange and fantastic character, who claimed to be, and for all I know *was*, the descendant in a direct line from barons who had possessed that castle for any number of years you please to name.

They had been queer characters, by all accounts. The best of them had been rough soldiers, rather brutal than not in their manner of warfare, and not over particular against whom they fought or how they carried on the strife. Some, however, had been much worse. Robbers, rebels, leaders of roving bands of marauders, and even a few acknowledged murderers went to make up the roll of the illustrious ancestors of the present Baron. Latterly, however, there had been no remarkable criminals of his race. Perhaps it was because the times had been less stirring, perhaps there was greater vigilance on the part of the authorities in looking after evil doers, or perhaps (to be as charitable as we can), the breed had really improved, and the more modern of the barons, repenting and regretting the deeds of their forefathers, had really become reformed characters, and set themselves down to lead regular and respectable lives.

Be this how it may, nobody had ever accused the baron of whom I speak of being anything more than eccentric; or, to speak more plainly, mad. No one exactly knew why they thought he was mad, but this made very little difference in the general opinion. There could not, indeed, be much evidence upon the question, because nobody ever saw him. He scarcely ever ventured beyond the spacious grounds of his castle, and when he did so, turned back immediately upon seeing anybody, and hastily regained the privacy of his own domain. He kept no servants except an old man and his wife who had been born and bred upon his estates, and who made it a solemn rule never to speak of their master and his family. They obtained such additional help as they required from some of the cottages near, but of those there were few, for the population of that country was thin and scattered, and there was no busy neighbourhood through which gossip about the castle and its inhabitants could circulate.

So time passed on, and but for the events which I am about to relate, the Baron and his castle might have passed on too, and faded away in good time without any record of them having become known to the world. There seemed no reason, indeed, why anybody should concern himself about either the one or the other. That country was full of castles and barons; most of the former were said to be haunted, and many of the latter were known to be eccentric, if nothing more, so that on looking back, one cannot form any accurate guess why this particular baron and this particular castle should have required a story all to themselves. So it is, however, and the story is like the Baron, of a somewhat remarkable character, if indeed, a story can be properly said to have any character at all.

The Baron's character was not a good one among other barons, for when a man holds himself aloof from the class to which he belongs, they are pretty sure to think and speak ill of him, and the present case was no exception to this general rule. Our friend had as bad a name among barons as anywhere else, and was never invited or received as a visitor in any of the other castles which were inhabited by persons of his own rank. In fact, for any reason to the contrary that I have been able to discover, he might have lived and died in the utter seclusion which he seemed to prefer, had it not been for one special circumstance which prevented such a result. That circumstance was the fact of his having no heir to inherit the broad lands which lay around the castle of his ancestors, and being able, so the world understood, to dispose of the same according to his own will and pleasure.

Now when a person, be he baron or peasant, simple or gentle, occupies this particular position, he sooner or later becomes an object of interest to the neighbourhood in which his lot happens to be cast. Had our hero been a poor man, with nothing to leave behind him, he might have left it when and how he pleased, and nobody would have troubled his head about the matter. It was different, however, when his retiring from the world would leave a castle and landed estates without an owner. So after the lapse of a certain time the circumstances and condition of the Baron de Grumpelhausen became the common subject of discussion in more than one household, and principally in those which were fortunate enough to contain unmarried members of the fairer portion of humanity.

Among these it was, strange to say, the pre-

valent, nay almost universal opinion that the Baron ought to marry, and as time passed on without his taking any step in this direction, the opinion of his madness became more than ever firmly established among the ladies. It was undoubtedly sad, if not mad and bad, most likely all three, that such a Baron should be without a wife, and such a castle without a mistress. Such, however, seemed but too likely to be the case at the time our story begins, nor did any of the fair creatures who lamented the probability feel able to avert so melancholy an occurrence.

Among those who took it most to heart was a respectable, I should rather say noble dame, who lived in another castle not many miles distant from that of the Baron. She was a lady of rank, and thought a good deal of it too, in which she was doubtless justified, as the Counts of Stuttenguttenheim had been counts ever since there were such things as counts at all, and everybody knows that the farther back you can trace your family and the more ancestors of rank you can reckon upon your fingers, the nobler, the wiser, the better, and the happier must you be. There is no doubt therefore, that the Countess of Stuttenguttenheim must have been noble, wise, good, and happy to a very great degree, since she could count back the ancestors of her house to a time more remote than I dare mention, for fear I should not be believed.

She was all this, I do not doubt, in spite of the trifling disadvantages of having a husband who was old, deaf, cross, very disagreeable, and as poor as a church mouse, though why a church mouse should be poorer than any other mouse I never could see, and I don't believe it.

You could not, with any approach to accuracy have called the Count of Stuttenguttenheim a church mouse, for the old heathen had never entered a church in his life; but you could make no mistake in calling him poor, and that in every sense of the word, for he had neither money, brains, or friends, which are three things without some one or more of which a man may be called poor indeed.

How he and his wife had managed to exist so long, I cannot say, but they did so, and moreover possessed olive branches in the shape of three daughters, by either of whom, had they been guided by the opinions of their parents, the name of Grumpelhausen would have been readily substituted for their own. But the daughters of an ancient house must not be dismissed in this summary manner. The respect due to their exalted rank compels a somewhat more detailed description.

Albertina, Gertrude, and Margaret von Stuttenguttenheim were maidens worthy of their race, and more than worthy of their parents, who were as frightful an old couple as you would come across in a long day's journey.

Their mother, indeed, tall, angular, and scraggy, had a sort of natural dignity about her, doubtless derived from an innate consciousness of the grandeur of her position in society, which carried off, to a certain extent at least, or at all events went far to moderate the first impression made by her extreme ugliness. But their little, short, podgy father had no redeeming quality apparent to the eye of the beholder, and looked very much more like a broken-down tallow-chandler than a man of family and position. But the daughters were somehow or other of an entirely different model.

It is very odd that this should be, as it sometimes is, the case, and that remarkably ugly parents should have children of ravishing beauty. In the instance of which we are now speaking there could be no doubt at all upon the subject, one way or the other. The father and mother were as ugly as sin, and the daughters as beautiful as the contrary of sin, whatever is the best word to express it.

Albertina was tall and fair, with light blue eyes, clear transparent skin, finely moulded limbs, graceful action, pleasant manner, and agreeable conversation. Gertrude was shorter and plumper than her sister, but equally fair, with an expression of countenance which spoke of a nature essentially good-humoured, and a frank liveliness about her which was extremely taking. Margaret was the dark one of the party, with masses of raven hair, rich brown complexion, beautiful figure and fit to be an empress, if there had happened to be a place of that kind vacant at the time of which we write.

Such were the three daughters of this ancient

183

house, and it was on their account that the old dame, their mother, took so strong an interest in the case of our Baron.

Why indeed should she not do so? Here were three charming girls, there an unmarried man rich and titled. What mother could sit still and see time gliding by without an attempt made to bring together elements which seemed intended to be combined, but which accident or fate had hitherto kept asunder? But whether the old Countess sat still to see this or not, the facts remained the same, and the difficulty before her was one which she did not perceive the way to overcome.

In our day the matter would have been comparatively easy. She would have managed to bring the Baron over to a croquet or lawn-tennis party, prepared a picnic or even given a ball, and at all events worried him with invitations till he had been forced out of his shell, and been brought in contact with those three charmers, of whom one or the other would certainly have enslaved him; or she would have made an expedition to see his castle, pretending to have been informed that he was away from home, and by clever management have brought him suddenly face to face with the beauties.

But these were not things which could be done in the days of which we write. Croquet and lawn-tennis were not known in that part of the world, picnics in secluded places would have been dangerous, as liable to interruption from bears, wolves, and robbers, whilst a ball would have been an event utterly unheard of, and in fact, from badness of roads and scarcity of neighbours, quite impossible to accomplish. No: if the thing was to be done at all, some other means must be found; some scheme planned which should be promptly and vigorously carried out, and to this the fertile brain of the old countess again and again reverted.

For some time the only thing that occurred to her was the good old-fashioned plan of attacking and plundering the castle, carrying off its owner as a captive, and releasing him only as the husband of one of his vanquisher's children. The only, or at least the principal objection to this scheme was to be found in the fact that the Baron's castle was strong, and that his means of defence were so much greater than the count's means of attack, that any attempt of the sort would probably meet with failure as complete as ignominious.

This idea, therefore, had to be abandoned, and the old lady racked her brain for another to no purpose. At last she bethought her of having recourse to magic, which was an art much held in esteem in those days, although very imperfectly understood. If any one has a turn for the thing in our days, it is well known that the best, if not the only way to proceed, is by spirit-rapping or table-turning, both of which are said to be healthy and innocent recreations, if not always as efficacious as might be desired. But in those old days spirits had other things to do than to rap their knuckles against walls or wainscots, and tables were in the habit of standing still in their proper places and doing the duties for which they had been made, without indulging in gymnastic exercises which had never been expected of them.

Those who wished to employ magic for any purpose in those days, generally did so in a regular and straightforward way, going off to consult a witch or a warlock, or a respectable demon of some kind or other, of whom there were always plenty to be found, as there probably are still if we only looked for them in the right places.

These creatures being regular dealers in the commodity of magic, were of course ready to supply any quantity of it upon the shortest notice, and it was in this direction that the Countess of Stuttenguttenheim at length determined to turn for assistance.

The Rhine has always had plenty of spirits on its banks and in its waters, and there could therefore be no difficulty about the matter. goblins, water-sprites, and merry little devilets were always as plentiful as blackberries in the locality of which we are now speaking, and the only question was as to the best way of getting hold of one of the best of them, without his getting hold of *you.* For, of course, any one who wanted some great deed accomplished by the aid of one of these gentlemen, whether it was the removal of some enemy or the acquisition of riches, or any trifle of the kind, was very likely to have to sign some awful bond—

possibly with his own blood, which might be inconvenient as well as alarming—and find himself engaged in some consequent disagreeable entanglement at a future period of his existence.

Now, this was not at all what the old Countess wanted ; in fact, she altogether objected to the kind of thing, and had no intention of signing anything except, if she could manage it, the register of the marriage of one or other of her three daughters. All she wanted from the dealers in magic was a little information as to the best way of getting access to the Baron, for if this could once be accomplished, she had unbounded confidence in her own resources and the charms of her children.

In order to obtain the desired boon she determined to inquire of the very best demon who could be had for money, for although the latter article was very scarce in the family, yet any which might be forthcoming could surely be expended in no more legitimate way than by forwarding the fortunes of a daughter of the house.

With this object in view the old Countess had her bath-chair drawn up and down the banks of the river for several consecutive days, anxiously looking out for demons, but with a total want of success.

When this had gone on for the best part of a week, one of the under-housemaids, who had once had an aunt in the witch business, and therefore knew something about it, told the upper-housemaid, who told the cook, who mentioned it to the lady's-maid, that there was a cave further down the river, and not far from the Baron de Grumpelhausen's castle, where people went to consult a spirit who dwelt there, and who was most obliging in the way of telling them a number of things they wanted to know, and who had consequently a great reputation.

The lady's-maid, of course, mentioned this to her mistress that very evening whilst doing her hair, and the Countess immediately sent for the girl, and having heard all she knew, and scolded her as in duty bound, for knowing anything about such matters, seeing that her knowledge ought to be entirely confined to dusters, broomsticks, and slop-pails, determined forthwith to visit the cave and consult the oracle.

184

Accordingly, the very next day she disguised herself in an old bonnet and a dark gray cloak which entirely enveloped her, and set out for the cave, attended only by her faithful maid Dorothy. This damsel was much younger than her mistress, and a comely lass withal, and to say the truth, she was not particularly delighted with the expedition. These kind of things always have to be done in the evening, when all kinds of disagreeable people are about, let alone demons, and the banks of the river were not in those days (whatever they may be now), the place upon which a respectable young woman would prefer to take her walk at that period of the day. However, the Countess so settled it, and mistress and maid set off together, starting sufficiently early in the afternoon to arrive at their destination shortly before sunset, which they did without any interruption or adventure of any kind.

The cave to which they had been directed was situate but a short distance from the river banks, and was very easy to discover, from the circumstance of there being no other cave near it. There was a path which led to it from the river, from which people used to land upon the shore and proceed by the said path to the cave. The entrance was also not difficult to find. You had only to walk straight on, and presently you saw immediately before you a gully, into which you entered (unless you happened to be frightened at this point and consequently turned back), and at the end of the gully was the entrance into the cave, just for all the world as if a railway tunnel had been bored into the mountain, only that it stopped when you had gone a few yards, and the faint glimmer of light from the outside showed you rough and rugged rocks and great masses of stone cast here and there, which showed very clearly that no railway engineer had constructed the place, and no railway train could go far without very fatal results to all concerned.

At this place the mistress and maid duly arrived, and (rather to the disgust of the latter) walked straight into the cave. Before they had proceeded many yards, however, they came to a rock which barred their advance, unless they could manage to climb over it,

which would have been a troublesome and unpleasant operation.

According to the housemaid's instructions, this was fortunately unnecessary, for she had told them that when they were well in the cave they had only to ask, and they would be answered by the being who dwelt there. They must ask in rhyme, she had been told, or at least those who did so always got the quickest and best answers. It was certain that they were "well in the cave" now, or at all events they were in it, though Dorothy had her doubts whether it was "well" to have come at all. So the old Countess prepared herself for the coming interview with great deliberation. She coughed, drew herself up to her full height, looked carefully forward (which was perfectly useless, as it was too dark to see anything a yard in front of you), cleared her throat again, coughed once more, and then gave utterance to the following lines which she had, after much thought and labour, composed on the previous day, and of which she was not a little proud—

" Whoe'er thou art, oh mighty one ! that dwellest in this cave,
Thine be the will and thine the strength, to grant me what I crave.
Three daughters have I—lovely (though by mother this is said),
And charming : but by some ill luck, they none of them are wed.
My Albertina holds herself as well as any queen—
My Gertrude is the dearest duck that ever yet was seen.
These two are blonde—then Margaret, the only one that's dark,
Has charms to raise in ev'ry heart love's instantaneous spark.
Yet they've no chance of finding mates, for, living where we do,
The eligible men alas ! are very, very few.
Yet one there is. Hard by the stream, amid his woods and dells,
Spouseless and lonely in his life, the Grumpelhausen dwells.
How can I get him for my girls ? that is, for one or t'other,
That one may win a loving spouse, and two may gain a brother !"

She spoke, and for a moment nothing was to be heard save the water slowly trickling along the sides of the cave from the mountain, finding its way out to the river, and having nothing at all to do with magic. Then presently there came a low voice from the interior of the cave. It seemed to come from some place very near the two women, as if the speaker was just behind the rock opposite to which they had stopped. There was nothing very remarkable about the voice, save that it was rather like some one whispering very loudly. And it replied to the demand of the Countess in such a manner as to make its meaning easily understood.

" Secrets of import dire can I reveal
To those who at my shrine submissive kneel,
And hidden mysteries can I disclose,
And call dead mortals back from death's repose.
But 'tis a task unsanctioned by the Fates,
To find for three young maidens fitting mates ;
And they must act like fairies, nymphs, and elves,
Keep good look-out, and find them for themselves !
Yet, to a mother's feelings am I kind,
And willingly some remedy would find ;
And could I but myself three people be,
I'd rid you of your girls, and wed the three !
But, failing this, I would not that to-day,
Unanswered and repulsed you went away ;
So listen to my words : to-morrow morn
Bid thy retainers come with hound and horn,
The wolf through all these woodland glades to chase,
And they shall meet the Baron face to face.
Let thy three daughters come and boldly ride,
I cannot talk of bridegroom or of bride,
But they shall meet the Baron in the dell,
And then, the consequences who can tell ? "

The Countess listened to these words with the deepest attention, and, upon the whole, was not dissatisfied with what she heard. It was true that the retainers of her husband were but few in number, they had no hounds worth much, and their performance in the hunting line was therefore not likely to be remarkable for its success. This, however, was a matter of very small importance, for as she understood the words of the voice, the hunting was to be a mere pretext, by means of which her daughters were to obtain the Baron's acquaintance. She therefore began to express, in such rhymes as she could manufacture on the spur of the moment, her cordial thanks to to the Being, whoever or whatever he was, who had responded to her demand in a manner so prompt and courteous.

Scarcely, however, had she got out more than a line or two, when a frightful roaring

proceeded from behind the rock in front of the old lady, which so terrified her that she immediately seized Dorothy's arm, and beat as hasty a retreat as possible, fully persuaded that she was about to be devoured that very instant. She need not have been in the least degree alarmed, first because no wild beast, whether in the flesh or in the spirit, could possibly have desired to touch so old, tough and skinny a creature as she was, and secondly, because, had she considered for a moment, she would have remembered that the housemaid had told her that the spirit of the cave always intimated by roaring his desire to put an end to an interview which he thought had lasted sufficiently long. At any rate, he was successful in getting rid of his visitors on the present occasion, and the countess made the best of her way home and related what had happened with great satisfaction.

Of course there was no doubt as to obeying the commands of the spirit of the cave, for as commands they were considered by her to whom they were addressed. Every retainer, therefore, was summoned to attend on the morrow, and every hound that could be produced was to be pressed into the service. Owing to the poverty of the count, his band of retainers had dwindled down to a very small number, and neither in dress, arms nor discipline were they such as befitted a nobleman of his rank and position. But, after all, a hunting expedition was not quite the same thing as an advance to battle, and neither discipline, arms, nor dress were deemed of much importance on the present occasion. A motley crew assembled at the Count's, or rather, at the Countess's commands, and the dogs were of as mixed and curious a character as the men, various breeds, from the large boar-hound down to the snapping little mongrel, being represented in that strange pack. But men and hounds mattered but little, so that the three young ladies could be furnished with the excuse for the ride which was to bring them into contact with the head of the House of Grumpelhausen. They were all dressed alike, and each was mounted upon her own steed, for no poverty had prevented the Count from keeping horses for his daughters, though they were not such as he might have preferred had his means been sufficient to enable him to exercise a wider choice. Albertina's sorrel was very old, Gertrude's chestnut was blind of one eye, and Margaret's bay mare was generally lame. This day, however, they were all put in requisition, and the old Countess herself would have mounted a horse too if she could, in order to have seen the result of the undertaking. This, however was impossible, partly on account of her having long given up riding, and partly because there was no fourth horse at her disposal. The only equipage was a gigantic bath-chair, in which she was occasionally drawn about, but rather for appearance than for any other reason, since she could walk as well as most persons of her age, as had recently been shown by her expedition to the cave. However, to put the best possible face upon it, she went out in her bath-chair to see the party start, under the direction of old Karl the huntsman, and having wished them all possible good luck, returned to the castle to await the result of her scheme.

The morning was fine, the scenery beautiful, and the three young ladies remarkably cheerful as they rode forth. I regret to inform my sporting friends that I am unable to give them any such accurate account of the hunting as I could wish to have done. No authentic record of the event has come down to us, and being personally unacquainted with the nature and habits of the wolf, and the particular method adopted in that country for hunting him down, I am unable to invent any details upon the subject. I only know that the hunting party found one wolf, if not more, and, for all I know, a bear or two.

At all events, the hunt went on, and the usual train of circumstances followed, namely, that the young ladies got separated from their retainers, and found themselves riding in the woods, they knew not exactly where. Being bold, high-spirited girls, this accident did not much distress them, but when Albertina's girths broke, Gertrude's chestnut got into a bog from which it could not get out again, and Margaret's bay mare fell so lame that it could not be made to move another inch, things began to look rather serious. The sisters all dismounted and held a serious consultation together.

187

What was to be done? They could hardly pass the night in the forest, for besides the cold and general unpleasantness which would be consequent on such an arrangement, it was possible that some of the hunted wolves might take an unhandsome advantage of their situation, and turn the tables upon them by an evening maiden-hunt, which might amuse them as much as a wolf-hunt had amused the maidens in the morning. But if they did not intend to be the objects of such a pastime for the wolves, it was evident that they must take some immediate action in order to save themselves from such a contingency.

Where should they turn, and what should they do? For a few moments they looked at each other in sad perplexity, and no idea suggested itself to any of the three. They looked first one way and then another, up at the sky (so far as they could see it through the tops of the high trees), and down on the ground, and could see or imagine no way of escape from the fate with which they were threatened.

Suddenly they perceived some object moving among the trees, and in another instant discovered that it was an old, a very old man, The weight of years upon his back, together with a faggot he was carrying, bent him almost double; a long white beard fell forward over his breast, scarcely could he drag one aged limb after the other, and his whole appearance indicated extreme age and poverty combined. As, however, he seemed to be the only living being near them, the sisters lost no time in accosting him, which they did all at once, one asking where they were, another if there was any house at hand, and the third which was the best way out of the forest?

The old man stared from one to another, doubtless surprised at the sight of so much beauty in such a strange and wild place. Then he replied in the feeble and tremulous tones of old age that he could not direct them, but that he was going home, and if they liked to follow him they could do so. As this appeared to be their only chance of escape from the dangerous situation in which they found themselves, the young ladies thankfully accepted the offer, and followed the slow steps of the old peasant through the trees and brushwood as well as they were able.

During their walk he asked them who they were, and how it was they came there, and they, seeing no object in concealment, told him the truth, so far, at least, as concerned their names and rank, and the fact of their having come out to hunt the wolves, for it was unnecessary to let him know that they were hunting a husband also. The old fellow asked them several questions about their family and themselves, all of which they answered with good nature and affability as became noble ladies, and he seemed to be much impressed with their rank and dignity. At last, after having passed for some way through the forest, they suddenly came upon a small cottage built into, and forming part of a wall which seemed to be the boundary of some park or pleasure ground. The old man opened the door of this place and bid them enter, which they accordingly did, and found themselves in a small passage passing quite through the cottage; at the other end of the passage was another door, which stood open, and disclosed a magnificent view beyond.

The sisters all hastened forward immediately, and found that they were looking upon the castle and domain of Baron de Grumpelhausen, which they recognised at once from having seen it at a distance from the river, although the view from thence was so intercepted by thick foliage and large trees, that they had formed little idea of its size and grandeur. It

was very large, very finely situated, very grand altogether, although bearing the unmistakable signs of great antiquity, and an involuntary cry of surprise and pleasure broke from the three sisters as they gazed upon it. The view was indeed lovely, for they had ascended through the woods by an almost imperceptible rise in the ground until they were now nearly on a level with the castle, from which the ground fell away to the river which they saw below, although the trees of course intercepted their view to such an extent that they could only here and there catch the silvery glitter of the water in the distance.

It was, indeed, a beautiful sight, and the view from the castle itself must be still finer. The young ladies turned round to speak to their conductor and guide, but found to their surprise that he had disappeared; not knowing his name, they called him frequently by various different appellations, none of which produced the slightest effect. They searched the cottage to no purpose. It was a very ordinary cottage, with very common furniture, but seemed to contain no living creature of any kind. They went back through the door by which they had entered from the forest, but he was not there, and they stared at each other in the greatest surprise, wondering what the old man's motive could be for deserting them, and that, too, when he might reasonably have expected some reward for the service he had already rendered.

(*To be continued.*)

189

JUNE.

Allegretto. Music by **T. Crampton.**

June the mer - ry, she is here. Hear her ca - rol far and near!

Thir - ty days of per - fect weather! Birds and children glad to - ge - ther!

June the mer - ry wel - come here! Joy and sun - shine with thee bear!

2.

See her flowers fall in showers,
Gay and fair and every where,
On the bushes light the roses,
And the grasses twink with posies.
  June the merry, &c.

3.

Girls and birdies on the bough,
Not a word is heard there now,
Bill and mouth erewhile so merry,
Stuff'd and stain'd with juicy cherry.
  June the merry, &c.

4.

From the tree-top both have sped,
Gone to pilfer strawb'ry bed,
O the joy of sweet June weather,
Birds and children know together.
  June the merry, &c.

189

JOHNNY IN THE GARDEN.

JOHN-NY IN THE GAR-DEN.

FOR VE-RY LIT-TLE FOLKS.

OHN-NY was a round-faced fat lit-tle lad of se-ven years old ; full of fun, and just such a chub-by jol-ly child as a boy of that age ought to be. He lived with his Aunt Nan-cy in a pret-ty coun-try house, with a nice gar-den. Now Aunt Nan-cy was a prim old maid, and though she liked him to a-muse him-self, she could not bear to see him dir-ty or un-ti-dy.

One e-ven-ing in June, when the gar-den was rich in blos-som, and the air full of sweet-ness, when each flow-er and plant seemed blow-ing and grow-ing its ut-most, John-ny stood watch-ing Thom-as, the gar-den-er, wa-ter-ing the flow-ers, and at last could not help ask-ing if he might help him. Now both the gar-den-er and John-ny knew that Aunt Nan-cy would not like it, but the lit-tle boy begged hard, and the gar-den-er gave way, on-ly say-ing, " You must be care-ful, Mas-ter John-ny, how you point the hose, for the wa-ter squirts out a long way."

John-ny took off his jack-et that he might be more like a real gar-den-er, and set to work with a will, only he wa-tered his own legs and feet al-most as much as the flow-ers. Pre-sent-ly Aunt Nan-cy tapped at the draw-ing-room win-dow, but the naugh-ty boy went on with his work, pre-tend-ing not to hear her. Then she came out in-to the gar-den, and Mas-ter John-ny, turn-ing round quick-ly as she ap-proached, ac-ci-dent-al-ly raised the mouth of the hose, and sent a show-er of wa-ter all o-ver her, just as if she had been one of the plants.

She was ve-ry an-gry, as you may sup-pose, and thought at first it had been done on pur-pose ; but John-ny was ve-ry re-pen-tant, and was at last for-giv-en.

PUZZLES.

CHARADES.

1.

My whole is a fruit which doesn't entice,
For, to tell you the truth, it's not very nice.

My first an expression of thanks is reckoned,
Which is lisped by young children to my second,
My third is a covering, thin or thick,
As soft as a plum or as hard as a brick.

2.

My whole you never should forget,
For it is now important,
My first is the way that goods are got,
My second is an insect.

3.

My first is often seen by night,
My whole is seen flying by day,
My second is a fish,
So find me out I pray.

4.

My first is a flower of many a hue,
My second a name well known to you,
My whole is a plant sweet-smelling and green,
Which in our gardens is often seen.

5.

My first is a tree,
My second a joint,
My whole is a town of England.

6.

My first is some animals
You may have often seen,
My second is an entrance
Leading to pastures green.
My riddle is so easy,
I have not the least doubt
But what you may my whole
Quite easily find out.

ENIGMAS.

1.

One fourth of dart, one fourth of cart
And then one fifth of giver,
One fifth of night, one fourth of kite,
My whole will name a river.

2.

One fifth of light, one fourth of dike,
And then one fifth of frown,
One third of pea, one third of sea,
My whole will name a town.

3.

My first is in vanity, not in pride,
My second in river, also in Clyde,
My third is in night, not in day,
My fourth is in spring, not in May,
My fifth is in city, not in town,
My sixth is in smile, not in frown.

HIDDEN RIVERS.

1. The broom is here.
2. The kettle, Gerald, is boiling.
3. Your allowance is due.
4. He sang the ode rightly.
5. Ethel began to cry.

Answers to Puzzles on Page 160.

CHARADES.

1. Harvest-home.
2. Hare-bell.
3. Steeple-chase.
4. Counter-pane.

ENIGMAS.

1. A nail.
2. A coal.

192

HOODIE.

By Mrs. MOLESWORTH, *Author of* "*Hermy*," "*The Cuckoo Clock*," &c.

" The little stars are the lambs, I guess,
The fair moon is the shepherdess."
                                                NURSERY SONG.

FEW mornings after the story telling in the garden, as Miss King was passing along the passage on her way down to breakfast, she overheard tumultuous sounds from the direction of the nursery. She stopped to listen. Various little voices were to be distinguished raised much higher than their wont, and among them, now and then, Martin's rather anxious tones as if entreating the children to listen to her advice.

" I don't care," were among the first words Cousin Magdalen made out clearly, " there isn't two trues, and what I'm telling is real true *true*, as true as true."

193   O

The speaker was Hoodie. Then came the answer from Maudie.

"Hoodie how *can* you?" she said in a voice of real distress. "I think it's dreadful to tell stories, and to keep on saying they're true when you know they're not. It wouldn't have mattered if you had explained it was a sort of fairy story like what Cousin Magdalen told us the other day, for of course that wasn't true either, only in a way it was."

"And Hoodie didn't usplain a bit, not one bit," said Duke virtuously. "Her keeped on saying it were as true as true."

"And we is too little to under'tand, isn't we?" put in Hec. "If Hoodie had toldened us she was in fun——"

"But I *wasn't* in fun, you ugly, naughty, *ugly* boy," retorted Hoodie, by this time most evidently losing her temper. "And if peoples 'zinks so much about trues, they shouldn't vant me to say what isn't true about being in fun when I wasn't in fun. The moon *does*——"

A choky sound was now heard, caused by Maudie's putting her hand over her sister's mouth.

"Hoodie, you're *not* to say that again," she exclaimed, no doubt with the best intention, but with an unfortunate result. Hoodie turned upon her like a little wild cat and was in the act of slapping her vigorously when Miss King hurried into the room.

"*Hoodie!*" she said reproachfully.

Hoodie looked up with a mixture of shame and defiance.

"Oh, Hoodie, I am *so* sorry. I thought you had quite left off everything like that," said her cousin.

One or two big tears crept slowly out of the corners of Hoodie's eyes.

"They shouldn't say I was telling untrue things," she muttered. "'Tisn't my fault."

"Oh! Miss Hoodie," said Martin injudiciously, "how *can* you say so? I'm sure Miss," she went on, turning to Magdalen, "no one said a word to put her out. She was telling fairy stories like, to Master Duke and Master Hec, and they began asking her to explain, and she would say it was quite true, not fairy stories at all. And Miss Maudie just

194

tried to show her she shouldn't say that and then you see, Miss, she flew into a temper."

"What were the stories about, Hoodie?" inquired Miss King, kindly.

Hoodie vouchsafed not a word in reply.

Magdalen glanced at the others.

"*I'll* tell," said Duke. "They was about things up in the sky, you know."

"Angels, do you mean?" said Miss King.

"Oh no, not angels," said Maudie. "It was about the stars and the moon. Hoodie has a fancy——"

"It *isn't* a fancy," put in Hoodie fiercely.

"Hoodie says," continued Maudie calmly, "that the moon and the stars and all of the things up in the sky, know each other and talk to each other, and that she has heard them. The moon takes care of the stars, she says, and early in the morning when it is time for them all to go away the moon calls to them. I mean Hoodie says she does."

"Cos she *does*," replied Hoodie, before any one else had time to speak. "She calls to them and they all come round her together, and then they all go away like a flash—so quick, and it is so bright."

Her funny eyes gleamed up into Magdalen's face. In the interest of what she was telling she forgot her temper.

"Was it that that you saw?" asked Magdalen, gravely. "The flash of their going, I mean?"

"Yes," said Hoodie, "I've seen it lots of times, and I try to keep awake on purpose. It passes—the flash, I mean—it passes by the little window near my head. The little window for seeing up into the sky, you know."

Magdalen nodded her head.

"I know," she said, "I had a window like that in my room when I was a little girl, and I was very fond of it. But I don't think I ever saw the moon and the stars saying goodnight, or good-morning—which is it? And are none of the little stars ever left behind?"

The whole of Hoodie's face lighted up with a smile, but the rest of the faces round Miss King looked grave and rather puzzled. Was she really going to encourage Hoodie in her fancies—thought Maudie and Martin?

"I don't *zink* so," said Hoodie, "but I'll look the next time."

"Cousin Magdalen," whispered Maudie, gently pulling her godmother's dress, "it *isn't* true. You don't want Duke and Hec to think it is."

"I don't think it would matter much if they did," replied Magdalen in the same tone. "Thinking little fancies like that true would do them far less harm than thinking their sister was telling falsehoods. But I will try to explain to Hoodie that perhaps it is better not to say any more about it to the little boys. Only, Maudie dear, I think you are old enough to understand better that Hoodie was not meaning to tell untruths."

"She said she heard the moon and the stars *talking*," remonstrated Maudie.

"Well—what if she did? Many a time when I was a little girl I have thought I heard the wind say real words when I was lying awake in my little bed. Of course I know better now, but so will Hoodie, and if these fancies please her and keep her content and happy, why not leave her them?"

"*Martin* doesn't think so," said Maudie, rather mortified that her efforts to bring Hoodie to a sense of her wrong-doings were so little appreciated.

"Miss Maudie, dear!" exclaimed Martin, "I never said so, I'm sure. I don't think I rightly understood what it was all about. I'm sure I don't want to be sharp on any of you for fancies that do no one any harm. I had plenty of them myself when I was little."

"You see, Maudie, Martin does understand," said Miss King. "I'll try and explain about it better to you afterwards, but just now I really must hurry down to breakfast."

She was turning away when a clamour of little voices stopped her.

"Won't you come back after breakfast, Cousin Magdalen?"

"Oh do tum back."

"It's such a wet day and we've nothing to do, 'cause it's Saturday, and Saturday's a holiday."

"Do you want me to come and give you lessons then?" said Magdalen, mischievously.

Dead silence—broken at last by Duke.

"Couldn't you tum and tell us more stories?"

Magdalen shook her head.

"I haven't got any ready. Truly I haven't," she said. "It takes me a long time to think of them, always. But I'll tell you what we might do. I'll come up after breakfast with my work and you might all tell *me* stories. That would amuse everybody. Each of you try to think of one, but you mustn't tell each other what it is."

Hoodie's face lighted up, but Maudie looked rather lugubrious.

"*I* can't think of one," she said.

"Oh yes you can if you try," said Magdalen cheerfully.

"Must it be all out of my own head?" Miss King hesitated.

"No, if you can remember one that you've read that the others don't know, that would do."

Maudie looked relieved.

"*I* don't need to remember one," said Hoodie. "I know such heaps. My head's all spinning full of them."

"So's mine," said Duke, jumping about and clapping his hands.

"And mine too," said Hec. "Kite 'pinning full."

"What nonsense," said Hoodie. "You *don't* know stories. It's only me that does."

"Hush, hush," said Miss King. "My plan won't be nice at all if it makes you quarrel. Now I *must* run down."

The children were very quiet through breakfast time. Every now and then the little boys leant over across their bowls of bread and milk to whisper to each other.

"Wouldn't that be lovely?" or

"That'd be a vezy pitty story," till called to order by Martin, who told them that spilling their breakfast over the table would not be at all a good beginning to the stories.

"'Twouldn't matter," remarked Hoodie, philosophically. "The cloth isn't clean; it's Saturday you know, Martin."

"Saturday or no Saturday," replied Martin, "it isn't pretty for little ladies and gentlemen to spill their food on the table. And it gets them in the habit of it for when they get big and have their breakfasts and dinners down-stairs."

"Doesn't big people *never* spill things on the cloth ?" inquired Hec, solemnly.

"Mr. Fielding does," said Hoodie. "One day when he was here at luncheon, he was helping Mamma to wine, and he poured all down the outside of her glass. I think he's dedfully ugly. I wouldn't like ever to be a big people if I was to be like him."

"Miss Hoodie," remonstrated Martin, hardly approving of the turn the conversation was taking, "do get on with your breakfast and you'd better be thinking about your stories than talking about things you don't understand."

Hoodie glanced at Martin with considerable contempt.

"I'd like to make a story about Beauty and the Beast," she said. "I know who'd be the beast, but *you* shouldn't be Beauty, Martin."

"Shouldn't I, Miss Hoodie ?" said Martin, good-naturedly. "Miss King would make a nice Beauty, to my mind."

Almost as she spoke the door opened, and Cousin Magdalen re-appeared.

"Children," she said, "your mother says we may have the fire lighted in the billiard-room because it is such a chilly day, so I am going to take my work there and you may all come. Martin will be glad to get rid of you, because I know Saturday's a busy morning for her always."

The news was received with great satisfaction, and before the end of another half hour the four children were all under their cousin's charge in the billiard-room, for an hour or two, greatly to Martin's relief.

"What pretty work you are doing, Cousin Magdalen," said Maudie, stroking admiringly the large canvas stretched on a frame at which Miss King was working.

"I am glad you think it's pretty," said her godmother. "I think it is very pretty ; but the colours are not very bright, and children generally like very bright colours. The pattern is copied from a very old piece of tapestry."

"What's tapestry ?" said Hoodie.

196

"Old fashioned-work that used to be made long ago," said Miss King. "It was more like great pictures than anything else, and such quantities of it were made that whole walls were covered with it. Once when I was a very little girl I slept in a room all covered with tapestry, and in the middle of the night——"

She stopped suddenly.

"*What ?*" said Hoodie eagerly, peering up into her face. "What came in the middle of night ?"

"I didn't say anything came," said Cousin Magdalen, laughing. "I stopped because I thought I could make it into a little story and tell it to you afterwards. But we are forgetting all about your stories. Who is going to begin ? Eldest first—you Maudie, I suppose."

Maudie looked rather melancholy.

"I can't tell nice stories," she said. "I've been thinking such a time, and I can't think of anything except something very stupid."

"Well let us hear it, any way," said her cousin, "and then we can say if it is stupid or not."

"It was a story I read," said Maudie, "or else some one told it me. I can't remember which it was. It was about a very poor little girl—she was dreadfully poor, just as poor as you could fancy."

"No clothes—hadn't she no clothes ?" asked Duke.

"And nucken to eat ?" added Hec.

"Very little," said Maudie. "Of course she had some, or else she would have died. She hadn't any father or mother, only an old grandmother, who wasn't very kind to her. At least she was very old and deaf and all that, and perhaps that made her cross. And the little girl used to go messages for a shop—that was how she got a little money. It was a baker's shop near where they lived, and it was rather a grand shop—only they kept this little girl to go messages, not to the *grand* people that came there, you know, but to the people that bought the bread when it wasn't so new—and currant cakes that were rather stale—like that, you know. And on Sunday mornings she had the most to do, because they used to send a great lot of bread very early to a room where a kind lady had breakfast for a great many poor people—for a treat because it was Sunday. They used to have lots of bread and butter and hot coffee—very nice. And Lizzie, that was the little girl's name, liked Sunday mornings and going with the bread to that place, because it all looked so cheerful and comfortable, and the smell of the hot coffee was so good."

"Didn't they never give her none ? " asked Duke.

"No, I don't think so. At least not before what I'm going to tell you. You should wait till I tell you. Well, one Sunday in winter, it was a dreadfully cold day ; snowing and raining, and all mixed together, and wind too, I think —dreadful cold wind. And Lizzie nearly cried as she was going along to that place. She had such dreadfully sore chilblains on her feet and on her hands too. She got to the place and emptied the basket and she was just coming away at the door, when a carriage came up and she stopped a minute to see the people get out. The first was the lady who gave the breakfast. Lizzie had seen her before, for she came sometimes—not every Sunday, but just sometimes— to see that the breakfast was all nice for her poor people. But this day, after she got out, she turned back to lift a little boy out of the carriage. And Lizzie had never seen this little boy before, because this was the first time he had ever come. His mother had brought him with her for a great treat. He was a very pretty little boy and his name was Arthur, and he was about six, I think it said in the story. The lady went into the room quick without noticing Lizzie, as she was in a hurry not to be late for the poor people, but Arthur stayed behind a minute and stared at Lizzie. She was so very cold, you know, she did look miserable, and then she had cried a little on the way, so her eyes were red.

"Arthur went close up to her, staring all the time. Lizzie didn't mind. She stared at him too. He was so pretty and he had such pretty clothes on. When he got close to her, he looked sharp up into her face and said—

" ' What is you crying for ? '

"Lizzie had forgotten she had been crying,

so she said, 'I'm not crying. I'm only very cold.'

" ' Poor little girl,' said Arthur, ' I'll ask Mamma to give you a penny.'

"He ran after his mother who was wondering what he was staying for, and in a minute he came back again and put a little paper packet into Lizzie's hand.

" ' That's all mother's got in her penny purse,' he said, and he ran off again before Lizzie had time to thank him.

"She was going to open the packet and see how much there was, but just then one of the men who helped to put out the breakfast came past and told her not to loiter about. So she took up her basket and ran away, for people often spoke crossly to her and she was easily frightened. All the way home she kept thinking about her pennies and what she would buy with them, but she didn't open the packet, because the way she had to go there were so many rude boys about that she was afraid they might snatch it from her. And when she got to the shop where she had to take her basket to, the baker sent her another message, so it wasn't till much later than usual that she got home. And all this time she had never opened the packet, at least it said so in the story, though I think *I* would have peeped at it before—wouldn't you, Cousin Magdalen ? "

"I'm not sure," said Magdalen. "I think if one has something nice it is sometimes rather tempting to keep it for a while without looking it all over. It is something to look forward to."

"Yes," said Hoodie. " *I'd* have keepened it for alvays wrapped up, and then I could have alvays thought perhaps it was a fairy thing like."

"You silly girl," said Maudie, "you're always fancying about fairies."

"Maudie, *dear*," said Magdalen, "do try not to say things like that. You are telling the story so nicely and we're all so happy. Please don't spoil it by saying unkind little things."

"I didn't mean to be unkind," said Maudie penitently.

"Pease 'do on with the story," said the little boys.

"Well, when at last she got home, she opened

the little packet," continued Maudie, "and what *do* you think she saw? Instead of two pennies and a halfpenny perhaps, or something like that, there were—let me see—yes, that was it—there were a gold pound, a half-a-crown, and a shilling. Just fancy! Lizzie was so surprised that she didn't know what she felt—she looked at them and looked at them, and turned them in her hand, and then all at once it came into her mind that of course the lady had given her them by mistake, and that she should take them back to her. And she jumped up very quick and said to her grandmother there was another message she had to go, and without thinking anything about whether the lady would still be there or not, off she ran back again to the place where the poor people had their breakfast. She ran as hard as she could, but of course when she got there it was too late—the breakfast was done long ago, and all the people away and the doors locked, and there was no one about at all to tell her where she could find the lady. And Lizzie was so unhappy that she sat down on a step and cried. You see it was such a disappointment, for she couldn't tell how much the lady *had* meant to give her and so she didn't like to take any. Besides she felt that it would be better to give the packet back just as it was, only she had so wanted the pennies, for she never had any. The baker's wife always paid her grandmother, not Lizzie herself, for Lizzie's going messages.

And after she had cried a good while she got up and went home. But just as she got near the baker's shop she thought she might ask there if they knew the lady's name, so she went in to ask. There was no one in the shop but the young woman who helped—the others had gone to church."

"How was it the shop was open, then, as it was Sunday?" asked Magdalen.

"It wasn't open, only there was a sort of door in the shutters that Lizzie always went in and out by on Sunday mornings. I know that, because there was a picture of it—I remember now where I read the story—it was in a big picture magazine when I was quite a little girl," said Maudie. "And this young woman was tidying the shop a little, and just going to shut it altogether when Lizzie went in. She was a

198

good-natured young woman and she looked in the money books for the lady's name, but it wasn't in—only the name of the man the room belonged to where the breakfast was—and then she asked Lizzie what she wanted to know for, and Lizzie told her. The young woman told her she was very silly to think of giving it back. She said to her that certainly the lady had *given* it her, it wasn't even as if she had found it. And Lizzie could not say that was not true, and she felt so puzzled at first that she didn't know what to say. The young woman offered to change it for her so that nobody could wonder how she had got a gold piece, but Lizzie said she would think about it first. And then she went home and thought, and thought, till at last it came quite plain into her mind that though it was true that the lady had given it her, still it was *more* true that she hadn't meant to give it her. And then she didn't feel so unhappy."

Maudie stopped for a moment. It had turned out quite a long story, and she was a little tired.

"And what did she do then? Quick, Maudie," said Hoodie.

"What did her do? Kick, kick, Maudie," said the little boys.

"Hush, children, don't hurry Maudie so. Let her rest a minute," said Cousin Magdalen; "she must be a little tired of speaking so long."

"No, I'm not tired now," said Maudie, "only I want to remember to tell it quite right, and I couldn't quite remember what came next. Any way, she couldn't do anything more that day. But she wrapped up the money again quite safe, and put it in another paper, outside the one it had, and—oh, yes, that was it, she settled that she would wait till the next Sunday, and then stand at the door of the breakfast place to see the lady again. She didn't like telling any more people for fear they might take the money away from her, or something like that, and she couldn't think of anything better to do. Well, the next Sunday morning she took the bread as usual, and then she waited at the door for the lady to come, but she never came. Lizzie waited and waited but she never came, and all the people had gone in and the breakfast was nearly done, but the lady never came. And at last she went and asked somebody if the lady wasn't coming—the woman who poured out the coffee, I think it was—and she told her no, the lady wasn't coming that day, and wouldn't come again for a great long while, because she was going away somewhere a good way off. Lizzie was so sorry, she began to cry, so the woman asked her what was the matter, and she told her, and the woman was so pleased with her for being so honest, that she gave her the lady's address and told her to go at once to the house, for perhaps she wouldn't have gone yet. But it was only another disappointment, for when poor Lizzie got there she found it was all shut up; they had gone away the day before."

"Poor Lizzie," said Magdalen, "what did she do then?"

"Poor Lizzie," said Hec and Duke, "and didn't she never get the real pennies?"

"It wasn't pennies she wanted so much," said Hoodie, "she wanted the lady to know how good she was."

"She wanted to *be* good, don't you think that would be a nicer way to say it, Hoodie?" said Cousin Magdalen. "You see, being so poor, it must sometimes have been very difficult for her not to use any of the money."

"Yes," said Maudie, "it said that in the story. Well, any way she *was* good. She sewed the money up in a little bag and put it in a safe place, and tried not to think about it. And all that winter she kept it and never touched it, though they were very poor that winter. It was so very cold, and poor people are always poorer in very cold winters, Martin says. Often they had no fire, and Lizzie's chilblains were dreadful, for her boots didn't keep out the rain and snow a bit, and often she was very hungry, too, but still she never touched the money. And at last, after a very long time, the winter began to go away and the spring began to come, and the woman who poured out the coffee told Lizzie she had heard that the lady was coming home in the spring. So Lizzie began to wait a little every Sunday morning when she had given in the bread, to see if perhaps the lady would come. She waited like that for about six Sundays, I think, till at

last one Sunday just as she was thinking it was no use waiting any more, the lady wouldn't be coming, a carriage drove up to the door, the very same carriage that Lizzie had seen come there before, and—and—the lady—the real same lady, and the real same little boy, got out! And Lizzie was so pleased she didn't know what to do, for though she had only seen them once before, she had watched for them so long that they seemed like great friends to her. But though she was so pleased, she began all to tremble and at first she couldn't speak, her voice went all away. She just pulled the lady's dress and looked up in her face but she couldn't speak. At first the lady didn't understand, though she was a kind lady she didn't like a dirty-looking little girl pulling her dress, and she looked at her a little sharply. But the little boy understood, and he called out—

"'Oh mamma, mamma, it's the same little girl. Don't you remember? I wonder if she's been waiting here ever since.'

"*That* was rather silly of him; of course she couldn't have been there ever since, but he was quite a little boy. And then the lady looked kindly at Lizzie and Lizzie's voice came back, and she said—

"'Oh ma'am, this is the money you gave me by mistake. I've kept it all this time,' and she put the little packet into the lady's hand. And then something came over her; the feeling of having waited so long, I suppose, and she burst into tears. And what *do* you think the lady did? She was so sorry for poor Lizzie, and so pleased with her, that she actually kissed her!"

"Aczhally *kissed* her," repeated Hoodie, Hec, and Duke. "That dirty girl!"

"No," said Maudie, "she wasn't dirty. She was poor, but she wasn't dirty."

"You said she was, once," said Hoodie.

"Well, I didn't mean dirty, really. I meant she looked so, because her clothes were so old. And any way the lady did kiss her, and then she was so kind. She had never thought of having given Lizzie the money. It was some she had put up to pay a bill with, and she had meant to put it in her other purse, and when she couldn't find it, she thought she had lost it somehow. And though she was sorry, of course it didn't matter so very much. And she said if she had known she would have written a letter to the coffee woman to tell her to spend it for warm clothes for poor Lizzie. But after all, it all turned out nice. The lady was very kind to Lizzie after that, and paid for her going to school and being taught all nice things, so that when she got a little bigger she was a very nice servant. I think it said in the story that she learnt to be a nurse, and she was a very kind nurse always."

"Like Martin ?" said Duke.

"Yes," said Maudie.

"Perhaps she was even kinder than Martin," suggested Hec. "Perhaps she was *awful* kind."

"Nobody could be kinder than Martin, except when we're naughty," said Duke, reproachfully.

"Don't you think we should all thank Maudie for telling us such a nice story?" said Magdalen. "*I* thank her very much."

"So do I," said Duke.

"And me," said Hec.

"And me," said Hoodie, "only I want to tell a story too."

"We're all ready to listen," said Miss King, "but it mustn't be *very* long. I've to go out with your mother this afternoon, so I must write some letters before luncheon. And Hec and Duke have stories to tell, too, haven't they? So fire away, Hoodie."

(To be continued.)

SUMMER-TIME.

In summer-time, in summer-time, How pleasant 'tis to play, In meadows bright with sunshine, And sweet with new-mown hay. To watch the sil-ver fishes Dart in and out the reeds, Or play at hide and seek be-low, A-mongst the dark green weeds. In summer-time, in sum-mer-time, How pleasant 'tis to play, In meadows bright with sunshine, And sweet with new-mown hay.

2.

To sit upon the soft long grass,
And pluck the dear wild flowers,
Or read some tale of fairy-land,
To while away the hours.
In summer-time, in summer,
The whole world seems so gay,
The sunny months they fleetly pass,
And seem like one long day.

In summer-time, &c.

TOO FOND OF WAR.

TOO FOND OF WAR.

EORGE and May are broth-er and sist-er. They love each o-ther dear-ly, and are al-ways to-ge-ther. Their fa-ther, who is dead now, was a sol-dier, and George is to be the same when he is grown up. He de-lights now in no-thing so much as what he calls fight-ing toys. He has quite an ar-my of toy sol-diers, be-sides drums, trum-pets, swords, mus-kets, and pis-tols. May joins in his play, and is al-most as fond of mi-mic war as he is. One day he bought a lit-tle brass can-non ; it was a mo-del of a real can-non, as the shop-man told him, and might be fired off with gun-pow-der. Of course George want-ed to try it, and ask-ed his mam-ma if he might, but she said "No" at once. Then what do you think these naugh-ty chil-dren did? I will just tell you.

George con-trived to get hold of a pow-der flask be-long-ing to the gar-den-er, who some-times shot lit-tle birds that peck-ed at the fruit, and he and May went off to-ge-ther in-to a field be-yond the gar-den. There he load-ed his can-non, cram-ming it full of pow-der, and push-ing a lit-tle stone in at the muz-zle to serve as the ball. Then light-ing a long ta-per, which he had brought out on pur-pose, he fired off his can-non.

There was a loud noise ; the lit-tle can-non burst in-to pieces, and poor May was thrown down by the force of the ex-plo-sion. The sound brought mam-ma to the spot. George was not hurt, but when he saw his sis-ter ly-ing sense-less on the ground, he was bit-ter-ly sor-ry that he had dis-o-beyed mam-ma. May soon got well, but George did not for-get the les-son. So much for being too fond of war !

THE POULTRY YARD.

BY THE AUTHOR OF "AUNT EFFIE'S RHYMES," ETC.

IT was a bright morning that first of July,
When we both sallied forth, little Maudie and I,
The child with a basket slung over her arm,
To gather fresh flowers, and to visit the farm.

And first to the yard where the poultry are kept,
To see how the ducks and the chickens have slept.
" Mr. Cock, did the foxes disturb you last night?"
" Haugh, haugh, little lady, all's right, all's right."

Sir Chanticleer drew up his neck in his pride,
Just glanced at the meek-looking hens at his side,
And spurring his wing with as gallant an air
As a knight could assume to his lady fair.

"Cock-cock; cock-a-doodley-doo," exclaimed he;
"I am lord, I am master of all I can see;
If any one thinks of disputing my right,
I am ready for battle, come on, let us fight."
204

Then up got the gander, and down sat the goose,
He was polished, and oiled, and uncommonly spruce.
"Sir Gander," said I, "do I see you in health?"
He eyed us askance, with a side look of stealth.

Three dubious steps, a deliberate stride,
And a furious rush brought him up to our side,
Where, with shoulders set up, and with head poking down,
He cackled and hissed like an ill-mannered clown.

And poor little Maude, with a wail of dismay,
Took straight to her heels to get out of his way.
Oh, could I but echo his shriekings profuse!
But no one can mimic the screech of a goose.

Then the pigeons came down, and like melody sweet
Was the sound of their wings as they dropt at our feet.
"Cuttery-coo, how do you do,
Turn about, round about, cuttery-coo."

Oh what a quantity pigeons can eat,
As they patter about on their rosy feet.
"Piddy-widdy," said I, "you are eating the best."
"Of course," said the pigeon, "the fowls eat the rest."

The Poultry Yard.

"While you think us greedy, our Father above,
Says wise is the serpent, and harmless the dove,
He knows why we swallow the most and the best,
For the sake of the two little doves in the nest.

For pleasure, for fame, or for profit you seek,
We care for the helpless, the homebound, the weak.
Cuttery-coo, cuttery-coo,
Turn about, round about, do as we do."

A flock of black turkeys, some large and some small,
Had been sunning themselves by the poultry yard wall,
But seeing the poultry yard breakfast begun,
They all started off in a shambling run.

The turkey cock last, in the height of his pride,
Came rolling along with a self-conscious stride,
His great warty face growing fiery and red,
When he saw how the ducks and the chickens were fed.

Little Maudie was watching with childish delight,
A flock of young ducks that were hatched over night;
Snugged up in a corner the little ones lay,
While the good mother duck kept the poultry at bay.

The dear little duckies were huddled together,
Like soft bits of fluff without tail or wing feather,
"Sississy, sississy, dear mother," they cried,
And they kept their beaks warm in the warmth of her side.

When mighty old turkey-cock came on the ground,
Transforming himself to a terrible round,
With circles of feathers all standing on end,
In a temper on which one could never depend.

207

"Stand back, little people," said he, "and give place,
Sir Bubbly-jock needs an unlimited space."
And with a fierce gobblety-gobble, and splutter,
He heltered and skeltered them into the gutter.

But Maudie stretched out her wide skirts at each side
And made a snug nook where the ducklings could hide,
And there sat the little ones safe in the corner,
As snug and as happy as little Jack Horner.

"Peep, weep," said a turkey hen,
"How selfish and thoughtless are women and men!
For pigeons perhaps good enough it may be,
But to think of providing tail barley for me!

When I and my turkey-poults lived in a pen,
It was not long ago," said the querrulous hen,
I used to be fed on delectable messes,
Of meal, and of milk, with chopped nettles and cresses.

Said the guinea fowl, ready as usual and plucky,
"Come-back, come-back, the happy go lucky!
When we desire dainties, my husband and I,
Have to search and to hunt for our ant's egg or fly."

And she gave a loud scream, it was piercing and shrill,
'Tis the way Mrs. Guinea-fowl makes known her will
To her husband, who flew from the woods at her cry,
"Come-back, come-back, here am I, here am I."

Aloft, on his favourite perch on the wall,
Stood the peacock complacently viewing us all,
But the peahen, who thought it her duty to hide,
And to keep out of sight, she was not by his side.

Like an Indian prince in his jewels of state,
He shared not his throne with a beautiful mate,
So the dusky peahen was content to abide,
Unseen, and unheard, like an Indian bride.

The blue and the purple, the green and the gold,
Of the peacock's soft robe was a sight to behold ;
No wonder that even a bird should be vain
Of the fringes that bordered his wonderful train.

"Pea-awe," said the peacock, "pea-awe, pea-awe,
I'm the grandest of monarchs, a prince, a pashaw."
And all of a sudden espying his bride,
He hastened his pace and came close to her side.

"Cock," said the lady, "pea-cock, pea-cock,
You're a handsomer bird than the Bubbly-jock."
"Than the Bubbly-jock ! I should think so," said he ;
"Is that the best praise you can think of for me ?"

Said he, "I'll astonish the lady's weak mind,
And show her my plumage before and behind ;
I'll spread out my train like a circle of glory,
And surely she'll tell me a different story."

So he tucked in his beak, and he set up his crest,
And he smoothed down the plumes of his beautiful breast,
And with one exclamation of pride and delight,
He threw up his train, and turned round to the light.

"Oh where is the peacock ?" said Maude with surprise,
"And what is that curious screen full of eyes ?
He was slender, and long, with a very long train,
Do you think that the beauty will come back again ?"

"Pea-awe," said the peacock, "pea-awe, pea-awe,
I'm the grandest of mortals, a prince, a pashaw."
"At least you're the vainest," said Maudie with glee.
"Can you spare any long peacock's feathers for me ?"

"And now for the garden, dear Maudie," said I,
"It is time we should say to the poultry good-bye."
And the drake said "quake," and the duck said "quack,"
But the guinea-fowls cried "come-back, come-back."

TALKS ABOUT THE MONTHS.

JULY.

By Mrs. GEORGE CUPPLES.

"Then came hot July, boiling like to fire,
   That all his garments he had cast away;
Upon a lion raging yet with ire
   He boldly rode, and made him to obey:
Behind his back a scythe, and by his side
Under his belt he bore a sickle circling wide."

ULY, the second summer month, is generally the hottest in the year, so that we feel we cannot stay in the close towns any longer, but must hasten away to the seaside or to some shady country village. Who can work comfortably when the sky is so azure blue and the earth so full of gleaming flowers, and glancing wings, and beauty and joy on every side? At noon we seek the pleasant shade of the trees, so richly clothed with bright foliage, lying under them, if possible, near a river or brook, watching the trout and other fish jumping to catch the numerous flies and insects of all kinds that are hovering about. How refreshing it is to see the lovely water-lilies in the reedy ponds and streams, or to sit under some high cliff by the sea-shore and watch the waves stealing in round some point, and dashing up against a rock so fresh and cool and white with spray. Perhaps we enjoy it all the more if we listen to the merry shouts of laughter that are coming from the hay-fields, for the farmer is taking advantage of the dry hot day to get in his crops of hay, and to finish the hay-harvest.

In July we are refreshed by cooling and juicy fruits, which fortunately are ripe at the time they are most wanted, such as currants, raspberries, gooseberries, cherries, and strawberries, pleasant and wholesome all of them. The woods and moors are alive with busy groups of young and old, gathering bilberries, cranberries, and other wild berries, to carry to the large towns where they are much sought after. In the early morning, too, the mushroom-gatherers are early astir carefully picking each plant, for they know that if they made any mistake they might poison people if they pulled the wrong fungus.

Why are the ducks and geese so busy poking their bills into the grass instead of swimming about the river? Because they know that the tadpoles have now become young frogs and have quitted the water, and are therefore to be found in thousands in the gardens and fields. The bees are busy too expelling or killing the drones, and the labouring ants are turning out the males and females from their little colonies. The poor males, after being driven away from the nests, wander about for some time and then die, but the female ant scoops out a hole in the ground, and lays her eggs in it. Some hundreds of these are hatched into labourers before winter, when the mother dies.

It is during the sultry weather of July that bathing becomes a refreshing and a healthful exercise. It is a most desirable thing to learn to swim, and as early in life as possible, so that we may have perfect confidence in the water; but we must not try to do it without some instruction, for we cannot support ourselves

in water without practice. No one, therefore, should be tempted by the heat of the weather or by the example of companions, to venture into deep water before he is sure he can swim. Many lives are lost every year for want of due caution in this respect, amongst boys, who rush out of their depth and then loose their self-confidence. In many a pleasant nook the sheep washing is going on this month. It is almost as merry a time as hay-making, for there is a large amount of fun going on as the sheep are dipped and hunted about from one to the other, to be rolled to and fro till they are thoroughly immersed. Now and then the sheep turn wild, and down go the washers in turn, causing a burst of laughter from the spectators. Then the busy time of "clipping" comes a week after, and by night the barn looks like a large wool warehouse, so high rise the piles of rolled up fleeces. The poor little lambs are sadly puzzled at sight of their mothers, and go smelling about them, bleating pitifully, till the mother answers them with her deep "Ma-ba," when the little lambs give a skip and a jump, for they know the well-known voice, and their hearts are glad in spite of the changed appearance of their dams.

This month was named July by Mark Antony, in memory of Julius Cæsar, as a tribute of respect to the man who had performed the great service of reforming the confused and imperfect Calendar. It was his natal month, and he it was who had restored it to thirty-one days. Our Saxon ancestors called it *Hey Monath*, because in this month they mowed their meadows, and made hay. Afterwards they altered it to *Math-Monath*, from the beautiful appearance presented by the fields, which at this season are covered with flowers.

In the beginning of July the bright star Canicula—the Little Dog—is in coincidence with the sun. On this account the time between the 3rd of July and the 11th of August is called Dog-Days. It was formerly believed that this star was the bringer of all sorts of evils when near to the sun. It was said " to make the sea to boil, wine to become sour, dogs to go mad, and all other creatures to languish, while in man it produced fevers and other disorders." These fancies are now in a great measure removed, but to this day magistrates of towns order dogs to be muzzled about the beginning of July, and all stray dogs to be taken by the police and poisoned.

We must not forget to take out with us on the 15th of the month as large an umbrella as we can find, for this is *St. Swithin's Day*, and we may be caught in a very heavy shower. There is a common saying, that if it rain on this day, it will rain for forty days more or less, and without attaching any degree of credit to the legend of St. Swithin, observations on the weather have shown, that if rain does set in about this time, it often continues to fall at intervals for several weeks. This of course depends on natural causes, and has nothing to do with St. Swithin. Still you may like to hear the legend that has been handed down to us from monkish ages.

It was common for the monks to refer almost every appearance or change in the seasons to one saint or another; and it is to this custom that we owe the following story—

St. Swithin, Bishop of Winchester, was a man equally noted for his uprightness and humility. So far did he carry the latter quality, that on his death-bed he requested to be buried not within the church, but outside in the church-yard, on the north of the sacred building. His lowly request was complied with, and in this neglected spot his remains reposed till about a hundred years afterwards, when a fit of indignation seized the clergy at the body of so pious a member of their order being allowed to occupy such a position; and on an appointed day they all assembled to convey it with great pomp into the adjoining cathedral of Winchester. When they were about to commence the ceremony, a heavy rain burst forth, and continued without intermission for the forty succeeding days. The monks interpreted this tempest as a warning from Heaven, and instead of disturbing the remains of St. Swithin they erected a chapel over his grave, "at which many astonishing miracles were performed." From this circumstance arose the popular belief of the anniversary of the attempted translation of St. Swithin; and, says vulgar tradition, for ever after this forty days rain has been renewed.

212

" In this month is St. Swithin's Day,
On which, if that it rain, they say,
Full forty days after it will,
Or more or less, some rain distill.
This Swithin was a saint I trow,
And Winchester's bishop also,
Who in his time did many a feat,
As Popish legends do repeat :
A woman having broke her eggs,
By stumbling at another's legs,
For which she made a woeful cry.
St. Swithin chanced for to come by,
Who made them all as sound or more
Than ever that they were before.
But whether this were so or no
'Tis more than you or I do know.
Better it is to rise betime
And to make hay while sun doth shine
Than to believe in tales and lies
Which idle monks and friars devise."

One thing about St. Swithin we are all glad to hear, that while Bishop of Winchester, through his endeavours great improvements were effected in the city. Several churches were erected, and the Itchin was spanned by a fine stone bridge, the first of its kind which had been seen in these parts.

The 25th of July is dedicated to St. James the Great, the patron saint of Spain. It has always been considered an auspicious day to the Spanish arms. The shrine of St. James at Compostella was a great resort of pilgrims from all parts of Christendom, and the distinguishing badge of pilgrims to this shrine was a scallop shell worn on the cloak or hat. There is a saying that whoever eats oysters on St. James' Day will never want money, and it is curious to think that it is customary to begin eating oysters in London on this day, though they are much dearer than afterwards. There is a custom in London in which we can trace the ancient association of the apostle with pilgrim's shells. In a few days after the 25th, the children of the poor employ themselves in collecting the oyster shells which have been thrown out from taverns and fish-shops, and of these they make piles in various forms. When they have them in nice order in some quiet nook or corner of a court, they stick a candle on the top to be lighted at night, and as you pass along you come upon a group of them who dart out with their importunate claim, "Mind the grotter, please to mind the grotter."

The penny is supposed to be required for the candle, and at a distance of more than 300 years from the Reformation, we have a relic of the habits of our Catholic ancestors still kept up in these little shell grottoes.

The fishermen of Cornwall have been keeping a sharp look-out from the tops of the hills on the coast for the first appearance of the shoals of that migratory fish, the pilchard. They can make out their approach at a great distance by the colour of the waves where they swim, and even before the little grottoes are being raised, every child in the fishing villages is actively engaged in helping to pack and send away this much-prized fish.

You see that in spite of the heat there are busy workers everywhere, who hail this month as much for the work it brings to them, as you do for the holiday season. There are bands of workers out in the turnip-fields hoeing and weeding, and the bird-boys are busy with their wooden rackets defending the corn crops from the birds, and, as we said before, the wild berry gatherers are abroad. The busy song of summer is loud everywhere,

" The smallest breeze can find a tongue :
While insects of such tiny size
Grow teasing with their melodies."

Very few people complain of summer heats, for without them we should want many of those natural productions which add greatly to our comforts; our harvests would fail, our fruits would not ripen, and instead of the country having a luxuriant appearance, which it does in autumn, it would look cheerless and barren if the heat of summer were less than it is. The number of insects in our climate, and the heat we suffer in July, is trifling when compared with that which is seen and felt in the summer of the West Indies. Beetles, scorpions, mosquitos, and hosts of others unknown to us even by name, fill every corner of the houses, whilst the heat of the sun is so intense, that it resembles the suffocating vapour which arises from hot coals. And then think of our delightful cool afternoons and evenings, when the sun declines.

" Noon swoons beneath the heat it made,
And flowers e'en within the shade,
Until the sun slopes in the West,
Like weary traveller glad to rest,
 *   *   *   *
A requiem to the day's decline,
Whose setting sunbeams coolly shine,
As welcome to day's feeble powers
As falling dews to thirsty flowers."

" Hot July brings cooling showers,
Pleasant shades, and leafy bowers."

THE RHINE CASTLE.

By the Right Hon. E. H. KNATCHBULL-HUGESSEN, M.P., *Author of "Uncle Joe's Stories," &c.*

CHAPTER II.

OWEVER, it was useless to speculate and guess on such a subject, and they soon turned themselves to the more practical consideration of what they should do next. The cottage, it was true, was better than the forest as far as

shelter was concerned, but, for all that they could see, it contained not a scrap of food of any description, and they all three began to feel hungry. It was already long past their usual luncheon hour, and their long ride and subsequent walk through the woods, had given all three a good appetite which ought certainly to be satisfied as soon as possible. The question was how this was to be managed, and it was not long before they all three came to the same conclusion.

Why not go boldly up to the castle? Of course they had heard of its being haunted, but that was not enough to stop three high-born ladies, especially when they had had no luncheon. Besides, it was still broad daylight, when no ghosts would be likely to be about. Moreover, this was the castle of the very man whose acquaintance their mother was so anxious they should make, and it really seemed as if the Fates had purposely arranged the matter in order that her wish should be gratified. So gathering up their riding apparel as well as they could, the three young daughters of the House of Stuttenguttenheim tripped lightly over the park, and made the best of their way to the castle of the Grumpelhausen.

As they approached it, they were struck with the grandeur of its position and general appearance, but each girl thought within herself that if *she* were the mistress of the place, it would be smartened up and repaired within a very short time. It certainly required some such process, for it would be no exaggeration to say that in some parts it was positively ruinous. The ivy with which it was covered had grown to an enormous size, and had eaten into and weighed down the wall at many points, whilst the neglect of all repairs during a long series of years had told upon the ancient fabric, and reduced it at certain points to a lamentable state of decay.

Still, there was a good deal of it in sufficiently fair condition, and perhaps after all, things were worse to the eye than in reality, for the walls were so massive that the crumbling away of some of the outside stones still left a good barrier against wind and weather.

The sisters marched boldly up until they came to the drawbridge, over which they passed, and without more ado pulled the handle of the bell which they saw immediately before them. They had scarcely done so when the door was thrown open, and an aged domestic stood before them, clad in faded livery, but evidently in his best dress, prepared to wait at dinner or perform any other similar function which might be required of him. He appeared in no degree asto-

215

nished at the sight of the three ladies, altho' one would have imagined that it was about as unexpected a sight as he could well have seen. He showed, however, no signs of being taken by surprise, but on the contrary, bowed in the most polite and deferential manner, and asked whether they would be pleased to take luncheon at once. As nothing could have been more agreeable to their feelings than this proposal, the sisters readily accepted the invitation, and forthwith entered the castle.

The old servant led the way to a spacious banqueting hall, in the centre of which stood a table, loaded with food of a substantial nature, which was exceedingly tempting to them at that particular moment. Two other servants appeared at the summons of the first, and if they were not quite as polished and handy as pattern London footmen might have been, they performed the duties before them with a cheerful alacrity which atoned for other deficiencies. The three girls were somewhat astonished at finding everything ready for them, but their astonishment did not perceptibly affect their appetites, and they made a hearty meal without the least hesitation or bashfulness, doubtless feeling that either of these would have been entirely out of place.

When they had concluded their repast, the old servant who had first received them respectfully opened a door on one side of the banqueting hall, and held it open for them to pass through, which they accordingly did, and found themselves in a large, rather dark drawing-room, somewhat scantily furnished with heavy, old-fashioned furniture, but possessing as its greatest attraction three windows which commanded the most superb view toward the river. From the middle of these windows the sisters looked out upon the scene with delight, and again the same thought crossed the mind of each, and each fancied herself the happy mistress of that magnificent place. As, however, the master had not appeared, and, as far as matters had yet gone, gave no sign of any intention of appearing, the chance of winning him for a husband was still somewhat remote.

The young ladies began indeed to reflect that they were in a very curious, not to say awkward position. They had left their father's house with no means that they knew of by which to return, and had entered the house of a stranger without having even seen him, partaken of his hospitality with great readiness, and up to that moment had no idea whether he was at home or knew of their coming, or whether when he came home (supposing him to be absent), he would not be excessively annoyed at their intrusion.

As these considerations passed through their heads, they began to feel rather uncomfortable, for the situation was one in which none of them had ever been before, and might at any moment become exceedingly unpleasant. They consulted together as to what they had better do, and at last settled that it would be best to ring the bell and ask whether the master of the house was at home, and if not, when he was expected.

They were on the point of carrying this intention into effect, when the door opened and in walked a respectably dressed old woman, who came up to them, dropped a low curtsey, and asked whether they would like to see their rooms. The sisters were much surprised at the inquiry, which, like the circumstance of their having found luncheon ready for them, seemed to show that they, or some other guests had been expected.

Albertina, therefore, as the eldest, thought herself bound to prevent any possible mistake by asking the old woman a few questions concerning the matter. The servant listened with great respect, but replied that she really knew nothing except that she was directed to prepare for three young ladies that day, and had accordingly done so. No other answer of any sort or description would she give, and all attempts to discover anything about the owner of the castle utterly failed.

The rosy Gertrude tried her hand next, but with no better success, and the lovely Margaret fared no better in the attempt. As, however they had no means of getting home, and must evidently remain where they were for the present, the sisters thought that they could do no better than allow the old woman to show them their rooms as she had offered to do.

They accordingly followed her up a grand

flight of stairs and along several passages until they came to a gallery, into which opened a number of bed-rooms. Into one of these she conducted the young ladies, and they found everything prepared in that and in two adjoining rooms, as if they were expected to occupy them as a matter of course.

The sisters looked at each other in astonishment, and the same thought crossed the mind of each at the same moment. They had no clothes but those they were then wearing! How could they possibly manage? What could they possibly do? Should the Baron suddenly return, all might depend upon his first impressions. A chance which, once taken and properly improved, might lead to the most fortunate and desirable of results, might on the other hand be lost for ever, should the Baron first see them in the costume in which they had traversed the woods, and walked through brake and briar for so long a time.

Never were three young ladies in a more extraordinary position, or one more difficult to extricate themselves from in a manner which should be satisfactory to themselves. However, as the old woman, after respectfully asking them whether they wanted anything, stood waiting for a reply, they thought they could not do better than explain their difficulties to her, and ask her counsel and advice.

She listened with respectful attention, and at once generously placed the whole of her wardrobe at the disposal of the sisters. Unfortunately, however, the aforesaid wardrobe was both limited in its extent, and what there was of it was hardly suitable to the quality of the daughters of the House of Stuttenguttenheim. The garments, in fact, were scanty, and their material coarse, not to mention the trifling inconvenience of their none of them fitting any one of the young ladies, in consequence of having been made for a much smaller person.

They were therefore compelled to reject the proffered kindness of the old domestic, which they did as gracefully as they could, and determined to make the best of it without change of raiment. Fortunately they were dry, so that they ran no risk of cold or rheumatism from damp garments. Moreover, brushes and combs were in their room, by the aid of which, and by assisting each other in tidying their hair, a very few minutes enabled them to present an appearance which, if it was not all that they themselves could have wished, would have been considered eminently satisfactory by the great majority of beholders, especially if the latter had belonged to the male portion of humanity.

Having thus completed their toilet, the sisters thought that it was foolish to remain in their bed-rooms, as it was a fine autumn afternoon, and they had some little curiosity to see the castle and its grounds.

They therefore descended to the drawing-room in which they had previously been, and seeing nobody to either direct or interrupt them, passed thence into a large room adjoining, which appeared to have served, if indeed it did not still do so, as a kind of armoury for the Barons of Grumpelhausen. Upon its oaken walls were hung numerous old-fashioned implements of warfare, helmets, swords, coats of mail, pikes, spears, and a variety of unpleasant weapons of that description. Over the mantelpiece, however, which was a curious specimen of old marble, was the huge picture of an armed man, inclosed in a magnificent and elaborate frame, which was fashioned also of oak, most fantastically carved into the heads of men, horses, and dogs, which ornamented the wall and gave it a somewhat grotesque appearance.

The picture itself was remarkable for nothing but its size, for the subject of it was neither beautiful nor prepossessing, while as a work of art it was below mediocrity. However, when the girls had glanced at the armour which hung upon the walls, and made the natural observation of young ladies in a large room, namely, that if all the rubbish and furniture were cleared out, it would make a capital room for a dance, they approached the mantelpiece and began to examine the picture.

"What a curious old frame" remarked Albertina.

"Yes," chirped Gertrude, "and do look at the heads of the men and animals all round it. How funny they are."

"And how well carved," observed Margaret.

"There is not much beauty in any of them, however," said the elder sister. "I think I never saw such a collection of frights in my life."

"Not more frightful than the old fellow in the picture, though," laughed Gertrude. "He is the ugliest old thing—"

"Thank you!" suddenly said a deep voice which apparently proceeded from the picture which they were thus criticising. The sisters all uttered a slight scream of affright, and hastily retreated several paces from the mantelpiece. "Thank you!" repeated the voice gruffly; "you are rather cool hands, though, to come into a fellow's house and abuse him before his face in this manner."

This remark astonished the girls almost as much as the voice, for they saw nobody, and had certainly abused nobody and nothing but the picture, which could scarcely represent the owner of the castle, as it was evidently that of a man who had lived at least a century before, and was clad in the warlike costume of a period long past. Being richly endowed with the courage of their race, and feeling moreover that politeness required some observation upon their part, they looked at each other for a moment, and then Albertina spoke.

"Sir," she said, ("for your voice lends us to believe that you are a gentleman, although we have not the advantage of seeing you), my sisters and I intended no disrespect to the owner of this beautiful castle, nor were we aware that he was present in the room."

"Well, I didn't say he was," responded the picture. "I'm his great-great-grandfather, though, which comes to the same thing, and you insult him when you abuse me."

The girls were more than ever astonished at this speech, and began to feel rather uncomfortable, as was perhaps not unnatural under the circumstances of the case, which were somewhat peculiar. Things were come to a pretty pass, if you might not express an opinion unfavourable to the personal beauty of a man's great-great-grandfather without being thought to have insulted the man himself, and if the picture of the aforesaid relative resented such a criticism, it was evidently the beginning of a state of things which would render visits to picture galleries extremely delicate undertakings, and prevent a great deal of innocent enjoyment and pleasant conversation about the merits of the pictures. They were at once

217

distressed and alarmed at the occurrence, and Albertina, having regained courage, again addressed the invisible speaker in extenuation of the fault which they seemed to have committed.

"Sir," said she, "believe me when I tell you that we were quite unaware either of your relationship to the owner of the castle, or of your power to understand what we were saying. Had it been otherwise, we should certainly have refrained from making any observations which could by any possibility have wounded the feelings of such a respectable old gentleman."

"Old!" shouted the voice in a tone of anger as she concluded. "What the plague do you mean by calling me old? I died, or rather was killed, before I was fifty, and you don't call *that* old? Time don't count after one's dead, you know, and this happened less than two hundred years ago. And then to call a Baron 'respectable!' 'Respectable' indeed, as if one was a master tailor! Really you ought to know better—you have no manners at all!"

The sisters listened to these words with increased awe and astonishment; they had evidently come into a strange place, but they had never read or heard of a ghost who spoke in so extraordinary a manner, or who made such little mystery about himself, and seemed to be possessed of all the feelings of an ordinary mortal. They began to think that they had better escape from his presence as soon as they could, but did not like to do so whilst he was so angry, nor did Albertina quite relish the idea of his having the last word, which, as is well known, it is the woman's right to have in every controversy. So, in spite of her growing alarm, she once more addressed the picture in these words—

"Really, sir, I sincerely beg your pardon, in my own name and in that of my sisters. We intended no harm and meant no disrespect. If we have done the one, and apparently implied the other, pray forgive us, and attribute our having done so to our ignorance, and not to our design."

"Now you speak well," immediately returned the picture, "and in consequence thereof I will give you some information. The next room is

the tapestried chamber; a visit to it will repay you. Spend ten minutes there, and then go out on the terrace-walk. Proceed to the end thereof, and you will see the whispering grotto. No one comes here without going to see *that*, and you may probably find it useful to do so."

Delighted at the change of tone in which these words were uttered, the three girls all joined in a chorus of thanks to the picture, who, however, said no more, but looked as ugly as ever as he seemed to glare at them out of his frame. They deemed it best to follow his advice as soon as possible, and were not sorry to get away from him, which they did as soon as possible. Opening a door which they supposed to lead to the chamber which he had told them to visit, they judged that they had made no mistake when they found themselves in a spacious apartment, entirely hung round with tapestry of a character marvellous and an appearance richly beautiful.

This they vastly admired, and would probably have stayed much longer than ten minutes in the room, had it not been for the words of the picture, which they feared to disregard, lest he should say or do something disagreeable in consequence. So, having observed glass doors opening from a corridor close to the drawing-room, and evidently leading into the garden, they returned thither, casting furtive looks round at the picture as they hurried through the armoury, not without some apprehension that they might again be accosted by that ghostly voice. The Baron's great-great-grandfather, however, said nothing this time, and the sisters passed through the room, and came to the corridor of which I have spoken.

Sure enough, the glass doors opened on to a short flight of broad stone steps, after descending which, a few steps brought them to the terrace-walk, which was a promenade in front of the castle, commanding a grand view, and terminated at one end by a stone wall which separated it from the park, and at the other by large trees, the commencement of the forest, which approached close to the castle grounds at that part.

But among the trees, which cast their dark shadows over it, was a kind of natural cave or grotto formed in the rock, which at that particular point rose somewhat abruptly for the space of fifty or sixty yards right and left, jutting upon the one side close to the castle walls which were there built upon it. This was doubtless the whispering grotto of which the picture had spoken, and which of course the sisters felt bound to visit, though with a somewhat vague idea of how they might find it useful. However, as they walked on the terrace-walk, they discussed again the nature of their present position.

It was getting late in the afternoon, and they must before this have been missed at home. What steps would their mother take? I do not think they gave their father a thought; *he* would do nothing if left to himself, but wait till they came back of themselves, and perhaps be rather sorry if they never came back at all. But their mother would be anxious. If she knew where they were, she would probably send after them. Unfortunately, however, there was no one whom she could very well send; every possible retainer and every available horse had been taking part in the hunt that day, and fresh men and horses were not to be had for the wishing.

They felt sure that no one could or would look for them until the next day, so that they would certainly have to pass the night in the castle. And even when next day came, how was their mother to discover where they were? This was the subject of their discourse as they slowly advanced towards the grotto, which was an ordinary place enough, with a little fountain at the back, over which a stone nymph presided, holding in her hand a huge stone shell into which the water lazily trickled from the spring in the side of the cave. The floor was paved with small stones, but the whole place had evidently been neglected for many years, and the first thought of the girls was that it had in it the making of a charming summer-house, if properly set to rights, but that at present it bore a somewhat damp and uncomfortable appearance.

They entered it, however, and standing before the fountain, looked around them. As it was rather dark, and there was nothing to see, it is not surprising that they saw nothing. Then they took some of the water in the palms of

their hands, and tasted it. It was cold and pure, as is not unfrequently the case with water taken fresh from a spring in the rock. They bathed their foreheads with it and felt it refreshing, which is also not an uncommon attribute with fluid of this kind. Up to this time they had not spoken since they entered the grotto, but now Gertrude observed with a laugh—

"What a quaint old place! I wonder who made it, and when it was made, or whether it came here naturally, without being made at all!"

Scarcely were the words out of her mouth, before a voice came from the nymph, or from some one close to her, speaking in tones which though low, vibrated through the whole grotto and startled the girls not a little, although they had made up their minds to be startled at nothing else after their extraordinary interview with the picture. And these were the words which the voice spoke, or rather sung to a peculiar tune—

" Three sisters came roaming out into the wood,
    Out into the wood with the hound and horn,
  They thought they would catch if they possibly could,
    A wolf and a husband the very same morn.
  For girls are fair, and lovely, I ween,
    And oftentimes men are uncommonly green,
      And a mother is always crafty !

" The wolves they were wild and ran howling away,
    Ran howling away from the hound and horn,
  And the sisters were forced in the castle to stay,
    In the very same clothes that all day they'd worn.
  For girls are fair, and lovely, I ween,
    And oftentimes men are uncommonly green,
      And a mother is always crafty !

" Three bodies were floating a-down on the Rhine,
    A-down on the Rhine without hound or horn,
  And the father is drowning his sorrow in wine,
    And the mother she wishes she'd never been born !
  For girls are fair, and lovely, I ween,
    But men are not *always* uncommonly green,
      And a mother may be too crafty ! "

As the voice sang these verses, the unhappy girls exchanged looks of horror. Here, in verse sang by some mysterious being, was their mother's plan openly disclosed; a plan in which they had joined, and which really looked contemptible when thus plainly stated by another. Not only so, but if there was any meaning in words, the prophet, or spirit, or wizard, or whatever it was that spoke, clearly intended to state that the result of their attempt to secure the Baron as a member of their family would be their own destruction and the ruin of their parents' happiness. For the "three bodies" evidently referred to themselves, and they began to feel as if they were already in the river.

The prospect before them was certainly not re-assuring, and, so far, their visit to the "whispering grotto" appeared to be anything but useful to them, and thus distinctly to belie the words of the picture. Trembling they stood before the fountain after they had heard the verses which the voice recited, but they had sufficient sense to know that to stand there trembling was of no use whatever. So Margaret, who was supposed to be rather a poet in her way, plucked up courage and thus replied to the invisible speaker of the grotto—

" Three sisters are we : 'tis a true indictment,
Yet what you say we hope, Sir, isn't *quite* meant !
To hunt down wolves, and other forest vermin,
Is what no judge will as a crime determine,
Nor will the law with angry eyes behold us :
We've only acted as our mother told us !
If we are wrong, forgive ! and in forgiving
Say how we may remain among the living.
You frighten us—tho' perhaps you don't intend to,
And drowning is so *very* sad an end, too !"

She spoke, and after a very brief interval of suspense the same voice replied to her appeal in the following words—

" For life, your one remaining hope and chance is
Dependent on the Grumpelhausen's fancies.
By forest-law you're his—and must obey him—
Here none can interfere—no hand can stay him.
Unless he speaks the word and bids them spare you,
The castle goblins will in pieces tear you.
Or, since you've ventured to come here so madly,
You'll starve, or drown, or somehow perish sadly.
If quite submissive to his will and pleasure,
Of mercy you may perhaps obtain a measure.
Some folk he *cannot* spare, but then he *can* some,
Provided they afford sufficient ransom ;
And if you're good and reasonable creatures,
Your case is not without redeeming features—
The Baron's short of servants—wil't annoy you
In scullery or kitchen to employ you ?
Or would you think it better, and a higher place,
To dust the furniture and clean the fireplace ?
220

To do a little wholesome household duty
Will neither hurt your health nor spoil your beauty ;
And if content with work that's thus assigned you,
What matter if your parents never find you ?"

It may be easily supposed that these words were not calculated to restore confidence to the young ladies, to whom there was nothing attractive in the idea either of being drowned, or of becoming household servants to the Baron. What were they to do ? The night was now approaching, no assistance was to be procured, and they saw nothing for it but to return to the castle and make the best of it. Before doing so, however, Margaret fired one parting shot at the spirit of the grotto who had made such unpleasant proposals. With pouting lips and eyes full of tears, she thus made her protest against the treatment with which she and her sisters were threatened—

" Sir Spirit, or by whatsoever name
They call you when at home (it's all the same),
We high-born damsels deem it only right
To tell you that you're very unpolite.
We lost our way, and here for shelter ran,
Thinking your Baron was a gentleman—
And, as I tell you boldly in your grotto
' Noblesse oblige '—a very famous motto.
But if he acts as you suggest he will,
Don't fancy that we then shall think so still ;
His conduct will be infamous and low,
And I, for one, won't fail to tell him so !"

As soon as she had pronounced these words. (which she did with some emphasis), the indignant girl turned round, and the three sisters left the grotto together. With no very pleasant feelings they retraced their steps to the castle, and although they found a repast set out for them in the banqueting hall, none of them felt at all able to do it justice. Their hearts were heavy, and full of direful and sad forebodings. And in this state we must unfortunately leave them, whilst we return to the home which they had quitted on the morning of this eventful day.

The old Countess had awaited with much anxiety the result of the hunting excursion, fully relying upon the promise given to her in the cave, and thinking it far from improbable that the Baron de Grumpelhausen, having been captivated at first sight by the charms of one or other of her daughters, might return with

The Rhine Castle.

them to a family repast after the chase. As the day wore away, she began to wonder why they did not return, and when some of the hunting-party came in, then some more, and gradually most of the retainers found their way home, and none of them could give any intelligence of the young ladies, her anxiety began to take a different turn.

They must have fallen from their horses and been hurt, or they had been seized by robbers, or devoured by wolves, or drowned in the Rhine. Certainly some terrible accident had befallen them, or they must have returned long since. The old lady was in a great state of alarm, and when they went to dinner without their daughters, for the first time for many years, the Count was forced to take three extra bottles of Rhine wine to get rid of the low spirits which such a circumstance produced.

Dinner past—still no daughters—the few people about the house were sent out in every direction, but nobody liked to go far, and nobody found anything. In fact, no news arrived until near sunset, when the three horses came in covered with mire, all more or less lame, and bearing evident marks of having had a rough journey. Then the mother gave way to despair and went at once into hysterics, on partially recovering from which, she clutched her husband's wig from his head, scratched him severely down one side of his face, and said it was all his fault, which the unhappy man did not attempt to deny, although there was not the shadow of a foundation for the charge. Then she wanted everybody to go everywhere at once, and do everything directly, the natural result being that nobody went anywhere or did anything. All was bustle and confusion, however, and nobody had any sleep in the castle that night.

Next morning the same sort of thing went on, the count hiding from his wife in abject terror, whilst she gave all kinds of contradictory orders, and really seemed to be half beside herself with alarm and distress. The only cool head about the place was the maid Dorothy, who was not only comely, as has been said, but had a great deal of common sense about her. Being moreover very fond of the three sisters, she was sincerely distressed at

221

the thought that some evil might have befallen them, and most anxious that nothing should be left undone in order to obtain news of them.

She advised her mistress to send scouts in every direction (though, alas! there were but few to send), and further suggested that she should again consult the spirit of the cave from whom she had previously sought advice. Now this was the more good of Dorothy, inasmuch as she had not at all liked the former expedition, and had no wish to repeat it. But she saw the absolute necessity of doing something, and of employing the superfluous energies of the old Countess during this time of trial, and she therefore urged her to the step.

The old lady, however, flew into a passion at the suggestion, declaring that their misfortune was all because of their taking the spirit's advice, for he it was who had suggested the hunting-party, hinting at "consequences," indeed, but in such a way as naturally led her to suppose they would be such as she should desire, whereas, so far as she could see, they had probably been utterly disastrous.

She abused the spirit in no measured language, loudly declaring that he was no better than an old rascal, who had intentionally misled her, and vowing that she would have no more to do with him. After a while, however, as Dorothy reminded her that they did not actually know that evil had happened to the young ladies, and that it might possibly turn out for the best after all, and the spirit of the cave be less guilty than she supposed, the Countess began to soften down. She could not, however, bring herself to pay a second visit to the cave, and it ended by her requesting Dorothy to go alone, which the damsel did not much fancy, but eventually undertook to do.

That very same afternoon, therefore, the good girl set out, unattended by any one, and unprotected by anything save those invisible beings which always watch over youth, innocence, and beauty, and thus she walked along the banks of the river, and reached the cave in due time without encountering any adventure. She approached the dread spot in the same manner as she had done before when in company with the Countess, entered the cave, walked up

to the big rock, and having been carefully in-
structed by her mistress how to address the
being whom she had come to consult, pronounced these words in a low but firm tone—

" Great sir ! the Countess very much afraid is
Some evil has befallen our young ladies ;
They hunted, yesterday, as you desired,
But were not with us when the day expired ;
And tho' we've searched o'er forest, hill, and plain,
Alas ! they have not yet been found again !
Wherefore I've come to humbly ask for aid,
And pray that succour may not be delayed."

As soon as Dorothy had spoken thus, she
paused for a reply, for which she had not long
to wait. The same voice, proceeding from the
same place, and speaking in the same tone as
before, thus answered her inquiries—

" 'Tis not for man to penetrate
The hidden mysteries of fate,
And yet, fair maid, to thee I'd fain
Thy wishes grant and all explain.
Then listen, maiden, whilst I speak
True words of those for whom you seek.
The sisters, hunting yesterday
Became the Baron's lawful prey,
And in his castle now abide
Upon the lofty mountain side.
The captives of his bow and spear
With whom durst no man interfere."

Dorothy listened to this statement with
equal surprise and regret. She could not help
feeling that the spirit of the cave, though
doubtless an excellent fellow in his own way,
had dealt rather hardly with the family of
Stuttenguttenheim in the present instance. It
was distinctly by his advice that the hunt had
been arranged, and he now seemed to take it
quite as a matter of course that it should have
turned out in the disagreeable manner which
it had done. She was, of course, not aware of
the extreme inaccuracy of the statement that

the sisters were the captives of the Baron's
bow and spear, neither of which articles as we
have seen, had been employed in the matter,
but even if it had really been so, this would
not have absolved the spirit from the grave
charge of having deceived the old Countess to
the destruction of her daughters.

Dorothy felt, therefore, rather indignant at
the cool way in which the invisible being seemed
to take it, and although she was well aware
that individuals of the spirit class have a code
of law and morality peculiarly their own, and
are not amenable to the laws by which the
proceedings of ordinary beings are regulated,
she could not help feeling that this was rather
a special and exceptional case, and that she was
bound to make some sort of protest against the
course which the dread inhabitant of the cave
seemed inclined to follow. So she thought for
a few seconds after the voice ceased, in order
to be sure of her rhymes, and then resumed the
conversation as follows—

" Dread Sir, when here my Lady came with me,
You told us both, as plain as plain could be,
That the young ladies, if they hunting went
Should meet the Baron ; and whate'er you meant,
No man or woman either, in their senses,
Could doubt your meaning as to ' consequences.'
'Twas not that they his captives should be led,
But one of them should capture *him* instead ;
And if the contrary has fallen out,
The fairness of the act I more than doubt.
What can I tell my mistress ? that she err'd
In acting on th' advice which here she heard—
That she, in fact, in your good words believer,
Was only trusting to a gay deceiver ?
It cannot be ! I'm sure you cannot mean
So far the spirit office to bemean,
As thus t'entrap a dame of her position,
And bring her into such a sad condition !
Pray tell her what to do and how recover
Her daughters—even tho' they get no lover ! "

(*To be continued.*)

PICTURE PAGE WANTING WORDS. (FOR PRIZE STORY.)

PUZZLES.

CHARADES.

1.

My first, the name by which are known
The lands which man doth sway;
My second is a common thing,
You meet him every day.
My third, with sails set to the breeze,
Fades slowly from the sight;
My whole directs and rules my first
With subtle unseen might.

2.

My first has neither body nor life,
But still it comes and goes:
And it comes, like Christmas, but once a year,
In the land of eternal snows.
Under my pleasant second I sat,
To make myself cool I reckoned;
But I snored away as my first came on,
For my first is nothing but my second.
My whole is a thing that has substance and life,
Though it never has walked or run;
It is not good to eat, but if eat it you dare,
Your career, like my puzzle, is done.

3.

What blighted our first parents' innocence,
What caused the flood, what made the nations
burst
All bounds of shame; all wickedness immense,
Are in one name included in my first.
I put my hand into my pocket—oh!
My purse is gone, and in its place, I trow,
My second now has come. No loss 'tis reckoned,
Because my purse held nothing but my second.
My third and last you will find hard I trow,
For metal never is found soft, you know.
My whole some call a Paradise, I own,
But really 'tis an Asiatic town.

4.

My first was on the table, when I sat down to tea,
My second was walking on it and looked so gay
and free;
But now look in the garden, among the pretty
flowers,
My whole is flitting in and out among the rosy
bowers.

ENIGMAS.

1.

My first is in glove, but not in hand,
My second in cornet, but not in band.
My third is in crow, but not in rook,
My fourth is in river, but not in brook,
My last is in wild but not in tame:
Wait just a moment and more I'll explain:
I am twice in you, and once in me.
Once in shrub and twice in tree.
I am once in dog, and once in cat,
Twice in collar, and once in hat,
I am in your garden, house, or book,
And in this one if you look.
I think I've explained enough to you now,
So I'll take up my hat and make my bow.

2.

I am thick, and I'm thin,
Sometimes fit to please a king,
And indeed I am prized by the ladies;
I am green and I'm blue,
And every colour too,
And am almost always present where much
trade is.
If you drop me on the ground,
I break with a sound,
For I'm not very strong, you must know.
Perhaps I am wrong
To say I'm not strong,
For, to break, I must fall or have a blow.

BURIED RIVERS.

1.

The Dutch are an ingenious and industrious
people.

2.

Have you written your French exercise?

3.

Will you send me a letter, John?

4.

Go in by the side entrance.

5.

Did it not blow yesterday?

Answers to Puzzles on Page 192.

CHARADES.

1. Tamarind.   2. Important.   3. Starling.
4. Rosemary.   5. Oakham.   6. Ramsgate.

ENIGMAS.

1. Trent.   2. Lewes.   3. Venice.

HIDDEN RIVERS.

1. Ebro.   2. Eger.   3. Ural.   4. Oder.   5. Elbe.

HOODIE.

By Mrs. MOLESWORTH, *Author of* "*Hermy*," "*The Cuckoo Clock*," &c.

"I almost think a robin
To a fairy I prefer."

HOODIE gazed round her condescendingly.

"I've such lots of stories in my head," she said. "They knock against each other. Well—I think I'll tell you a story of two little goblins. They lived in a star, and they were just e'zackly like each other. As like as two pins, or as like as a pin is to itself if you look at it in the looking-glass. They lived all alone in the star, and all day they stayed asleep like we do all night, but all night they were awake like we are all day, 'cos you see all day the star was shut up—like a shop you know, only with curtains all round—all the stars are shut up like that all day, you know, and at night the moon wakes up and

225   Q

sends round to draw the curtains and all the stars come out, rubbing their eyes."

"They hasn't any hands—how can they rub their eyes?" objected Duke.

"You silly boy," said Hoodie, very sharply. "How do *you* know? You've never been in the stars?"

"But you hasn't neither," he persisted.

"Never mind. I know, and if I didn't I couldn't tell you. That's how people can tell stories. Well, the stars come out, lots and lots of them, and go running about all night, and then in the morning the moon sends round to draw all the curtains again and they're all to go to sleep."

"But some nights the moon isn't there and the stars are there without her. How is that, Hoodie?" said Cousin Magdalen, rather mischievously.

"You think so 'cos you don't know; but I do," said Hoodie, nodding her head sagaciously. "The moon's *always* there, only sometimes she has a cold, and then she wraps up her white face in a shawl and you can't see her."

There was a twinkle of fun in Hoodie's green eyes as she said this that showed her cousin that her little teasing was understood.

"Oh indeed," she said, gravely, "I did *not* know. Thank you, Hoodie, for explaining to me."

"And so," continued Hoodie, "the goblins never saw anything of day things, but they saw very funny things at night when they went sailing about on the star."

"Stars don't go sailing about," objected Maudie. "They're always quite still."

"They're *not* then," said Hoodie, "that shows you don't listen, Maudie. I heard Papa say one day that the stars are going as fast as fast, only they go *so* fast that we can't see them."

"What nonsense! Isn't it nonsense, Cousin Magdalen?" pleaded Maudie.

"No," said Miss King. "It is true they are moving faster than we can even fancy, but the reason we can't see them moving isn't *exactly* what Hoodie says."

"What is it then?"

"I can't explain it to you just now—it would not be very easy for you to understand,

and if I explained it, it would take too much time and we shouldn't hear the rest of Hoodie's story. I think we should let poor Hoodie go on with her story now without interrupting her any more."

Hoodie required no further bidding.

"Well," she said, "all night long the goblins went sailing about in the star and sometimes they saw very funny things. They were up so high that they could look down and see everything, you know. They could see the big ponds up in the sky where the rain is made, and the *awful* big windmills up there where the wind blows from, and the cannons that bum the thunder down."

"Could they——?" began Duke, timidly, and then he stopped.

"Could they what?" said Hoodie rather snappishly. "If peoples interrumpt, I wish they'd finish their interrumpting and not stop in the middle."

"I didn't like to say it," said Duke. "I only wanted to know if they could see right into the middle of the sky where the angels are."

"No," said Hoodie, decidedly, "they couldn't. They was goblins; they wasn't angels at all, so they didn't want to see angels. It isn't that kind of story, Duke— I'll tell you one like that another day—Sunday perhaps. Now I want to go on about the goblins. What they liked best was to peep into the windows and look at people and play them tricks sometimes. They was awful fond of playing tricks; goblins always is. But sometimes they gets tricks played them, and that's what my story's about. There was a window up in a house that they wanted to look in at, but they couldn't ever get quite high enough up, 'cos the window was at the top of the house, you see. It was the window of a witch, but the goblins didn't know that. She was a witch that lived all alone, and there wasn't anything she cared for except playing tricks, she was always playing tricks. She knowed the goblins wanted to peep in at her window, she knowed everything, 'cos that's what it means to be a witch, that and playing tricks. And she set herself to play a trick on the goblins—a reg'lar good trick, 'cos she didn't see what they was always wanting to peep in at her window for."

Hoodie paused for a moment to take breath.

" I *wonder* what the trick was," whispered Duke and Hee under their breath, evidently very much impressed.

" Yes, you may wonder," said Hoodie, majestically. " You'd never guess. Not in a milliond guesses. Well then, one night when the goblins was twisting and turning theirselves about on the very edge of the star, trying to peep in at the window, all of a suddent the witch's house turned right round, so that the window came to the side instead of up at the top, and one of the goblins gave a great jump and screamed out to the other—

" ' I say brother, we can see into the witch's house now.' "

" But you said the goblins didn't know it was a witch that lived there," said Maudie.

" Well, they didn't know *at first*, but when they saw the house turned round, of course they knowed it must be a witch that lived there. Nobody else could turn their house round," said Hoodie, composedly. " And so they both *screamed*, they were so pleased, and all the time the witch was settling about the trick she'd play them. Now I must tell you what the trick was. The witch wasn't all a bad witch—she was a little good too, and there was a little girl lived in the room next to her that liked her very much, 'cos the witch was very good to her and used to tell her funny stories. And that was why the witch didn't want the goblins to peep into her room, 'cos she thought perhaps they'd steal away the little girl for a trick, for she was very often in the witch's room, and goblins is *awful* fond of stealing children and taking them up into the stars to live with them, so she—the witch, I mean—was sure that they'd try to steal her little girl once they saw her. So when the little girl came to see her that night, she made her go to bed in a nice little bed she'd made for her, and told her she was to be quite still, for perhaps a' ogre was coming to see her. The little girl was a little frightened but not very, for she knowed the witch would take

227

care of her even though she knowed the witch had got very funny friends, ogres you know, and black cats that was really fairies, and all creatures like that—it's rather a dedful story, isn't it ?—but you needn't be frightened Duke and Hee, it'll come unfrightening soon. And so the little girl got into the little bed and cuddled herself up just like the witch had told her. And the goblins came sailing and sailing up on the star ; they was working it like, to make it go quick you know, like a boat with men oaring it you know, and they was oaring and oaring so hard, they was as hot as hot. And at last they got the star right up to the edge of the window, but they made a little noise and the little girl was startled and jumped up in bed, just what the witch had not wanted her to do, and the goblins when they saw her forgot all about the witch and called out, ' Oh what a nice little girl to steal,' and they were *just* going to jump in and catch her up and steal her, when—what *do* you think ?—the witch jumped out of the corner where she had been watching them and caught hold of them fast, one in each hand, and put them—where *do* you think ?—one into each of the little girl's eyes ! And they couldn't ever get out again, for there's a fine little glass lid in people's eyes that nobody could open but a witch, and she shut it down on them tight, and there they were ; they couldn't do anything but peep out, and there they were for always, peeping out."

" But didn't it hurt the little girl ? " asked Maudie. " It would hurt dreadfully to have the least thing put in your eye."

" Oh no," said Hoodie, " it didn't hurt her —not a bit—she just thought a fly had tickled her eyes, and she winkled them, and the witch said to her, ' You may come out of bed now, my dear. The ogre won't be coming to-night.' And so the little girl got out of bed, and when she came up to the witch, the witch looked at her and laughed, and the little girl couldn't think what she was laughing at, and she never knowed about the goblins being in her eyes till one day when her little brother was playing with her, he peeped in her face and said, ' I see two goblins in your eyes.' "

" That was me," exclaimed Duke. " It was

one day I looked in Hoodie's eyes and I saw two goblings in 'zem, I did. Hoodie's made the story about me."

"I hasn't," said Hoodie, indignantly. "I've got stories enough without making them about silly little boys like you. Of course you saw the goblins in mine eyes—there's goblins in every little girl's eyes ever since the witch put them into her little girl's. It's comed to be the fashion, and now you know how it was, and that's the end of the story."

"Thank you for telling it, Hoodie," said Magdalen. "We're all very much obliged to you, and another day I hope you'll tell us some more. Now Duke and Hec, are your stories ready?"

Hec looked exceedingly solemn.

"I only know one," he said; "Duke knows lots."

"Well, which of you is going to begin?"

"Hec," said Duke.

"Duke," said Hec.

"Mine isn't ready," said Duke. "Hec, you begin. If you only know one it must be always ready."

"Mine's only about a little dog," began Hec, modestly. "It was a little dog that had only three legs."

"Only three legs!" exclaimed Magdalen. "My dear Hec, are you sure you haven't made a mistake?"

"Sure," said Hec, "the housemaid had broke its leg off a long time ago, when she was dusting the mantelpiece, so the Mamma gave it to the little boy because it was spoilt for the drawing-room. And the little boy was very fond of it—it was made of hard stuff, you know, all white and shiny, and it had blue eyes. It was *very* pretty. Martin told me the story. She knowed the little boy. And one day the little boy lostened the little dog. He always had it on the nursery table at breakfast and dinner and tea; and he used to 'atend to feed it. Sometimes he put it on the edge of his plate, and sometimes if he 'atended it was 'firsty he put it on the edge of the milk-jug. And one day he lostened it. It was there at the beginning of tea he was sure, but at the end it wasn't there. And he looked and looked and looked, but he couldn't find it; and the

228

nurse looked and looked, but she couldn't find it. So the little boy cried. He cried dedfully, but he couldn't find it. And the nurse was vexed 'cos he wouldn't stop crying. She wasn't as kind as Martin. So he had to go to bed crying, and the next morning when he got up he cried again for his little doggie. And his Mamma said she would buy him another, but he didn't care for that. He said he wouldn't like any but his own dear doggie with only three legs. Well, that day they had rice-pudding for dinner. The little boy kept crying even when he was eating his dinner, and they zeally didn't know what to do with him. But what do you think came? He put some pudding in his mouf, and there was somesing hard. He thought it was a stone, and he feeled to see what it was, and it was his little dog that had been cooked in the pudding—aczhally cooked in the pudding."

"Like Tom Thumb," said Magdalen. "Yes it was very funny. But it must have been a very little dog, Hec, to go in the little boy's mouth?"

"Oh yes, littler than Martin's fimble. She showed me," said Hec. "It was quite a little wee doggie. And Martin said it had got into the pudding, 'cos it had been on the edge of the milk-jug and had felled in, and so it went down to the kitchen in the milk-jug, and the cook had put the milk that was over, to make a pudding. The little boy was so dedfully glad, you can't fancy. He never lostened the little dog again, Martin said, and he said he would keep it till he was a big man. That's all my story."

"Thank you, dear. You've told it very nicely. Hasn't he?" said Miss King.

"Very nicely," said Maudie.

But Hoodie tossed her head rather contemptuously.

"*I* like stories that peoples make out of their own heads," she said.

"So do I," said Duke. "I've been making mine while Hec was telling his; I didn't need to listen, for I've heard the story of the little dog before. Now I'll tell you mine. Onst there was a ogre that lived in a castle, and the castle was on the top of a big, big hill—such a awfully big hill that nobody could ever get up it—not the biggest person that ever was made couldn't get up it."

" How did the ogre get up it then ? " said Hoodie.

" He didn't. He'd always been there and he had a' ogre's wife to cook his dinner, and he had a—a—oh yes, I know, he had a awful big billiard-table, and he used to use little boys' heads for the balls," continued Duke, his eyes wandering round the room for inspiration, as he proceeded. " And," he went on, as he caught sight of a large mirror at the end of the room, " he was so big he couldn't get any plates big enough for him to eat off, so he used to have big looking-glasses for plates, and—and—he had a coal-box for a salt-cellar, and when he had a' egg for breakfast he had the shovel for a' egg spoon, and—and—the white muslin curtains was his pocket-hankerwitches, and——" here Duke came to a dead stop, but another gaze round the room provided fresh material, " and," he proceeded energetically, " the Venetian blind sticks was his matches, and his ogre's wife used to wash his hankerwitches in a lake, and that was his basin ; and for soup she used a—oh I don't know what she had for soup—never mind that. But she had beautiful big earrings," his eyes at this moment happening to catch sight of Magdalen's sideface, " beautiful big earrings made of two shiny glass and goldy things for candles, like that one hanging up there, and —"

" You're just making a rubbish story, Duke," said Maudie. " You just put in whatever you see. I don't call that a proper story at all. Is it, Cousin Magdalen ?"

" You're very unkind, Maudie," said Duke, dolefully, before Magdalen had time to reply. " It isn't a rubbish story. I was just going to tell you about one day when the ogre was very hungry——"

" Well, what did he do ? "

" Well," repeated Duke, somewhat mollified, " one day when the ogre was very hungry, he couldn't find nothing to eat, and he said to his wife, ' Ogre's wife, I'll eat *you*, if you don't get me somefin to eat too-dreckly.' And his ogre's wife cried, and she said she'd go to the greenbaker's and see if she couldn't get somefin for he to eat."

229

" Go to the *where*, Duke ? " said Magdalen, looking up from her work.

" To the green-baker's, that's where they sell apples and pears and p'ums," said Duke.

Maudie burst out laughing.

" He means the green-*grocer's*," she said. " Oh, Duke, how funny you are ! "

" And how could the ogre's wife go and buy him things at shops if they were up on the top of a hill so big that nobody could get down ? "

" Oh," replied Duke, " 'cos there was andnother hill just a very little way off that they could get on quite easily, like steps, and there was lots of shops on the nother hill —all kinds."

" All shops for ogreses ? " inquired Hec timidly.

" No, in course not. Shops for proper people. But when the ogre's wife went to buy somfin for him to eat she had to buy a whole shop-ful—lots and lots—but I zink I've toldened you enough for to-day. I must make some more up first."

" Very well, dear, perhaps it will be better, and thank you for what you've told us to-day," said Cousin Magdalen, beginning to fold up her work. " I must try now to get my letter written before luncheon. I hope it's not going to rain all the afternoon."

One or two of the children ran to the window, as she spoke, to examine the state of the clouds. Suddenly, as they stood there, something, a small dark thing, was seen to fall or flutter to the ground, a short way off.

" What was that ? " said Hoodie, whose quick eyes always saw things before any one else.

" What ? " said Duke deliberately.

" Didn't you see something fall, stupid boy ? " said Hoodie politely.

" Yes, I saw somefin, but perhaps it was only a leaf."

" But perhaps it wasn't only a leaf," said Hoodie impatiently. " There now, look there, don't you see it's moving ? Over there by the little fat tree with the spiky leaves—oh, oh, oh ? It's a bird—a poor little innicent bird— that's felled out of a netst," screamed Hoodie, in tremendous excitement, which always upset her English. "Oh, Cousin Magdalen, quick, quick! open the door, do, do, and let Hoodie go and fetcht the poor little bird."

She danced about with impatience, her eyes streaming—for in curious contrast with Hoodie's scant affection for her fellow human beings was her immense tenderness and devotion towards dumb animals of every kind. She "would not hurt a fly" would have very poorly described her feelings. She had been known to nurse a maimed bluebottle for a week, getting up in the night to give it fresh crumbs of sugar—she had cried for two days and a half after accidentally seeing the last struggles of a chicken which the cook had killed for dinner, and had she clearly understood that the mutton-chops she was so fond of were really the ribs of "a poor sweet little sheep," I am quite sure mutton-chops would in future have been cooked in vain for Hoodie.

Cousin Magdalen had not hitherto seen much of this side of the little girl's character, and she looked at her with some surprise, not sure if there was a mixture of temper in all these dancings-about and callings-out. But she came quickly across the room all the same, to the window, or glass door rather, where all the children were now assembled—

"What is it?" she said. "Hoodie, dear, why do you get into such a fuss?"

"'Cos I want to go out and pick up the little bird, poor little innicent thing, that's felled out of the tree. Oh Maudie's godmother, do open the door—quick, quick, and let me out," said Hoodie, still dancing about. "The bird will be lying there thinking that nobody cares."

Magdalen quietly unfastened the door, which was bolted high up, out of the children's reach, and led the way out into the shubbery. The rain had left off, but it had warmed rather than chilled the spring morning air, and a delicious scent of freshened earth met the little party as they came out of the billiard-room. Magdalen would have liked to stand still for a moment and look about her, and enjoy the sweet air, and listen to the pretty soft garden sounds— the crisp crunch of the heavy roller which the

men were drawing over the damp gravel of the drive, the voices, further off, of the school children running home, for it was twelve o'clock,—prettier still, the faint cackles from the poultry-yard, and the twitterings, gradually waking up, of the birds, whose spirits had been depressed by the heavy rain—but where *Hoodie* was, such lingerings by the way must never be thought of! The child darted on the moment the door was opened, and rushed across the grass-plot just in front—heedless of the soaking to which this exposed her feet and legs up to her knees, for the grass hereabouts was allowed to grow wild, and in the corners near the wall was mixed with coarse ferns and bracken, through all of which Hoodie determinedly ploughed her way.

"Oh dear," exclaimed poor Magdalen, "how *silly* I was to open the door! Just look at Hoodie, Maudie. She will be perfectly drenched. Martin really will have reason to think I am not fit to take care of you."

"And she has her *best* house shoes on," said Maudie, lugubriously. "Martin put them on when she made us neat to come down to you, Cousin Magdalen, because one of her common ones wanted stitching up at the side, and Martin always says mirocco shoes never *are* the same again after they get soaked."

"I must go after her, at all costs," said Magdalen, lifting up her long skirts as well as she could to prevent their getting any *more* than their share of drenching. "Now, Duke and Hec, stay where you are, whatever you do, or better still, go back into the billiard-room. I trust you, Maudie, to take care of them. I am afraid their feet are wet already."

"Yes, and Hec gets croup when his feet are wet," replied Maudie, consolingly. "Never mind though, Cousin Magdalen. I'll take him in, and take off his shoes and stockings by the fire and dry them."

"Thank you, dear," said Magdalen, at the bottom of her heart, though she would not have said so to the children, considerably relieved that Martin need not be summoned to the rescue. "She would really feel that I could not be trusted with them, and it would be such a pity, just when I wanted so much

Hoodie.

to bo of use and to help Beatrice." (Beatrice was the name of the children's mother.)

It was no very pleasant business following Hoodie across the long, soppy grass; even if one were quite careless of the effect on one's clothes, the soaking of one's feet and ankles was disagreeable, to say the least. But Magdalen faced it bravely, and found herself at last beside her troublesome charge. Hoodie, not content with having thoroughly drenched her fat little legs and feet in their pretty clothing of open-work socks and "mirocco" slippers, was actually down on her knees in the wet grass, tenderly stroking the ruffled feathers of the little bird whose misfortunes had aroused her sympathy, while tears poured down her face and her voice was broken with sobs as, looking up, she saw her cousin, and cried out—

"Oh Maudie's godmother, him's dead. The innicent little sweet. I do believe him's dead, or just going to deaden. I daren't lift him up. Oh dear, oh dear!"

It was impossible to scold her—her grief was so real; so with one rueful glance at the destruction already wrought on the nice blue merino frock and frilled muslin pinafore, Magdalen set to work to soothe and comfort the excited little girl.

"Hush, Hoodie dear," she said. "You really mustn't cry sb, even if the poor little bird is dead."

"But Hoodie can't help it, for you know, Maudie's godmother, little birds doesn't go to heaven when they's dead—not like good people, you know, so I can't help crying."

To this reason for Hoodie's tears Magdalen thought it best to make no reply, but she stooped down and carefully lifted up the little bird. It was a pretty little creature—its wings and breast marked with delicately shaded colour, though just now the feathers were ruffled and disordered—a very young bird; and Magdalen's country-bred eyes, recognised it at once as a greenfinch.

"Poor little birdie," she said gently, as she held it up to examine it more closely. "I wonder if its troubles are really over," she added to herself softly, not wishing to rouse Hoodie's hopes before she was sure of grounds

231

for them. "No—it is not dead. It certainly is not—only stunned and terrified. Hoodie, the little bird is not dead. Leave off crying dear, and look at it. See, its little heart is beating quite plainly—there now, it is moving its wings. I don't think it is even much, or at all hurt."

Hoodie drew near, her tear-stained cheeks all glowing with eagerness, holding her breath just as she did when her father for a great treat let her peep into the works of his watch.

"Him's not dead," she exclaimed. "Oh, Cousin Magdalen, are you sure him's not dead? Oh, what can we do to make him quite well again?"

She clasped her hands together with intense eagerness, and looked up in Magdalen's face as if her very life hung upon her words.

"It must have fallen out of the nest," said Magdalen, looking up as she spoke at some of the trees near where they stood. "Still it seems fully fledged, and it should be quite able to fly—most likely its parents suppose it is out in the world on its own account by now, and even if we could find the nest, it is pretty sure to be deserted."

"You won't put it back in the netst, Cousin Magdalen—you don't mean that? It wouldn't have nothing to eat, and it would die," said Hoodie, the tears welling up again, for she hardly understood what her cousin was saying.

"No, dear. I don't think it would be any good putting it back in the nest, and it would be very difficult to know which was its nest, there must be so many up in those trees," said Magdalen. "Besides, as you say, it wouldn't get anything to eat, for if all its brothers and sisters have flown away, the parent birds will not return to the nest. No, I think we had better take it into the house and take care of it till it gets quite strong. See, Hoodie, it is beginning to get out of its fright and to look about it."

"The darling," said Hoodie, ecstatically. "It's cocking up its sweet little head as if it wanted me to kiss it. Oh, dear Cousin Magdalen, isn't it sweet? Do let me carry it into the house."

But Magdalen told her it was better to leave

the bird for the present in her handkerchief, which she had made into a comfortable little nest for it, "till we can find a cage for it; there is sure to be an empty cage of some kind about the house. And then we must see if your mother will give you leave to keep it for a while."

"For alvays!" said Hoodie. "I must keep it for alvays, Maudie's godmother. Maudie

has two calanies in a cage, so I might have *one* bird—mightn't I, Cousin Magdalen?"

"We'll ask your mother," repeated Magdalen, afraid of committing herself to a child like Hoodie, who never, under any circumstances, forgot anything in the shape of a promise that was made to her, or had the least mercy on any unfortunate "big person" that showed any signs of "crying off" from such.

(To be continued.)

JACK AND JILL.

Presto.

Jack and Jill went up the hill, To fetch a pail of wat - er;

Jack fell down and broke his crown, And Jill came tumb - ling af - ter.

JACK AND JILL.

TALKS ABOUT THE MONTHS.

AUGUST.

By Mrs. GEORGE CUPPLES.

"Golden wheat and poppies red,
Grow together side by side;
Fruitful corn with drooping head,
Brilliant poppies open wide.
Not the brightest, not the proudest
Are of greatest service here,
But the bowing heads of harvest
That with plenty crown the year."

IIE delightful feature of this month is Corn Harvest, a time for gladness and joy in all the rural districts. For once more has the husbandman's labour been crowned with success, and the bountiful Creator has again provided for the sustenance of all His creatures by causing the earth to produce a number of substances fitted for their food. August is the third of our summer months, and in its begin-

234

ning there is generally very fine weather. The calmest part of our year happens about this time, and it is very favourable for ripening corn and fruit. But though little regular rain falls, and the summer sun dries up the land, the dew gives us plenty of moisture, and on these calm and still nights of August we often find it bathing everything, and making the ground look as if a heavy shower of rain had fallen. How fresh and beautiful the country looks on a calm morning in August, when there has been a copious fall of dew; the rays of the rising sun tinging the dew-drops with the most brilliant colours.

"August brings the sheaves of corn
When the harvest home is borne."

The days are perceptibly shortening, but the sky is blue and clear; and though the sun at noon is strong, there is a light breeze during the day, so that the heat is not so oppressive as during July, and the evenings are delightful. In addition to the wheat, oats, and barley, which are harvested this month, the hops are now gathered. In the English counties in which hops flourish, the hop-gardens present a most animated scene, full of men, women, and children, seated in the open air, busy picking the hops from the long poles that have been pulled up covered with their rich and fragrant burden. The air is full of their merry laughter and the sweet singing of birds, for now it is holiday with all the little songsters, both old and young. Those birds that have their favourite haunts near the moors of the northern counties, will soon have their joy turned to fear and dismay, for the rich sportsmen are already seeing to their guns in readiness for the 12th of the month, when the season for grouse shooting commences. They may try to hide themselves among the long grass or heather, but the sharp noses of the dogs soon sniff them out, and away they go up into the air with a loud whirr, and then snap, bang, and down goes the poor bird, perhaps into the very centre of a "fairy-ring." If the fairies are out dancing round these bright green circles so often seen during the month of August in the fields, how sorry their little hearts must be to see the poor birds laid low. No doubt they

leave the moors as fast as their little legs or wings will carry them, to hide in some of the wild-flowers they find in the woods, till they are driven from there some weeks after, when the pheasant shooting begins. Where will they hide themselves then? perhaps in the water-lilies. No, *they* will all be gone; more likely they will take themselves off to the sea-side, and creep into an empty sea-shell, where they will shake their kind little heads over the cruelty of man, glad in heart that the noise of the waves drowns the sound of the fearful guns.

The month of August has its present name from *Augustus Cæsar*, who took one day from February and gave it to August after Julius Cæsar's death. This great ruler was born in September, but a number of "lucky" things had happened to him in August, so this month has borne his name over since among all nations deriving their civilisation from the Romans. Before this time it had been called Sextilis, or sixth month, because it was the sixth month after March. The Romans dedicated August to Ceres, the goddess of corn, and celebrated it by many games and observances. But in all ages this has been a time of rejoicing, as it is the season of harvest when the fruits of the earth become ripe.

The 1st of August is called *Lammas Day*, a name which has come down to us from Roman Catholic times, when it was customary on this day to offer at the altars of the cathedrals two young lambs. It was one of the four great pagan festivals of Britain, the others being on the 1st February, 1st May, and 1st November. Lammas was a festival to celebrate the first fruits of the earth, and particularly the grain harvest. When Christianity was introduced, the day was still observed on these grounds, and from a loaf being the usual offering at church, the day came to be called Half-mass, and then was turned into Lammas. A relic of the ancient pagan festival, we are told, was practised in Lothian till about the middle of the eighteenth century. From the uninclosed state of the country, the tending of cattle then employed a great number of hands, and the cow-boys being more than half idle, were much disposed to unite in seeking and creating amusement. In each little district, a group of them built, against Lammas-day, a tower of stones and sods in some conspicuous place. On Lammas morning they all assembled, bearing flags, and blowing cow-horns. After a hearty breakfast of bread and cheese, they set out in procession or march, which usually ended in a foot-race for some trifling prize. But as one part of the day's entertainment consisted in one party trying to knock down the towers of stones and sods belonging to another, the consequence was, there was much brawling and quarrelling, which was a thing greatly to be deplored.

The 24th of August was the date of a striking historical event. On this day, in the year 1572, the Massacre of St. Bartholomew took place in France, when upwards of 40,000 persons were barbarously murdered. There used to be a great fair held in London on the anniversary of St. Bartholomew's Day, established for useful trading purposes. The fair was always proclaimed by the Lord Mayor, and there used to be a good deal of fun, for the boys especially, for after the games of wrestling were over in the tents that had been pitched for the accommodation of the people, a number of live rabbits were turned loose among the crowd, and after them the boys ran with many shouts and much laughter, as they tried to catch them. It was a gay time the fair at Smithfield in those old days, lasting at one period for fourteen days when all the theatres in London were closed and the actors and people of all classes flocked there to exhibit and to see the puppets and shows of all kinds, and the most wonderful sights that could be seen, such as wild beasts, learned pigs, giants, dwarfs, mermaids, and many other astonishing things besides.

And as we walk abroad in the lanes and fields during August, what do we see? that all the early flowers are gone, and only sun-flowers, marigolds, amaranths, and dahlias are left, but these are gradually losing their splendour. The ferns, however, are in perfection in August, and afford shelter to many of our smaller quadrupeds and birds. The different sorts of heaths are in flower, and give a rich purple tinge to commons and waste lands.

236

In the beginning of August, the first broods of swallows and martins collect together in large flocks, and fly about in the morning and evening, as if exercising their wings ; great numbers of them are caught by hawks and other birds of prey, which easily carry off as many as they please, for their victims have not got the full command of their wings. The swift, or long-wing, the largest of all the swallows leaves us about the middle of August. These birds are seen soaring high in the air in the still, warm evenings, and as the insects on which they feed, are now becoming scarce, both old and young wing their way to a warmer country in the sunny south.

However bright and warm the weather, we are reminded that summer is very nearly over, and that autumn is approaching, by hearing the singing of the robin-red-breast. It has finished its spring and summer labours, its young are no longer dependent on it, but have left the nest to seek food for themselves ; so, perched on some lofty branch near our habitations. it warbles forth its agreeable song.

All the country seems to be astir gathering in the harvest, and if you pass through a village it seems as if it were deserted totally, for even the babies have been carried off to the wheat-field, and only the very aged are left at home to nod in their chairs, and dream of the days when they too were amongst the busiest and the happiest. It is a season of joyfulness to all, for in spite of the hard work the harvest brings, every one is pleased and glad to be out in the field, sickle in hand. And then to notice the splendid appearance of the harvest moon. No moon during the year can bear any comparison with it. How anxiously does the farmer look out for its rising, for he knows

" If the moon shows like a silver shield
Be not afraid to reap your field,
But if she rises haloed round
Soon you'll tread on deluged ground."

And haven't we all noticed how large and round, and like a silver shield the harvest moon is.

" And lo ! behind yon branching pine,
Broad, red, and like a burning sun,
Comes up the glorious autumn moon,
God's creature, like a thing divine !

The peasant stands beside his door,
  To mark thee in thy bright ascent ;
The village matron 'neath her tree,
  Sits in her simple piety
  Gazing in silent wonderment.
A world self-balanced thou appearest,—
An ark of fire, thou onward steerest
  Thy upward, glorious, course aright ! "

It rises for several nights successively almost at the same time, in all its beauty, immediately after the sun sets. How delightful it is to walk home along the lanes on these clear balmy evenings, with the sounds of voices coming on the still air from the distant fields, making us think of the glad hearts there ; and of our bountiful Creator, how He has provided for the sustenance of all His creatures by causing the earth to produce such a number of substances fitted for their food. And, besides, these long twilight evenings make us think of how highly favoured we are in our own country, for in very hot countries the summer heats are so great, that man cannot labour except in the morning and evening, and if he is long exposed to them, he is liable to die. Travellers there are all obliged to rest during the day, and to proceed on their journey at nightfall. Travelling becomes unhealthy on account of the heavy dews and vapours which then cover the ground. Noon in these places, is almost as still and quiet as in our climate, for both birds and beasts shelter themselves from the intense heat in the densest parts of the woods and forests.

In very cold countries the summer is short, though hot and bright, but nothing is seen of the gradual changes of the seasons as is the case in our country. Winter yields at once to spring, and spring to summer. Budding, leafing, growing, and reaping time are all crowded into three or four months, and the harvest is liable to be destroyed by the return of cold weather even a few days before the usual time. The seasons in our country have, however, been so arranged by God's good providence, that the heat is seldom excessive ; we may almost always bear it with comfort by suiting our dress to it.

" Now Autumn strews on every plain
  His mellow fruit and fertile grain ;
  And laughing plenty crowned with sheaves,
  With purple grapes and spreading leaves,
  In rich profusion pours around
  Her flowing tresses on the ground.
  Oh, mark the great and lib'ral hand
  That scatters blessings o'er the land ;
  And to the God of nature raise
  The grateful song, the hymn of praise."

THE OWL'S GOOD-NIGHT.

THE OWL'S GOOD-NIGHT.

FOR VE-RY LIT-TLE FOLKS.

" OOD-NIGHT, lit-tle child-ren," says old Mr. Owl,
        As he opens his fun-ny big eyes;
        "Be sure you are good, and go to bed soon;
        Then like Owls you will some day be wise.

" Young Owl-ets we man-age with ve-ry great care,
        They sleep when you child-ren a-wake,
But then through the night they are livel-y and bright,
        And sweet sounds of mu-sic they make.

" We think that young Owl-ets are bet-ter by far
        When they spend all the day in their nest,
They might meet rude child-ren and copy their ways;
        To keep out of their path we think best.

" Young Owl-ets, you know, quick-ly learn to obey,
        At their moth-er's com-mands they all fly,
They agree in their homes, do not squab-ble or fight—
        We peck them quite hard if they cry.

" We're su-pe-ri-or, dear child-ren, you plain-ly see that,
        Our young Owl-ets are pat-terns for you;
Per-haps you would scorn to copy young birds,
        But it is the best thing you could do.

" If you're ve-ry good child-ren, some soft moon-light
            night
        I'll just let you say—' How d'ye do,'—
Just peep at my nest; and the Owl-ets, you'll hear,
        Will an-swer ' Tu-whit' and ' Tu-whoo'."

239

LITTLE TROTS.

LITTLE TROTS.

BY THE EDITOR.

T is nearly the end of summer; the heat is intense, the birds are silent, and the fields are rustling with yellow corn ripe for the sickle. Indeed the reapers are already hard at work in some parts of the country : the sun-burnt arms, wielding their sharp reaping hooks, have already laid low millions of heads of heavy wheat and horned barley.

But in the field with which we have to do just now, great kingly golden ears stand proudly yet upon their tall strong stems. So tall, that little Trots, carrying her father's dinner along the field path from the village, is quite overtopped by the large gold tassels, and says to herself—"What a little thing am I!" as the corn, on either side, waves and nods a welcome to her with its myriad heads.

Dear little Trots! She is only five years old, but for wisdom and goodness she might be fifty. Little Trots has many pleasures it is true, but she has her cares as well, for mother is often ailing and Trots is the eldest of four, so perhaps she is more thoughtful than is usual with little persons of her age. At all events she walks along now anything but carelessly; she notices with quite a thoughtful air the pretty wild-flowers in her path. She stops a minute to look at the deep lilac corn-cockles hiding amongst the wheat; at the large ox-eyed daisies as they seem to watch her pass; at the scarlet poppies and the blue cornflowers. Our little maid, too, listens to the murmuring of the great gold-belted humble-bees. The sound seems to her pleasant and summer-like, and summer is really the time of happiness to little village children.

Trots had not reached quite the middle of the field when she saw a great gap where the tall nodding corn had been laid low. As she approached the gap she heard men's voices and exclamations of surprise or dismay : at the same time there was a sudden stop in the swish, swish, of the reaping-hooks. Trots feared there was something the matter, and hurried on as fast as her sturdy little legs could carry her. Reaching the open space she found there was indeed something very sad the matter, for Trots' own dear father was sitting on the stubbly grass almost fainting. His reaping-hook had slipped while he was at work, and he was badly cut above the knee.

The sight of his dear little daughter made poor Edward Marchmont smile in spite of his pain; but the little chubby face he loved so well grew double its length when Trots saw father in such trouble. He cheered her up as well as he could, and one of the other reapers bound up his leg, advising him at the same time to keep quiet, and assuring poor frightened Trots that the wound was not dangerous.

"You make father rest a bit, dear," said the man. Then turning to the wounded man he added; "See, Ted, what a nice dinner your little maid have brought you. Make father eat it, my dear, and then we'll see about helping him home."

Trots seated herself with her quiet old-fashioned air close to her father, and untying her handkerchief produced a delf bowl, whence came a savoury smell. It was a simple dinner enough : a basin of broth containing some fine wholesome potatoes and a very little meat, then there was plenty of bread to make up in quantity. Father enjoyed his dinner in spite of his hurt leg, and the more that little Trots shared it with him.

After dinner, when the other reapers—who had all dined at the same time as Trots and her father—returned to work, Edward Marchmont and his little girl rested a while, lying on

R

a soft piece of grass which skirted the field. The other men had helped him there before dinner. When the poor reaper tried to rise he found that it was impossible for him to get on at all, even with the kind help of his clever little daughter, who, being but five years old, was not quite a Samson.

Edward Marchmont groaned as he felt how stiff his hurt leg was, for he thought of all the dear ones depending upon his labour; and how was he to work for wife and children with such a terrible game leg? Trots had to give her father up to the care of a stronger prop, in the shape of a stalwart Irish reaper, and she ran along beside her father with that peculiar little trot, which had earned for her her nickname—her real name being Susan.

Gloom and trouble overspread the Marchmont cottage when the head of the family returned in such a crippled state. Mrs. Marchmont settled her good man at once in bed, and then leaving the other children in the charge of Trots, with orders to look after them and keep them quiet, so that father might not be disturbed, the anxious wife hurried off to the doctor to beg him to come and cure her husband as quickly as possible. Mother had scarcely left the cottage when little Trots discovered that she had left behind her, in the cornfield, both the handkerchief and the basin in which she carried her father's dinner. She thought to herself that as soon as mother returned she would run back into the field and look for them. When mother did return, however, and Trots heard that the doctor was coming soon she thought she would wait a little longer to hear what he said, and her anxiety was rather relieved when she heard him say that her father would be all right again in three or four weeks if he only had rest in the meantime.

At last when Trots started on her search, the evening was closing in : the shadows had grown long, the air blew freshly on her chubby cheeks, and the reapers had left the field. Neither the handkerchief nor the basin were any longer in the place where they had dined, but she still looked about, thinking that the reapers might have merely moved them out of the way of their work.

Now this field was divided from the next by a small stream, and the footpath was continued over the stream by a plank of wood which formed a sort of rustic bridge, and was reached by a stile. Trots seated herself on this stile, and was still looking about wondering what could have become of the objects of her search, when she caught sight of something glittering in the muddy bed of the stream. She soon clambered down the bank with her sturdy little legs, to see what this shining thing might be, and, when she reached it, found, to her surprise, that it was a purse, the bright steel edges of which had attracted her notice.

Trots had to work hard with her fat little fingers to dislodge the purse which had evidently lain in its muddy bed for some time. She took it up, and examined it, without knowing how it opened ; but she could feel through the leather that it was full of money. Suddenly it seemed to open of its own accord, and showed to her astonished eyes five bright gold pieces besides white money as she called silver.

The first feeling that rose in our little friend's heart was one of pride and joy, at being the lucky finder of such a prize. She knew mother could buy many things they wanted with this money. And, then too, did she not remember father's deep sigh when the doctor told him he would not be able to work for some time, and his sad voice and wistful look when he said, "It is of the wife and children that I think."

Our little friend's first feeling, as I say, was one of joy that father would not need to work, with all these gold pieces. But then came a second thought, and the question arose in her mind, "Whose money is it?" She remembered that her father had once told his wife and children that he had picked up something of value and he had added, "Of course I found out who it belonged to, and returned it." Then somehow a vision of the village church rose up before the little child : she thought of the commandments written on either side the altar, and of all the words of wisdom and goodness she had heard from clergyman and teacher. Small as she was, Trots quite understood the difference between right and wrong.

Little Trots.

"Miss Blanche will tell me what to do," thought little Trots, "I will go to her."

Miss Blanche was the clergyman's daughter, and lived at the Rectory; she was Trots' teacher at the Sunday school.

Off to the Rectory marched the child, important with her new-found treasure, forgetting all about her delf bowl and handkerchief, in her hurry and excitement. Her friend Blanche was at home, and came to her at once. Little Trots explained all the events of the day at great length, and when at last Blanche understood her, she was first filled with sorrow for the poor father, and then with surprise to hear of Trots' lucky find.

"Give me the purse, Trots," said Miss Blanche, "I will ask papa about it."

She left the room but soon returned with the rector, and it appeared that the purse belonged to the rector himself. He had dropped it a few evenings before, when returning from a visit to a sick parishioner. He was pleased with the little child for bringing it, and spoke very, very kindly to her; so kindly that Trots always remembered how kind he was, even when she grew to be a woman.

I need hardly tell you that the five gold pieces in the purse managed to find their way in another shape from the rector's pocket to Trotty's father: for thanks to the care of the rector and his family, the poor man was nursed well, fed well, and his mind was well at ease during the whole time of his lying up with his wounded leg. And all this he owed to his own little Trots who had been such a good and honest little girl.

GRASSHOPPERS.

BY THE AUTHOR OF "AUNT EFFIE'S RHYMES," ETC.

RICKETY-CRACK and away,
Springing about in the hay,
With its legs and its wings
The Grasshopper springs.
Crickety-crack and away.

Camping in sunniest hedges,
Clinging to slenderest sedges,
Springing from narrowest ledges.
Crickety-crack and away.

Every one at its side,
Carries its grasshopper drum,
No one can tell where they hide,
Beating their crickety strum.

Come from the hedges and ditches,
Come from the vetches and twitches,
Come in your green leather breeches.
Crickety-crack and away.

When the cool leaves of the clover
With tiniest dew-drops are spread;
When all the stars, big and little,
Come twinkling out over head,
When, like a wandering rover,
The long reeds and grasses hang over,
Among the green leaves of the clover
The Grasshoppers creep into bed.

There they all sleep and are happy,
Like good little children up stairs,
(Not quite, for the queer little crickets
Omitted the hymn and the prayers,)

Hush, for the Fern-owl is whirring,
Hush, for the Land-rail is burring,
The glorious Nightingale stirring
Our souls with melodious airs.

Only asleep till the twilight
  Creeps up the red clouds in the east,
To open the wonderful skylight
  That rouses the bird and the beast.
Then up start the blithe little crickets
  To welcome the coming of day,
One bound—and they clear the grass wickets.
  Crickety-crack and away.

245

THE RHINE CASTLE.

By the Right Hon. E. H. KNATCHBULL-HUGESSEN, M.P., *Author of "Uncle Joe's Stories," &c.*

CHAPTER III.

HE spoke in an earnest tone, and with a courage which deserved great praise, since she knew that she ran great risk of offending the spirit of the cave in accusing him of having deceived the old countess, as he certainly had done, and if he should become really angry,

there was no knowing whether he might not inflict upon her some disagreeable punishment then and there. But being both courageous and faithful, the fair Dorothy spoke as I have said, and having done so, awaited the reply with heightened colour and beating heart, but quite prepared to take the consequences of her boldness, whatever they might be.

246

In a very short time the voice replied, and that in no angry manner, but in rather a melancholy tone, as that of one who grieved at having offended the person he addressed; these were his words—

" The secrets of the spirit-world are grave ;
In open air or in the sacred cave
They cannot be revealed—yet they exist,
Believe me, maid—and to my counsel list.
Be not too rash the spirits to reprove
(Tho' courage they respect, and beauty love),
But think and know, since thou canst understand,
They hold not fate's decrees within their hand ;
They but interpret things which may be known,
And show what is permitted to be shown.
What chanced on yesterday you know not yet,
And when you know—perchance may not regret—
Then judge not harshly, ere you know the end ;
But would you the imprison'd girls befriend—
There is a way—safe, certain, sure, and true,
And their release, fair maid, depends on you.
Hie to the Baron's castle in the morn
(You need no aid from men with hound and horn),
Demand their ransom boldly, and forsooth,
You'll see I'm only telling you the truth ;
And if the damsels thus you nobly save,
Come here and thank the spirit of the cave ! "

Dorothy paid great attention to this speech, but was rather alarmed at the advice which it contained. She was very ready to do anything in her power to help the Countess to recover her daughters, but at the same time she did not particularly desire to be destroyed in the attempt. She could not but feel, moreover, that if the Baron had really carried off and imprisoned three damsels in his castle, another more or less would probably make no difference to him, and the result of her obeying the directions of the spirit might be that she would share the captivity of the sisters without being of the smallest use to them.

She hesitated for a moment, therefore, as to whether she should not ask whether there was no other way by which their release could be equally well effected, without her being called upon to run what she felt to be a great risk. Remembering, however, that spirits are queer customers to deal with, and that she had certainly obtained direct, positive, and definite information from this one, she deemed it better, on the whole, to be content, and not to go on asking questions which might possibly arouse

him to wrath. Besides, she was nearly at the end of her rhyming powers, and, should she attempt to continue the conversation, and break down in doing so, who could answer for the consequences ? So she murmured a few words of grateful and proper acknowledgment, and forthwith quitted the cave.

It must be confessed that during her homeward walk, sundry doubts arose within the damsel's breast. If the spirit had wilfully misled and deceived the mistress, it was possible that he might be intending to play the same game with the maid. This was not a pleasant reflection, and there was another which she could not help making within herself. Why should she tell the Countess the last advice of the spirit ? He had told her where the young ladies were, which was the particular piece of information, to obtain which she had been sent to the cave; would not the countess be satisfied with this, and was there any occasion to tell her the whole conversation ?

But the thought of concealment was banished as soon as it was entertained, or rather it never was entertained at all, but only flashed across the girl's mind. Dorothy was too honest and truthful to hide anything of the sort, and the very first thing she did when she got back was to seek the presence of her mistress, and give her a full, true, and particular report of everything which had taken place in the cave.

The old lady listened with feelings of a varied character. She was very angry that things had not turned out exactly as she had expected. Still, she could not feel sorry that the Baron's acquaintance had at all events been made, and being of a sanguine temperament, hoped that all would eventually turn out for the best. She would rather that the Baron had himself sent, as a gentleman should have done, to inform the Count and herself of the fact that their daughters were in his castle, and invited them to come there too, and reclaim them in a proper manner.

But as the Baron had taken no step of the kind, it seemed certainly desirable to follow the advice of the spirit, and let Dorothy proceed to the castle in which the poor girls were immured. In fact, there was nothing else to be done, unless the Countess went herself, and in her own opinion this would have been the better and more desirable course, if the spirit had given directions less positive and definite. But if, after having designated one person to perform certain duties, they were undertaken by another, there would be an excuse for the adviser if things went wrong, and it was evidently better to follow implicitly, if at all, the advice which had been given. There was, moreover, something appropriate in the idea of sending a maid to imprisoned young ladies, although indeed the fair Dorothy could hardly be called an ordinary servant, being rather more of a companion to the Countess, and altogether a superior sort of person.

It was very soon settled that she should obey the directions which had been given, and accordingly the next morning she set forth. It had occurred to the mother of the lost damsels that the messenger charged with such an important mission as the recovery of her daughters, should go in proper state, and therefore the family coach of the Stuttenguttenheim's was ordered to be got ready. Unfortunately, however, it was so long since this had been used, that there were considerable difficulties in obeying the order. The wheels refused to act, and the body seemed inclined to come to pieces. So at last they brought out an old cart, into which they yoked an older horse, and in this vehicle Dorothy was driven to the gates of the castle of the Baron de Grumpelhausen, where she alighted and rang the bell, not without some little beating of the heart at a faster rate than usual.

During the interval for which we have left the three sisters to their fate, their adventures had doubtless been of an exceedingly interesting character. But, unluckily, there has never been an account given of them upon which the veracious historian could positively rely. I confess that I have always wondered how they managed without any change of dress, and with no clean things, and can only imagine that the wardrobe of the old woman who had shown them their rooms proved, on closer investigation, to be more ample than had at first appeared to be the case, or that some other female inhabitant of the castle must have turned up to help them.

248

Certain it is, at any rate, that they contrived to get on, somehow or other, and that their imprisonment was not one of a very dreadful character. They were neither starved, drowned, nor tortured, and in some respects had no cause to regret the change from the paternal mansion, since the food was better and more plentiful in their present abode. What little there is to tell, being entirely derived from the gossip of the country afterwards, may or may not be entirely correct, and must be accordingly received with caution.

It is rumoured that the castle nobly vindicated its reputation for being haunted. Strange noises sounded at the most unexpected times and places; white figures peeped round corners suddenly, the rustling of stiff brocade dresses was distinctly heard in passages where nothing was to be seen, and the distant clanking of chains, and groans which were scarcely human, were only too plainly audible in the dead hours of the weary night. But somehow or other the sisters survived it all, and the second morning of their sojourn in the castle found them still alive, and as cheerful as could have been expected under the circumstances.

The odd thing was that the master of the castle had so far never appeared. Save the old retainer who had first received them, and the venerable dame, who turned out to be his wife, they had seen none but domestics of an inferior grade, and no great number of these.

It may be asked why, under these circumstances, they did not attempt to quit the castle. It must be obvious, however, to any one who takes the trouble to think about the matter, that there were evident objections to such a course. Even if no one had offered opposition to such a step, it was not very safe or very pleasant for three young ladies again to traverse the forest unattended, and was a step not to be taken if it could be avoided. Besides this, the words they had heard in the "whispering grotto" had so distinctly informed them that they were prisoners, that it never entered their heads to doubt the fact, and they would probably have waited some days longer before they had become sufficiently desperate to attempt an escape.

They were rather pleased, however, to find

that in spite of the alarming words which had fallen upon their ears, nobody endeavoured to impose upon them the performance of those household duties or menial employments with which they had been threatened. They had, in short, been allowed to do pretty much as they pleased, subject always to those ghostly visits of which I have been unable to obtain an account which I could conscientiously present to the public as undoubtedly accurate.

Upon the morning of Dorothy's arrival the three sisters had breakfasted in the banqueting-hall, and were standing at the bow window of the adjoining room, looking out over the river, when the loud peal sounded at the gate, and their hearts beat high in the hope of deliverance from a situation which was worse from its uncertainty than from anything else. Presently the door opened, and the same old domestic introduced Dorothy into the apartment. With a cry of joy the girls rushed to meet her, and after tenderly embracing her in the delight of seeing a home face again, eagerly asked after the welfare of their parents, whom they naturally imagined to be overwhelmed with grief at their loss.

Having reassured them as far as she was able, the damsel began to question the sisters as to their own condition, and the conference would doubtless have continued for some time, had it not been interrupted by the sudden opening of the door which led into the armoury, and the unexpected appearance of a personage whom they had not yet seen.

It was a tall man who entered, clad in armour from head to foot, as if immediately about to enter battle instead of walking into a room which contained nothing but members of the softer sex, although it may be that he feared an encounter with such more than with mailed warriors.

His head alone was unprotected by warlike or any other covering, so that it could at once be seen that he was a man of middle age, not unprepossessing in appearance, though withal of a somewhat grave and stern aspect, as one who had known and felt something of the cares and troubles of life. His beard cut into a point, hung, as beards not unfrequently do, down upon his breast, adding much to the dignity of his

appearance, and the eagle glance that shot from his proud eye betokened one of noble birth and high position.

He strode forward into the room for several paces, and then halting, looked upon the four damsels who stood before him, marvelling who or what he was. For some moments he regarded them without a word, and then haughtily waving his hand, he thus addressed them.

" I hope, fair dames, that ye find the castle to your liking. In me you behold its owner. But how comes it there are four of you ? I fancied I had but three captives."

At this Albertina immediately interposed.

" We be no captives, Sir Baron," she said, " if that you be Baron, but three maidens who have lost our way in the woods, and taken refuge in your castle. We pray you send us home to our parents, therefore, without delay. This is our mother's handmaid, Dorothy, who has come to fetch us, and is no captive either."

The Baron smiled grimly, but answered in a sportive tone—

" Dorothy, Dorothy, my mother's maid,
　She stole oranges, I am afraid,
　Some in her apron, and some in her sleeve,
　She stole oranges, I do believe."

" Sir ! " cried Dorothy, indignantly stepping forward at this supposed imputation upon her honesty. " I never stole anything in my life, and it's a shame for any one calling himself a gentleman to say so ! "

" *I* never called myself a gentleman," replied the Baron, "inasmuch as a man's own testimony in such a case goes but for little; but, fair maid, I did but quote from an ancient song, and if you ever stole anything it was more likely to be a heart than an orange, and *that* you could not help. No, mistress Dorothy, you are no captive, having come here on a lawful errand. But for these young ladies, who had no business to be hunting in my woods at all, they are certainly my captives, and belong to me absolutely, unless I choose to let them be ransomed."

Margaret's dark eyes flashed fire at these words.

" It is no such thing ! " she said. " Are we in a civilised country, that such claims should be made? What have we done wrong ? What right has any man to capture free-born damsels, and require ransom before he lets them go?"

The Baron again smiled.

"Might, sweet child," he remarked in a sarcastic tone, "has ever prevailed over right in this land; and the will of the Grumpelhausen must not be questioned here. You and your sisters are mine. Ye cannot escape me, and had better submit with patience to the power which you are unable to resist."

"I never heard of such a thing!" cried Albertina, indignantly.

"Probably not," rejoined the Baron; "but we live and learn, you know."

Then little Gertrude took up the discourse.

"Sir," she said, "it is really a great shame for you to treat us thus——"

"Have you been treated badly?" interrupted the Baron.

"No, sir, it is not *that*," replied the girl, "but it is too bad for you to call us captives when you know quite well we are no such thing. Why can't you send us home quietly, like a good respectable baron?"

"But," gravely returned the other, "I never pretended to be a good, respectable baron. Who can have told you such nonsense about me? Good and respectable, indeed! I am the very reverse. A bad, loose-lived, robber-baron if you please, doing what I please and when I please it, restrained by no law, a dealer in unlawful things with unlawful people, a regular demon, if you like to call me so; but good and respectable! not *that* if you please!" and a sardonic smile sat upon his countenance.

The sisters knew neither what to say nor do as they listened to these strange observations of their host. They therefore remained silent, and looked one at the other in dire dismay. Then Dorothy stepped boldly forward and spoke with head erect, and eye that sparkled with honest indignation.

"Sir," she said, "you cannot mean what you say. No true nobleman would capture and detain helpless damsels in the way you threatened but now. Surely you spoke but in jest. Suffer me to take back word to the Countess that her daughters will be speedily restored to her."

"I have never had any other intention," observed the Baron composedly, "as soon as the proper ransom shall be forthcoming. You would not have me give up my prize for nothing?"

And without another word he turned round and re-entered the armoury, closing the door behind him. As soon as he was gone the three sisters fairly broke down and burst into tears. It really seemed as if their hunting expedition would cost them dear, and that their captivity was only at its commencement. What ransom could their father pay? Nothing, as they well knew, which could satisfy the rapacity of the Baron. There seemed to be no way out of the difficulty, and their prospects were as gloomy as well could be the case.

Dorothy, however, did her best to cheer up the poor girls, telling them that when things were at the worst they often mended and took a turn for the better, and exhorting them to keep up their hearts and make the best of it. They dried their tears after a while, being brave damsels, and then held a consultation which lasted several minutes, at the end of which they came to the conclusion that it would be desirable to ascertain what sort of a ransom the Baron would actually take. So they followed him into the armoury, but he was not there, and they knew not where to look for him. Whilst they stood in doubt upon this point, Dorothy walked up to the mantel-piece and began to look at the carving and the picture. As she was contemplating the latter, to her intense surprise a deep voice proceeded from it, and abruptly asked her the question—

"Well, how do you like me?"

Overcome with astonishment (for the sisters had not told her of their conversation with this self-same picture), Dorothy could at first make no reply, upon which the picture, as if impatient of delay, gruffly observed—

"Have not you got a tongue in your head, that you can't answer a civil question? How do you like me?"

"Very much, sir," replied Dorothy, thinking it best to sacrifice truth to politeness at that moment, and making a curtsey to the picture as she spoke.

"I'm glad of that," remarked the picture quietly, "for I like *you*, too—very much."

"Thank you, sir," replied Dorothy, still more surprised and confused, whilst Albertina, Gertrude, and Margaret stood listening in amazement.

"Yes, I do," continued the picture. "You are just the sort of girl I *do* like, to tell the truth."

This repeated assurance of regard on the part of the picture gave Dorothy fresh courage, and she began to think that she might possibly be able to turn it to account in furthering the escape of the three young ladies from the castle. So she looked up at the picture, as if its addressing her had been the most ordinary, every-day occurrence in the world, and making another respectful curtsey, demurely said—

"If you really like me, sir, it would be very kind if you would help me to get my young ladies home, away from this castle and its owner."

"You mean my great-great-grandson," remarked the picture. "Well *that* is easy enough to be accomplished, at all events."

"Please tell me how, sir," asked the girl.

"Why," said the picture promptly, "*you* must take their place, of course. One can see with half an eye that the Baron likes the looks of you, and if you will stay in the castle, there is no doubt but that he will let the three ladies go."

"Oh sir!" replied Dorothy, "how can you say such a thing? I'm sure the Baron would never want a poor girl like me, or count me equal to three such young ladies as these."

"Just you try him," responded the picture, and at the same moment the three sisters all came forward and cried with one voice—

"Oh Dorothy, if you could save us so!"

"What?" asked the poor girl trembling all over, "*I* stay all alone here with this terrible Baron? Why even if he wanted me, I should be frightened to death, and he couldn't *really* want me, you know."

"But his great-great-grandfather wouldn't say so if he didn't," observed Margaret.

"Of course I shouldn't," said the picture.

"I never heard of such a thing," sobbed Dorothy.

"But would you do it to save us, dear, kind, good, sweet Dorothy?" said Gertrude eagerly.

251

"I would do anything for *you*, dear," answered the girl.

"Then do it!" said the voice in a tone more cheerful than it had hitherto used, and at that moment the picture swung round upon hinges moved by hidden springs, and the Baron himself stood before the astonished girls.

"After Dorothy's last speech," said he, "further concealment is unnecessary. I love her, and if she will consent to remain in my castle, it shall be as its Baroness, a position which I am confident she will adorn, and make happy a home which has too long been desolate and lonely. Young ladies, your hunt in the forest will thus have borne good fruit after all, and your excellent mother will have so far carried out her benevolent intentions in providing the Grumpelhausen with a wife."

The girls were all so much amazed as to be unable to speak for some seconds. When they had sufficiently recovered their presence of mind, Albertina replied with a dignity befitting her rank and family.

"Sir Baron," she said, haughtily regarding him, "so that you forward our return to our parents, it is no concern of ours whether you wed or not; and if you are bent on doing so with one beneath your own rank, you could find no better mate than Dorothy."

"That he couldn't, I'm sure!" cried the good-natured Gertrude, and Margaret likewise gravely nodded her assent to the proposition.

Meanwhile the person chiefly concerned in the proposed domestic arrangements of the Baron was perplexed and amazed beyond measure. How, when, and where the head of the House of Grumpelhausen should have seen and taken such a fancy to her, as he had evidently done, was a thought which puzzled her extremely, and the change in her prospects was so great, so sudden and unexpected, that she felt perfectly bewildered.

Had the three sisters resented the proposition of the Baron as in the slightest degree insulting or annoying to themselves, I really believe that Dorothy would not have entertained it for a moment, so fond was she of the young ladies, and so loyally attached to the ancient house of Stuttenguttenheim. But, since their attitude was entirely different, the damsel could not help seeing the advantages which were offered her in the proposed change of her condition. From being the handmaid of the old Countess, loved and trusted indeed, but still a servant, she would be raised to a rank and position superior to that of her mistress, to whom she might still be a useful friend and valuable neighbour. True it was that she did not know much of the Baron, nor had he encouraged her much by the character which he had given himself, but after all, his acts might belie his words, and his decided preference for her was very flattering to say the least of it.

Hardly knowing what to say or do, Dorothy did the most natural thing in the world, namely, burst into tears. The sisters comforted her, and the Baron said all he could think of with the same view, and at last, after sundry denials and doubts, she gave her consent to the settlement of the matter in the manner which he proposed. Upon this the Baron embraced her tenderly, and being a just and impartial man, saluted the three sisters also, one after the other, saying that it was the invariable custom of his family on such occasions.

Thinking it useless to resist, the girls submitted without a murmur, and this ceremony having been completed, the question of their getting home had next to be discussed. The cart which had brought Dorothy was still waiting, and it was agreed that they should all go back in it, Dorothy having stipulated with the Baron that she should accompany them, which he permitted upon her promise being given that their wedding should be very shortly celebrated. The Baron was very anxious to come too, but from this he was dissuaded by Dorothy, who foresaw that his reception by the old Countess might not be exactly what could be wished. In this surmise she was undoubtedly right, as will be seen immediately.

The cart bore its precious burden safely to the abode of the Stuttenguttenheim family, and the parents of the lost damsels were doubtless overjoyed at their return. But no sooner had the old Countess heard the whole story than she flew into a furious passion, calling the Baron every bad name she could lay her tongue to.

What! her peerless Albertina, her sweet

Gertrude, her queenly Margaret, were none of these good enough for his high-and-mighti-ness, but he must take up with a low-born wench, forsooth, who ought to be their scullery-maid! Then she turned upon Dorothy herself, and gave her what she called "a piece of her mind," and a very disagreeable piece it was, too. She accused her of fraud and deception, of having laid herself out to entrap the Baron, and employed her situation about the young ladies as a means to wheedle them out of the position which one of them had a right to expect.

The girls were quite ashamed of this harsh and unjust language, but poor Dorothy bore it meekly, and after the storm was over the old lady relieved herself by a great gush of tears, and was afterwards quieter and more composed. Then she took to declaring that she should never be able to spare Dorothy, and that she must really tell the Baron that she had changed her mind upon the subject of matrimony, and could not agree to marry him.

Dorothy, however, having once given her promise, was determined to keep it, and gently reminded her mistress that, but for this, she would not have recovered her daughters so easily. The latter, too, joined in the opinion that faith must certainly be kept, especially as a contrary course would raise up a powerful enemy to their house in the person of the justly provoked Baron. So the old lady was forced to give in, and a messenger was sent to inform the Lord of Grumpelhausen that he might visit his intended bride when he pleased.

He pleased very soon, and was received by the old Countess with more urbanity than might have been expected. The fact is, that after giving the matter full consideration, the good lady had come to the conclusion that there was more to be gained by being friends with the Baron than by quarrelling with him, and that if she had failed to secure him as a son-in-law, the next best thing was that he should wed some one who was attached to her family. So matters being thus set right, all went smoothly and well, and the wedding was duly celebrated within a very short space of time, for people in those days, and in that part of the world, seldom delayed these matters when they were once determined on.

When the nuptials were over, and she had a little time to think about all that had occurred, Dorothy remembered that upon her second visit to the spirit who had directed the hunt, and afterwards the method by which the lost girls should be recovered, he had intimated that if her attempt succeeded, she should "come and thank the spirit of the cave." Accordingly, having asked her husband's leave overnight, she set off in the morning, alone as before, safely reached the cave, and walking up to the same place as before, thanked the spirit in the following appropriate terms—

"Oh dread inhabitant of this dark cave,
Thou aidest me the missing ones to save.
From servant I've become a noble dame,
And thank you very kindly for the same!"

Immediately the voice answered—

"And dost thou thank me, who hast others saved,
Only alas! thyself to be enslaved,
Tied to a robber-baron for thy life,
And doomed to be his miserable wife?"

At these words Dorothy became very angry, and instantly replied—

"I am not miserable—not a bit—
And, spirit tho' you be, 'tis most unfit,
This charge against my husband dear to bring;
He's *not* a robber sir, nor no such thing;
And if he was, in spite of that, or you,
I'd be to him a loving wife and true."

"I am very glad to hear it," replied the Baron in his natural voice, and suddenly stepped from behind the rock and stood before his astonished wife. Having first reassured her by a tender embrace, he then proceeded to explain to her several things which the accomplished reader has already guessed.

He, the worthy Baron de Grumpelhausen, was the spirit of the cave, as well as of the whispering grotto, and had moreover represented the departed soul of his great-great-grandfather in the recess behind the picture of the latter. A secret passage from the castle communicated directly with the grotto, and by means thereof the Lord of Grumpelhausen had often been able to utter prophecies and commands which were more or less useful to his family and himself.

As to the cave, its mysteries were also well known to his illustrious house. It has been said that the Baron was eccentric, and one of his fancies was to act the part of the spirit of the cave, and amuse himself with the visits paid to it from time to time, by the scattered population around. It was by accident that he was there upon the occasion of the first visit of the old Countess, unless indeed he had received secret intelligence of her coming, and of this I am not certain.

At that time he was very much struck with the appearance of Dorothy, and in fact, fell violently in love with her at first sight. Fate placed in his hands the means of making her acquaintance very speedily, and that, as we have seen, under circumstances which enabled him to prosecute his suit to a successful issue without let or hindrance. So the charming handmaid of the old Countess von Stuttenguttenheim became Baroness de Grumpelhausen in the manner we have seen.

She amply realised the fond expectations of the Baron, and made him an excellent wife. Moreover, in her prosperity she did not forget her old friends. In spite of its ghosts and goblins, she made the castle quite gay with the festivities which she introduced into it. Balls, parties, gatherings for croquet and lawn-tennis, even football and cricket matches, each in the proper season of the year, were arranged by the indefatigable Baroness, and attended by all people for many miles round who were fortunate enough to be upon her visiting list.

The result was natural. The three sisters of the House of Stuttenguttenheim came to all these entertainments, and not only came, but saw and conquered too.

The adorable Albertina married an officer of high rank, who lived but on her smiles. Gertrude went to cheer the home of a merchant of immense wealth, who lavished it upon her with the generosity of devotion, whilst Margaret became the wife of a nobleman of ancient lineage and vast estates, who worshipped the very ground she trod on.

Baroness Dorothy was well satisfied in having promoted these three marriages, and none the less so because the old Countess took the whole credit to herself, and moreover went so far as to state—and that so often that it is charitable to suppose she quite believed it—that to her foresight, advice, and good management was due the marriage of Dorothy herself to the Baron de Grumpelhausen. How she made it out I do not exactly know, but as her doing so satisfied her, and did no harm to anybody else, it did not much matter. At all events, she held and spread abroad this view of the case until the day of her death, which did not occur until she had dandled upon her knees several grandchildren, and told them the adventures of this story with additions and exaggerations which doubtless rendered the narrative attractive beyond measure.

The Count preceded his wife to the family tomb by some years, having eaten unripe pomegranates in larger quantities than prudence would have dictated, and afterwards drank his claret without having the chill taken off. So it took *him* off, and nobody missed him when he was gone. There is very much more to be told about the castle and its inhabitants, but it is well to leave them at the particular point which we have now reached. When people are happily married they like to be left alone sometimes, and so we will leave the Baron de Grumpelhausen and his Dorothy to themselves.

It was a happy match in every respect, and the Baron never had cause to regret the eccentricity on his part which had led to it. The only difficulty I have in saying good-bye to the happy pair is that of drawing a moral from their story. There is one to be drawn, no doubt, but it cannot be that we should all frequent mysterious caves or whispering grottos, because very few of us are ever likely to have the opportunity of doing so. It cannot be to avoid husband-hunting, because, in the result, those who followed this interesting occupation were as well provided for as she who did not, and therefore no particular lesson can be learned upon this point, nor can it be any of those ordinary morals which are drawn from ordinary stories, because this is in fact one of rather an extraordinary character. So I think the best thing to do is to leave the moral alone, and let people try to find one out for themselves if they want one; and if writers of stories would take this course rather oftener than they do, it is my private opinion that they would please their readers a great deal more than they do, and would at the same time save themselves an infinite amount of trouble which produces no adequate result. And with this sentiment I bid farewell to the Baron and Baroness de Grumpelhausen.

(*Conclusion.*)

A MONKEY'S TALE.—In Six Chapters.

1.

Mamma, papa, and little Jock,
A tiny imp without a frock,
Went out one morning for a walk,
And as they went were full of talk.

2.

"What's that!" cried out young Jock's mamma;
"Let's go and see!" said Jock's papa;
And leaping o'er each other's back,
They hasten'd down the stony track.

3.

They soon arrived upon the ground,
Where lay a basket broad and round;
They view'd it both inside and out
And then they pushed it all about.

4.

At last young Jock got shut inside,
"What fun!" his pa and mamma cried;
And as Jock's tail a hole came through,
They pulled it till he screamed "Boo hoo!"

5.

His cries disturbed a dreadful foe,
Who prick'd his ears and said, "Hullo!"
And then, without a moment's pause,
Mamma and pa were in his claws!

6.

Young Jacko in an awful fright,
Within the basket stayed till night;
Then cautiously, I need not say,
He scrambled out and fled away!

PUZZLES.

CHARADES.

1.

My first is very valuable to my second.
My third is always used by my second.
And three combined will make an art.

2.

My first is a preposition.
My second is a temporary habitation.
My third is a pronoun.
My fourth is a preposition.
My whole, if a good one and well kept, is a
first rate thing.

BURIED TOWNS.

1. Burgundy wine is very dear.
2. That is the kettle we sold you.
3. He loses and owns it directly.
4. Does zero mean nothing?
5. Would you like an orange? No: an apple please.
6. Here is an iceberg.

DIAMOND PUZZLES.

1.

1. A consonant.
2. Part of the verb "to be."
3. A ring.
4. A pastime.
5. Plural of an expanse of water.
6. A river.
7. A consonant.

2.

1. A consonant.
2. A useful article of commerce.
3. A set of people inhabiting a country of Europe.
4. A country of Europe.
5. To accomplish.
6. Part of the verb "to be."
7. A consonant.

BURIED RIVERS.

1. He is a dangerous enemy to deal with.
2. Tell the boy never to do such a thing again.
3. Have you finished entirely what I set you about?
4. He sent both a message and a note inviting him to dinner.

SQUARE WORDS.

1.

1. A garment.
2. An imaginary monster.
3. An open space.
4. A farmer's waggon.

2.

1. Gone by.
2. A fruit.
3. A chemical.
4. A sign of grief.

Answers to Puzzles on Page 224.

CHARADES.

1. Statesmanship.
2. Nightshade.
3. Singapore.
4. Butterfly.

ENIGMAS.

1. Vowel.   2. Glass.

BURIED RIVERS.

1. Indus. 2. Exe. 3. Ouse.
4. Dee. 5. Wye.

256

HOODIE.

By Mrs. MOLESWORTH, *Author of* "*Hermy*," "*The Cuckoo Clock*," &c.

CHAPTER IX.—THE GOLDEN CAGE.

"Here secure from every danger,
Hop about, and chirp, and eat."

"YES," repeated Hoodie to herself, as she followed her cousin into the house, "I'll keep the little bird *always*, and I'll teach it to love me; I'll be so *vezzy* kind to it."

And as they entered the billiard-room where, true to her charge, faithful little Maudie was drying and warming the twins' feet by the fire, Hoodie exclaimed with great triumph—

"It's a bird, Maudie, a most *bootiful* bird, and I'm going to have it all for my *vezzy* own and keep it in a cage *always*. Cousin Magdalen is going to ask Mamma. May I go

s

and tell her to come now quick, Cousin Magdalen?"

"No, my dear, certainly not. Your mother's busy and must not be interrupted. You may go and ask for a little milk and a bit of bread, and I'll try if I can make the little bird eat something. It's opening its mouth as if it was hungry. But no—stop, Hoodie. I was forgetting what a state you are in. Maudie, take off her shoes and stockings too—that's a kind little girl. I'll help you in a minute when I've found a safe place for the little bird. There now—that'll do beautifully," as she spoke taking the skeins of wool out of her little workbasket and putting the bird in instead and carefully closing the lid. The children looked on with great interest.

"Is him always to live in zere, Cousin Magdalen?" inquired Hec.

Magdalen was by this time employed in examining into the state of Hoodie's garments. It was rather deplorable!

"It's no good, Maudie," she exclaimed at last. "She must be thoroughly undressed, for she's damp all over. I *must* take her up to Martin—oh dear, what a pity! Just when we had had such a nice morning."

"But it was a vezzy good thing I saw the little bird felling down, wasn't it?" said Hoodie complacently, as she trotted off with her cousin's hand. "And Martin won't 'cold *me*, 'cos it was your fault for letting me go out in the wet; wasn't it, Cousin Magdalen?" she added with great satisfaction.

Magdalen, to tell the truth, found it rather difficult to keep her temper with Hoodie just then.

"*Hoodie*," she said, sharply. "It is not right to speak like that. You *know* you ran away out before I could stop you."

"But if you hadn't opened the door, I couldn't have goned," was Hoodie's calm reply, with mischievous triumph in her bright eyes.

Martin received the misfortune very philosophically—perhaps she was not sorry, at the bottom of her heart, that some one else should have some experience of the trials she had with Hoodie.

"Not that she means always to be naughty,

258

of course, Miss," she explained to Magdalen. "But she's that heedless and tiresome—oh dear! Though one could manage that if it wasn't for her queer temper—*queer* indeed! queer's no word for it."

"Martin, Martin," came in Hoodie's shrill voice from the inner room, where she was sitting, minus the greater part of her attire, while Martin "aired" the clean clothes, unexpectedly required, at the nursery fire. "Martin, you must go down to the kitchen *at oncest*, and get some bread and milk for my bird. I'm going to keep it *always*, Martin, and you mustn't let Duke and Hec touch it never."

"Well, well, Missie, we'll see," said Martin; "you must get your Mamma's leave first, you know."

"By the bye, I'd better go and speak to her about it," said Magdalen. "Shall I tell the other children to come up stairs, Martin? And my poor letter," she said smiling rather dolefully, as she went out of the nursery, "I'll never get it written before luncheon, for I must superintend the feeding of the bird, otherwise the children will certainly kill it with kindness."

Magdalen had a good deal of experience in rearing little birds and little lambs and all such small unfortunates. She had always lived in the country, and having neither brothers nor sisters her tender heart had given its affections to the dumb creatures about her. It was fortunate for the foundling bird that it fell into her hands, as had it been left to Hoodie's affectionate cares its history would certainly have been quickly told. She was very indignant with Magdalen for the very tiny portions of bread and milk, which was all she would allow it to have, and asked her indignantly if she meant to "'tarve" the poor little pet.

"Hush, Hoodie," said her mother, who had come to see the little bird. "If you speak so to Cousin Magdalen I certainly will not let you keep the bird. You should thank her *very* much for being so kind to you and giving up all her morning to you."

Hoodie did not condescend to take any notice of her mother's reproof.

"Hoodie," said Mrs. Caryll, "do you not hear what I say?"

No reply.

"*Hoodie,*" more sternly.

Hoodie looked up at last.

"Mamma dear," she said sweetly, "may I keep the little bird for my vezzy own? Cousin Magdalen said she would ask you if I might."

Her mother looked puzzled.

"If you are good perhaps I will let you keep it," she replied.

Hoodie looked up sharply.

"Did Cousin Magdalen ask you to let me keep it, Mamma?" she inquired.

"Yes," said her mother.

Hoodie turned to Magdalen.

"Thank you, Maudie's godmother," she said condescendingly. "I thought perhaps you had forgotten."

"And you wouldn't thank me till you were sure—was that it—eh Hoodie?" said Magdalen.

One of her funny twinkles came into Hoodie's green eyes.

"I like peoples what doesn't forget," she remarked with a toss of her shaggy head.

Magdalen turned away to hide her amusement, but Hoodie's mother whispered rather dolefully, "Magdalen, was there *ever* such a child?"

And Hoodie heard the words, and her little face grew hard and sullen.

"I'm always naughty," she said to herself. "Naughty when I tell true, and naughty when I don't tell true. Nobody loves me, but I'll teach my bird to love me."

"What is to be done about a cage for this little creature?" said Magdalen, looking up from her occupation of feeding the greenfinch with quillfuls of bread and milk. "Isn't there an old one anywhere about, that would do?"

"I'm afraid not," said Hoodie's mother. "What can we do?"

"Leave it in the basket for the present," said Magdalen. "And—if Hoodie is *very* good, perhaps——"

"Perhaps what?" said Hoodie, very eagerly.

"Perhaps some kind fairy will fly down with a cage for the poor little bird," said Magdalen mysteriously.

Again Hoodie's eyes twinkled with fun.

"*I* know who the kind fairy will be," she said, skipping about in delight. Then suddenly she flung herself upon her cousin and hugged her valorously.

"I do love *you*, Cousin Magdalen," she whispered. "I do. I *do*. And I'd love Mamma too," she added—her mother having left the room—"if she wouldn't *alvays* say I'm naughty."

"But Hoodie, my dear little girl, do you really think you are always good?" said Magdalen.

"In course not," said Hoodie, "but I'm not *alvays* naughty neither."

Just then the luncheon-bell rang and the interesting discussion, greatly, it is to be feared, to Hoodie's satisfaction, could not be continued.

"You're going to be very good to-day, any way, aren't you, Hoodie?" whispered Magdalen as they went into the dining-room, where the children dined at the big people's luncheon.

"P'raps," replied Hoodie.

"Because you know the kind fairy can't give you the cage if you're not," said Magdalen, smiling.

"I forgot about that," observed Hoodie, coolly.

And her behaviour during the meal left nothing to be desired. But to do her justice, her naughtiness did not as a rule show itself in such circumstances, and according to Martin this was the "provokingest" part of it. "That a little lady who could be so pretty behaved if she chose should stamp and scream and rage like a little wild bear"—though where Martin had seen these wonderful performances of little wild bears, I am sorry to say I cannot tell you —*was* aggravating, there is no doubt. And as Magdalen watched Hoodie through luncheon, and saw her pretty way of handling her knife and fork, and noticed how she never asked for anything but waited till it was offered her, never forgot her "if you please's" and "thank you's," and was always perfectly content with whatever was given her, she repeated to herself in other words Martin's often expressed opinion.

" What a nice child she might be! What a nice child she *is*, when she likes! Oh, Hoodie, what a pity it is that you ever let the little black dog climb on to your shoulders or the little cross imps get into your heart! "

Just at that moment Hoodie caught her eye. She drew herself straight up on her chair with a little air of inviting approval.

" Am I not *rezzy* good? " Magdalen could almost fancy she heard her saying, and in spite of herself, she could not help smiling back at the funny little girl.

Luncheon over, the children were dismissed for their walk, for the rain was now quite over and the afternoon promised to be fine and sunny. As they were leaving the room Hoodie threw her arms round Magdalen's neck and drew her head down that she might whisper into her ear.

" Will the fairy come, does you think? " she asked.

" I hope so," said Magdalen, in the same tone; " but Hoodie, you must promise me one thing. You must not touch the little bird while I am away. I have put it on my table in the basket and it will be quite safe there. You may go in to look at it with Maudie, but you must not touch it."

" Won't it be hungry? " inquired Hoodie.

" Oh no, I'll give it a little more before I go out, and then it will be all right till I come in. You promise, Hoodie? "

Hoodie nodded her head.

" P'omise," she repeated.

Magdalen looked after her anxiously.

" Poor little Hoodie," she said to herself, as she watched the neat little figure tripping out of the room. Just then the children's mother came over to her.

" Magdalen, my dear child," she said, " you must not worry yourself about these children. You have been looking quite careworn all the morning, and I can't have it."

" But I wanted to help you with them, so that you might have a little rest and get quite strong again, dear Beatrice," said Magdalen. " You have never been really well since your

illness last winter, and Mamma and I thought I should be able to help you—and—and—" the tears came into Cousin Magdalen's pretty eyes.

" Well, dear, and who could have done more to help me than you, since you have been here? I shall miss you terribly when you go, especially about Hoodie," and in spite of her wish to cheer Magdalen, Hoodie's mother gave a little sigh.

" It was about Hoodie I was thinking," said Magdalen. " I was so anxious to do her good."

" And don't you think you have? "

Magdalen hesitated.

" I don't know. Sometimes I think I have made an impression on her, and then it seems all to have gone off again. She is such a queer mixture—in some ways so old for her age and in some ways such a baby."

" Yes," said Mrs. Caryll. " It is so very difficult to know how to treat her. But she is very fond of you, Magdalen, and I am so glad to see it. We really used to think it wasn't in her to be fond of any one."

" But I am sure it *is* in her," said Magdalen, " only—I hardly can say what I mean—if she could be made to believe that other people love *her*, that she could be of use to others—I think that would take away the sort of defiance and hardness one sees in her sometimes. It is so unlike a child. She is always imagining people don't care for her, and then she takes actual pleasure in being as naughty as she can be."

" Yes," said Hoodie's mother ; " there really are days when she goes out of her way to be naughty, one might say,—when it is enough for Martin to tell her to do or not to do *any-thing*, for her to wish to do or not to do the opposite. Still she *has* been better lately, Magdalen, and it is all thanks to you."

" Poor little Hoodie! " said her cousin, " I wonder why it should be so very difficult for her to be good. But we must get ready now, must we not, Beatrice? And *whatever* I do I must not forget the cage, or any good I can ever hope to do Hoodie will be at an end! "

" But she is only to have it if she really has been good? " said Mrs. Caryll, who was sometimes afraid that Magdalen was rather inclined to spoil Hoodie.

"Only if she has been good, you may be sure," said Magdalen. "And there is one thing about Hoodie—she does keep a promise."

"You think she is honest and truthful?" said Mrs. Caryll.

"By nature I am sure she is. But her brain is so full of fancies that she hardly understands herself, that I can quite see how sometimes it must seem as if she were not straightforward. Not that the fancies would do her any harm if they were all happy and pretty ones—but I do wish she could get rid of the idea that no one cares for her. It is *that*, that sours her and spoils her, poor little girl."

Hoodie's mother looked affectionately at Magdalen.

"Where have you learnt to be so wise about children, Magda?" she said. "You seem to understand them as if you had lived among them all your life."

"It is only because I love them so much," said Magdalen, simply. "And often somehow ——" she hesitated.

"Often what?" said her cousin, smiling.

"I was going to say—but I stopped because I thought perhaps you would not like it as we were talking of your children who have everything to make them happy—" said Magdalen. "I was going to say that sometimes, often, I am so very, very sorry for children. Even their naughtinesses and sillinesses make me sorry for them. They are so strange to it all —and it is so difficult to learn wisdom."

Hoodie's mother smiled again.

"You are such a venerable owl yourself, you funny child," she said. "However, I do understand you, and I agree with you. I do feel very sorry for poor Hoodie sometimes, even though she really goes out of her way to make herself unhappy. But what *is* one to do?"

"Yes, that is the puzzle," said Magdalen. "In the first place any way, I am going to buy her a cage for her bird—it will be good for her to take regular care of the bird. I am so glad you said she might keep it."

"I only hope we shall be able to rear it," said Mrs. Caryll. "Hoodie would indeed think

all the powers were against her if it died. That is the worst of pets."

"I think this bird will get on, if it is taken care of and not over-fed," said Magdalen. "It is a greenfinch, you know, and greenfinches take kindly to domestic life. Besides, it is not so very young a bird, and it looks quite bright and happy now that it has got over its fright," and so saying she followed Hoodie's mother out of the room to prepare for their drive.

It was nearly five o'clock in the afternoon when they returned. Cousin Magdalen ran joyously up stairs to the nursery carrying a very funnily shaped parcel in her hand. The children were all at tea. She heard their voices and the clatter and tinkle that always accompanies a nursery meal as she came along the passage, and she opened the door so softly that for a moment or two she stood watching the little party before any of them noticed her.

How nice and pretty and happy they looked! Martin, a perfect picture of a kind, tidy nurse, sat pouring out the tea, looking for once quite easy-minded and at rest; Maudie, a little model of neatness as usual, her small sweet face wearing an expression of the utmost gravity as she carefully spread some honey on Hec's bread and butter; Duke, frowning with eagerness to understand some mysterious communication which his neighbour Hoodie was making to him in a low voice, her eyes bright with excitement, her cheeks rosy and her pretty fat shoulders "shruggled" up, as she bent to whisper to her little brother.

"*What* do you say, Hoodie? I don't understand. How could it be all of gold?" were the first words that met Magdalen's ears.

"*Hush*, Duke," said Hoodie, placing her sticky little hand on his mouth, "you're *not* to tell. I didn't say it would be all gold. I said p'raps the little points at the top would be goldy—like the shiny top of the point on the church. But you're too little to know what I mean. You must wait till— Oh!" with a scream of delight, "*there's* Maudie's godmother! Oh Maudie's godmother, Maudie's godmother, *have* you got it?"

She was off her seat and in Magdalen's arms in an instant—hugging, jumping, kissing, dancing with eagerness. It was all Magdalen could do not at once to hold out to her the parcel, but her promise to Hoodie's mother must not be broken.

"Yes," she said, "I have got it. But first tell me, Hoodie dear—have you been really a good little girl all the afternoon? Has she, Martin?"

"Oh, trually I've been good—rezzy good—haven't I, Martin?" said Hoodie.

"Yes, Miss. I must really say she has been very good. I don't remember ever having a more peacefuller afternoon," said Martin with great satisfaction.

"I am so glad," said Magdalen. "And you didn't touch the bird, Hoodie?"

"No, oh no, I didn't touch it one bit," said Hoodie earnestly. "I went and lookened at it, but I didn't touch it. Martin will tell you."

"No, Miss, she was quite good. She just stood and peeped at it, but she didn't touch it, I'm sure, for I went with her to your room and stayed there a few minutes while she looked at the bird."

"That was very nice," said Magdalen.

"We didn't let Hec and Duke go," said Hoodie, "for they'd have wanted to touch the bird, wouldn't they? They're so little, you see, and Hec says he likes smoowing down the feavers on little birds's backs, so Martin and me thought we'd better not let them be temptationed to touch the bird."

"Ah, yes, that was very wise. And as Martin stayed with you, you weren't temptationed either, were you, Hoodie?"

Somewhat to her surprise, at this Hoodie grew rather red.

"I didn't stay all the time, Miss," said Martin. "I heard the little boys calling me, so I left Miss Hoodie for a minute or two feeling sure I might trust her."

"So there's nothing to prevent my giving you the cage. That's very nice," said Magdalen. She lifted the funny-looking parcel on to the table and unfastened the paper. There stood the cage—and such a pretty one! It was painted white and green, and greatly and specially to Hoodie's satisfaction the pointed tops of the pagoda-like roof were gilt.

"Didn't I tell you so," she said to Duke in a

262

tone of great superiority, "I told you there'd be goldy points on the top."

"Yes," said Duke, much impressed; "I wonder how you knowed, Hoodie?"

Hoodie tossed her head.

"Knowed, in course I knowed," she said.

Only Hec did not seem as much interested and delighted as the others. He just glanced at the cage and then subsided again to his bread and honey.

"What's the matter with Hec," said Cousin Magdalen. "He doesn't look as bright as usual, does he, Martin?"

"He's been very quiet all the afternoon," said Martin, "but I don't think he can be ill. He's eaten a good tea, hasn't he, Miss Maudie?"

"Very," said Maudie. "Three big slices first—only with butter, you know, and then six with honey. We always have to eat three plain first, on honey days," she added by way of explanation to her cousin.

"Nine slices," said Magdalen, opening her eyes. "Martin, isn't that enough to make him ill?"

"Bless you, no, Miss," said Martin, laughing. "As long as it's bread and butter, there's not much fear."

"Or bread and honey," corrected Hoodie. "One day Duke and Hec and me—Maudie wasn't there—one day Duke and Hec and me eatened firty-two slices—Martin counted. It was when we was at the sea-side."

"My dear Hoodie!" exclaimed Magdalen, and the astonishment on her face made them all laugh.

The consumption of bread and butter and honey seemed however over for the present, so Magdalen led the way to her own room, followed by Hoodie carrying the precious cage which she would entrust to no other hands, Maudie, the twins, and Martin bringing up the rear.

Magdalen opened the door and crossed the room, which was a large one, to the side window, on the writing-table, in front of which she had left the basket containing the bird. She had placed it carefully, with a little circle of books round it to prevent the bird's flutterings knocking it over. As she came near the table, she gave an exclamation of surprise and vexation. The circle of books was still there undisturbed, but the basket was no longer in the centre—indeed, at the first glance Magdalen could not see it at all.

"Oh dear!" she exclaimed. "Where can the basket be? Hoodie, you *surely* didn't touch it?"

The moment she had said the words she regretted them—but just at first she had not time to look at Hoodie to see how she had taken them, for another glance at the table showed her the basket peeping up behind the edge where it had slipped down, though fortunately the table was pushed too near the wall for it to have fallen quite on to the floor.

Magdalen darted forward and carefully drew out the basket, in considerable fear and trembling as to the state of the little bird inside. But to her relief it seemed all right. It had had another fright, no doubt, poor thing—it must have thought life a very queer series of falls and bumps and knocks, I should think, judging by its own experience, but still it seemed to have a happy faculty of recovering itself, and though its position in the toppled-over basket could not have been very comfortable, it looked quite bright and chirpy when Magdalen gently lifted the lid to examine it.

"It is hungry, I'm sure," she said; "can't you give me a little bread soaked in milk for it again, Martin? There's some milk on the nursery table, isn't there?"

"To be sure, Miss," said Martin, starting off at once. To her surprise, as she left the room she felt a hand slipped into hers. It was Hoodie's.

"I'll go with you," said the child, and Martin, thinking she only wanted to go with her to see about the bread and milk, made no objection. It was not till they reached the nursery that Martin noticed the expression of the little girl's face. It was stormy in the extreme.

"I won't go back to Maudie's godmother's room," she exclaimed. "I won't have the cage. I won't speak to her—nasty, *ugly*, Maudie's godmother."

"Miss Hoodie!" said Martin in amazement and distress. "You speaking that naughty way of your cousin who has been so very nice and kind to you."

263

"I don't care," said Hoodie, fairly on the way to one of her grandest tempers, "*I* don't believe what I say. I *toldened* her I didn't touch the basket, and she said I did."

"Oh no, Miss Hoodie, my dear, I'm sure she didn't say that. She only asked you if you were quite sure you didn't. And who could have done it, I'm sure I can't think," said Martin, herself by no means satisfied that Hoodie's indignation was not a sign of her knowing herself to blame. "No one was in the room but you and me this afternoon, for none of the servants ever go near it till dressing time. Besides, they wouldn't go touching the bird. If it had been one of the little boys now. It's just what they might have done, reaching up to get it. But they weren't there at all."

"*I* don't care," reiterated Hoodie. "I didn't do it, but Maudie's godmother doesn't believe me. *I* don't care. But I won't have the cage." And in spite of all Martin could say, the child resolutely refused to leave the nursery.

Hoodie sat there alone, nursing her wrath and bitter feelings.

"I don't care," she kept repeating to herself. "Nobody likes me. I'm always naughty. What's the good of being good? I did so want to touch the bird when Martin went out of the room and left me alone, but I didn't, 'cos I'd p'omised. I might as well, 'cos Maudie's godmother doesn't believe me. It's very unkind of God to make it seem that I'm always naughty. It's not my fault. *I* don't care."

In Magdalen's room Martin was relating Hoodie's indignation.

"Oh, how sorry I am for saying that," said Magdalen. "It will just make her lose her trust in me. And I do believe her. I'm sure she didn't touch it. Don't you think so, Martin?"

Martin hesitated.

"Yes, Miss, I do think I believe her. Only didn't you notice how red she got when I said I wasn't with her *all* the time in your room this afternoon?"

"Yes," said Magdalen; "but I thought it was just that she felt so eager for me to know she had kept her promise. I *don't* think she

Hoodie.

touched it, Martin. I really don't. But I am afraid it will be difficult to make her believe I don't."

Just then a sudden sound of weeping made them all start, thinking for a moment that it must be Hoodie herself, who had run back from the nursery. But no—it was not Hoodie— It was Hec. The little fellow had crept under the table unobserved, and there had been listening to the conversation.

"What's the matter, dear? What's the matter, my darling? Don't cry so, Master Hec," said Martin, as she drew him out.

"Poor Hec! Poor little Hec! Has he hurt himself?" exclaimed all the others.

"No, no, I hasn't hurt myself," sobbed Hec. "I'm crying 'cos it was *me*. It was *me* that tumbled the basket down and Cousin Magdalen 'colded Hoodie. It wasn't poor Hoodie. It was all me."

And for some minutes, conscience-stricken Hec refused to be comforted.

(To be continued.)

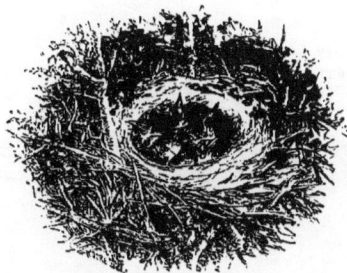

264

BUMBLE BEE.

Bum - ble Bee su - perb - ly dressed In vel - vet, jet, and gold; Sailed a - long in ca - ger quest, And hummed a ballad bold. Morn - ing - Glo - ry cling - ing tight To friend - ly spires of grass; Blush - ing in the ear - ly light, Looked out to see him pass.

2.

Nectar pure as crystal lay within her ruby cup:
Bee was very glad to stay, and tried to drink it up.
"Fairest of the flowers," said he, "it was a precious boon,
May you still a glory be, each morning, night, and noon."

ROSA.

ROSA.

T was quite a dreadful place to live in, Rosa thought, although most people thought quite differently. She had not been very well that spring, so that when the warm weather came, and Rosa still seemed to droop, and did not care to eat, although it must be confessed that she sometimes felt very hungry whilst she was hanging her head on one side and saying " No thank you! " in a weak voice as an invalid should; and as, above all, she could not *do her lessons*—the doctor said the country would be the best place for her. So she was sent to stay with her godmother in the country.

This godmother was quite an old lady, living alone in a large house in Kent. The house was old and full of low dark rooms with deep window-seats and heavy curtains. The chairs were so heavy that they never tipped over, although Rosa in her restlessness would climb all over them like a monkey; the rest of the furniture was pretty solid too, except some little tables loaded with ornaments, one of which generally seemed to stand just in Rosa's road if she happened to want to make a dash across the room. And there were such quantities of things ready almost to break if you only *looked* at them, that after a very few days' experience Rosa began to creep about as if she were afraid to move, in her real anxiety to "take care."

From the very first day her visit had been marked by a succession of mischief, and she began to feel rather like a big brown bee which had caused one of her many misfortunes, and which she had watched afterwards as it blundered about the room, first coming with a thump and a whirr against one thing, and then against another. Only, in the bees' case, he generally seemed to get the worst of it, as he would always sit still and rub his head with his forelegs for a minute or two before opening his wings again, whereas if Rosa came full tilt against a table, or knocked down a vase, the

table went over, and the vase was broken, or at least all the water spilt, whilst Rosa herself was none the worse.

The first thing that had happened was this. Rosa had been running about all the morning in the high grass, scrambling over the fence which divided the garden from the pasture-land beyond, and picking all the flowers which grew in places very difficult to get at—across a muddy ditch for instance, or *on the other side* of a clump of brambles—not that these flowers were really better, but because, somehow, the difficulty gave them a sort of superiority over the flowers which you had only to stoop to gather.

This spirit of enterprise had resulted in Rosa's appearance in the luncheon-room adorned with a long tail, composed of torn flounce and a long trail of bramble, the whole well coated with wet mud.

Being promptly sent off to change her frock, Rosa discovered a long track of mud from the hall-door to the dining-room. In her anxiety to remove the cause of this last mischief she flew up the stairs, and on returning presently, very shiny in the face, with a clean dress and pinafore, and very much on her good behaviour, she found to her dismay a second track rather more muddy than the first. With all this on her mind, her glass of port-wine was very difficult to manage, and the tablecloth, somehow, drank more than half of it; but these things were mere trifles compared with the catastrophe of the afternoon.

Rosa had taken a book as she had been told, and had curled herself up in a window-seat, from which she could look out over the garden and towards the wood beyond. There was a wistaria in full bloom clustering round the window, and a banksia rose mingled with it, and all sorts of sweet flowers grew just outside, round which a whole crowd of bees were humming happily. Rosa watched and listened lazily at first, then she yawned and opened her book, but very soon the birds' song sounded fainter and further off, and the bees seemed to hum very loudly, and Rosa fell asleep.

She sat there so quietly that the bees skimmed past her in and out of the room, but presently, one big brown fellow, so heavy that he could not manage himself very well, whizzed his soft velvet body against her eye with a pretty hard thump. Up sprang Rosa in a fright—down went her book, and down, too, went a beautiful china jar, all over dragons, that had stood close to the window-curtain.

"Take care! take care! whatever is the matter with the child?" cried her godmother. But though, as usual, there was nothing whatever the matter with Rosa, there was a great deal amiss with the jar. There it lay, broken into pieces, and all the sweet dried leaves it had held were drifting over the carpet.

It had been so clearly an accident that, although Mrs. Leslie loved her china almost as much as her godchild, she refrained from scolding her, but it went to the little girl's heart to see the old lady down on her knees beside the ruin of her beloved jar, picking up the fragments with her feeble fingers and trying to fit them into each other.

You should always make an extra strong resolution whenever your last has proved a failure; and Rosa made a very very strong one on the spot, not to meet with another accident, *if she could help it.*

The next day she determined, as she was allowed to roam where she liked in the house and grounds, to keep as far as she could away from the rooms which held the possibility of so many disasters. The housekeeper had given her two kittens to play with, one tabby and one white, with the fluffiest tails, the roundest eyes, and the weakest legs imaginable. Rosa was perfectly happy, and it is to be hoped the kittens were happy too. At all events she paid them a great deal of attention—never by any chance allowing them to waddle off on their own account, as they endeavoured to do fifty times every five minutes, always finding a much better thing for them to play with than anything they had chosen for themselves, and vigorously shaking a ball of wool or a piece of paper before their eyes whenever

268

they seemed inclined to be lazy and to go to sleep.

In the afternoon Mrs. Leslie went out in the carriage, but unfortunately she could not take Rosa with her, as she was going to see a sick friend.

"I only hope that when I come home I shall find the kittens alive and my china safe," said the old lady, shaking her head. "But those kittens must have a dozen lives each I'm sure, and I haven't had time to put all the china under lock and key."

Rosa felt a little crushed, but she promised to be very careful, and the carriage drove away.

At first Rosa went to the housekeeper's room to play, but after a time she found that very dull work. The housemaid was there making some tablecloths, and had a long story to confide to the housekeeper. It would not have been a bad story, as there seemed to be plenty of wicked people in it; but just at the most interesting parts she would break off and glance at Rosa, and screw up her mouth, and shake her head. The housekeeper would stare at her for a second, and then screw up her mouth, and shake her head, and say, "Ah, dear! I understand. Go on." And then the housemaid would go on, without explaining herself further, until Rosa felt quite oppressed by all these mysteries.

So she packed up the kittens into a heap, and strolled out into the hall. Such a beautiful old hall, full of heavy carved presses and queerly-shaped chairs, and with stained-glass windows through which the afternoon sun streamed, painting bright patches of colour on the dark walls and dusky pictures.

Rosa stood still at the door in order to look about and see whether by any chance she could do any mischief here. Neither she nor the kittens could upset *this* furniture, that was certain at all events; there were some orange-trees in tubs, but they seemed pretty firm; the china—of course there was some of that dreadful china even here—was safe in the presses, except just one row of plates arranged on a ledge which ran round the hall.

Rosa took counsel with herself and decided that she need not retire because of these plates.

They were leaning against the wall at a good height from the ground and need not interfere with her nor she with them. So she tumbled the kittens down upon the floor and began to enjoy herself. But as ill-luck would have it, she felt a little tired presently, so she hoisted herself up into one of the big chairs and leant back dangling her feet lazily and dropping her arms, whilst the kittens had their own way for once and quarrelled comfortably in her lap.

Rosa had never noticed that the chair she had chosen was just under those precious plates —never reflected that she had taken up the only dangerous position in the whole hall, until at last a harder pat than usual from his brother, sent the tabby kitten flying, as best he could, first on to Rosa's shoulder, then on to the ledge where the plates were arranged. Another second and there was a roll and a clatter and a smash, and Rosa could see nothing but fragments of coloured china glistening all over the floor.

She was horrified. She stood quite still, seeing nothing but those bits of china, hearing nothing but imaginary carriage-wheels on the gravel outside, not thinking for a moment whether she should be punished or not, but only so dreadfully sorry! How would her godmother's kind old face look when she saw what Rosa was staring at now—what would she say—would she cry? She had nearly cried about the cats—would she ever trust her alone again? If only, after remembering to be "take care" for a full hour, she had not forgotten just at this minute!—if only she had sat in another part of the hall!

"*If only*" seem such little words, but they meant a great deal to Rosa just then. And people much older than she have found them the two saddest words in the language, in their time.

At this moment the sound of wheels did really come faintly through the open door, and the little girl fairly turned coward. She snatched up her hat and fled, leaving the kittens to take care of themselves; fled across the lawn just in time to avoid being seen, over a little bridge, and up a steep bank of nettles and high grass towards the oak wood at the end of the garden. She pushed at the gate which

led into the wood, but as she could not open it she scrambled over it, leaving a good deal of her dress amongst the bushes at the top of it, and hurried on, not caring where she went so long only as she could get well out of sight of the house.

The wood was a large one, so large that it would not have been difficult for a grown-up person to lose his way in it; and yet Rosa tore on through the underwood, not keeping to the path, but diving amongst the wild-rose bushes and ferns wherever the thicket was deepest, until at last, suddenly afraid of the silence and loneliness, she stopped short and looked round her with a beating heart.

The sky had clouded, and there was that heavy sweetness in the air which comes before summer rain; not a breath of wind stirred the leaves except those of the topmost branches, amongst which the birds were flying uneasily.

Rosa was panic-stricken. She had never ventured far into the wood before, for she had never been able in a calmer frame of mind to take three steps in a much more open part without encountering a fright of some kind or another—a bough would suddenly crack without any reason, or there would be a rustling close behind her so that she was afraid to look round, or a heaving in the long grass which was very alarming; and though the next moment perhaps a little brown rabbit would scud away as fast as he could, or a squirrel whisk up the nearest tree much more startled than the young lady, still she never knew what was going to happen next, and preferred to go where she could see her adventures coming if they *must* come.

All her old horror rushed back upon her now —now that she was she knew not how far from every one—all alone under the great silent trees and, perhaps, with all sorts of dangers quite close to her. She peered anxiously about to right and to left; there was not a vestige of a path to be seen. Then she made a few trembling steps and her feet sank ankle deep in black mud; then she crept back to dry ground, and tried to crush through the brambles. But still there was no path. The trees were a little thinner, but wherever she looked she found the same black swamp, and she was afraid to move more than a few steps in any direction

She began to forget all her former fears and her anxiety to escape, and to long more than she had ever longed for anything in her life for the hot nursery at home in London, with all her little brothers and sisters giggling and squabbling by turns, and the tea-table by the open window, and the rumbling of carriages in the street, and the faint scent of the lime-trees in the square. The sky was growing darker and darker; a few heavy rain-drops pattered down on her shoulders, and a sort of shiver was running through the leaves. Clearly it was going to rain fast, and poor little Rosa, all alone in the great wood, afraid to move or to cry out lest she should disturb some dreadful wild animal which might be close to her now for aught she knew, hungry, chilly, and despairing, felt as miserable as a little girl well could.

She tried to call for help, but her voice sounded so odd that it frightened her, and besides, those terrible rustlings began again at the noise. Once more she crept a little way, and this time finding dry ground under her feet, she gathered together what scraps of courage she could find and battled on bravely through the brambles. In the meantime the rain was coming down faster and faster, and presently there was a quick sudden gust of wind which so startled her that she stumbled forward against the root of a tree. The next moment she was down amongst the ferns, held fast by a dreadful something that had seized her ankle.

" Don't hurt me, please ; oh, don't hurt me ! " she screamed, not daring to lift her face from the ground. And whatever it was did not hurt her much, although she could not drag her foot away. Presently, as nothing moved, she cautiously raised her head, and saw, instead of the monster she had half expected, a rusty iron hoop which had closed round her ankle. It was a trap which some boys had set to catch a hare, and which had caught poor Rosa instead. Still things were bad enough. Her little fingers could not move the iron so as to release her foot, although fortunately a bit of stick had become wedged in at the hinges and so lessened the pressure. And besides all this, the trap was chained to a tree. There was nothing for

it but to sit still and call for help if she could find a voice to call with. Again and again she screamed as loud as she could, using any name that came into her head, but no one answered. And Rosa's screams subsided into sobs.

In the meantime the rain had ceased, and evening was coming on. The birds were still singing softly and dreamily, the leaves dripping with rain-drops rustled faintly in the breeze, but there was no sound of any one coming to help poor little Rosa. . . . .

The next morning the sun shone brilliantly. It poured into Rosa's bedroom, making diamond-shaped patterns on the window-blinds, which were still down, although the window was open and the breeze brought the scent of roses and honeysuckles to the little sleeper on the bed. For the little girl was safe and sound in her own bed, but with tumbled hair and a flushed face, and as she slept she moved restlessly and tossed about.

She woke up presently with frightened eyes ; but a kind old hand laid her head back on the pillow, and a kind old voice said,

" Go to sleep again, my little Rosa, you are quite safe now." And Rosa's eyes shut again, whilst a feeling of rest and comfort stole into her troubled little mind in the midst of its dreams, and her little hand closed tightly round her dear old godmother's fingers.

Rosa was very ill. She had caught a terrible cold, and for some days was not allowed to leave her bed. Nobody scolded her for her carelessness, nor even for running away; but at last, one afternoon when she was lying on the sofa feeling very weak and tired still, her godmother sat by her and talked to her very gently and gravely. ·

She told her how frightened she had been when evening had come on and still Rosa did not return. How she had sent all the servants to look for her, and had sat at home alone, trembling lest some one should come back and bring her bad news, and how at last the game-keeper had found Rosa amongst the ferns so sound asleep from exhaustion that they could hardly rouse her. And lastly, how fortunate it was that she had been held fast by that cruel trap, since just a few steps further on there was a deep pond with steep shelving sides, into which she might have fallen.

And then Mrs. Leslie went on to tell her that we should never fly from the consequences of a fault, and that in all things, great and small, the consequences of our own deeds *follow* us if we are not brave enough to stand and face them.

"But the plates, godmother, the plates?" said poor Rosa, anxiously, for nothing had as yet been said about *them*.

Mrs. Leslie was silent.

"We won't talk about the plates, my dear," she said presently, with rather an odd catch in her voice.

It was too much for Rosa. She threw both her arms round her godmother's neck, pulling her cap away, and without the least consideration for her spectacles.

"I'll never, *never* be careless again, dear, DEAR godmother!" she sobbed out—"*if I can help it.*"

And she kept her word.

EVENING.

THE day is past; the glorious sun
  Is sinking in the west;
And weary man (his labour done)
  May lay him down to rest.

The noontide heat is spent; and now
  A cool refreshing breeze
Plays softly round his careworn brow,
  And lightly stirs the trees.

The little birds from tree and bush
  Together join to raise,
In this sweet solemn evening hush,
  Their joyous notes of praise.

The bounteous Heaven a gracious shower
  Of gentle dew doth pour;
Still brighter glows each grateful flower,
  Content, nor craving more.

And now the slowly rising moon
  Sheds forth her silver light,
The shadows deepen; all things soon
  Will murmur soft "good-night."

ETHEL STREATFIELD.

TALKS ABOUT THE MONTHS.

SEPTEMBER.

By Mrs. GEORGE CUPPLES.

" Autumn's sighing, moaning, dying,
Clouds are flying on like steeds ;
Red leaves trailing fall unfailing—
Dropping, sailing from the wood."

EPTEMBER is our first month of autumn, and is one of the most interesting periods of the year. Though the days are getting shorter, and the mornings and evenings chill and foggy, the weather is generally mild and well fitted for out-door exercise and amusements. The different species of water-fowl are collecting together and drawing up in regular order, and under the leading of one particular bird they are about to wing their way from the Arctic regions across the dark

272

and stormy Northern Ocean, amidst tempest and fog, till they reach our coasts, islands, rivers and lakes, where they will find food and shelter during the winter.

" Warm September brings the pheasant,
When to gather nuts is pleasant."

The last month commenced with corn-harvest, this commences with partridge-shooting, and very busy have the sportsmen been, seeing to their dogs, guns and ammunition. The dogs are as impatient as their masters; whining and fawning, and endeavouring to tempt them abroad. When their kennel door is opened, away they bound with a joyous cry, running here and there in circles to show their delight, their masters scarcely having the heart to restrain them, for they, too, feel inclined to shout aloud to show their exultation that the day has come when the sport is free.

" High life of a hunter ! he meets on the hill
The new-wakened daylight, so bright and so still ;
And feels, as the clouds of the morning unroll,
The silence, the splendour, ennoble his soul."

A real sportsman is never cruel in his sport, and would scorn to keep his gun in practice by shooting at the swallows. This is not only inexcusable, but very wicked, for they are of great service to man in devouring the myriads of insects which would, were it not for them, be a torment to us and a ruin to the crops. To be insensible to the benefits conferred by their instrumentality shows that we have not the spirit of love and of kindness which should lift us above the inferior animals. No sooner have the swallows, and other birds which are unfit to endure the cold of our winter, departed, than their place is filled by troops of fieldfares, thrushes, and others, which find their food in hips, haws, and berries. We are cheered, too, by several of our native birds renewing their song now the labour of rearing their young brood is at an end, and they again pour out their song, though not in such joyous strains as during the months of spring.

Spiders are very numerous in September, and during a walk at this season we see many a bush covered by a most beautiful web, and on account of its regularity it is called the

geometric spider-web. Those we see in the hedges and stubble fields with long loose threads hanging from them are the webs of the gossamer spider, and very curious it is to watch the nimble little creatures floating at the end of the threads, like balloons. Another curious insect, the glow-worm, shines with great brilliancy during the evenings of September. It teaches us a lesson to be careful how we expose ourselves to the night air, for

" When the glow-worm lights her lamp,
Then the air is always damp."

If we have very sharp eyes we may see that man is not the only one who is attending to the harvest. The squirrels, field-mice, dormice, and many other four-footed inhabitants of the woods and hedges are as busy as the farmers in getting in their harvest. They store up corn, acorns, nuts, beech-mast and other hard seeds.

The name of September signifies the *seventh*, although now this month is the ninth of the year, and was dedicated by the Romans to Vulcan. Our Saxon ancestors called September *Gerst-monat* from the word gerst, signifying barley, because barley was then ready for the sickle. This grain was much cultivated by them, as they made from it a great part of their common drink. It was brewed and fermented, and the produce called *ael* and afterwards *beere*, so that this use of barley has come down to our times, and beer and ale have been called our national drink. In the warmer counties of Great Britain large quantities of apples are ripening fast, so that the grower watches the weather anxiously, in case it should be stormy and windy, when his fruit would be blown down and damaged, so he hums to himself no doubt

" September blow soft
Till the fruit's in the loft."

Throughout September we look for settled weather, either wet or fine, for, as the Portuguese say, "September dries up the wells or breaks down the bridges." Up in the northern counties every one looks out anxiously to see what kind of weather they are to have on Holyrood Day, which is on the 26th of September.

" If dry the buck's horn
 On Holyrood morn,
    'Tis worth a kist of gold ;
 But if wet it be seen,
 Ere Holyrood e'en
 Bad harvest is foretold."

But we must not forget Michaelmas Day. The 29th of September is so called from having been appointed as the festival of St. Michael and all the Angels. This feast was established in the year 487, for the purpose of keeping mankind in memory of the ministry of the holy Angels, as the messengers of God's will towards men. This is the third quarter-day in the year, and is still very often called by the old name Martinmas. Rent and other payments now become due, and, like the other quarter-days, it is a period of bustle and anxiety in money affairs. In many country villages however the good wives are early astir, for they must drive their geese to the goose fairs, and the payment received for the little flock will greatly help to make up the rent. There is not a happier time for all the little Sallys, and Pollys, and Emmas, for they see a smile of satisfaction on their mothers' faces, and they know that once the geese are sold, the sighs and fears about the rent will be over. Besides, they have always herded the geese on the common, and they know right well that even their mothers would never be able to drive them so quietly to market. Indeed, mother has quite enough to do to carry the baby, who is growing so fat and heavy, so Mary or Sally or Emma has the herding all to herself. No doubt the little girl speculates as they jog along as to the price to be given for each, and whether her geese will be the best at the fair, and a dozen other things ; besides the one that will come uppermost as to the delightful arrangement about every one having a goose for dinner on St. Michael's Day. Very likely little Emma knows nothing about the record that Queen Elizabeth was eating her Michaelmas goose when she received the joyful tidings of the defeat of the Spanish Armada; but one thing she does know, and that is, she is glad there is such a thing as a goose fair, for if the birds are sold well she will be sure to get a penny or two to herself to buy some tempting article at the booths.

274

The practice among the rural tenantry of bringing a good stubble goose at Michaelmas to the landlord when paying their rent, arose perhaps in the hope of making him kind to them if they could not pay all the money quite at once. Hence the lines

" And when the tenants come to pay their quarter's rent
 They bring some fowl at Midsummer, a dish of fish in
    Lent,
 At Christmas, a capon, at *Michaelmas, a goose,*
 And something else at New Year's tide, for fear their
    lease fly loose."

At this season, apart from its being a pleasant time, the weather is generally soft and mild and well fitted for out-door exercise and amusements. The days indeed are getting shorter and the mornings and evenings chill and foggy, but the sun still shines brightly, and it is pleasantly warm during many hours of the day ; and though we must be careful to have an extra wrap ready for the afternoons, we scarcely can realize that the summer is over and gone by, seeing so many butterflies and moths sporting about.

If we look closely in the hedges we may find too, several kinds of the ladybird—exceedingly useful little insects, especially in gardens and green-houses. We need not be afraid, when looking for the ladybirds, that we shall be startled by coming upon any snakes or vipers, for they betake themselves to hollows in the banks and elsewhere, to pass the winter in a torpid state.

If we happen to be staying by the sea-side we are certain to see the annual shoal of herrings filling every creek and bay. They have come from the northern ocean—where they always have abundance of food—to deposit their eggs in the shoal water, where the warmth of the sun can reach them, which it could not have done had they been laid in the deep sea. And if we are spending the holiday season near any oak or beech woods, we shall then see plenty of acorns and beech-nuts. There are still some forests remaining, particularly the New Forest, in Hampshire, where large droves of swine are fed for about six weeks in the year, from the middle of September to the end of October. The swineherd has often as many as five or six hundred under his charge, and though we may suppose it will be no easy matter to keep them in order, to him it is quite easy. At first he puts them into a temporary sty round a tree, gives them plenty of acorns, and blows his horn, which he always carries with him. This he does night and morning, till they get to understand that the blowing of the horn means supper or breakfast, and they at once return to the same place the moment they hear it.

September is the great harvest-time for the apple, one of the most useful fruits we have, and in several of the counties every one is busy making cider or apple wine, and many too in other parts are gathering the ripe elderberry for the same purpose. Every season brings its work, its pleasures, and its beauty. It is true that the beauty of summer is gone, so far as the flowers are concerned, but there are still a good many left, miniature, indeed, in size, but most delicate in form. And towards the end of the month the foliage of trees begins to wither, and the gradual decay of the leaves is marked by a variety of charming hues. Over the hedges the travellers'-joy waves its white blossoms, often in company with the wild hop. Blackberry bushes are covered with buds, flowers, and green and ripe fruit at the same time, and the ivy is putting forth its multitude of blossoms. We can still sing, however,

> " The violet by the mossed grey stone
>   Hath laid her weary head ;
> But thou, wild bramble ! back dost bring
>   In all their beauteous power
> The fresh, green days of life's fair Spring,
>   And boyhood's blossomy hour,
> To gird with thee the woodlands o'er
>   In freedom and in joy."

FAIRY TALES.

FAIRY TALES.

BY THE EDITOR.

NICE pleasant place on this hot summer's day,
A quiet delightful cool nook,
To rest from their play just under the wall,
With a wonderful fairy-tale book.

The summer breeze blows on their fair curly hair,
And fans them on cheek and on brow,
As they thrill with delight at the strange fairy lore:
Some marvellous legend, I trow!

Are they travelling with Sindbad his journeys again?
Are they following small Golden-hair,
As she wanders away from her own happy home
To take shelter in that of a bear?

I wonder what book 'tis the little lad holds;
Has Andersen written the tale?
Is it he that has woven the silvery web—
That enchanter who never can fail?

The great friend of children, past, present, to come,
Alas! though he lives, he is dead.
How we've dreamed, and we've laughed, at his fancies and fun,
How many the salt tears we've shed!

The sweet little Mermaid we never forget,
Her great love, her terrible pain;
The Angel, Lead Soldier, and dear Ole Luk Oie,
We can read them again and again.

Those tales of our childhood! How happy we were
In the hours spent o'er them—long past,
When reading of Bluebeard, or Wonderful Jack,
The minutes flew by us so fast!

And then Cinderella comes back to our minds,
And little Red Riding Hood too,
And Jack and the Beanstalk, and Hop-o'-my-thumb,
The old woman who lived in a shoe.

This boy in our picture is very intent,
He solemnly stares at the book;
While our fair little friend is excited indeed,
We can see by her rapt eager look.

THE HERMIT.

By the Right Hon. E. H. KNATCHBULL-HUGESSEN, M.P., *Author of "Uncle Joe's Stories,"* &c.

CHAPTER I.

THERE was once a cave in the very midst of a forest. The forest was very large and very thick, and had by no means a good reputation. It was said to be full of wild beasts, robbers, witches, evil spirits, and whatever other crea-

278

tures are likely to make a place disagreeable to live in. But the cave was the abode of a hermit, who did not care sixpence for any of these terrible things, but lived on very comfortably without being troubled by them.

The cave was in the side of a huge rock, and a stream of water trickled at the foot of the rock on its way through the forest, so near the

The Hermit.

entrance of the cave that the Hermit could sit with his feet in it if he pleased. He never *did* please however, for reasons of his own, into which we need not inquire, although I have no doubt that the principal one was a dislike to wet feet, and the uncomfortable position which he would have been obliged to occupy, in consequence of the edges of the rock at the mouth of the cave being sharp and jagged. So he preferred to step gently down and stride across the stream (which was narrow at that part), whenever he wished to go forth into the forest.

He was a curious fellow to look at, that Hermit. Tall, gaunt, with dark hair matted over his brows, and long rugged beard falling down his breast, he looked like some malefactor who had escaped from prison and sought refuge in the woods, or like some wild man who had never known the comforts and habits of civilised life. His frame indicated vast strength, his arms, longer than those of most men, displayed muscular development of no ordinary character, which his sinewy legs well matched; and his whole appearance was such as made you feel at the very first sight of him that he was a man whom you would rather have upon your side than against you in the event of a scrimmage.

There was no chance, however, of having to take sides in a scrimmage of any kind at the time my story begins, for, so far as one could see, nobody seemed likely to come near the cave with intentions either friendly or the reverse. In spite of all that had been said or could be said about the forest, it appeared as if anybody who chose to be a hermit therein might play the hermit to his heart's content without any interference. My Hermit certainly did so for some time, and but for one circumstance might have done so to the end of his days without anybody being a bit the wiser for it. What do you think that circumstance was? Well, it is no use trying to guess, because you would never do so if you tried until a week of Sundays came together, and we all know that such a happy and delightful event as *that* is entirely out of the question.

The circumstance was one which has probably never been mentioned before in the various

279

histories of hermits which have been told or written. Still it is a true circumstance, as is also the fact that this particular hermit was in most respects very like other men in his tastes and habits, thereby differing greatly from the popular idea of hermits as gathered from, and related in, the histories to which I have alluded.

These other hermits were all extraordinary men; they fasted frequently, which my hermit never did when there was anything to be had to eat; they spent long time in meditation and holy thoughts, in which respect my hero had but little in common with them, being altogether of a different temperament; they drank nothing but water from the brook, he never drank water at all when he could get anything better; finally, they frequently scourged and tormented themselves by way of penance, whereas the individual of whom I write always made himself as comfortable as he possibly could. And one thing he did, which leads me directly to the circumstance upon the occurrence of which the whole of this touching story is founded.

He smoked. Yes, he did. He smoked a pipe, and he wouldn't have given up that pipe for anything that you might have offered him. He thought—and there may have been reason for it—that there was to be found in his pipe a solace, a calming-down of troublesome thoughts, and a sweet forgetfulness of sorrow, which were to be found in nothing else.

Seated within the secret recesses of his cave, or reclining against the trunk of some ancient monarch of the forest, he would often sit for hours together with no other company than his pipe, musing over the past, and turning over in his mind many curious thoughts about men and things, which perchance would never have occurred to him but for that faithful friend.

A listless, dreamy existence you may deem it, and think that he was scarcely employing his time as usefully as he ought to have done. That may very likely be true, but the fact remains the same, and two closer friends never existed than my hermit and his pipe. It was indeed his only friend.

Some hermits, disgusted with mankind, have fled to dark woods and gloomy caves, and when there, finding it absolutely impossible to live quite alone, have chosen to associate upon intimate terms with some member or other of the brute creation. One has had a dog, another a cat, and I remember reading of one who made friends with a bear, though this intimacy, if I recollect right, terminated rather unfortunately, owing to the animal mistaking a bluebottle fly which settled upon the sleeping hermit's nose for a bee, and smashing in his friend's head with his paw in the kindly endeavour to prevent his being stung. But no animal could ever have been to my hermit what his pipe was. It soothed and consoled him, it was never cross to him, never answered him angrily, never teased and wearied him with conversation when he wanted silence, and never interfered with him when he desired to be left alone. It was his child—his own—his beloved—was this pipe to my hermit.

Unfortunately, however, pipes, being but mortal, I was going to say, but I suppose it would hardly be correct ; pipes, then, being, like mortals, generally dependent upon somebody or something else to keep them as they should be, this particular pipe became entirely useless one day on account of its owner having come to the end of his tobacco.

This was the circumstance to which I have already referred, and it certainly *was* a circumstance with a vengeance. A pipe without tobacco is like an umbrella without any covering to its skeleton frame, or like a woman without a tongue (even worse, some wicked folk might say), or like a house without windows, or like a bird without wings, or like a purse without money, or like anything else you please to mention, without that which constitutes its chief perfection or which alone makes it useful and pleasant.

How the misfortune happened I can briefly tell you, without going into a narration of the events of the early life of our hermit, which I am at present bound not to disclose.

It happened in a very natural way. It was not that he dropped his tobacco pouch into the stream—he was far too careful of the precious article for *that* - it was not that any robber of the woods had taken it from him by force, or any nightly thief had crept in while he slept and carried off the precious article ; no, it was

280

simply that he had not brought to the cave a sufficient quantity to last out, either because he had miscalculated the amount he *had* brought, or had not expected to stay so long ; and the consequence was that one fine morning, immediately after breakfast, when he went to his store to get out sufficient tobacco for the day's consumption, he found that he had only enough left to last him for another week.

This was, as I have remarked before, a circumstance with a vengeance. To do without his pipe, or without that which made his pipe valuable, was an utter impossibility. To get a new supply in the forest was equally out of the question. There remained, then, nothing for it but to return to the abodes of men in order to obtain that which was to him an absolute necessary of life.

But a man who has quitted society, given up the habit of associating with his kind, and adopted the life and assumed the character of a hermit, cannot easily retrace his steps. There are occasionally practical difficulties in the way. If he has not actually destroyed those garments which are deemed essential to persons entering or dwelling in a civilised community, he probably only possesses them in a state much worse than when he last wore them, entirely out of fashion, and not unlikely in an unwearable condition. Apart, moreover, from these technical considerations, the whole current of a man's thoughts when in such a position, his whole habit of life and the way of living into which he has fallen, render his return to civilised life extremely difficult.

Our Hermit felt all this, and felt it deeply. During the whole of that week he thought, and thought, and thought again, but with no other result than that to which he had come at first, namely, that the article he required must, somehow or other, be obtained. So determined was he upon this point, and so very difficult withal did the accomplishment of his determination appear, that I verily believe he would have turned robber forthwith, provided that the persons to be robbed had happened to be tobacco-merchants, or, at all events, persons well supplied with the article in question.

No such opportunity, however, offered ; no such temptation was thrown in his way, and all his musing and thinking brought him to the conclusion that there was nothing for it but to sally forth into the world in order to get that which he wanted. As day after day of that week slipped away, the thing appeared more and more difficult, and the thought of giving up smoking once actually crossed his mind, though only to be banished the next moment with the contempt it deserved.

The week at last was nearly out, and so was the Hermit's tobacco. Then he took up his big staff, which was so heavy at one end as to give rise to dark suspicion that it was loaded with lead ; he put on the old brown wide-awake which he constantly wore when he wore anything at all upon his head ; he wrapped round his manly frame a cloak of skins which would serve equally well for a coat by day and a blanket by night; he fastened on his sandals with due care, and stepped boldly out of his cave across the stream. Then, taking off his wide-awake, he stooped down, dipped his hand in the water, and passed it across his brow by way of refreshment, after which he rose, cast one look of fond and lingering regret upon the place which had been his home for many months past, and strode forward upon his journey.

Dense and dark was the forest for the most part, but the Hermit had started with sunrise, and the rays of the great luminary streamed in at intervals through the trees, and wherever they were less thickly planted he filled the forest with his glorious light, revealing a thousand woodland beauties and gladdening the eyes of him who beheld them. The way was in itself not without difficulties. Brakes and briars, tangled bushes, thorn-trees overcome by time which had bowed them to the ground, and seemingly resolved to vent their spleen upon the passing traveller by trailing their hidden branches, well studded with sharp spikes, upon the ground ; fragments of rocks half concealed by the luxuriant growth of fern and brambles —a sharp ascent here, there a fall in the ground so sudden as to be near akin to a precipice ; all these were features of the journey little calculated to make it more easy to the foot traveller.

The Hermit, however, seemed to make but little of them ; his strong arm brushed the

obstacles aside with apparent ease ; his well-sandaled feet resisted the insidious attacks of the thorn ; his sinewy legs bore him bravely up the hills, and his keen eye warned him in due time from the precipices, and so he pushed his way forward more rapidly than a man of less strength and determination could have done.

For several hours he proceeded through the forest without interruption of any kind, and indeed without encountering anything or anybody at all likely to interrupt him. Now and then a deer, startled from its lair by the unwonted intruder, sprang to its feet, regarded him for an instant with astonishment, and then darted away into the recesses of the forest ; anon a big bird, scared by his passage through the branches, burst out into the open air and sought safety in flight from the danger which its instinct taught it to expect, and here and there a snake, roused by the passing tread of the traveller, reared its head, fixed its basilisk eye upon him for a second, and then glided away to its refuge beneath the roots or within the adjacent rocks. But nothing stayed his onward course, and he pushed forward for some hours with the perseverance of a man who, having an object to accomplish, sets himself to the accomplishment thereof with the steady resolution which is the only sure method to obtain success.

The sun rose higher, the light grew stronger, animal creation throughout the whole forest began to stir and awaken into life, and still steadily onward strode the Hermit, never flagging, never wearying, never turning from his course, but always tending in the same direction and walking with the same vigorous stride.

At length he reached the mouth of a deep ravine, which appeared to divide the forest into two parts, beginning at a narrow outlet, and rapidly widening out on each side. As the traveller paused for a moment, he could see that the ground fell rapidly before him, that instead of huge trees, low and stunted bushes occupied the space upon which he was about to enter for some two or three hundred yards, whilst on each side the ground sloped upwards again, forming a kind of vast gorge down which, if he advanced and kept on his straight track, he must immediately descend.

He paused, I say, for a moment, as if unde-
cided whether to proceed or to turn aside, and
gazed into the ravine before him.

At that instant the silence and solitude of
the scene was suddenly changed. Wild figures
rose as if by magic from the brushwood and
stunted trees, as if disposed to bar his passage.
One of these immediately confronted him,
having sprung from behind a large bush where
he had lain concealed. It was a man, scantily
clad in garments made of the skins of animals,
and armed with a staff sharpened at the end
into a spear. He was apparently of about
middle height, and of no inconsiderable strength,
whilst his eyes, gleaming brightly from the
dark and bronzed countenance which they
adorned, had a wild fierceness of expression
which boded no good to the traveller. His hair
was matted upon his head, and surmounted by
a rough cap of fur, and altogether his appearance, quite as uncouth as that of the Hermit
himself, was anything but agreeable in the eyes
of the latter. Had the other been alone, indeed,
the Hermit would have cared but little for him
or his appearance, but he could hardly help
doing so when the bushes and brushwood
disclosed at least half a dozen figures of
a similarly strange appearance, armed with
sticks and clubs, if with no more deadly
weapon, and evidently disposed to dispute the
passage.

Our Hermit was no coward; great as was his
physical strength, it was equalled by the high
courage with which his heart was possessed,
and though the latter probably beat somewhat
quicker for the moment, it never quailed, nor
did he show aught of doubt or fear for a single
instant.

There was no mistaking the intentions of
those who thus interrupted his journey, for
without parley of any kind they rushed upon
him, the first man making a determined thrust
with his spear, which, had it taken effect as it
was intended, would have deprived the Hermit
of his life and the world of this story without any possible doubt. Fortunately for both
parties, however, it did no such thing. Our
Hermit, without the slightest hesitation, but
with no inconsiderable skill, parried the blow
with his staff, and immediately brought the

same implement down with a mighty thwack
upon his adversary's head.

Neither man nor beast could have withstood
the force of that blow. He went down like a
bullock before the deadly stroke of the butcher's
axe, and fell like a log upon the ground.

Whirling the staff round his head, the victor
turned to meet his other enemies, and gallantly
struck right and left as they closed in upon
him. For an instant it really seemed as if he
would prevail. So vast was the sweep of that
mighty arm, so powerful the weapon which it
wielded, and so dauntless the spirit of the man,
that it seemed as if, like one of the champions
of olden time, he was endowed with the mira-
culous gift of conquering any number of foes,
natural or supernatural, whom fate might bring
against him. The heavy blows which he dealt
as he swung his staff to and fro, and the unexpectedly resolute character of his defence, might
indeed, and probably would have gained him
the victory, had his enemies been less brave
and less numerous.

But however brave and strong a man may
be, it is heavy odds against him when he is
confronted and attacked by a dozen others, and
the bushes presently disclosed fully as many
enemies closing in around him, and fiercely
striking at him with their clubs and blud-
geons.

No aid was near, and only one result was
possible. Down they went, right and left, but
one struck as another fell, and no man can
resist his fate. It must moreover be remembered that our unfortunate friend was by no
means so fresh as when he had started that
morning: he had journeyed for hours through
thick woods and tangled brakes, and was
indeed beginning to think of a temporary pause
and rest at the very moment when he was thus
savagely attacked. His resistance, therefore,
could only be prolonged for a certain period,
and the more certainly was this the case, since
his enemies were able, from their number, and
the open nature of the spot upon which he
stood, to attack him on all sides at once, nor
could he ward off the blows of six or eight
strong arms striking at him at one and the
same moment.

So presently he got a nasty knock on the

head from a rascal who came treacherously behind him, then another from two or three blows aimed at the same time, and in the scrimmage that followed upon their coming to close quarters, he got so knocked about that before many seconds had passed he lay mute and insensible upon the ground.

And now comes what has always appeared to me the most incomprehensible and extraordinary part of the whole story. One would have thought that men, be they who they might, who had thought it worth their while to stop another man upon the highway—or rather in a place where there was no highway at all, but where each man had to make a path for himself — must have had some definite object in view, especially when the person stopped was tall, strong, and likely to resist.

If that object had been revenge, or the gratification of personal animosity towards their victim, one would have supposed that, having mastered and knocked him down, they would certainly have either made an end of him then and there, and, if employed by some rich enemy of the traveller, would have taken his head back to their employer as a proof of the fidelity with which they had discharged the duty they had undertaken, or would have carried him off bodily as a prisoner, and delivered him to those who had appointed to them their work.

If, on the other hand, the attacking party was composed of mere vulgar robbers, with no aristocratic revenge in question, but simply actuated by the desire of plunder, one would have imagined that they would either have destroyed the person they had attacked in pure disgust at finding upon him nothing valuable, or that if they had thought it worth while, they would have carried him off to their mountain fastnesses or forest caves, and held him captive in the hope of ransom, perhaps occasionally, in playful mood, sending a finger or two, or one of his ears, to his sorrowing relatives, in the hope of touching their hearts and opening their purses by this pleasing and simple plan.

The Hermit, for his part, certainly expected no mercy, and when he fell to the ground, had no sort of expectation that he should ever

again rise from it as a living man. But in this marvellous world of ours, the wisest and most scientific of us are frequently mistaken, whether we prophesy about the weather, or concerning public events which may happen to be passing around us, or with regard to something more directly relating to our own lives and actions.

In this instance, as an example of the same thing, our friend the Hermit was agreeably— well, not disappointed exactly—but mistaken in his expectation of ending his life under the bludgeon-blows of those who had assailed him.

To this hour I can never make out how or why it was that they did not effectually and for ever knock him on the head, and secure his silence with regard to a transaction which, even in that half-civilised country, might, if a one-sided statement should be made about it, entail unpleasant consequences upon themselves. Perhaps they did not think him worth the trouble ; perhaps they had still some mercy left at the far corner of their hearts, or perhaps (which seems to me most likely of all suppositions) they thought he was already dead, and required no more killing.

They might well have thought so, certainly, for the poor man had received blows enough, on head and body, to have killed half a dozen ordinary men, and lay there in his own blood, apparently as dead as Julius Cæsar.

It was remarkably lucky, moreover, that the robbers did not think it necessary to bury him, which would have been extremely awkward for him, and have silenced him with equal certainty. However they did no such thing, partly, I presume, because they thought it a needless ceremony, and partly because they were occupied in attending to their own wounded, inasmuch as, besides the leader, four or five of their number had suffered more or less from the violent resistance of the traveller.

They searched him, and found nothing that they thought worth taking, except his staff and his empty tobacco-pouch ; the former they carried off, but ere long threw away into the bushes as being too heavy for use save by a man taller than any of them happened to be ; the latter they thought might be useful, and so appropriated, and shortly afterwards left the spot.

It is impossible to say how long the Hermit remained insensible. It must have been for a considerable time, for when at length he opened his eyes, the sun was fast declining, and the shades of evening descending upon the forest.

For several moments our friend could not imagine where he was, or what had happened to him. He lay perfectly still, looking up at the skies, and trying to collect his ideas. Gradually, memory regained her powers, and the whole scene came back to him. His first thought was one of extreme surprise at being alive, mingled, let us hope, with gratitude to a Higher Power, which had spared his life in that hour of danger. His next thought was for his pipe.

Instinctively he felt for it, and as he raised his left arm to do so, the pain was so intense that he nearly fainted, and he became aware that it was either broken, or so bruised as to be but of little use to him. Under these circumstances, he not unnaturally tried the other arm, and to his great delight found that his faithful and beloved pipe was in its accustomed hiding-place, close to his heart.

Joy once more welled up within his breast, although the next moment came the rebound, as the miserable thought came across him that he had no tobacco, and a pipe without tobacco can be of little practical use, although indeed it may recall sweet memories of the past, and suggest pleasant anticipations for the future.

Having ascertained the safety of this valuable implement, he now began to turn his attention to matters which many people would have thought of before their pipe.

His condition was the reverse of agreeable, and could hardly be called safe. He was faint and weak—very weak. His head was bruised and beaten, so that if it had not been a remarkably thick one, he must certainly have been killed. He ached all over, and his limbs felt as if they could never again perform their duties towards his unfortunate body. Moreover, he did not know exactly where he was, and his journey forward, difficult even to a hale and strong man, had become positively impossible to one in his enfeebled and crippled

284

condition. He tried to raise himself up to a sitting posture, but fell back directly with a low groan. He endeavoured to creep to some better shelter, but the attempt gave him such pain, that he instantly desisted.

Then the terrible thought came over him that he should never leave that place alive. A horrid thought it was, enough to make the bravest heart shrink, for what kind of death had he to apprehend? Not the death of a brave warrior struck down in open fight by a fair foe, and breathing out his last sigh for the cause for which he had fought, conscious that to the last he had done his duty, and had at length fallen in its discharge. Not the death, either, which a hermit might naturally have expected, when his frame, attenuated with fasting and penance, had gradually worn out, and he lay upon his bed of leaves, peacefully and painlessly breathing out his soul.

Both these kinds of deaths our Hermit pictured to himself as he lay there, and fancied that either would have been easy to encounter.

But neither of these appeared likely to fall to his share. Felled by the blows of cowardly robbers, he had been left there in a position from which it seemed that death alone could release him, and that death would in all probability come either after many hours of suffering from starvation and thirst, or from the wild beasts of the forest, whose fangs he already fancied in his imagination fastened upon his helpless carcase, whilst the brutes snarled and snapped and worried over his still living self.

The idea was horrible, and his bodily weakness contributed to make it more so. He heartily wished that the robbers had done their work more completely, and that he had never waked from that sleep in which they had left him, for surely it would have been better thus than that he should have to meet such a fate as that for which he seemed destined. And as he lay and thought, the shades of evening began to close in, slowly but surely, and new sounds arose in the forest, whose animal life woke with the setting of the sun.

Far, far away, he fancied he heard a sound —a long, low sound, for which he listened again.

with a tension of nerves of which he had hardly been capable when in full strength. Again it sounded—and then again—and he knew but too well that it was the sound of the terrible panther of the forest, beginning his night-hunt for prey. He was answered by his mate, still in the far distance, and then came other sounds, little less alarming to the unhappy man.

The short bark of the wolf fell upon his ear, and as time passed on this sound came nearer and nearer, and other cries, of strange and wild animals, awoke the echoes of the forest. At last he felt as if he could bear it no longer: the suspense was too terrible—and he shouted aloud in desperation.

Weak as was his voice, from wounds and fatigue, it sounded loudly and strangely in that lonely place, and immediately afterwards the woodland cries seemed to increase, as if the wild beasts, recognising the voice of their enemy, man, were closing in around him with a view to his destruction.

Nearer and still nearer they seemed to come, and to the Hermit's excited imagination the leaves seemed to rustle and the dry sticks to crack before the advancing creatures. His head reeled again; his brain was on fire; his heart grew sick within him; strange, fantastically shaped reptiles seemed to crawl around, and over him; enormous snakes seemed to enfold him in endless coils; cruel faces seemed to peer out at him from the bushes on every side; bright, fierce, gleaming eyes seemed to glare upon him with ferocious expression, and he felt that a few moments more must end his existence, and blot him out from the earth. One more effort he would make—one more, and then sink back and die—with enormous exertion he raised himself upon his right arm, and once more shouted aloud.

Oh heavens! He was answered. A voice came back to him—no echo—no delusion, but an actual, undoubted, human voice, and it seemed near enough, too, to make it very certain that it was nothing else.

I cannot write for you in the language in which the voice spoke; at least I cannot carry on the conversation which ensued—if conversation you call it—in the language, because it

285

was Spanish, if I am not mistaken, and I don't know a word of Spanish, my ancestors having taken an active part in repelling the Spanish Armada, and having been so indignant at the invasion that they never allowed the children of their family to be taught the language, which did nobody any harm but themselves, and need not therefore be made a matter of accusation against them. However, in consequence of this, no doubt, I cannot speak or write Spanish, and so I prefer to pretend the people in this veracious history were all English, and in the English tongue I shall make them speak.

But all this time I am keeping the Hermit—and my readers also—waiting to hear what the voice said, which was really very little. "What cheer, comrade?" was what an Englishman would have said, and the owner of the voice said the equivalent to that in Spanish.

The Hermit, exhausted by the effort he had just made, could say no more, and the next moment the person who had answered him stepped forth out of the bushes.

He was a man somewhat above the middle height, with black hair cropped short round his head, handsome features, marvellous white teeth, swarthy complexion, a large gold earring in each ear, a curiously coloured shawl thrown carelessly over his shoulders and round his body after the fashion in which a Highlander wears his plaid, and the butts of several pistols appearing in the belt which it partially concealed.

He was a much smarter-looking fellow than any of the party who had first assaulted the Hermit, who were indeed a beggarly-looking lot in comparison with the new comer. Nor were his intentions unfriendly, as was immediately evident by his actions. He strode forward to the spot where the Hermit lay, and placing against a tree the gun which he carried in his hand, knelt down on the ground and began to examine his condition.

When he had satisfied himself as to the extent of the injuries which the other had received, he raised him gently in his arms and propped him up against an adjoining bush. Then he produced a small bag, from which he took a species of ointment, with which he began to touch the various bruises from which the Hermit had been suffering. He very carefully examined his head, and let fall upon it some drops from a small bottle which he produced from his bag—the relief was enormous.

The Hermit felt new life come into him as the stranger applied his remedies, and with freedom from pain and returning strength came, I am glad to say, a deep feeling of gratitude to the man who had indeed preserved him from a certain and horrible death.

(To be continued.)

PICTURE PAGE WANTING WORDS. (FOR PRIZE STORY.)

PUZZLES.

ENIGMAS.

1.

In Italy and sunny Spain
I'm the centre of attraction,
In Africa o'er many a plain
I'm surely found in action,
In France and Asia I am known,
So my origin now trace,
In America 'tis plainly shown
I hold a leading place,
In India, China, and Japan,
I'm certain to be found,
In Switzerland and Austria,
And England I'll be bound.

2.

So high is my post, so exalted my station,
That I'm sure to be found with the heads of
the nation ;
I'm sometimes as lonely as lonely can be,
And there's never a sigh but is uttered through
me,
But I'm sometimes so ugly and void of all
charm,
Though I do try my best not a heart can I
warm ;
By some men I'm treated quite harsh I declare,
But women protect me with infinite care ;
With watches and clocks too I'm sure to be
found,
Or useless 'twould be for their hands to go
round.

SQUARE WORDS.

1.

1. A plant. 2. Sour. 3. What I hope you
have never done. 4. Two thousand, five
hundred.

2.

1. A country. 2. Perceiving. 3. Rest.
4. A musical instrument. 5. To persist.
6. Actors.

CHARADES.

1.

Whole, I am a part of the human body,
Behead me, I am a conjunction,
Transpose me, I am a boy's name,
Behead me, I am an article.

2.

Whole, I am a tyrant,
Behead me twice, I am a mark,
Behead me, I am a vessel,
Transpose me, I am the summit,
Behead me and transpose me, I am a river in
Italy.

3.

Whole, I am to instruct,
Transpose me, I am a swindler,
Behead me, I am hot,
Behead me, I am to consume,
Transpose me, I am a drink,
Transpose and behead me, I am a preposition.

Answers to Puzzles on Page 256.

CHARADES.

1. Penmanship.   2. Intention.

BURIED TOWNS.

1. Ryde.   2. Lewes.   3. Sandown.
4. Rome.   5. Genoa.   6. Nice.

DIAMOND PUZZLES.

(1.)
```
        C
      A R E
    C H I M E
  C R I C K E T
    L A K E S
      L E A
        T
```
288

(2.)
```
          D
        T E A
      D A N E S
    D E N M A R K
      L E A R N
        A R E
          K
```

BURIED RIVERS.

1. Ouse.   2. Boyne.   3. Eden.   4. Thames.

SQUARE WORDS.

1.		2.	
1. Coat.	3. Area.	1. Past.	3. Soda.
2. Ogre.	4. Team.	2. Aloe.	4. Tear.

HOODIE.

By Mrs. MOLESWORTH, *Author of* "*Hermy*," "*The Cuckoo Clock*," *&c.*

"One flew away, and then there was none."
THREE LITTLE BIRDS.

HOODIE sat alone in the nursery, wrathful and sore. All the pleasure in the little bird and the beautiful cage seemed to have gone.

"I don't love her neither, not now," she said to herself. "I don't *think*—no I really don't *think* I love anybody, 'cos nobody loves me, and ev'ybody thinks I'm naughty. Never mind—I'll go away some day. As soon as ever I'm big enough I'll go kite away and never come back again and I sha'n't care what anybody says then."

There was some comfort though of a rather vague kind in this thought. Hoodie sat swinging her legs backwards and forwards, while queer fancies of where she would go—

289
U

what she would do, once she was "big enough," chased each other round her busy little brain.

Suddenly a sound in the passage outside the nursery door made her look up just in time to see the door open and Magdalen, leading tearful Hec by the hand, followed by Maudie, Duke, and Martin, came in.

Hoodie looked up with some curiosity.

"Hoodie," said Magdalen, "Hec wants to tell you how sorry he is that you have got blamed on his account. It was he that touched the basket and knocked it over. He ran into my room to look at the bird without Martin's knowing he had left the nursery, and he was so afraid that he had hurt the little bird, by knocking it over, that he didn't like to tell. Kiss him and speak kindly to him, poor little boy, Hoodie dear. He has been so unhappy."

Hoodie gravely contemplated her little brother, but without giving any signs of obeying her cousin's request.

"*I* have been unhappy too," she said, "and it wasn't my fault. It *was* Hec's."

"Well, then," said Magdalen, "it should make you the more sorry for Hec. He has had the unhappiness of knowing it *was* his fault, which is the worst unhappiness of all."

Hoodie threw back her head.

"*I* don't think so," she said. "I think the worst is when people always says you're naughty when you're not."

"I am sorry you thought I said you were naughty when you weren't, Hoodie," said Magdalen, "but you thought I meant more than I did. As soon as I thought about it quietly I felt sure you hadn't touched the basket—and even *more* sure, that if you had been tempted to touch it, you would have said so."

"'Cos Hec toldened you it was him," said Hoodie.

"No, before Hec said a word, I said to Martin I was sure it wasn't you."

Hoodie looked up with a new light in her eyes.

"*Did* you?" she said, as if hardly able to believe it.

"Yes, indeed, Miss Hoodie," said Martin, "Miss King did say so. And very kind of her, it was, to trust you so, for you did look very

290

funny when I said you had been a few minutes alone in the room.

Hoodie flamed round upon her.

"It's very nasty of you to say that, Martin," she exclaimed violently. "*Vezzy* nasty. You alvays think I'm naughty. I daresay I did look funny, 'cos I was temptationed, awful temptationed to touch the bird, but I wouldn't, no I *wouldn't*, 'cos I'd p'omised."

And at last her mingled feelings found relief in a burst of sobs.

The sight was too much for Hec, already in a sorely depressed and tearful condition. He threw his arms round Hoodie, nearly dragging her off her chair in his endeavours to get her shaggy head down to the level of his own close-cropped dark one for an embrace.

"Oh Hoodie, Hoodie, *dear* Hoodie, don't cry," he beseeched her. "It's all Hec's fault. Naughty Hec. Oh Hoodie, please 'agive me and kiss me, and I'll never, never touch your bird again."

Hoodie was quite melted.

"Dear Hec—poor Hec," she cried in her turn. "Don't cry, dear Hec," and the two little creatures hugged and kissed and cried, all in one.

"Let's kiss Maudie's godmother too. She didn't think you was naughty, Hoodie," suggested Hec, and Hoodie at once took his advice, so the kissing and hugging were transferred to poor Magdalen, who bore them heroically, till at last she was so very nearly smothered that she was obliged to cry for mercy.

"And let us go back to my room now," she said, "and introduce the little bird to its new house. It hasn't seen it yet, you know, Hoodie."

"*Hasn't* it?" said Hoodie.

"Of course not. The cage is yours—your very own. I waited for you to come before putting the bird in it."

"That was *rezzy* good of you," said Hoodie, approvingly, and as happy and light-hearted as if no temper or trouble of any kind had ever come near her, she took Hec's hand and trotted off with her cousin to help in the installation of the bird in its beautiful cage.

"What funny creatures children are," said Magdalen to herself, "and of them all surely Hoodie is the funniest."

It would be impossible to tell the pleasure that the possession of the little bird gave to Hoodie, and the devotion she showed to it. For some days its cage remained in Miss King's room that Cousin Magdalen herself might watch how the little creature got on, and there, as Martin said, "morning, noon, and night," Hoodie was to be found. It was the prettiest sight to see her, seated by the table, her elbows resting upon it, and her chubby face leaning on her hands while her eyes eagerly followed every movement of her favourite. She was never tired of sitting thus, she was never cross or impatient, nor did she ever attempt to touch the greenfinch without Magdalen's leave. And finding that the little girl was so gentle and obedient, and that the bird gave her such pleasure, Magdalen kindly did her utmost to increase this pleasure. She taught Hoodie how to tame and make friends with her pet, to call to it with her soft little voice—for no one could have a softer or prettier voice than Hoodie when she chose—always in the same tone, till the bird learnt to recognise it and to come at her summons. And oh the delight of the first time this happened! Hoodie was holding out her hand, the forefinger outstretched in the open door of the cage, half-cooing, half-whistling, in the pretty way Magdalen had taught her, when birdie, its head cocked on one side as if half in timidity, half in coquetry, at last mustered up courage and hopped on to the fat little pink finger.

Hoodie *nearly* screamed with delight, but recollected herself just in time not to frighten the bird.

"Oh Cousin Magdalen," she whispered in the most tremendous excitement, "Him is pouching, him's pouching on my finger. Oh the darling, —look, look, Maudie's godmother."

But before Maudie's godmother could get across the room to look, Mr. Birdie had hopped off its new perch, and the experiment had to be repeated.

"Come and pouch, birdie, dear birdie; *do* come and pouch on my finger?" said Hoodie, beseechingly.

"Call it the way I taught you," whispered Magdalen.

Hoodie did so, and at the sound of her well-

known call, the greenfinch cocked its head, looked round on all sides, appeared to consider, and at last condescended again to hop on to its little mistress's finger.

"Isn't it *sweet?*" said Hoodie ecstatically, though scarcely daring to breathe for fear of disturbing it.

"If you take care never to startle it," said Magdalen, "it will get in the way of coming regularly whenever you call it. Never let it hear you speaking angrily or roughly, Hoodie. That would startle it more than anything."

"*Would* it?" said Hoodie, regarding her pet with affection not unmingled with respect. "Would it know I was naughty? Cousin Magdalen," she added, looking up into her friend's face with considerable awe in her bright green eyes; "Cousin Magdalen, do you think *p'raps* my bird's a fairy, and that God sent it to teach me to be good?"

Fortunately by this time Magdalen's intercourse with Hoodie had taught her the necessity of great control of herself. Whatever Hoodie said or did, she must not be laughed at—not even smiled at, if in the smile there lurked the slightest shadow of ridicule. Once let Hoodie imagine she was being made fun of and all hope of leading her and making her love and trust you was over.

So Magdalen's face remained quite grave as she replied to Hoodie's question,

"I think that *everything* nice and pretty that comes to us is sent by God, dear. And He means them all to teach us to be good. But I don't think you need fancy your little bird is a fairy."

"It's *so* clever," said Hoodie. "Fancy him knowing when I call. Do you think some day it'll learn to speak, Cousin Magdalen?"

Cousin Magdalen shook her head.

"I'm afraid not. It isn't the kind of bird that ever learns to speak," she replied, as gravely as before. "But I shouldn't wonder if it learns to know you very well—to come in a moment when it hears you call, and to show you that it is pleased to see you."

"Oh how lovely that'll be," said Hoodie, dancing about with delight. "Fancy it coming on my finger whenever I say ' Birdie dear, come and pouch.' I'll *never* let it hear me speak c'oss,

Cousin Magdalen. Whenever I feel *it* coming I'll go out of the room and shut the door tight so it sha'n't hear me."

"Whenever you feel what coming?" asked Magdalen.

" *It.*" repeated Hoodie, " c'ossness, you know. It must come sometimes—*all* chindrel is c'oss *sometimes*," she added complacently.

" Well, but suppose some children were to make up their minds to be cross *no* times," said Magdalen with a smile. " Wouldn't that be a good thing? Suppose a little girl I know, not very far from here, was to set the example."

Hoodie laughed.

" Cousin *Magdalen*," she said with an accent on the name that she always gave when amused. " Cousin *Magdalen*, how funny you are! I know who you mean—yes, I do, kite well. But she couldn't, that little girl couldn't help being c'oss *sometimes.*"

She shook her head sagaciously.

"Well, any way," said Magdalen, "try and let the ' sometimes ' come as seldom as possible. Won't you do that, Hoodie?"

Just then there came a tap at the door.

"Miss Hoodie," said Martin's voice. "Come to tea, please. It's quite ready."

Hoodie gave an impatient shake. Fortunately the bird was no longer on her finger, otherwise its nerves would have been considerably startled. Hoodie had been on the point of putting her hand into the cage to entice it to hop on to her finger and thus to lift it out when Martin's summons came.

"I don't want any tea," she said ; "do go away, Martin. You *always* come for me when I don't want to go."

" Hoodie," whispered Magdalen, " the bird will be quite frightened to hear you speak like that."

Hoodie looked startled.

" Oh dear," she said. " I quite forgot. You see, Cousin Magdalen, it *will* come. There's no good trying to keep it away."

"Yes there is," said Magdalen. "There's good in trying to keep it away, and there's good in trying to send it away even after it's come. You're sending it away now, Hoodie. I think."

" Am I? " said Hoodie, doubtfully. Then with a sudden change of tone, " Well, I *will*

then. I'll go goodly with Martin. Martin," she said amiably, turning to her nurse, " I'm coming. I'll go out of the room kite goodly and quiet, and then perhaps birdie won't remember about my speaking c'oss."

"I daresay he won't," said Magdalen encouragingly. " I'll give him some fresh seed to eat, as it's rather low in his box, and that will give him something else to think of. But I won't speak to him, Hoodie. I never do, because I want him to learn to know your voice."

"That's out of the Bible," was Hoodie's parting remark, as she went off with Martin, quite " goodly," as she had promised.

Day by day Hoodie loved her bird more and more, and her love was repaid by great success in taming the little creature. It grew to know her wonderfully well, to hop on to her rosy finger when she called to it, adding always, " Birdie, birdie, come and *pouch*," with a soft. clear note of delight that it was quite a pleasure to hear. Its cage was placed in the window of a little ante-room out of which Miss King's room opened. There had been some talk of putting it in the nursery, but Hoodie pleaded against this. The cat *had* been known to enter the nursery, for Hec and Duke were rather fond of old pussy, and Prince was a frequent visitor there. And besides this, Hoodie could not feel quite sure that her little brothers might not be some day "temptationed " to touch her favourite. It was pretty clear any way that birdie's residence in the nursery would be a source of quarrels, so Mother and Magdalen and Martin agreed that the anteroom window would be the best and safest place.

" It isn't as if winter were coming instead of summer," said Magdalen. " In that case a room without a fire would be too cold for it. But every day, now, the weather is getting brighter and warmer. What are you looking so grave about, Hoodie? "

Hoodie looked up solemnly.

" I were just thinking," she replied, " what a pity it would be if winter comed back again instead of summer, just when we're settled about my bird so nicely—by mistake you know."

" But winter and summer don't come of

themselves, Miss Hoodie," said Martin. "You know God sends them, and He never makes mistakes."

"But *supposing* He did," said Hoodie, "you are so stupid, Martin. You might *suppose.*"

"Hoodie!" said Magdalen, warningly.

Hoodie gave a wriggle, but said no more. Not that she was vanquished however. She waited till bed-time and then, after saying aloud as usual her little evening prayer, added a special clause for Martin's edification. "And p'ease, dear God, be sure not to forget to send the nice warm summer for my little bird, and don't let cold winter come back again by mistake."

"It'll do no harm to '*amind* God, any way," she observed with satisfaction, as she lay down in bed and composed herself for her night's repose.

Weeks passed on and the nice warm summer came. Hoodie's devotion to her bird seemed to increase as time went on, and so much of her time was spent beside its cage that the nursery peace and quiet were much greater than before its arrival.

One day, just after the nursery breakfast, she hastened to her pet as usual. Rather to her vexation she saw that her two little brothers were standing by the cage, of which the door was open, Miss King beside them. Hoodie frowned, but did not venture to say anything.

"See, Hoodie," said Magdalen, "see how very confiding birdie has learnt to be. He has actually hopped on to Duke's finger when he whistled to him the way you do. It will do him no harm now to be friendly to other people too—now that he knows you so well. Look at him."

"See, Hoodie," cried Duke in delight, holding up his stumpy little forefinger, on which birdie was contentedly perched.

An ugly black cloud came over Hoodie's face. She darted forward, furious with anger.

"I *won't* have him pouch on your finger, Duke," she cried. "I won't have *anybody* call him but me. I won't. I won't—he's the only thing that loves me and nobody's to touch him. Go away, naughty Duke; ugly Duke."

293

She pushed Duke aside with one hand and with the other attempted, gently, notwithstanding her passion, to take the bird. The window was wide open, and the children were standing beside it. Magdalen, who was at the other side of the table on which stood the cage, hurried forward, but too late. Startled by Hoodie's loud voice, not recognising in the furious little girl its gentle mistress, and with some instinct of self-preservation, the greenfinch with a frightened uncertain note flew off Duke's finger, alighted for one instant on the window sill, from which it seemed for a moment to look at the group in the room, as if in farewell, then, before Magdalen could do anything, before Hoodie had taken in the idea of the misfortune that threatened her, raised its pretty wings with another soft reproachful note, and flew away—away out in the bright sunny garden, over the bushes and flowers, away—away—to some leafy corner up among the high trees, where there would be no angry voices to startle it, no quarrelsome children to frighten its tender little heart—no sound but the soft brush of the squirrel's furry tail among the branches, and the gentle flutter of the summer breeze. Away, away! But what did that "away" mean to poor broken-hearted Hoodie.

She stood motionless with surprise and horror—she did not dart to the window as one would have expected—ready almost to throw herself out of it in fruitless pursuit of her favourite—she stood perfectly still, as if turned into stone. But the expression on her face was so strange and unnatural that Miss King felt frightened.

"Hoodie," she exclaimed. "Hoodie, child, don't stand like that. Come to the window and call to your bird. Perhaps he will hear you and fly back."

She said it more to rouse Hoodie out of the depth of her misery than because she really thought the bird would return, for in the bottom of her heart she feared much that it had truly flown away, and that once it felt itself out in the open air its natural instinct of freedom would prevent its returning to its cage.

Hoodie started.

"Come back? Do you *think* he'll come back, Cousin Magdalen?" she exclaimed, and rushing to the window, and leaning out so far that Magdalen was obliged to hold her for fear she should fall over, she gave the soft clear call which her cousin had taught her—over and over again, till, tired and out of breath, she drew in her head and looked up in Magdalen's face despairingly.

"He won't come," she said, "he won't come. P'raps he's flied away too far to hear me. P'raps he can hear me but he doesn't want to come. Oh dear, oh dear, what shall I do? My bird, my bird—you always said he would fly away if he heard me speak c'oss, and I did speak c'oss, dedful c'oss. Oh! what shall I do?"

Hoodie sank down on the floor—a little heap of tears and misery. Hec and Duke flung their arms round her, beseeching her not to cry so, but there was no comfort for Hoodie.

"It was my own fault," she kept repeating, "my own fault for speaking so c'oss. The bird will never come back. Oh no, Hec and Duke, dear Hec and Duke, it isn't no good kissing me. I'll never, never be happy again, and it's my own fault."

It was impossible not to be sorry for her. Magdalen felt almost ready to burst into tears herself. She took Hoodie up in her arms and tried to comfort her.

"I don't think you should quite lose heart about birdie, Hoodie. He may come back again, once he has had a good fly. We must keep the window open, and you must keep calling to him every now and then, in the way he is used to. And perhaps it would be a good plan to go out in the garden and call—he may perhaps have flown up among the trees at the other side."

Hoodie was only too ready. Patiently, while her cousin went down to her breakfast, the little girl stood at the window calling to the truant. Every now and then the sobs that would continue to rise, made a sad little quaver in the middle, and once or twice poor Hoodie was obliged to stop altogether. But she soon began again, and every now and then between her whistles, she said in a beseeching, half heart-broken tone—

294

"Oh birdie, *won't* you come? Come dear birdie, oh *do* come and pouch on my finger. I'll never, never speak c'oss again—never, dear birdie, if only you'll come back and pouch on my finger."

It was very melancholy. Very melancholy too was the walking about the garden in vain hopes that birdie might be somewhere near and would fly down again. The whole day passed most sadly. Hoodie's eyes were swollen with crying, and she could scarcely eat any dinner or tea, and her distress naturally was felt by all the nursery party. It was one of the saddest days the children had ever known, and they all went to bed with sorely troubled little hearts.

Magdalen too was grieved and sorry.

"I blame myself," she said to Hoodie's mother. "Pets are always a risk, and Hoodie is such a strange mixture that one shouldn't run risks with her. I wish I had never suggested her keeping the bird as a pet, but I thought it might be good for her to have something of her very own to care for and attend to."

"And so it was," said Hoodie's mother. "It has done her a great deal of good; it has softened her wonderfully. We all noticed it. And even this trouble may do her good; it may teach her really to try to master that sad temper of hers."

"I had no idea she would have been so put out at Duke's playing with her bird," Magdalen went on, "or I would not have risked it."

"But she *should* not have been put out at it," said Mrs. Caryll. "You have nothing whatever to reproach yourself with, dear Magdalen. Hoodie *must* be taught that she cannot be allowed to yield to that selfish, jealous temper."

"I know," said Magdalen. "But how are we to teach her? that is the difficulty—the least severity or sternness which does good to other children, seems to rouse her very worst feelings and only to harden her. She is not hardened now, poor little soul, she is perfectly humble. Oh how I do wish I could find her bird for her!"

"Don't trouble yourself so much about it,

dear. You really must not," said Mrs. Caryll, as she bade her cousin good-night.

But unfortunately those things which our friends beg us not to trouble ourselves about are generally the very things we find it the most impossible to put out of our minds. Magdalen could not leave off "troubling" about poor Hoodie. She slept little, and when she did sleep it was only to dream of the lost bird, sometimes that it was found again in all sorts of impossible places—sometimes that Hoodie was climbing a dreadfully high mountain, or attempting to swim across a deep river, where Magdalen felt that she would certainly be drowned,—in search of it. And once she dreamt that the bird flew into her room and perched at the foot of her bed, and when she exclaimed with delight at seeing it again it suddenly began to speak to her, and its voice sounded exactly like Hoodie's.

"I have come to say good-bye to you, Maudie's godmother," it said. "Nobody loves me and I am always naughty, so I'd better go away."

And as Magdalen started up to catch the bird or Hoodie, whichever it was—in her dream it seemed both—she awoke.

It was bright daylight already, though only five o'clock. Outside in the garden the sun was shining beautifully, the air, as Magdalen opened her window, felt deliciously fresh and sweet, everything had the peaceful untroubled look of very early morning—of a very early spring morning especially—when the birds and the flowers and the sunshine and the breezes have had it all to themselves, as it were, undisturbed by the troubles and difficulties and disagreements that busy day is sure to bring with it, as long as there are men and women, and boys and girls, in this puzzling world of ours.

Though, after all, it is better to be a child than a bird or a flower—whatever mistakes we may make, whatever wrong we may do, all, alas, adding to the great mass of mistakes and wrong—whatever sorrows we may have to bear, it is something to feel in us the power of bearing them, the power of *trying* to put right even what we may have helped to put wrong—best of all the power of loving each other, and

295

of helping each other in a way that the happy, innocent birds and flowers know nothing about. Is it not better to be *ourselves*, after all?

Magdalen leant out of the window, enjoying the sweet air and sunshine, but thinking all the time how much more she would have enjoyed this bright morning but for her sympathy with poor Hoodie's trouble.

Suddenly a thought struck her. *Possibly* the bird, chilled and hungry after some hours' freedom, unaccustomed to be out in the dark, or to find food for itself—*possibly* he might have returned to his cage in the night. Magdalen threw on her dressing-gown and hurried into the ante-room. The window was open, the cage-door stood open too, everything was ready to welcome the little wanderer—fresh seed in the box, fresh water in the glass—Hoodie had seen to it all herself before going to bed—but that was all!

There was no little feathered occupant in the cage—it was empty, and with a fresh feeling of disappointment, Magdalen stood by the window again, looking out at the bright morning, and wondering what she could do to comfort poor Hoodie. Outside, the birds were singing merrily.

"Should I get her another bird?" thought Magdalen, "a canary, perhaps, accustomed to cage life? No, I think not. It might only lead to fresh disappointment; besides, I don't think Hoodie is the sort of child to care for another, *instead*. No, that wouldn't do."

Suddenly a sort of flutter in the leaves round the window-frame—Mr. Caryll's house was an old one; there were creepers all over the walls—made Magdalen look up.

"Can there be a nest in the eaves?" she said to herself, for the flutter was evidently that of a bird; and as she was watching, she saw it fly out—fly down rather from the projecting window roof, and—to her amazement, after seeming for an instant or two to hesitate, it summoned up courage and flew a little way into the room—too high up for her to reach however, and not far enough into the room for her to venture to shut the window. She stood breathless, for as it at last settled for a moment on the curtain-rod, she saw what at first she had scarcely ventured to believe, that it was Hoodie's bird.

It stayed a moment on the rod, then it flew off again—made a turn round the room—"oh" thought Magdalen, "if it *would* but settle somewhere further from the window, so that I could shut it in"—But no, off it flew again —out into the open air and Magdalen's heart sank. Patience! Another moment and it was back again, with designs on its cage apparently, but it hesitated half-way. Now was the critical moment. Magdalen hesitated. Should she risk it? She stretched out her hand towards the bird and softly and tremulously whistled to it in Hoodie's well-known call. The wavering balance of birdie's intentions was turned—it cocked its head on one side and with a pretty chirp, flew towards Magdalen and perched on her finger! Slowly and cautiously, whistling softly all the time, she slipped her hand into the cage, and quickly withdrawing it the instant birdie hopped off, he found himself caught.

But he seemed quite content, and in two moments was pecking at his seed as if nothing had happened.

(To be continued.)

ROGER'S STORY.

By the AUTHOR of "AUNT EFFIE'S RHYMES," Etc.

DEAR ROGER has come home from school,
   To the little ones' infinite joy,
He is first-rate at whipping up fun,
   A kind-hearted unselfish boy.

What help when the good-natured lads,
   For the fourteen long weeks that they stay,
Take a lift of the nursery babes
   In a story, a game, or a play.

"You said you would tell us a story
   The next time you came home from school,
Do tell it to-night—" said the Fairy
   Who perched on his boots for a stool.

"Yes now," said the six little voices;
   And one said, "Begin it to-day,"
Another said, "Make it so long
   It will last the whole time that you stay."

"Just so, to begin," said the brother,
   "You all take your seats and be still;
The Fairy may sit on boot laces,
   And you on the floor, Jack and Jill."

297

Now lest you don't know I must tell you,
  These two on the floor were the twins,
The two were the same age exactly,
  And like as a couple of pins.

And no one could tell which was which
  When asleep on their pillows they lay,
But one had blue eyes when they opened—
  Blue eyes, while the other had grey.

Now do not you think Jack and Jill
  Must have been most uncommonly wise
To be quite sure they knew their own selves
  When they never could see their own eyes?

To know one's own self is so hard,
  You may try, try again and yet fail,
It is just such a difficult thing
  As to hold a live eel by the tail.

So now let us turn from that subject
And sit down beside the small twins :
To hear what tall Roger their brother
Will say when his story begins.

"It happened a long time ago
And when nobody travelled by train,
For railways were only laid then
In clever Bob Stevenson's brain :

It happened that good Mrs. Whistles
Who wanted a new woollen gown,
Set out on a Saturday morning
To buy herself one in the town.

Old Pat, that is, old Mr. Whistles,
Had left her before it was light;
He started, as bird-catchers do,
In the very small hours of the night.

His clap nets, decoy birds and bundles,
He carried behind in a pack,
And beside him ran little Pat minor
With one empty cage on his back.

"It's myself," said old Pat to himself,
   "That's the luckiest cratur on earth
To have got such a wife as my Judie
   Without either fortune or birth."

"It's myself," said Pat Whistles again,
   "That's the luckiest cratur alive.
With my children all working together
   Like so many bees in a hive.

There's Illin and Katleen got married,
   And Morris and Tim gone to sea,
And no one but little Pat minor
   To look for his victuals to me."

And thereupon whistling a tune,
   He made three or four rounds of a jig,
'Twas as natural Paddy should dance
   As that small birds should hop on a twig.

"As a family always united
   Was mine from its earliest days,
For I managed to hold them together
   By sending them different ways.

And no doubt we'll have real luck
   At the catching," said he, "for the larks
Are all fast asleep in the heather
   And hungry as children or sharks."

"Yes, I'll wring their necks," said the boy,
   "But the linnets, we'll sell them alive;
And all in good time for the market
   We'll reach Covent Garden by five.

But when shall we get any breakfast?
   For if we meet Mother in town
And we all of us walk home together
   We'll take a long time to get down."

"Och sure, we'll dine first in the city,
   A glass of poteen and a snack;
And reversing the order, we'll breakfast
   At home when we all have got back."

300

While good Mrs. Whistles jogged on
  In the carrier's cart to the town,
She kept making long calculations
  Of lengths and of breadths for the gown.

"One breadth for the front, and the back,
  And a half breadth will do for each side,
And a yard and a half for the bodice
  Because the material is wide."

And then for the price, she would like
  That her very best dress should be good,
And so, to secure the best cloth
  She would give the best price that she could.

And then for the colour, old women
  Look better in browns or in greys,
"They look like old fools," said dame Whistles,
  "In colours of all the sun's rays."

She learnt this wise creed from wise neighbours
  Who saw that though prudent and kind,
She dressed in the gayest of colours
  Because she was born colour blind.

So she asked a smart youth in the shop
  To select for her soberest grey;
And she paid down the price in hard cash
  And then carried her parcel away.

"I'll make it myself," said dame Whistles,
"And no one shall see it or know
Till I put on my new Sunday gown,
For I've time both to wash and to sew."

When Whistles was going to be married
And buying his goods at a sale,
The Auctioner put up a mirror,
And said it belonged by entail

To a long string of Queens that had reigned
In the beautiful Emerald Isle.
"And the crown at the top makes that sartin,"
Said Pat to himself with a smile.

So the Auctioner lifted his hammer
And Pat gave a nod with his head,
And the glass was knocked down for a shilling,
Said Pat, "and he knocked it down dead."

"When Judie, my bride, stands before it,
Reflecting her body and mind
In the parts where the ancient quicksilver
Is not quite kilt off it behind,

What a beautiful cratur she'll look,
    For the glass is a beautiful green,
And I'll worship and kiss her reflection
    As if I was kissing the Queen."

But many a winter had passed
    Since the mirror was nailed to the wall,
And said Judie "The quacksilver's old,
    And it don't reflect beauty at all."

So Pat with his fertile invention
    Suggested the use of a spoon,
"In its hollow one looks like the sun,
    On its hill, like a slender new moon.

I shall use it myself when I shave
    If the barber should chance to be tight,
When I want to be smart on the Sabbath
    And have to get shaved overnight.

I likes to be cleaned up and tidy
    At church, when I chance to go there,
Though I can't say I find, like the priests,
    That the pomps give more vartue to prayer.

There's a silver-washed spoon in the cupboard,
    I swapt with that man at the fair,
When I gave him a wrinkle or two
    About catching small fowls of the air.

303

Avourneen make search, and you'll find it,
An illegant piece of old plate
Wrapped carefully up in the shammy
To ward off the tarnishing state."

Said Judie, "It's spoiled, but be easy,
And take things for best as they come."
Said Pat, "Won't I whiten the nigger
And polish him off with my thumb."

"There, now it's a piece of perfection,
Look into it, Judie, and say
If you ever beheld such a picture
As that which you're seeing to-day."

Said Judie, "The face that looks out
Is a forehead and chin without eyes;
But the phases of life that are spoonie
Are mostly addicted to lies."

"It's the wrong way, I'm thinking," said Paddy,
"Look into the spoon from behind,
And if it's true plate, the reflection
Is sure to smile friendly and kind."

Little Bob over grandmother's shoulder
Saw something distorted and dim,
That seemed to grow bigger and bigger
The nearer they thrust it to him.

"Oh, Granny, it's coming, it's coming
　To gobble and swallow me down,
It's the Punch that kills Judy, high up
　In the Punch-box that walks about town."

Says Pat, "Bless the child and behold him,
　His eyes are as round as the moon;
Why it's only the great Topsy-Turvey
　That lives in the heart of the spoon."

"We know him quite well," said the twins,
　"For we look for him every day
In the backs and the fronts of the spoons,
　And we turn them in every way.

But he turns overhead in the front,
　And if ever he's straight on the back,
He makes some queer ugly grimaces
　And hides in his mantle of black."

Said Roger, "You two little stupids,
　Turn hand over heels on the floor,
And see if the great Topsy-Turvey
　Dare play you such tricks any more."

Said the Fairy, " But Roger do tell us
The end of old Judie's new gown."
"Oh, only it proved a bright scarlet
Because the young shopman in town

Played good Mrs. Whistles a trick
When he found she took scarlet for grey,
And he gave her a dress like the Guards'
And then laughed when he sent her away."

"Oh Judie, you've been and enlisted,"
Said Pat, when he saw her come down
All ready for church in the morning
And dressed in her bright scarlet gown.

"It's I who can stand up in danger
And ne'er leave my wife in the lurch,
But I can't stand the laugh that will follow
My soldier and me into church.

So here's to you Judie, my darling,
I'm off to the fields for the day,
We're too late for church, but out yonder
We'll worship together and pray."

TALKS ABOUT THE MONTHS.

OCTOBER.

By Mrs. GEORGE CUPPLES.

" When the chill October wind
Oft is sadly sighing,
When the leaves in curlets fly,
All seems dead or dying.
Wild Rose, then thy ruddy leaves,
Scarlet berries shining,
Give bright glow to bare hedgerow,
And the year declining."

HE stormy weather usually attending the latter days of September have passed away, and we may expect the beginning of October to be mild and serene ; though the mornings and evenings are often very chill and foggy. Owing to the decay of nature, we cannot but have a melancholy feeling about this month, still we have occasionally in it some of the finest and most bracing weather of the year. There is often frost in the morning and evening, and warm sunshine in the mid-day, with a fine breeze; and it is considered the very best time of the year to enjoy a "sniff of the briny sea air."

At this time of the year, as well as in April, we often see in the fields marks of footsteps, in which the grass appears as if it had been scorched by heated iron. Ignorant people when they come upon these footsteps are very much afraid, as they suppose some hobgoblin has walked along that way; but the real truth is that when the grass is crisped by hoar-frost it is very brittle, and the weight of a man, or even of a child, breaks it down and kills it. So when the sun has thawed the "rime" from the fields, these spots look brown and bare in the midst of the surrounding grass.

It is during October that the leaves of trees and shrubs, after having taken on them their rich autumnal colours, begin to fade quickly and to fall off. The whole of this season is often distinguished by being called "the fall of the leaf," though the falling of the leaves more particularly takes place in the following month. But the hedges with their glowing berries of various hues in the midst of their fading colours cause the month to be called "golden October." The bright scarlet hips, the fruit of the wild rose; the haw, that of the hawthorn; the dark purple sloe, that of the blackthorn, together with the bright and beautiful berries of the honeysuckle, the privet, the elder, the briony, and the holly. It is these, and the berries of the ivy, which ripen at a later period, and the seeds of the innumerable grasses and plants, that supply our birds with their winter food.

October takes its name from two Latin words—one *octo*, eight, and the other *imber*, rain or *shower*. It was the *eighth* month of the first Roman year, and the word *imber* was joined to *octo* to point out the showery and wet weather which generally appeared about this time.

The Saxons called October *Wyn Monath*, or the Wine Month, because it is the season for pressing grapes and making wine. It was also occasionally called *Winter fulleth*, or coming winter, with the full moon of the month.

During this month there are several days dedicated to patron saints, and held as festi-

vals in one country or another. The 9th of October is *St. Denis's Day*, the patron saint of France, and the Romish writers gravely relate, that having been beheaded by the pagans, he took up his head in his hands, and carried it two miles, when he delivered it to "a good woman, called Catula," who buried it. The guardianship of France and England is expressed in the old ballad—

"St. George he was for England,
St. Denis was for France,
Singing, *Honi soit qui mal y pense.*"

The 12th day of October is worthy of being remembered as the day on which Columbus landed on the island of San Salvador, one of the Bahamas, the first land discovered in the New World.

Then there is St. Luke's day on the 18th, and St. Simon's and St. Jude's on the 25th, the latter disciples of Jesus and the former of the Apostle Paul.

The 25th is *St. Crispin's Day*. St. Crispin and his brother Crispinian were natives of Rome, and having become converts to Christianity, travelled northwards into France to propagate the faith. They preached to the people during the day, and at night earned their subsistence by the making of shoes, furnishing the poor with them at a very low price, for the legend adds an Angel supplied them with leather. This day in many places is still celebrated with great festivity and rejoicing. One special ceremony was a grand procession with banners and music, whilst various characters representing King Crispin and his Court were sustained by different members. At Tenby it was customary, on the eve of St. Crispin's day, to make an effigy of the saint, and suspend it from the steeple, or some other elevated place. In the morning it was formally cut down and carried in procession throughout the town. In front of every shoemaker's door the procession halted, when a document, purporting to be the last will and testament of the saint, was read, and in pursuance thereof some article of dress was left as a memento of the noisy visit. At length, when nothing was left but the padding which formed the body of the effigy, it was made into a football and kicked about by the crowd. As a sort of revengo for the treatment of their patron saint, the shoemakers hung up the effigy of a carpenter on *St. Clement's Day*, which was treated in a similar way. Shakespeare writes of this day:—

"This day is called the feast of Crispian :
He that outlives this day, and comes safe home,
Will stand a tip-toe when this day is named,
And rouse him at the name of Crispian.
He that shall live this day and see old age
Will yearly on the vigil feast his neighbours,
And say, 'To-morrow is Saint Crispian.' "

The 28th of October is kept in our memories as the one on which Alfred the Great died. Several of our wisest institutions date their origin from this Saxon monarch, and the various divisions into which our country is arranged were made by his order ; the names of these, very little changed, have come down to us as memorials of his attention to the welfare of his people.

But the night we all look forward to with most delight is the last night of October, the Eve of All Saints, or Allhallows' Eve. This night used formerly to be celebrated with rude sports and games, part of which consisted in diving for apples, and in burning nuts on the bars of the grate, when it is called by the vulgar name of *Nutcrack Night.*

"The auld gude wife's weel-hoordit nits
Are round an' round divided,
An' mony lads' and lasses' fates
Are there that night decided :
Some kindle, couthie, side by side,
An' burn thegither trimly ;
Some start awa,'wi' saucy pride,
An' jump out-owre the chimlie."

There is a remarkable uniformity in the fire-side customs of this night all over the United Kingdom. Nuts and apples are everywhere in requisition and consumed in immense numbers. Oh, how delightful to think of the Halloween nights, with the great tub of water in the centre of the floor full of large red-cheeked or brown apples floating about, and what fun to try to catch them with one's teeth ! What a sputtering and a choking when the apple bobs away, and the water rushes into one's mouth and up the nostrils ; but what a feeling of triumph there is when one manages to catch one securely ! After the apples have

all been caught there are still many other ceremonies peculiar to Halloween to be gone through. In some places there is the pulling of " kale-storks," or stalks of colewort, to see if one's future husband is to be tall or straight, little or crooked. If one comes up with a great deal of earth round the root then it denotes riches, and if the pith tastes sweet it shows that the husband or wife of the lucky individual is to be sweet also. Perhaps tho greatest fun of all is caused by the "Three Dishes," a ceremony never forgotten in the northern counties. Two of these are filled with clean and foul water and one is left empty. They are ranged on the hearth, when the parties, blindfolded, advance in succession and dip their fingers into one. If the finger goes into the clean water they are to marry a maiden or a young man, as the case may be ; if into the foul water, a widow or widower ; and if into the empty dish, then the person is destined to be a bachelor or an old maid.

It is to be hoped that none this Halloween will lose their temper, as they used to do in bygone days, when people were more superstitious than they are now, and actually believed in the customs, for we read—

"In order, on the clean hearth-stane,
The luggies three are ranged,
And every time great care is ta'en
To see them duly changed :
Auld Uncle John, wha wedlock's joys
Sin' Mar's-year did desire,
Because he gat the toom dish thrice,
He heaved them on the fire
In wrath that night."

Poor Uncle John ! It is to be hoped that the burning of the nuts, which always winds up every ceremony, put him in a better frame of mind, and that when he put his three nuts on the bars one of them at any rate did not crack and jump away from the one representing himself, but burnt steadily on to the end.

And what other things do we see in October ? The poor bees, having been busy all the summer storing their hive with sweet honey, expecting to enjoy it during the coming winter, are now being robbed of it. The way in which tho honey is taken away is to kill the bees by burning brimstone in the hive, the vapour from which suffocates them. If it is not meant to destroy them, care is taken only to stupefy them, and in this case enough of honey is left to feed them during the winter. This month is called the fungus month, and has a vegetation peculiarly its own, and one, too, full of beauty and design. Few of the summer flowers can show anything so splendid in colouring and so curious in form as some of the vegetable productions of this month. This consists of the family of the *fungi*, such as mushrooms, agarics, toad-stools, and a variety of others. Forest-glades, hedge-rows, wood-heaps, and dead trees, would at this season, when moistened by rain, poison the surrounding air and fill it with unwholesome effluvia, were it not that the putrefying mass gives birth and supplies nourishment to millions of *fungi*. These remove the dead matter, cover even corruption with beauty, and in their turn afford food to myriads of maggots. Some of them are also useful to ourselves as food; but in gathering them great caution is requisite, as the most serious consequences have in many cases followed from the poisonous sorts being collected by mistake. These *fungi* are of all shapes and sizes, from that of a pin's head to a foot in diameter. Some are round, some conical, some flat, some curled, and some divided in the most curious manner. Nor are their colours less varied than their forms. Some amongst them are very beautiful, of the most delicate shades of pink and yellow, whilst others are crimson, red, blue, or rose-coloured.

In October wild ducks are abundant in the markets. This plenty arises from the multitudes of these birds which are caught in *decoys*, the business of which is ordered by an Act of Parliament to commence on the first day of the month. The dark and glossy acorns lie scattered in profusion on the ground, the richly-coloured and veined horse-chestnuts glow in the midst of their rugged and spiny shells; the host of birds are enjoying a plentiful feast of beech-nuts in the tree-tops; and the squirrels beneath them, ruddy as the fallen leaves amongst which they rustle, and full of life and archness, are a beautiful sight.

"The greenwood! the greenwood! what bosom but allows
The gladness of the charm that dwells in thy pleasant whispering boughs!
How often in this weary world I pine and long to flee,
And lay me down, as I was wont, under the greenwood tree!"

THE HERMIT.

By THE Right Hon. E. H. KNATCHBULL-HUGESSEN, M.P. *Author of " Uncle Joe's Stories," &c.*

CHAPTER II.

T that moment, however, the danger did not seem entirely over. The sounds in the forest had continually drawn nearer, and there seemed a possibility that the beasts might devour both the travellers together. This, however, was by no means the intention of the new comer. He hastily collected a quantity of dried leaves and sticks, laid them in a circle round himself and his patient, and presently set them on fire by rubbing two sticks together in a manner which he appeared perfectly to understand. The fire

311

quickly blazed up, and the beasts which approached, as quickly beat a retreat when they perceived it.

There was danger, however, that other beings might perceive it too, and as soon as the Hermit found voice enough to speak, he felt it his duty to tell his new friend how and by whom he had been struck down, and that, for aught he knew, the robbers were still in the neighbourhood.

At this the other only smiled, but as soon as he had sufficiently doctored the Hermit's wounds, he assisted him to his legs and asked if he could walk. To his great surprise he found that he could do so, though weakly, and besides this, that his arm was not only less painful, but stronger than he could have expected. His new friend then told him to lean upon him and follow, which he accordingly did.

They went but a few steps before they reached an enormous tree, spreading out its branches on all sides. It was evidently a very old tree, as not only did its enormous bulk and vast roots testify, but the great hollow within it, as if Time had found it useless to work at it outside, and had therefore concentrated all his efforts to make it decay internally.

There was space enough inside that tree for a dozen people to have sat down to tea comfortably and without crowding, and the Hermit was not surprised when his companion stepped quickly into the hollow and assisted him to do the same.

What followed, however, *did* surprise him considerably, and so it would have surprised any one who had seen it, even if his intellects had not been previously confused and his perception dazzled by many knocks upon the head.

The Hermit's new friend proceeded to one side of the hollow, and clearing away some of the leaves which lay therein, disclosed a rope, at which he gave a pull, and immediately a large trap-door opened. He motioned the Hermit to descend a ladder which he now saw, and of course he instantly obeyed. Then his companion slowly followed him, having first made some arrangement by which the rope fell, so that it should not be perceived, upon the closing of the trap-door behind them.

They descended a few steps and found them-

selves again standing upon the ground, in a sort of passage which sloped rapidly downwards, and along which the Hermit followed his companion until it suddenly terminated in a large cave, which, at some time or other, had been either made, or more probably enlarged, by the hand of man. It was apparently not very far from the surface of the earth, for a faint light (as the Hermit afterwards found, for it was too dark then for him to make the discovery), streamed in from above at one corner, but this was the only communication with the outer air.

As soon as they had entered the cave, the Hermit's new friend felt about on one side of him and presently found what he was looking for, which was something (perhaps a lucifer match box) which enabled him forthwith to strike a light. This he did, and proceeded to light a curious, old-fashioned lamp which stood upon a roughly-made table in the centre of the cave.

By its light the Hermit was soon able to discover different objects around him. In fact, they were not very difficult to discover, being but few in number. There were a few dried skins of animals upon the ground, a couple of chairs manufactured in a primitive manner, and evidently by some hand little skilled in the trade of a carpenter, and a long barrelled gun leaning against the side of the cave.

This was all the Hermit saw as he glanced around him, and it must be owned that there was nothing very remarkable in the sight. A second glance, however, showed our friend that there was something more in the cave—something that moved in the far corner, and which presently came creeping forward, and disclosed to his astonished gaze the figure of an old—a very old woman.

Her appearance was not altogether inviting. She seemed to be composed of nothing more than skin and bones, bent nearly double with age, and with garments upon her which were, so to say, in tatters, kept together by a large wolf-skin wrapped around her in such a manner as to make it doubtful at first sight whether it was a wolf or a woman you beheld.

It was the latter, however, as you discovered when you saw her head, upon which was a small cap of faded red colour, fitting close, but from beneath which some straggling grey locks appeared. Her face was wrinkled, her teeth few, but prominent, whilst her nose and chin appeared, the one hooking down over her mouth and the other turning up, as if engaged in a continual effort to meet each other, in which they had nearly succeeded. But what struck the Hermit most was the fire which still sparkled in the eyes of the old dame, as if therein was concentrated all the life which remained to that venerable frame. They were very remarkable luminaries, and shone like a cat's eyes in the dark as she came scrambling and stumbling, creeping and crawling forward from the corner of the cave.

The Hermit's friend accosted her at once with great deference.

"Mother Breenwole," he said, "I've brought you a wounded man, knocked over by the Forest Robbers and nearly made an end of."

At these words the old woman emitted a sound which partook of the several natures of a groan, a sob, and a squeak, and answered, somewhat to the Hermit's disgust—

"Better so, son Pedro, better so than have shown the secret of the cave to a stranger," and she looked on the Hermit with an eye which made him feel glad that it was not she who had come upon him when lying wounded and helpless on the ground.

But Pedro, as we will henceforth call the Hermit's preserver, replied in cheery tones to the old hag—

"No harm done, Mother Breenwole; one more may know the secret without hurt, and this poor chap was a gone coon if I hadn't come along. We must set him upon his legs again now though, and who can do that better than you, mother?"

The old woman mumbled and muttered to herself as Pedro spoke thus, but raised no further objection; but when the Hermit, at his friend's request, had stretched himself down upon a huge skin which lay near, she shuffled up close to him and began to examine his wounds.

The Hermit experienced a queer sensation as he felt those scraggy, bony old fingers moving about his throat, but judged it best to show no

distrust, especially as it was impossible to believe that the man who had taken the trouble to save him would now permit him to be killed in cold blood.

After a short examination the old woman told Pedro that he had already administered the best remedies to the wounded man, and that the ointment—which was of her own making—could not be surpassed by any medicine in its efficacy in curing bruises and wounds. All the man now wanted was food and rest, but the former he must take sparingly lest the wounds should inflame.

With these words she shuffled back to her corner, and in a short time produced a wooden dish which contained some cold meat, apparently venison, which she placed on the table along with a loaf of bread, and invited Pedro to partake. A small slice she cut off and brought to the Hermit, bidding him remain where he was, and when he had eaten she shuffled off again, and presently returned with a pot of ointment.

She gave him water to drink from a spring which seemed to rise in one corner of the cave, and he thought he had never tasted anything more delicious. Then she put some more ointment upon his wounds and bruises, chanting to herself in a low, weird tone as she did so; in a language perfectly unintelligible to the Hermit. Presently she passed her lean skinny hands to and fro close over his face, several times, and gradually he felt a heavy, drowsy feeling steal over him, until little by little the scene seemed to fade before him, everything became indistinct, and he sank into a deep sleep.

How long he remained in that condition I cannot say, but probably it was the very best condition in which he could have been. No man, however strong his frame and vigorous his constitution, can stand such a knocking about as our friend had that day received, and but for Pedro and the old woman's ointment, together with the rest afterwards, it would certainly have gone hard with him.

The Hermit slept, as I have said, but it was not altogether a quiet sleep. Knocks on the head, if administered with sufficient force by a thick stick and a strong arm, are apt to produce a confusion in the brain and a strange jumbling up of ideas in the mind of the person who has received them, which no ointment, however powerful, can entirely prevent. So as our friend slept, wonderful thoughts crowded upon his brain, the imagination was active although the body was still, and extraordinary dreams took the opportunity of paying him a visit.

The days of his childhood came back to him as vividly as if he was really living them over again; people who had long been dead talked with him as familiarly as when they were alive, without exciting in him the least surprise at their being present, and things of the most curious kind happened without seeming otherwise than perfectly natural to him. He dreamed that he was seated upon a footstool at his mother's knee—that beloved mother whose pure spirit had long fled to a brighter and better world—and he seemed once more to hear, teaching her boy the first lessons of gospel truth and heavenly love, the tender accents of the voice that was hushed for ever. Then again he played upon the terrace and in the shrubberies of the old place which had once been his home —he played, and not alone—there were three sisters and a brother—the playmates of his happy youth—alas! where were they now? But in his dream they all lived, joyous and loving as in the old days, and he laughed and talked with them as then. Again, he was a soldier, fighting gallantly for his country, beloved by his comrades and honoured by all who knew him; and then came a change, a dark, troubled dream in which everything seemed confused and mixed, and whispers seemed to fall upon his ear, whispers of shame, disgrace, degradation, and a horrible time from which his mind recoiled as if it would shut and blot out that part of his life altogether. And then he fancied himself once more in his cave, with solitude for his comforter, with only the birds and wild animals to talk to, free from the wiles and hypocrisy, the schemes and plots of man, free from the restraints and unreality of what men' distinguish by the name of Civilisation, from which it seemed to him was banished much of that which most ennobled and most blessed man, and into which much was imported which most enslaved and degraded him.

So dreamed our Hermit as he slept, and

tossed uneasily in his sleep as he did so, until at last consciousness gradually came back to him, and he remembered, little by little, the events of the past day, and knew where he was and all that had happened to him.

When he first half opened his eyes, he was scarcely quite awake, and before he was so, the sound of voices fell upon his ear, and with the habitual caution of one who had lived so long in the woods, he shut his eyes again and listened attentively without giving the least sign that his slumbers had come to an end.

The voices he heard were those of Pedro and the old woman, but to these was added another, which somehow or other seemed to chill the listener's blood, and to awaken within him feelings of bitterness and hatred which he had thought were extinct. It was the voice of a man, not a harsh or angry voice, but on the contrary smooth and soft, but it had a peculiar kind of lisp in it not easily to be forgotten. To be sure the words it uttered were neither smooth, soft, or at all reassuring to the Hermit, for the first which he could distinctly hear had reference to himself, and were spoken in no friendly spirit.

"The old woman is right," said the speaker. "Better to have knifed the fellow where he lay, or left him to the wild beasts, than run the risk of the secret of the cave being betrayed. But since you have saved him, Captain Pedro, the mischief is done, and cannot be helped, unless indeed——" and here the man paused, significantly touched his dagger with one hand, and with the other pointed to the sleeper.

Then came the voice of Pedro in reply—

"No, no, Baron," said he, "none of that— the poor fellow will do no harm, and if there is gratitude in man, will never betray those who saved his life. I could not leave a human being to the wolves and panthers, being human myself, and he who would harm him now must harm me too. Besides, he may be useful some day, who knows?"

The other muttered something between his teeth which the Hermit could not catch, and then the old woman chimed in, recommending the stranger to be off, and not to remain until the sleeper awoke, as it might be better that he should not be seen. Thereupon the man who had been addressed by Pedro as " Baron " arose, and stealthily crept to the side of the cavern opposite that on which the Hermit and his preserver had entered on the previous evening.

As he did so, our friend took the opportunity of peeping at him from beneath his eyelids, for the voice had sorely perplexed him, recalling memories of the past which it had been his constant endeavour to stifle, and reminding him forcibly of one whom he not only believed to be dead, but in whose well-deserved death he had himself borne a share.

As the man passed along, the Hermit could see him, though but imperfectly, by the faint light of the lamp. He was about the middle height, and limped slightly on his left leg. He had on a large slouched hat which half concealed his face, but enough of it was seen to show a large, long gash upon one side, extending from forehead to chin, and entirely disfiguring what might otherwise have been handsome features. A heavy, drooping moustache, a chin closely shaven, and eyes that flashed beneath overhanging eyebrows, completed the picture, as far as the face of the stranger was concerned, and his figure was so entirely enveloped in a dark cloak, that the Hermit could only obtain, in his momentary glance, the sight of a belt in which several pistols and daggers seemed to be sticking, ready for immediate action if occasion should require.

The Hermit was a brave man, but an involuntary shiver ran through him as he looked at the figure which passed before him. It was that of a man to whom he owed the greatest misfortune of his life—the worst—the deadliest—the bitterest enemy he had ever known. But surely that man was not alive. His own right arm had struck him to the ground in fair fight, and he had seen the warm life-blood welling up from the fatal wound, and the ashen pallor of death creeping over the face which, even so, scowled upon him with savage and bitter malignity.

What did it all mean? Was he awake, or was this still some horrible dream — some strange production of his still heated brain? With a mighty effort he recovered his calmness, but before he had resolved on any definite

course of action, the figure had passed from his sight. It had disappeared upon the other side of the cave—disappeared so suddenly and completely that he began to think that it was certainly only in a vision that he had seen once more that hateful face. Still, it was strange—passing strange—and all the more so as he now felt perfectly awake, and, in spite of the feverish nature of his sleep, very much the better for his rest.

He therefore began to yawn and stretch himself, as if he had just opened his eyes, and thus very soon attracted the attention of Pedro and the old woman. They invited him to arise and join them in their morning meal, for it was now past the break of day, and Pedro informed our friend that if he meant to journey in their company, he must be ready to start in an hour's time. The Hermit therefore arose, and felt much fresher and stronger than the night before. He thanked his entertainers warmly for their care of him, and assured them of his desire to make any return that should hereafter be in his power.

In answer to his inquiries, Pedro informed him that he was bound for the sea-coast, and that he expected to find a vessel there which would convey him to a port not many miles distant from the forest, from whence he could make his way where he would. This seemed to the Hermit as good a way as he was likely to find of supplying the want which had caused him to leave his cave, and he therefore consented with readiness to accompany his companions.

They advanced to the other side of the cave, and then for the first time our hero was able to account for the sudden and mysterious disappearance of the figure which he had seen in the early morning. At one place the rock projected into the cave, and on rounding the angle thus formed a narrow opening became perceptible, through which a man could easily pass, and immediately this was left behind there appeared a passage similar to that by which the Hermit and Pedro had entered on the previous day. This ran on in a straight line for some little way, and then turned suddenly to the left. Then the passage was no longer smooth, and fashioned into a pathway which might be easily trodden. Stones lay upon the ground, and these became more numerous and larger for some twenty yards or so, and then the passage seemed almost blocked up by them. Still, it was just possible to squeeze oneself between the large stones and the main rock, and having done this for the space of two or three more yards, a faint light began to glimmer from above, the ground sloped upwards, and presently the three travellers crept out into a deep, dense thicket, in and round which lay scattered enormous masses of stone and rock, of such a mixed and curious character, that the casual observer might well doubt whether he stood upon the ruins of some mighty fortress or palace of ancient times, or whether some freak or strange convulsion of nature had cast about and left in that spot the vast boulders of rock and massive blocks of stone with which the place was choked.

When they had emerged, the Hermit perceived that the entrance to the cave from that side, though open, was extremely difficult of discovery, owing to the thickness of the brushwood around it, in the first place, and in the second, to the narrowness of the mouth, and the extreme probability that, even if any one discovered it at all, they would never guess that a regular passage lay behind the scattered fragments of rock which I have described.

His companions halted as soon as they were out of the passage, and indeed it was time that the old woman should do so, for she had come so far with difficulty, and was quite out of breath. It was not, however, as Pedro soon informed the Hermit, her intention to accompany them any further. In the neighbourhood of the spot upon which they stood there were other caves and hiding-places, in one of which she expected to find friends with whom she would be welcome. This was all that the Hermit was told, and as he had neither seen nor heard anything of Mother Breenwole to induce him to desire her further acquaintance, he was by no means sorry to be quit of her company.

He and his companion now pursued their way for a short distance through the thicket until they suddenly came out upon a sort of cart-track, down which Pedro turned, and which was easier walking than the brushwood

316

which they had just left. They followed this for half a mile or so, and then the trees began to be thinner, vegetation less luxuriant, and in a short space of time they came out upon the edge of the forest full in sight of the sea.

From the large pine-trees which skirted the forest there was a space of a few hundred yards only, of broken ground and sand-hills, interspersed with brambles and thickets here and there, and then came the gentle slope down to the beach, on which the sea was gently rippling with a faint, pleasant murmur as if trying to keep itself awake on that warm, long day.

The two travellers paused for a moment to gaze upon the scene before them, and then Pedro spoke. "The ship is not here," he said. "We are before our time—let us sit and talk a while under the shade of this pine-tree." The Hermit readily consented, and the two sat down side by side.

At first they did not find much to say to each other, but it was different when, after a few moments, Pedro lugged out from his pocket that which proved to be neither more nor less than a huge pouch of tobacco.

Not having been able to make use of his pipe for more than two whole days, the Hermit, as you may well suppose, was transported with joy at the sight, nor did his pleasure diminish when, having filled his pipe at the invitation of his companion, who speedily followed his example, he found the mixture to be one of which he thoroughly approved. The two men sat and smoked there for some time in silence, until the charms and soothing influence of the fragrant weed unlocked the secret caverns of their hearts, and made each inclined to be somewhat communicative towards the other. The Hermit was the first to speak, feeling indeed a remarkable sensation of gratitude towards the man who had first saved his life, and then ministered to the principal pleasure which made that life endurable. He asked his companion to tell him, if he had no reason to the contrary, how it was that he happened to be alone in the forest on the previous night, and what was his object and pursuit in life.

"To tell you the honest truth," replied the other, "I have for some time been thinking whether or no I should put a somewhat similar question to you. I cannot imagine what could have brought you into the middle of the forest where I found you—where you were going, and what pathway you meant to follow—you were heading for the sea, but no regular boat comes here—you could not know of my ship—and in short I don't understand it."

The Hermit took his pipe out of his mouth, emitted a whole volume of smoke, and answered his companion at once.

"I am a hermit," he said. "I live in a cave some miles further in the forest than where you met me, and where I should be at this moment if it had not been that I cannot exist without my pipe, and I had exhausted my supply of that precious herb which makes it so delightful."

"That may be all very well," returned the other. "But why are you a hermit? I have always understood that hermits are people who, worn out with the vanities and struggles of the world, retire to pass their time in prayer and meditation, and think of nothing else, banishing altogether such trifles as pipes from their consideration."

"Possibly," observed our friend, "this may have been the case with hermits in ancient times, but the world grows wiser as it grows older."

"True," responded Pedro, "but somehow or other you do not look to me the sort of fellow that should be a hermit. You look more like a soldier. Tell me if I have not guessed right?"

The Hermit heaved a deep sigh as his companion spoke, and after a short pause replied to him in the following manner.

"I had almost vowed that I would tell my tale and open my heart to no one. I have suffered—suffered deeply—and I have left the world behind me just as much as many of those old hermits of whom you were speaking just now. But you have saved my life, and if you really desire to know anything of my past history, I do not think I should be right in refusing to tell you, provided always that you solemnly engage not to disclose it to any one else without my consent."

Pedro having readily given the desired promise, the Hermit proceeded to tell him his story.

"I was born," he said, "of noble parents in a distant country. I had a happy home, and a joyous boyhood. My father and mother were devoted to their children, of whom I was the eldest. I had one brother and three sisters, and a more attached family can never have existed. We were together whenever it was possible, and loved each other with the truest affection.

"My mother died when I was about seventeen, and my eldest sister two years younger. A profound grief seized upon my father. He shut himself up in a country villa which he possessed, refused all consolation, would see none of his friends, join in no amusements, and follow none of his usual occupations. The result was that he died within the year, and we were left orphans.

"It was about this time that we became acquainted with Count Benjanisi—who or what he was I hardly know, but he apparently had great command of money, of the value of which I myself knew little or nothing. He professed the greatest admiration for my sister Angelina, and at the same time threw himself as much as possible into my society, apparently as a means whereby he might obtain access to her he loved. He encouraged to the utmost extent of his power an unhappy propensity for gambling which I had somehow acquired, and endeavoured in every way to poison my young mind, and corrupt my morals. Meanwhile he had effectually succeeded in gaining my sister's affections, and she, poor girl, loved him devotedly, and believed him to be little short of perfection.

"Somehow or other, however, I obtained a knowledge of some conduct of his which gave me warning in good time, so far as my finances were concerned, and I cautiously held aloof from the Count. He saw that I avoided him, suspected or ascertained the cause, and became from that moment my deadly enemy.

"At that time a war had recently broken out, our country having been invaded by a neighbouring monarch. A military ardour seized me, and although I might have escaped the service on account of my wealth and rank,

I joined the army, and became an officer in the king's guards. In a skirmish which shortly took place, I was fortunate enough to distinguish myself, and to attract the notice of our general. All seemed to prosper with me, and to add to my good fortune, I fell deeply in love with Bianca, the general's daughter, who returned my affection with all the impulsive love of a young heart.

"Bianca! my soul bleeds as I pronounce thy name, and my tongue refuses to continue the narration of the misery which followed. Would to heaven I had died when first I saw thy sweet face!"

Here the Hermit paused, seemingly quite overcome by the depth of his feelings. Large tears forced their way from his eyes and ran down his bronzed cheeks, and his whole frame quivered visibly from the internal emotion he experienced.

"Cheer up, mate!" interposed his companion, with rude good-nature; "cheer up, unburden your soul, and hap 'twill relieve you after all."

The Hermit gulped down his rising feelings, took a long pull at his pipe, and continued in the following words—

"My Bianca was beautiful as a flower in early spring, and pure as the dew that kisses the rose-buds at dawn of day. She was promised to me, and our future apparently lay before us as safe, and smooth, and happy as the life of mortals may be. But listen to the melancholy sequel.

"The traitor Count Benjanisi belonged to my regiment. Envy at my success in love as well as war added to the bitter hatred he already felt for me, and deepened his resolve for vengeance. He first strove to detach from me the affection of my betrothed. In this he signally failed, but his neglect and cruelty to my sister, whom he openly abandoned, broke the poor girl's heart, and she died, the victim of his heartlessness.

"I had, I thought, a right to revenge my poor Angelina, but it was pointed out to me that the faithlessness of lovers was but too common, and that any measure which I took against the villain could only expose my sister's memory to unjust reproaches, since she, poor child, had perhaps built too much on his attentions, and he could excuse himself in the eyes of the world by saying that he had meant no more than ordinary civility and was not to blame if a girl chose to break her heart on his account. Therefore I could do nothing but trust that Providence would in good time repay the villain for his perfidy. But worse was to come.

"Enraged at the unsuccessful issue of his attempt to wean my Bianca from me, he laid his plans to ruin me with diabolical craft. I still played high, and was always rather fortunate in my dealings with Fortune. But all at once, I perceived—or thought I perceived—a certain unwillingness on the part of my comrades to play with me. Little did I know that the demon Benjanisi, paving the way for his great attempt to destroy me, had set afloat, but so craftily that I could not detect it, a report of mal-practices on my part, which had created, almost insensibly, a prejudice against me. Yet my character stood so fair, and I was so popular with my comrades, that his machinations would have been of no avail had he not resorted to a still more diabolical expedient. I afterwards discovered that he had bribed my servant, and it was with the connivance and assistance of the latter that he carried out his nefarious plot.

"One day we were playing cards, some of my brother officers and I, when Count Benjanisi lounged in. I took but little notice of him, but afterwards recollected that he stood for some little time near the door on which our overcoats hung. There was a good deal of smoking going on, and, owing to this and the excitement of our play, he might have easily tampered with my coat, as he doubtless did, without my detecting him in the operation.

"Presently he came forward and stood behind me. Fortune had as usual favoured me throughout the evening, and I was in high spirits. At that moment I was dealing, and the atmosphere was tolerably thick, as you may imagine. I turned up a king. At the same instant another king dropped upon the table, and the hand of Count Benjanisi seized my wrist with a grip of iron; naturally I shook it off in fury, but in the confusion the cards got mixed, every one rose and there was a violent altercation. The Count swore vehemently that he had seen me drop a king from my sleeve and pretend to have fairly turned it up.

"I knew well enough that the card had dropped from his hand and not from mine, and loudly declared this to be the case. Who was to decide between us? The base villain avowed his belief that if I was searched then and there, proof would be found of my guilt. Of course I submitted willingly, when in one of the pockets of the coat I had on, two marked cards were found, and a whole pack in the pocket of my overcoat."

(To be continued.)

BABY'S BATH.

ABY, baby, in your bath,
   Do you make a splashing?
Do you kick and clap your hands,
   Round you water dashing?

Do you say you'll come out good,
   And bargains drive with mother,
To have your duckies in your bath,
   And sister play with brother?

Do you laugh when in your bath?
   Little face all merry!
Do you cry when you come out?
   Naughty child then—very!

319

PUZZLES.

CHARADES.

1.

My first is in silver but not in grey,
My second in spoon, but not in tray,
My third is in mirror but not in vain,
My fourth is in money but not in gain,
My fifth is in red but not in blue,
My sixth is in crimson, but not in hue,
My seventh is in penny but not in pound,
My eighth is in tone but not in sound ;
If these letters you place aright
A county of England will come to sight.

2.

My first is a cave. My second an impression.
My whole is a kingdom in Europe.

3.

My whole it is a Bible name,
It tells us of much strength,
My first it is a Christian name
But not of any length,
My second is what every man
That is now living is ;
Be he heathen or a Turk
This title still is his.

4.

My first is a subject to talk about,
My second is used when we take stout,
Look at my whole when you go out.

5.

My whole carries my first, and my second is
my whole.

DOUBLE ACROSTICS.

1.

1. A flower.
2. A robber.
3. A coarse kind of bread corn.
4. A strong motion of the air.
5. An animal.
6. Woollen thread.

The initials, read down, give the name of one
country in northern Europe ; and the finals,
read down, give the name of another country
in northern Europe.

2.

My finals, read down, are the capital of my
initials, read down.

1. A magistrate.
2. A kind of stone.
3. To settle on.
4. Seldom.
5. An engraved gem.
6. A messenger.
7. A town in Northumberland.

WORD SQUARES.

1. I, oft-times, am seen in the night.
2. My next a story should be.
3. An expression of grief ; not delight.
4. My last's the remainder you see.

Answers to Puzzles on Page 288.

ENIGMAS.

1. The letter A.   2. A face.

SQUARE WORDS.

(1.) 1. Balm.   (2.) 1. Servia.
      2. Acid.   2. Eyeing.
      3. Lied.   3. Repose.
      4. M.D.D.D.   4. Violin.
                          5. Jurist.
                          6. Agents.

CHARADES.

1.

Hand (And, dan, an).

2.

Despot (Spot, pot, top, Po).

3.

Teach (Cheat, heat, eat, tea, at).

HOODIE.

By Mrs. MOLESWORTH, *Author of* "*Hermy*," "*The Cuckoo Clock*," &c.

CHAPTER XI.—HOODIE'S DISOBEDIENCE.

" Where are the pretty primroses gone,
    That lately bloomed in the wood!"

NOTWITHSTANDING her troubles, on account of them partly, perhaps, for nothing tires out little children more than long crying, Hoodie slept soundly that night. She was still sleeping when at seven o'clock, Magdalen, already dressed and with the cage in her hand, came into her room to watch for her waking.

Martin, who had heard the joyful news an hour ago, stood with Miss King beside the little girl's bed and looked at her. Poor Hoodie! Her rosy face still bore traces of yesterday's weeping, and now and then through her sleep one heard that little sobbing catch in her breathing which is, to my thinking, one of the most piteous sounds in the world. "She's tired herself out," said Martin. "She may sleep another hour or more. You'll be tired standing there, miss. Who would think Miss Hoodie had it in her to take things to heart so, for to see her sometimes she's like as if she had no heart or love in her at all."

"I think I'll put the cage on a chair beside the bed," said Magdalen, "and then she'll be sure to see it the moment she wakes."

She did so and went quietly away. Half-an-hour later coming back again to see if Hoodie was still sleeping, she heard as she opened the door the sound of the little girl's voice. She had just awakened and had discovered the return of her bird. She was in an ecstasy of delight, very pretty to hear and see.

"Oh my darling little bird," she was saying, "oh my sweet, innocent pet, have you come back? oh my dear, *dear* bird! You didn't mean to go away from Hoodie, did you? You lost your way, didn't you? Hoodie will never speak c'oss again, birdie, *never*. I do think God is vezzy kind to send you back again, and I *will* try to please Him by being good, 'cos He's so kind."

Magdalen stood still and watched her, with pleasure, but with a strange sort of slight sadness and misgiving too. There was something almost startling in the little girl's extreme love for the bird, and it made her cousin wish it could be bestowed on a higher object.

"Why can't she love her sister and brothers more?" she thought to herself. "I do not know what she would do now if anything again happened to the bird. I wonder if it would have been better if it had not come back. But no, I must not think that. *All* love must do good to a nature like Hoodie's, and her love for the bird may teach her other things. And oh, I should have been sorry to leave her while she was as unhappy as she was yesterday."

Then she came forward into the room and when Hoodie saw her, there was a fresh cry of delight, and Magdalen had to tell her over and over again exactly how it had all happened;

322

how it was that she was up so early, how birdie flew in and then out again, and how Magdalen feared that after all she might not be able to catch him, and how delighted she was when she felt sure she had got him safe.

"I was so glad to think how pleased you would be, Hoodie, dear!" she said.

"Thank you, cousin Magdalen, you are vezzy kind," said Hoodie. "And I think God is vezzy kind too, for you know I said my prayers to Him last night to send birdie back again, so He must have told him to come. P'raps He sent a' angel to show birdie the way. I'm going to be vezzy good now, cousin Magdalen, *awful* good, alvays, 'cos God was kind and sent birdie back. *Won't* God be glad?"

"Yes dear, God is always glad when His little children are good. He likes them to be happy, and being good is the only way," said Magdalen.

"But won't He be *dedfully* glad for me to be kite good?" said Hoodie, seemingly not quite satisfied with her cousin's tone. "I wouldn't have tried so much if He hadn't sent birdie back, but now I'm going to try awful hard."

"But Hoodie, dear, even if God hadn't sent birdie back it would have been right to try as hard as ever you could," said Magdalen. "That's what I wish you could understand—even when God *doesn't* do what we ask Him we should try to please Him. For He loves us just the same—better than if He did what we ask, for He knows that sometimes what we ask wouldn't be good for us. I don't think you understand that, Hoodie dear. You think when your mother or Martin perhaps, doesn't do all at once what you ask, that it is because they don't love you. You mustn't feel that way, dear, either about your friends here, or about God, your best friend of all."

Hoodie looked up, rather puzzled. Magdalen feared she had not understood what she said and almost regretted having said it. And afterwards she wondered what had put it into her mind to try to explain to the little girl what puzzles and bewilders far wiser people, but by the time that "afterwards" came she no longer regretted having said what she had.

"I do think God loves me now," said Hoodie, sturdily, "'cos He's sent birdie back, and so

I'm going to try to be good. But if I was God I'd *always* do what ev'ybody asked me, and I'd *make* it be good for them, and then ev'ybody would be so pleased, they'd always try to be good." .

" I'm afraid not, Hoodie," said Magdalen with a slight smile. "I'm afraid if everybody always got what they want there would soon be very little goodness left anywhere."

Hoodie at this looked more puzzled than before, but Magdalen who had been speaking more to herself than to the child this time, did not try to explain any more. She bent over Hoodie and kissed her.

"Any way don't forget about trying to be good, and ask God to help you," she said.

The next day "Maudie's godmother" went away. She had stayed longer than she had intended, and now her father and mother could spare her no longer. The children were greatly distressed at her going. Maudie cried gently, the boys more uproariously, and all three joined in reproaching Hoodie for not crying at all. Hoodie seemed quite indifferent to their remarks.

"Why should I cry?" she said. "It would be very silly to cry when cousin Magdalen is going back to her father and mother. Crying isn't any good."

"You don't love Cousin Magdalen," said Maudie, "if you did you couldn't help crying."

"I *do* love her. I love her as many times as you do, ugl——"

She stopped—Magdalen was looking at her with a look that Hoodie understood. Hoodie ran to her and threw her arms round her neck.

"I *do* love you, Cousin Magdalen," she whispered. "Don't you believe me? I do love you, and I'm trying dedfully to be good, to please you and God, 'cos of birdie coming back."

"I do believe you, dear," said Magdalen, and Hoodie glanced round with triumph.

I am coming now to a part of Hoodie's history which I cannot prevent being rather sad. I wish, for some reasons, I could prevent it. But true stories must be told true, and even fancy stories must be told in a fancy true way, or else they do not suit themselves.

When I was a little girl I never cared for the new-fashioned "Red Riding Hood" story; the one in which she was *not* eaten up at the end after all, but saved by a woodcutter at the last minute. Of course it was very nice to think of poor Red Riding Hood not being eaten up, if one could have managed to believe it. But somehow I never could, and even now whenever I think of the story the old original ending, dreadful as it was, always comes back to me. So now that I am telling you about— not Red Riding Hood—but my queer, fanciful, but still I hope lovable, Hoodie, I feel that I must go straight on and tell you what really happened, even though it makes you rather sad.

For some time after Miss King left, things went on pretty smoothly, very smoothly perhaps I should say. Hoodie did not forget about trying to be good, especially in her bird's presence. It became a sort of conscience to her, and as, by a law which is a great help in learning to be good,—though also a danger the more in learning *wrong*—by the law of *habit*, every time one tries to keep under one's ill temper, makes it easier for the next time, it grew really easier for Hoodie to check her naughty cross words and looks from the way she kept them down when beside her little pet. And Martin and every one began to think it had been a happy thing for Hoodie and those about her that her cousin had taught her how to tame and care for the pretty greenfinch.

It was so pretty, poor little birdie! It grew so tame that, with the window shut of course, it spent a great part of its time flying freely about the ante-room where stood its cage. It would "pouch" not only on Hoodie's finger but on her shoulder, her head—any where she chose to place it. And in an instant, at the sound of her call, it would fly to her. Every morning it was her first thought, every night her last. And night and morning when she said her prayers, she never forgot to thank God for being "*so* kind as to send birdie back again," and to beg Him to keep birdie safe and well.

One evening—how it happened I cannot tell, —it was very hot and sultry weather, with thunder about, and at such times people are careless about closing doors and windows—one evening, by some mischance which no one ever could explain, the window of "birdie's room," as it had come to be called, was either left open, or flew open in some way. Hoodie was sure she had closed it when she went to bid her pet good-night, but it was what is called a lattice window, and these are apt to fly open unless very firmly shut. Birdie was safe in his cage however, and the door of *that* was fortunately—even when you hear what happened, children, you will agree with me that that part of it *was* fortunate—quite fastened. Early the next morning, one of the servants who slept in an attic above the ante-room, heard a noise below. She was a kind-hearted girl, and her first thought was of Miss Hoodie's bird. She got up at once, and hurrying down stairs—it was not so very early after all, nearly six o'clock—ran to the ante-room. As she opened the door, to her horror a great big strange cat jumped out of the window.

"Oh dear, oh dear," said Lucy, "can he have got at birdie?"

The cage was not to be seen—but in another moment Lucy spied it on the floor, knocked down off the table by the cruel cat. He had not got at birdie—birdie lay in one corner, quite still as if dead, and yet when Lucy with trembling fingers unfastened the cage door and tenderly lifted out its little occupant, she could see no injury, not the slightest scratch.

"His heart's beating still," she said, "perhaps it's only the fright of the fall," and she was turning to the window to examine birdie more closely, when a sound behind her made her start, and turning round she saw in the doorway the bird's little mistress, poor Hoodie herself. She was in her nightgown only—she had run from her room with her little bare feet, having heard Lucy passing down stairs, with an instinct of fear that some evil had befallen her pet.

"Lucy, Lucy," she cried, "what is the matter? It isn't anything the matter with birdie. Oh dear Lucy, *don't* say it is."

Her voice somehow, as Lucy said afterwards, sounded like that of a grown up person—all the babyishness seemed to have gone out of it —she did not cry, she stood there white as a

sheet, clasping her hands in a way that went to Lucy's heart.

"Oh Miss Hoodie," she replied, the tears running down her face, for she was very tender-hearted, "oh dear, Miss Hoodie, don't take on so. I hope birdie's not badly hurt. The cat didn't touch him. It knocked over the cage and it must have been the fall; but *perhaps* he's more frightened than hurt."

"Give him to me, Lucy," said Hoodie. "Let me hold him in my own hands. Oh birdie dear, oh birdie darling, don't you know me?" for birdie lay still and limp—almost as if dead already. Hoodie, forcing back the tears, whistled her usual call to him, and as its sound reached his ears, birdie seemed to quiver, raised his head, feebly flapped his wings, and tried, with a piteous attempt at shaking off the sleep from which he would never again awake, tried to rouse himself and to struggle to his feet.

"Oh Lucy," cried Hoodie, "he's getting better," but as she said the words, birdie fell over on his side, uttered the feeblest of chirps, and with a little quiver lay still—quite still— he was dead. The fright had killed him.

Hoodie looked up in Lucy's face with tearless eyes.

"Is he dead?" she said.

"Yes, Miss Hoodie dear," said Lucy softly stroking the ruffled feathers, "he is dead, but oh dear, Miss Hoodie, it isn't so bad as if the cat had torn and scratched him all over. You should think of that."

But Hoodie could think of nothing in the shape of comfort. She held the little dead bird out to Lucy.

"Take him and bury him," she said. "He can't love me any more, so take him away. All the loving's dead. He was the only thing that loved me. I won't try to be good any more. God is very unkind."

"Miss Hoodie!" exclaimed Lucy, considerably shocked. But Hoodie just looked at her with a hard set expression in her white face.

"You don't understand," she said. "Take him away and bury him."

She turned to the door and left the room. She went slowly back to her own room, and got into her little bed again. Then, like the old

Hebrew king, poor little English Hoodie, "turned her face to the wall," and wept and wept as if never again there could be for her brightness in the sunshine, or love and happiness in life.

"My bird, my bird," she moaned. That was all she could say.

She refused at first to get up and be dressed. Then, with an idea perhaps that if she did so she would be more independent, than if staying in bed, with papa and mamma and Martin and everybody coming to talk to her, and try to comfort her, &c., she slowly got out of bed and let Martin dress her. But when it came to saying her prayers, she altogether refused to do so, and on this point there was no getting her to give in. She did not refuse to eat her breakfast, because she had sense enough to know that sooner or later she would be obliged to eat, but the moment it was swallowed, she took her little chair and seated herself in the corner of the nursery, her face to the wall, crying, crying steadily, and hopelessly, turning like a little fury upon any one who ventured to speak to her, only moaning out from time to time—

"My bird, oh my bird!"

They were all very sorry for her. Maudie's tears and those of the little boys had flowed freely when the sad story was first told to them; they had all rushed to Hoodie to try to kiss and comfort her. But her extreme crossness, or what any way looked like it to them, sent them away puzzled and hurt. Hoodie's mother had proposed that the little girl should spend the whole day down stairs with her, have dinner at the dining-room luncheon, and go a drive in the afternoon, but to all this Hoodie only replied by a determined shake of the head, as well as to her father's offer of a new bird, or two if she liked, the prettiest that could be bought.

So they were all really at their wits' end.

It was very sad, but one must also allow that it was very tiresome. Martin began to fear that the child would really make herself ill, and as was Martin's "way," her anxiety began to make her rather cross.

"I wish Miss King had never put it into the child's head to have a pet bird," she muttered

to herself as she was washing up the tea things that evening, glancing at Hoodie's disconsolate figure still in the corner of the nursery. "Miss King may be all very well and kind, but she's no knowledge of children, how should she have any? I think it's much best to leave children to them that understands them; though indeed as for any one's understanding Miss Hoodie——!"

Fortunately it did not occur to Hoodie to make any objection to going to bed, and it was a relief to every one to know of her being there and safely asleep, "forgetting her troubles for a while," as Martin said. The next day was very little better. Hoodie did not cry quite so much, but she still sat in a corner doing nothing, and when any one attempted to speak to her, however kindly, she turned upon them with fierceness, like a little ill-tempered cat.

Yet it was not ill-temper; it was really misery, or at least it was ill-temper caused by misery. But as no gentleness and patience, no sympathy or attempt at comforting her did any good, but harm—and as any approach to reasoning with her, or scolding her, seemed to harden her already embittered little heart more and more, what was to be done, what could be done, but leave her alone? She continued determinedly to refuse, night and morning, to say her prayers, and refused too to say grace at the nursery table when it was her turn. But of all this Mrs. Caryll wisely desired Martin to take no notice, and not to try to force the child to any formal utterance of words in which her heart had no part.

"It *must* be all right again soon if only we are patient with her," said Hoodie's mother, more cheerfully than she was really feeling, for she saw that Martin was very much worried and distressed about Hoodie, and she was anxious to encourage her.

"It is to be hoped so, ma'am, I'm sure," was Martin's rather hopeless reply.

Somewhat to everybody's surprise, on the third day Hoodie condescended to ask a favour. Might she go out for a walk alone with Lucy? Everybody was so enchanted at her seeming to take interest in anything or wishing for anything, that with some conditions her request was at once granted. It was arranged that she should set off with Lucy and go wherever she wished, with the understanding that she would meet Martin and the other children at four o'clock at a certain point on the road, as it was not convenient that Lucy should stay out longer. To this Hoodie agreed.

"I'm going through the wood," she said. "I want to get some flowers that grow there, and Lucy must take a basket and a knife to dig them up, and then I'll tell her what to do."

"Very well Miss Hoodie," said Martin, but privately she told Lucy not to let the little girl go to the cottages at the edge of the wood, for Martin had never forgotten the fright of Hoodie's escapade several months ago. "If she gets in the way of going to that young woman's cottage, she'll be for ever running off," she said. "So silly of the people to encourage her, when they might see we didn't like it. We met the young woman the other day, and she actually stopped short in the road and began asking when Miss Hoodie was coming to see her again."

"But mamma says they're very respectable people, Martin," said Maudie, who was standing by. "I don't think she would mind if Hoodie did go to see them. Papa said one day he wished the young woman's husband was one of our men. He's so steady."

"Hold your tongue, Miss Maudie," said Martin with unusual sharpness. She knew that what the child said was true, but she had taken a prejudice against the little family in Red Riding Hood's cottage, as the children always called it, and when a good conscientious woman of Martin's age and character once takes a prejudice, it is rather a hopeless matter!

Poor Maudie slid away, feeling in her turn that things were rather hard upon her. She had been very patient and gentle with her strange-tempered little sister these three days, and had tried not to feel hurt at Hoodie's indifference to all her small overtures of sympathy. And now to be told by Martin to hold her tongue when all she meant was to try to make things better, was not easy to bear.

326

"I'm sure Hoodie wants to get flowers to put on birdie's grave," she thought to herself, as she wiped away the tears called forth by Martin's sharp words. "I think she *might* have told me about it and asked me to go too."

But she said nothing about it and set off uncomplainingly on her solitary walk with Martin, for the two little boys were spending the afternoon with the children at the Rectory.

Hoodie marched Lucy straight off to the wood. Primroses were the flowers on which her heart was set, for birdie's grave, as Maudie had guessed. She had seen them growing in the wood in the spring in great numbers and beauty, and no flower, she had settled in her mind, could look so pretty on birdie's grave. She said very little to Lucy, having satisfied herself that the knife to dig the roots up with, and the basket to carry them home in had not been forgotten, she walked along in silence. But when they reached the wood and had gone some little way into it and no primroses were to be seen Hoodie looked very much disappointed.

"There were such lots," she said to herself.

"Lots of what, Miss Hoodie?" asked Lucy, thinking her charge the oddest child she had ever had to do with.

"Of p'imroses," said Hoodie. "That's what I came for, to plant them on birdie's grave, you know, Lucy."

"Primroses," repeated Lucy. "Of course not now, Miss Hoodie. They're over long ago. See, these are their leaves—lots of them." She stooped as she spoke, and pointed out the primrose plants clustering thickly at their feet. Hoodie stooped too, to look at them.

"Oh dear," she exclaimed. "Are the flowers all gone? What shall I do! If we unplanted one, Lucy, and took it home and watered it *lots*, twenty times a day p'raps, wouldn't more flowers come?"

"Not this year, Miss Hoodie," said Lucy. "Not all the watering in the world would make any flowers come before the spring, and watering too much would kill the plant altogether."

"Oh dear," repeated Hoodie, "what shall I do?"

"Won't no other flowers do?" said Lucy.

" There's violets still, and lots of others in the garden that Hopkins would give you—much prettier than primroses."

"No," said Hoodie, shaking her head, "none but primroses would do. Birdie liked them best, I know, for when I put some once in the wires of his cage, he chirped. When will the spring come, Lucy?"

"Not for a good bit, Miss Hoodie," said Lucy, "it's only July now. There's all the summer to go through, and then autumn when it begins to get cold, and then all the cold winter, before the spring comes. A good while—eight months, and there's more than four weeks in each month, you know."

"I can't help it," said Hoodie, "only primroses will do. Please dig some roots up, Lucy, and we'll plant them on birdie's grave. The green leaves are a little pretty, and in the spring the flowers will come. And if I'm dead before the spring," she added solemnly, "you mustn't forget to water them all the same."

"Miss Hoodie!" said Lucy reproachfully, "you should not talk that way really. Your mamma wouldn't like it."

"Why not?" said Hoodie, "there's lots about deadening in the Bible and in the church books, so it can't be naughty. I wouldn't mind, if only I thought birdie was in heaven."

"We'd better be going on," said Lucy, rather anxious to give a turn to the conversation, "or we'll be late for Martin and Miss Maudie. I've got up two nice roots, and we may see some others that take your fancy as we go on."

They made their way slowly through the wood—Hoodie peering about here and there in search of primroses still, some two or three might, she thought, possibly have been left behind, or some buds might by mistake have bloomed later than their neighbours. For Hoodie, as you have seen, was not easily convinced of anything that she did not wish to believe.

But all her peering was in vain; they reached the end of the little wood without a single primrose showing its pretty face, and Hoodie was obliged to content herself with the brightest and freshest plants they could find, which Lucy good-naturedly dug up for her.

At the edge of the wood, the path led them in front of the cottage to which three or four months ago Hoodie's memorable visit had been paid. Lucy walked on quickly, talking of other things in hopes of distracting the little girl's attention till the forbidden ground was safely passed. Vain hopes. Hoodie came to a dead stand in front of the little garden gate.

"That is the cottage where baby and its mother and the ugly man live," she announced to Lucy. "Once, a long time ago, I went there to tea. Baby's mother asked me to come again some day."

"But not to-day, Miss Hoodie," said poor Lucy, nervously, "we'd be too late if we stopped now."

"No, not to-day," said Hoodie. "I don't want to go to-day. I'm too unhappy about birdie to care for cakes now. I don't think I'll ever care for cakes any more. Besides," with a slight hesitation, "she won't have any ready. She said I was to let her know. P'raps I'll let her know some day."

She was turning to walk on, immensely to Lucy's relief, when the gleam of some pale yellow flowers growing close under the cottage walls, up at the other end of the long narrow strip of garden, caught her glance.

"Lucy," she cried. "I see some p'imroses in the garden. I must run in and ask baby's mother to give me some. I'm sure she will."

She unfastened the wooden gate and was some steps up the path before Lucy had time to reply.

"They're not primroses, Miss Hoodie," she said. "Indeed they're not. I can see from here. They're quite another kind. Oh do come back, Miss Hoodie."

"I won't be a minute," said Hoodie. "I'd like some of the flowers any way," and she began to run on again.

"Miss Hoodie," cried Lucy, driven to despair, "Martin said you mustn't on no account go into the cottage."

Hoodie's wrath and self-will were instantly aroused.

"Well then, Martin had no business to say so," she replied. "Mamma never said I wasn't to go. She said I should go some day to see the baby again and to thank baby's mother."

"But not by yourself—without Martin, Miss Hoodie. Your mamma always tells you to be obedient to Martin, I know."

Hoodie vouchsafed no answer, but marched on, up the little garden path towards the house. Lucy looked after her in dismay. What should she do? Following her and repeating Martin's orders would probably only make Hoodie still more determined. Besides, Lucy was a very gentle, civil girl; it was very disagreeable to her to think of going into the cottage and telling the owners of it that the child had been forbidden to speak to them, and she gazed round her in perplexity, heartily wishing that Miss Hoodie had not chosen her for her companion in her walk. Suddenly, some distance off, coming across the fields, she perceived two figures, a tall one and a little one. Lucy had good eyes.

"Martin and Miss Maudie," she exclaimed, with relief, and just glancing back to see that Hoodie was by this time inside the cottage, she ran as fast as she could to meet the new comers and tell of Hoodie's disobedience.

She was all out of breath by the time she got up to them, though they hastened their steps when they saw her coming—and at first Martin could not understand what Lucy was saying. When she did so, she was exceedingly put out.

"Run into the cottage, has she, Lucy?" she exclaimed. "And after all I said! I really do think you might have managed her better, naughty though she is. Oh dear me, I do wish she hadn't been allowed to come out without me."

Maudie stood by in great trouble at Hoodie's misdoing.

"Martin will be so cross to her," she thought, "and Hoodie will speak naughtily I'm sure. I'll run on to the cottage first and tell her how vexed Martin is, and beg her to come back quick and say she's sorry."

And before Martin and Lucy noticed what she was doing, she was half way across the fields to the cottage.

The door stood open when she got there. Maudie peeped into the kitchen but saw no

one. "Hoodie," she called out softly, "are you there?"

No answer.

"Hoodie," called Maudie again, more loudly, "I've come to fetch you. Martin's just coming."

Then Hoodie's voice sounded from above.

"I'm up here, Maudie. I came up here 'cos there was no one in the kitchen. And baby's mother doesn't want me to stay 'cos poor baby's ill, so I'll come."

Maudie could not however clearly distinguish what Hoodie said, so, guided by the sound of Hoodie's voice she in turn mounted the ladder-like staircase which led to the sleeping room above. Hoodie was just preparing to come down, but when Maudie made her appearance she drew back a little into the room.

"Baby's mother won't let me nurse baby," she said, "'cos she's ill, though I'm sure I wouldn't hurt her. Do look at her Maudie. You can't think how pretty she is when she's well—but her face is very red to-day—baby's mother thinks she's getting her teeth."

Maudie approached rather timidly. Certainly the baby's face was very red.

"Please miss," said its mother, "I think you'd better not stay. It's very kind of you, and I'm that sorry I can't tell you, to ask you to go."

"I've only *just* come up stairs," said Hoodie, "I waited ever so long in the kitchen, 'cos I thought baby's mother was out and that she'd come in soon. And then I called out and I heard she was up stairs so I came up, but she won't let me touch baby and I can nurse her so nicely."

"It isn't for that miss," said Mrs. Lizzie in distress; "it's only *for fear* there should be anything catchin' about her. Doctor saw her yesterday and thought it was only her teeth, still it's best to be careful."

"Yes, thank you," said Maudie, "I think we'd better go. Perhaps we'll come again when baby's better. Come, Hoodie."

With some difficulty she got Hoodie away, for though considerably offended with baby's mother, Hoodie was much more inclined to stay and argue it out with her, than to give in quietly. At the foot of the stair they met

Martin; Maudie explained things to her, and Martin's face grew very grave. She was too really alarmed to be cross.

"Run out at once," she said. "both of you into the open air, and stay in the field till I come: I have sent Lucy home. Better know the worst at once," she added to herself, as she climbed the steep little stair, "oh dear, oh dear! who ever would have thought of such a thing?"

(To be continued.)

"SIR," SHE SAID.

Allegretto Moderato.

Music by T. CRAMPTON.

"What are you do-ing, my pret-ty maid?" "Us-ing my nee-dle, sir," she said,

"Sir," she said, "Sir," she said; "Us-ing my nee-dle, sir," she said.

"What are you mak-ing, my pret-ty maid?" "Mak-ing a man-tle, sir," she said; "Sir," she said,

"sir," she said; "Mak-ing a man-tle, sir," she said.

"Who is to wear it, my pretty maid?"
"'Tis for a princess, sir," she said,
"Sir," she said, "sir," she said;
"'Tis for a princess, sir," she said.
"What is her name, then, my pretty maid?"
"Her name is Alice, sir," she said;
"Sir," she said, "Sir," she said;
"Her name is Alice, sir," she said.

"Where is she living, my pretty maid?"
"Living in Doll-land, sir," she said,
"Sir," she said, "Sir," she said;
"Living in Doll-land, sir," she said.
"Then I won't have her, my pretty maid."
"Nobody asked you, sir," she said,
"Sir," she said, "Sir," she said;
"Nobody asked you, sir," she said.

THE TAME LION.

THE TAME LION.

"WON-DER" says Mr. Li-on, "what you small peo-ple think of me. You see I am hand-some and ve-ry large, but you have no i-dea how strong and ac-tive li-ons are when you on-ly see them at a show of wild beasts. The li-on is the king of beasts, and makes them all fly before him in his na-tive fo-rests. I know a great deal a-bout my-self and o-ther a-ni-mals, for I have heard my mas-ter tell peo-ple a-bout things which I can-not re-mem-ber, and could not learn from a-ny-one but him. It was he who caught me in a great fo-rest of A-fri-ca, when I was but a lit-tle cub, and my poor mo-ther had been shot. I am fond of my mas-ter, and o-bey him : I am glad al-so to see you lit-tle ones watch me as I per-form my tricks ; though some-times I am ve-ry wea-ry of you all, and e-ven feel in-clin-ed to bite off my mas-ter's head when he puts it in-to my mouth. But I am glad that I have ne-ver done so, for I do not a-lways feel cross.

"I have heard my mas-ter say that we li-ons be-long to the cat tribe, though I can scarce-ly be-lieve it, for cats, leo-pards, and e-ven ti-gers, who, he says, are of the same fa-mi-ly, are all poor crea-tures com-pared to li-ons. Now I don't want you to go away and say that I am a vain beast, you child-ren ; but I ask you—is not a li-on the fi-nest and grand-est-look-ing of all crea-tures? What o-ther beast has such a mane as I have, or such a hand-some tuft at the end of his tail ?"

LITTLE KNICKERBOCKER BOYS.

BY THE AUTHOR OF "AUNT EFFIE'S RHYMES," Etc.

ITTLE Knickerbocker boys,
  When you're playing here and there,
If you chance to find a little cap
  Lying anywhere—
I counsel you to cry, Hurra!
  And toss it in the air.

Little knickerbocker boys,
  A somebody unknown,
Is sure to say the cap is his,
  And claim it for his own.
'Tis better not to handle it—
  To let the thing alone.

Little knickerbocker boys,
  I have heard the story read,
Of Touchy Tom who found a cap,
  And picked it up, instead,
Said he, "I do believe it fits,
  I'll try it on my head."

332

Little Knickerbocker Boys.

The cap was ready-made you see,
　And proved a little tight,
And as his head grew hot it shrank,
　And pinched his brow outright,
And Tommy longed to tear it off,
　And tugged with all his might.

Said he, " You horrid cap, I'd like
　To thrash the man who made you."
The man who chanced to pass just then,
　Said, " Little sir, what said you?
I never bade you wear that cap,
　It was yourself that bade you."

TALKS ABOUT THE MONTHS.

NOVEMBER.

By Mrs. GEORGE CUPPLES.

"Dull November brings the blast;
Then the leaves are whirling fast."

THIS month is the pioneer of winter, month of fog and rain, of dirty days and dark nights.

" No sun—no moon—no morn—no noon—
No dawn—no dusk—no proper time of day—
No comfortable feel in any member—
No shade—no shine—no butterflies—no bees—
No fruits—no flowers—no leaves—no birds—November."

"Oh, dear," I hear some one say, "what a dreary prospect; have you nothing good to say about November at all? How can there be windy weather and foggy at the same time? Why I have been told that dense fogs are never seen except when the weather is very still and calm."

All very true, and yet as a general rule we

have foggy days so dense and thick as even to obscure the light of day, and force us to light candles and burn gas or lamps in our rooms even at noon. We have often a great deal of rain at this time, though there are now and then gleams of clear and pleasant weather. Ice frequently encrusts shallow ponds, and crackles under foot early in the morning, but rarely remains during the whole day, as the sun still shines with some degree of warmth.

November was the ninth month of the Roman year—hence its name. The Saxons styled it *Wint Monat*, or Wind Month, from the gales of wind prevalent at this season that complete the fall of the leaf. On every side trees stretch out their naked arms, and heaps of leaves choke the walks, and fill the ditches and hollows. The mulberry, though the latest in putting forth its leaves in spring, is one of the first to lose its foliage ; and by the end of the month our gardens look desolate. The country roads are so soft that we think twice before we take a walk out of doors, as we are apt to stick in the mud at every step.

The many little animals that have been busy during the autumn in laying up stores for winter are most of them asleep, with their tails curled cosily round their necks and over their noses to keep " Johnnie Frost " from pinching them. If a fine day happens to come in the middle of the gloomy weather, then many of them wake up and take a nibble at the store of food they have saved with so much industry and trouble. What an example the long-tailed field-mouse is to us. Think what a tiny creature it is, and yet it is a well-known fact that it stores its granaries as well as any of the torpid animals. Nothing comes amiss to it, ears of corn, nuts, acorns, and these gathered from the woods often five hundred yards distant from its nest.

But let us take a glance at the towns now at this season. The weather it is true is as bad, and the fog denser, and the side paths very dirty and disagreeable to walk along ; still there seems to be a good deal of mirth and laughter going on down the side alleys, or in some quiet crescent, and out-of-the-way corners. If we turn down one we come upon a group of boys all busy dressing up a figure, and we all know that this is the effigy of Guy Fawkes, that is

335

to be paraded through the streets on the fifth day of the month, and afterwards burned. The well-known festival of Guy Fawkes' Day is observed by English juveniles as one of the most delightful and joyous days of the year. The general mode of practising the custom through all parts of England is the dressing up of a scarecrow figure in all sorts of cast-off clothing, the head-piece generally a paper-cap painted and knotted with paper strips in imitation of ribbons. Of course those forming the procession try to have as many fancy articles of clothing on too, such as false faces, cocked paper hats and other things. The figure of Guy Fawkes is seated in a chair, carrying a dark lantern in one hand and a bunch of matches in the other, to show that he was a conspirator, and the procession visits the different houses in the neighbourhood repeating the well known rhyme :—

" Remember, remember !
The fifth of November,
The gunpowder treason and plot ;
There is no reason
Why the gunpowder treason
Should ever be forgot."

Then comes the " Pray remember Guy," or " Please to remember the bonfire," and he *is* a cross-patch indeed if he refuses a penny to help the merry-makers.

The bonfires kindled nowadays are very small in comparison with what used to be in former times. The largest we read about was at Lincoln's Inn Fields, when two hundred cartloads of fuel would sometimes be consumed, while upwards of thirty Guys would be suspended on gibbets and committed to the flames. Then a very large pile was heaped up by the butchers in Clare Market, who paraded through the streets at night playing the famed marrow-bone-and-cleaver music amidst great confusion and uproar ; the church-bells ringing out merry peals but by no means drowning the noise from the mob.

Do any of the children in the northern counties ask, But why do they burn the " Guys," and why do they have bonfires on the fifth of November ? Because that day marks the anniversary of the discovery and prevention of the gunpowder plot. Ever so many wicked men managed to get a quantity of gunpowder placed in a vault under the House of Lords and their intention was to set fire to it when the King, Lords, and Commons were all assembled, and blow them all up. This plan was found out in time, and when the soldiers marched into the vault they found Guy Fawkes there ready, when the signal was given, to light the match. He was at once taken prisoner and all the other conspirators fled. You will not wonder now why the fifth of November is a special day of rejoicing to the inhabitants of London especially, and why the children there as well as elsewhere in various parts of England chaunt and sing till their throats are sore—

"This is the day that God did prevent
To blow up his king and parliament,
The fifth of November
Since I can remember
Gunpowder treason and plot."

No sooner have the ashes of the Guy Fawkes bonfires been swept away from the streets and alleys of London or wherever they have been placed, than all the little cousins from the country are roused up early on the ninth of November to set out in good time to see the Lord Mayor's Show. On that day the Mayor of London is sworn into office and goes in procession through London to Westminster. It is not nearly such a great show as it used to be, but little country cousins and town ones too think it a fine show enough, and hail it as quite a bonny coming in the gloomy foggy month. Then we must not forget Martinmas Day, for though it is rent-day in many of the northern counties, and a day rather dreaded by the poor, still it is held as a festival over most parts of Christendom. It happens to be the season when the new wine is drawn and tasted, when cattle are killed for winter food, and fat geese are in their prime, so that it is regarded as quite a feast day. St. Martin used to be regarded as the saint of the beggars for the legend about him is that he halved his cloak with a beggar, and in the old pageants connected with this day, when the procession walked to Guildhall we read that a "multitude of beggars were in the crowd, howling most lamentably," and following the saint till the procession stopped in St. Paul's Churchyard. Then the represent-

ative of St. Martin, drawing his sword, cut his rich scarlet cloak into many pieces which he distributed among the beggars who ceased their howlings.

The last of the saints' days is St. Andrew's, the patron saint of Scotland, and is held by many Scotchmen in England and abroad as an occasion of reunion, social and national. The commencement of the ecclesiastical year is regulated by the feast of St. Andrew, the nearest Sunday, to which whether before or after, constitutes the First Sunday in Advent or the period of four weeks which heralds the approach of Christmas. St. Andrew's Day is thus sometimes the first and sometimes the last festival in the Christian year.

Poor November, after all we have tried to say in its favour, it is a gloomy month! but one way of keeping out the dulness is to be extra busy. We must think too of the poor who are already beginning to feel the pinch of hunger and cold, for work is becoming scarce in many places and at any rate the aged poor are likely to be suffering. The German children have a very good custom and that is to prepare a number of useful warm things to hang on a little tree. This tree they carry away at Christmas to the house of the poorest family they know about, and thus they have a good Christmas indeed, for by making other people happy we become far happier ourselves.

"It is such a pity," said a little girl the other day, "that people's skins don't grow thick like the animals when the cold weather comes. I do hate to sew so many flannel petticoats for the poor women."

She had been reading that during October and November many animals put on their winter clothing, more especially in the more northern countries, and she thought it would be a very good thing indeed if people were saved the trouble of sewing, by their skins getting thick as a protection against the cold. It is quite true that horses, cows, sheep, and many wild quadrupeds, have a growth of long coarse hair at this season, and in the arctic regions most animals become white during winter, because this colour preserves their heat, which a darker colour would allow to escape. But as God has not made us with such thick skins we must do our best to keep out the cold by healthy exercise and by being industrious during the summer and autumn to have a good supply of warm clothing ready for the cold gloomy days.

In the farming districts November is an active month. The land is ploughed and wheat-sowing finished, the winter fallows turned up and the fields drained, when the farmer lays aside his implements till the following spring. During November the wood-pigeon, or stock-dove, the latest of our winter visitants, makes its appearance. Formerly, when this country was more covered with woods, vast flocks of these birds came hither from Sweden and other northern parts. They fly in long trains of thousands upon thousands, and multitudes are destroyed by fowlers, who watch the time of their alighting. This month is a busy time with fish. Many of them deposit their eggs in shallow pools and the higher parts of rivers; for that purpose salmon come from the sea, and force their way up the most rapid streams, to reach fit *spawning* places.

Few flowers are to be seen at this time of the year. Here and there a solitary bluebell is found drooping in the shade, or a daisy with its flowerets just closed, but they give little variety to the landscape. But the gardens have still the cheery golden chrysanthemum.

> " When grey winter comes apace,
>   And the summer flowers are gone,
>   Golden brightness in thy face
>   Then we gladly look upon.
>   May we all thy teachings heed—
>   That, in paths of sombre care,
>   There is hope in darkest need,
>   And some brightness even there :
>   Golden rays of faith and worth,
>   Springing from the dust of earth."

LILY.

A SNOWY flower pure and white.
  A child as fair, who glads our sight—
        Called Lily!

The child is looking at us now,
With clear bright eyes and open brow—
        Fair Lily!

The pure still flower's the garden's light,
The graceful child of home the glory bright—
        Dear Lily!

VIOLET.

THOUGH lilies are, of flowers, most fair,
   I think I'd almost rather wear
      The Violet.

My little friend, whose earnest look,
Meets yours from out the open book,
      Is Violet.

She robbed the flower of her name
And sweetness too, 'twas quite a shame,
      Miss Violet !

THE HERMIT.

By the Right Hon. E. H. KNATCHBULL-HUGESSEN, M.P., *Author of "Uncle Joe's Stories," &c.*

CHAPTER III.

"NOW came into play the fiendish machinations of my enemy; the reports which he had sedulously spread were remembered and believed, and when, on searching my quarters, another pack of marked cards, and also some loaded dice, were found, nothing could save me.

340

" I need hardly tell you that it was through the villainy of my servant that all this had occurred. Believe me or not, but before you refuse to do so, think what object I can have in telling you the story at all, if my version is not true. It was in vain that I protested and swore ; even the previous high character which I had borne could not stand against proof so apparently strong.

The Hermit.

"I was turned ignominously out of the regiment, and my career in life ruined for ever. At once I challenged my vile traducer and offered to decide the matter by fair fight. He replied, with a sardonic smile upon his sallow features, that 'he did not fight with cardsharpers,' and even to this I had to submit.

"Great heaven! what agony did I endure. My brother and young sisters alone believed in my innocence. It maddens me to think of that which happened next. Without my knowledge, my brave young brother picked a quarrel with the demon Benjamin, to avenge the insult which had been offered to his family. My first intelligence of the matter was that the boy—for he was little more—had been brought in, run through the chest, and dying from the effects of the wound inflicted by the superior strength and skill of his adversary. One of my remaining sisters, delicate from her youth, soon followed to the grave the brother to whom she had been devotedly attached. The other—my last relation—entered a convent, and sought in the consolations of religion that comfort which the world denied.

"I was alone, and had but one object in life —revenge upon the author of my misery and the destruction of my family. I watched for an opportunity—days, weeks, months—but none occurred. The wary villain avoided me, and I discovered moreover that he had actually formed a plot to have me assassinated, and thus removed from his path for ever.

"I have not yet mentioned the deadliest blow of all. My Bianca was lost to me. Poor girl! I hope—I know—I feel that she loved and trusted me still. But her father was inexorable. Himself the soul of honour, he could not tolerate the bare suspicion of its absence in the heart of another. As soon as my disgrace had been accomplished, he forbade me his house and refused me permission to see or to approach his daughter. I was in despair. Count Benjamin took the opportunity of eagerly urging his pretensions to Bianca's hand. Her father supported his pretensions. My brave girl resisted all pressure, and at length took refuge in the same convent as my last remaining sister. Nothing daunted, the villain now formed the project of carrying

341

her off from the convent. He laid his plans well, but happily I discovered them. My resolution was soon taken. This should serve to supply the opportunity for which I had so long waited.

"I had money—for the demon who had ruined my honour had not been able to deprive me of the poor dross which is valueless without it; nay, I am wrong, not wholly valueless; at least it was not so in my case, for, by a liberal use of my wealth I hired a small band of men to waylay the count and his party upon their expedition. You need not shudder: murder had no place in my thoughts—all I wanted was to compel him to the combat which he had declined. I succeeded. The party with him were well-armed, but they were engaged in a nefarious deed, and had probably no great heart in their enterprise. They fled upon the first attack of my men, which was made not far from the walls of the convent, which their leader had intended to scale.

"I took good care that my enemy did not join in their flight. He was left alone with only two companions, whilst I, with a dozen men at my back, could have had him surrounded and slain at a word from my lips. I scorned such a proceeding. Nay, more; I told my people that I was about to engage in single combat with that man, and I charged them to let him depart without injury if he should overcome me. Murder was ever abhorrent to my feelings, and it was not his death but my revenge that I craved. Traitor to the last, he fired a pistol at me whilst I was actually giving my men these directions, but fortunately his coward heart made his hand tremble, and he missed me. Then I called on his two friends to stand back as mine had done, and I attacked him.

"It was a fair fight; he had a sword and so had I, but I had right on my side and the deep sense of bitter injury, whilst he had a bad, black heart, and the knowledge that he was face to face with the man whom he had bitterly and cruelly wronged. Could there be a doubt as to the issue of such a combat? After a very few passes, I broke through his guard, and, having him momentarily at my mercy, I slashed his face from ear to chin and gave him a mark which he will carry to his grave."

The Hermit.

At this point of the hermit's story Pedro gave a sudden start, but immediately resumed his former attitude of earnest attention to the recital.

"Furious with pain and rage," continued the hermit, "the count redoubled his efforts, and rushed upon me with the fury of a madman. But I parried his blows without difficulty, and he almost ran of his own accord upon the point of my sword, which passed clean through his body. He fell upon the ground and lay at my feet covered with his own blood. I stood by, and soon saw that no more was necessary. I was rid of my enemy for ever.

"For a few moments I stood over him hoping that he might speak, and perhaps say some words of repentance for his crime, and give me some clue by which even then I might have re-established my position and regained the honour of which he had so basely robbed me. But as I gazed upon the dying wretch, no sign of repentance or softness came over his features, over which the ashy pallor of death was already spreading. On the contrary, a look of unextinguishable hatred seemed to disfigure still more his wounded face, as he passed away from a world which his crimes had disgraced. He lay dead at my feet, and the sight was not one which I cared longer to look upon.

"I left his body where it lay and departed with my companions. But I had nothing left to live for, and life seemed to me a weary burden. I determined to quit for ever the haunts of men, and bury myself in the solitude of some wilderness or forest, where the sin and misery of man might cease to torment me. I roamed listlessly at first from place to place, until at last I heard of this forest which we have just quitted together. Therein I wandered, caring little whether the robbers who frequent, or the ghostly creatures who are said to inhabit it, should dispute my right to do so. Neither the one nor the other, however, troubled me until the occasion which has led to our acquaintance.

"I found a cave in the middle of the forest, wherein I took refuge, and which has been my home for many months. One companion alone I had—my pipe; one solace remained to me—tobacco. By the aid of this soothing weed I have

often been able to forget my sorrows—so far as such sorrows can ever be forgotten. Seated in or near my cave, with my pipe in my mouth, I have mused on the past with a bitterness rendered less intense as the sweet influence of the charm stole over me, and ever and anon has seemed even to inspire me with some faint hope for the future.

"Fancy then my sadness when I found that the large stock of tobacco which I had brought with me to the forest began visibly to decline. I eked it out as long as I could, but at last it vanished, and I was without my only consolation.

"I tried to bear it ; but man is only man after all, and it was impossible that I could do so. Therefore I resolved to make one more visit to the haunts of men, in order to supply myself with that which had become for me a necessity. Unfortunately, my wanderings had been quite desultory on first entering the forest ; I had gone hither and thither for some miles before I stumbled upon the cave, and consequently I had no idea which was the shortest way out into the open country again. So I could only march straight on, and hope for the best.

"I need tell you no more ; you know the sequel of my story, and how that, but for your kind assistance, I must certainly have perished. Now you know all that I have to tell, and the woes and misfortunes which have made me what I am."

Whilst the hermit was speaking, his companion listened with the utmost attention, and when he had ceased, remained silent for a few moments, as if buried in thought. Presently he lifted his head which he had allowed to sink forward into his hands, which rested upon his knees, and looked steadily at the other.

"I believe you," he said at length ; "I believe every word which you have told me. But there is one question which I desire to ask you, and I beseech you to answer me truly. Have you ever had any reason to believe that this precious Count Benjamin of yours was not dead after all—or is there any person of your acquaintance who at all resembled him in appearance ? "

"Friend," returned the hermit, speaking with the solemnity of one who felt he was.

touching upon subjects of a deep, if not sacred nature, "I will even answer you as freely and fairly as you ask me. I never knew any person who resembled that fiend, and I vow to you that, twenty-four hours ago, I would have sworn that he was not only dead, but that these eyes witnessed his death. Even now I know not how to doubt it. The gulf which separates the living from the dead may be deep or shallow—wide or narrow. No mortal man can say that it is impossible for one who has once left this world to reappear therein. I may have seen a spirit: I may have been under some strange delusion, but I do truly say and swear to you that the first doubt of the count's death which ever crossed my mind arose this very morning in the early twilight, before I joined you at your breakfast.

"Awakened by the sound of voices, I fancied that I heard that voice, whose tones I remembered but too well, and when, shortly afterwards, a figure crossed the cave, the height, the general appearance, the manner of walking, all reminded me forcibly of the man. Still I was so firmly convinced of his death that I should have thought it a strange but passing fancy of my brain, had I not had a glimpse of his face, and of a scar so exactly like that which must have resulted from the wound which I myself inflicted, that I confess my mind to have ever since been filled with doubts and misgivings."

"You do well to speak thus frankly," remarked the other, "and in return for this and your story I will in a few words relate to you my own. I am of an ancient but decayed family, and have knocked about the world since the age of fourteen, when my father's death turned us young ones adrift. It is not necessary to tell you of my adventures since then, both by sea and land. Suffice it to say that they have been many and perilous. At last, some three years ago, I became the captain of a small ship, with as gallant a crew as ever sailed on the blue sea. Why should I hesitate to tell you the whole truth? I am a rover—a pirate, if you like the name better. I love the ocean. I love the excitement of the wild, free life I lead; but I vow to you that, save in fair fight, no man has ever fallen by my hand, and no such

343

cruel actions as those of which you sometimes hear in old stories of buccaneers, have been perpetrated by my crew.

"Some time since, we discovered the caves and recesses with which this forest abounds— or at least those which lie within easy distance of the shore. We determined to make use of these as hiding-places, wherein our plunder might be secure until we gave up our roving life, or went off to some other part of the world. There are several caves more or less like that which we quitted this morning, and a large treasure, belonging to me and my crew, is deposited in these.

"I came on shore three days ago, to tell you the truth, in order to give a meeting to that very person whose presence has filled you with such strange emotion. I will tell you at once that he is no old acquaintance of mine. I met him first at a masquerade ball in a sea-coast city not far from this shore, about two years ago. He gave the name of the Baron Ferdinando, and seemed anxious to make my acquaintance, and that of two of my officers who were with me. In this he succeeded: we sailormen are not hard to know, or difficult to get on with when you know us. Since that time he has given us information of booty to be captured, which has been accurate and useful, and on one occasion he made a short expedition with us. Now that I think of it, he advised killing the prisoners, after we had captured a small vessel, and was not much pleased at the manner in which I at once negatived the proposal.

"To cut a long story short, he gradually made himself friends among my crew, among whom, by the by, he entered a fellow of his own—a sullen dog, whom I like but little, and whom they call Philippo. By this means he became acquainted with our course of life, our plans, our ways of living, and even of the position of those caves in which our treasure is hid. I have had my doubts about him once or twice, but when he appointed a meeting with me yesterday, I did not like to decline, especially as he stated that he had something of importance to communicate. That something was that a large merchant vessel, with a very valuable cargo, will pass off this coast some time to-morrow. The Baron's information has hitherto always been so correct, that I have no reason to doubt its accuracy on the present occasion. Yet I did not quite like the bearing of several questions he put to me as to the treasure—which cave held the most? of what did it exactly consist? had we thought of the difficulty of moving it when we wished to do so? The questions were asked in a simple and natural manner, but experience has made me suspicious.

Now if this man turned out to be your confounded Count come to life again, I should be more suspicious still. Suppose he is treacherous—he might bring us into trouble easily enough, and who but he would get the treasure afterwards? He did not recognise *you*, certainly, or he would probably have tried to pay off old scores, and verily he would have had a good opportunity. As it was, he suggested putting a knife into you, and if he and the old hag you saw (who lives in these caves and looks after them a bit for us) had been alone, I would not have given much for your chance. But it was not likely that I had saved a fellow's life to let him be butchered by an ugly, ill-conditioned son of a gun like that. He excused himself from joining us in this expedition, but said he would not be far off, and could be of more use on shore. I want no unwilling hands in *my* vessel, and he may come or go just as he pleases. But if he means treachery ——"

Here Captain Pedro clenched his fist and shook it, softly and silently, before him, in a manner which betokened no good to the individual of whom he spoke, if he should bring himself within its reach after having given occasion of offence to its owner.

Both men sat silent for a short time, and then the Hermit said—

" Whether he be Ferdinando the Baron, or the Count Benjamin come back to life, is more than you and I can tell. But if there be treachery in the world, it is written on that man's face. It is your duty—and it will be your wisdom—to guard against it."

" True," replied the other, " but how is this to be done? Every minute I expect to see my vessel rounding the bay. I invite you to come on board. Close to the shore we must await

344

the arrival of the merchant vessel. I see now what treachery Ferdinando can practise upon us, since he will not be with us. My crew are faithful and brave. Suppose that he is really villain enough to intend to carry off our treasure from the caves, he will find himself terribly mistaken if he thinks to escape our vengeance. We should follow him to his death—and it would be but justice to slay him."

As the two conversed, a small vessel was seen rounding the bay from the direction in which Pedro had told the Hermit he expected his ship to come, and the captain soon recognised it as his own. They descended to the shore, and a boat was presently sent off, in which they rowed back to the ship.

The crew appeared to be a reckless, merry set of fellows, but treated their captain with respect, and evidently regarded him with affection. He invited the Hermit to come down into his cabin, and when there, suggested to him a plan which had come into his head.

" It is possible," he said, " that if Ferdinando and Benjamin are one and the same person, you may recognise the man he has put aboard this ship as one of my crew. He is but a poor sailor, anyhow, but may be a good man for all that. Now do you stand at my cabin door, or rather just behind it, so that you can see well, and I will call this man with several others, from the end of the passage, so that they must pass the door in coming to me. Note them well, and see if you remember the face of any one of them."

Accordingly, the captain went a little way from his cabin, and (using nautical phrases which I forbear to repeat, for fear of making a mistake in them) called several of the crew by name, whilst the Hermit stood in such a position as enabled him to see them without being seen.

Captain Pedro then returned to his cabin and found the Hermit pale with emotion. In the man Philippo he had recognised the servant who had betrayed him to Count Benjamin, and enabled the latter to carry his abominable designs against him to a successful issue. He no longer doubted that the villain Count intended treachery also in the present instance. What was to be done? They might seize

Philippo and endeavour to wring from him a confession of his master's schemes. But to this there were two objections.

First, that he might not know them, and secondly, that the crew might dislike the arrest of one of their number upon the mere word and suspicion of a stranger. This notion, therefore, was at once discarded.

Captain Pedro's chief apprehension was for the concealed treasure. After hearing the Hermit's story, he had come to the conclusion that Count Benjamin—for he no longer doubted the identity of Baron Ferdinando with the villain—had a design upon the contents of the various caves, and that he might possibly have confederates in the forest at that moment, and intend to carry off the treasure whilst he knew that the pirates were engaged upon their present scheme. The more he thought it over, the more likely did this appear, and he expressed to the Hermit his doubt whether it would not be better to land a portion at least of his crew in order to visit and guard the caves.

To this, however, there were also weighty objections. The crew barely numbered seventy men all told. If the Count had really concealed friends in the wood—and how could they tell but that the very people who had attacked and left the Hermit for dead might belong to his party?—was it not probable that they would be in sufficient numbers to be able to overcome any such small detachment as could be well spared from the crew? It would be useless to send less than twenty-five or thirty men to make the thing tolerably certain, and the caution of the pirate captain forbade him to attack any vessel with such a reduced number of sailors as would then be left in his vessel. This plan, therefore, was also ultimately abandoned, and none other seemed to suggest itself.

At last it occurred at the same time to both the Hermit and Captain Pedro that there would be great advantage in the adoption of a middle course. The Hermit was of little use on board ship, nor indeed was he by any means anxious to join in a piratical attack upon peaceful traders. At the same time, he felt bound to render any service he could

345

legitimately afford to the man who had saved his life. He was therefore quite willing to land again upon the shore, accompanied by three of Captain Pedro's most trustworthy men, who knew every corner of the caves in which the treasure was hid, and could conduct him safely thither. It was settled that they should at once proceed to the nearest cave for the purpose of discovering whether there was anything suspicious, or whether things were all right, after which they were to return to the shore and signal the vessel by means of a white handkerchief if the latter, a red if the former should turn out to be the case.

Accordingly, without the crew being generally informed of what was going to be done, the Hermit and his three companions were quietly sent off in a boat and landed upon the shore, the former being much gratified by the present of a quantity of the best tobacco sufficient to last for a couple of days even if he should make a continuous use of his pipe.

The small party advanced to the edge of the forest, which they cautiously entered, and proceeded by a narrow pathway which the pirates were able to discover by marks made by them on former visits to the same place. When they had gone some distance, they stopped, and the eldest of the three, a wary old sailor named Stefano, told the Hermit that they were now within a few hundred yards of the entrance to one of the caves, wherein a large quantity of their valuables was hidden. He proposed, with the Hermit's permission, to go forward alone from the point at which they then stood, in order to see whether they might safely enter the cave. Presently he returned, and told them that all seemed safe, but that he could perceive that some one had visited the spot since they were last there.

The four men advanced, and presently arrived at a small opening in the side of a large rock, much overhung with branches of trees, which had to be pushed aside before it could be well discovered. Here they paused, and Stefano pointed to the ground, whereupon were impressed the marks of footsteps, evidently of tolerably recent date. They listened attentively, but could hear no sound, so they crept quietly forward into the cave.

All was still and silent as death. The passage into this cave was but short, and the cave itself appeared to have no other egress than the aperture by which they had entered. One of the pirates now struck a light, and for a moment the sudden change from darkness to light dazzled them all.

As soon as they were able to see more clearly, an exclamation of surprise and wrath burst from the three pirates. Their treasures had been buried on either side of the cave, or thrust away in various recesses around it. But the place was not as they had left it. The hand of the spoiler had been there. Many things of little value appeared to have been contemptuously tossed aside, but the best part of their treasure seemed to have disappeared. Nor did it seem as if the robbery had been perpetrated in a hurry. The earth had been carefully dug up, bags and boxes of coin and other valuables abstracted, and a thorough search made over the whole cave. Who, then, were the robbers?

Stefano, who had been informed by Captain Pedro of his suspicions concerning the individual whom the pirates knew as Baron Ferdinando, had no doubt at all in the matter, and at once informed his comrades of the same. Loud and deep were their threats and curses upon the head of the supposed robber. He had certainly, however, not been alone, nor could the robbery have been perpetrated by one person only. The question was, how many assistants had he with him? Then, how had they conveyed away their booty, and in what direction had they gone?

Further examination answered the second of those questions.

Although no other opening appeared at first sight, by which men could enter the cave, it seemed that at the far end there was an aperture leading into another place of the same kind, wherein the ground sloped upwards at the further end, and allowed of the easy passage of more than one man into a wider and larger excavation, from which it was not difficult to pass out into the forest. The footprints here showed the Hermit's party that it was by this means their treasure had been carried away, and also that some half-dozen persons

at least must have been concerned in its abstraction. Outside the cavern, moreover, they perceived the footprints of some beasts of burden, and the mystery was so far solved. Whoever it was who had visited their hiding-place and taken away their goods, had doubtless provided himself with horses or mules, which he had laden with the proceeds of his expedition.

What were they to do? If they pursued the robbers, they would probably overtake them, but the result of their doing so might not be entirely advantageous, as, considering the probable number of the party, they would run no inconsiderable risk of losing their lives as well as their property.

Meanwhile time had been slipping away. I do not think I have clearly stated that which was the fact, namely, that the Hermit had passed an afternoon and night on board Captain Pedro's vessel, and that it was in the early morning that he had again been put on shore. Since that time several hours had elapsed, and the captain would doubtless soon expect news of their expedition. As they could evidently do nothing by themselves, they judged it best to return to the shore without further delay, and communicate with the vessel.

In a very different frame of mind, therefore, from that in which they had landed a few hours before, they began rapidly to retrace their steps to the shore. They had accomplished something more than half the distance when the loud sound of cannon broke upon their ears. The pirates looked at each other with a smile, and remarked that the captain was speaking to the merchant ship, and that they should just be in time for a share in the plunder, which might help to make up for that which the crew had lost by the treachery which had despoiled their cave. The firing continued as they hastily pushed their way through the forest, and the men remarked to each other that the ship which they had attacked must be making a better fight than common, but that it would be of no avail against Captain Pedro.

Presently they came out upon the beach, and approached near to the water's edge. An unlooked-for, and no less unwelcome sight met their eyes. Instead of seeing their own ship proudly clinging as it were to the side of her enemy, and the flag of the latter hauled down, as her crew fled before the pirate boarders, a totally different state of things seemed to exist. Captain Pedro's vessel appeared to be sheering off from the merchant ship (which was much the larger of the two) as well as she could, whilst the deck of the latter seemed to be thronged with men, who were keeping up a heavy and continuous fire of musketry upon the baffled pirates, whilst every now and then came a puff of smoke from the side of the larger ship, followed by a flash, and then a deep, rolling sound as of distant thunder rolling up the bay.

It was evident that Captain Pedro had "caught a Tartar," and the Hermit's companions cast looks of blank dismay upon the scene before them. It was not of very long duration. They could distinctly hear the cheers and shouts of the enemy as they maintained their fire upon the pirate vessel, and it became soon apparent that she could only escape by a miracle. As miracles do not generally occur on behalf of respectable people, much less in aid of those who live by plundering others, it was hardly to be expected that this channel of escape would open before Captain Pedro and his crew. Nor indeed did it do so.

They returned a feeble fire for some time, but gradually it slackened, and after a tremendous volley from the merchantman's defenders, and a few more discharges from her heavy guns, the pirate vessel slowly toppled over on one side, and appeared to be about to settle down and disappear. No white flag had been shown—no signs of surrender given—perhaps because it was known to be useless, but more probably because those who manned that vessel knew not what yielding meant. But as soon as the fate of their beloved ship appeared to be beyond all doubt, the two younger of the Hermit's companions threw themselves on the ground and fairly wept with shame and rage. Old Stefano roused them from this condition.

"Up! men," he cried, "there is something yet to be done! see, some of our men have escaped from the ship, they may yet be saved!

Courage! do not give way to despair which can help nobody!"

With these words he encouraged his two mates, and at the same instant the Hermit perceived that which the more experienced eyes of the old sailor had discovered before, namely, that from amid the smoke and spray which surrounded the sinking vessel, a boat was emerging, rapidly pulled by strong arms towards the shore. The same causes prevented her being seen by the crew of the larger vessel until she was half way between the ship and the beach. Then they raised a loud shout, and directed their fire upon those who were evidently the only survivors of the pirates.

But the boat kept on her way until within some forty or fifty yards of shore, when a lucky shot seemed to strike her, and with a loud shriek from some of those on board, she broke up, and her crew were in another instant struggling in the water.

Up to this moment the Hermit and his companions had remained stationary, silent, but deeply interested spectators of what was going on. But when they saw the boat thus swamped they could restrain themselves no longer, and leaving their posts, they rushed down eagerly into the sea, as if to meet and save any of their comrades who might yet be alive.

It was a moment of suspense, of excitement, even of agony. At that particular spot the trees and shrubs came more nearly down to the water's edge than at any other point, since the boat's crew had naturally steered for the landing-place where they might most quickly find shelter from the enemy's bullets. It was soon evident to those on shore that some at least of their friends would reach them in safety. The merchantman was too far to render it probable that many men, if any, would be hit whilst swimming singly in the water, and before long one after another landed and joined the Hermit's party.

Their attention, however, was specially directed to one man who was gallantly supporting another as he made his way to the safety of the shore, and as they rushed to relieve him of his burden they discovered that it was none other than Captain Pedro himself, supporting the almost lifeless body of Philippo.

The latter had escaped all the previous dangers of the fight, and was among the crew of the boat who seemed so nearly free from further peril, when the shot which capsized the boat drove a splinter into his body, inflicting a wound which utterly prevented his attempting to swim to shore.

His was the shriek which had reached the ears of the Hermit's party when the shot struck the boat, and without any doubt he must have perished then and there, but for the resolution and bravery of Captain Pedro. The latter, seizing the wounded man, plunged with him into the sea, and by dint of almost superhuman exertions, succeeded in bringing him to land.

Out of twenty men who had manned the boat, ten were saved besides these two, the others perished either from injuries received before or after the shot struck the boat, or else because, being unfortunately unable to swim, they had nothing for it but to be drowned.

No sooner were the survivors on shore, than they hastened to seek the friendly shelter of the trees already mentioned, carrying Philippo with them. Before anything else was said or done, they watched with deep anxiety the conduct of their foes, who, they apprehended, might follow them on shore. They were, however, soon relieved from this fear. The pirate vessel had settled and gone down like a log. The boat which had attempted to reach the shore had also been destroyed, and although the victors might have seen, or at least might have expected, that some of her crew must in all probability reach the shore, they did not feel inclined to follow them into the depths of a forest wherein the risks they would possibly encounter would be greater than any advantage

to be derived from the capture or destruction of the few survivors of their enemies. So they made no sign of pursuit, or even of approaching any nearer to the shore, and as soon as this had been satisfactorily entertained, the Hermit began to inquire anxiously into the causes of the disaster.

It was soon explained. The merchantman had been no merchantman at all. Disguised as such, she carried guns far superior in weight to those of the pirate, and was manned by a crew at least four or five times as numerous as that of Captain Pedro, and had soldiers, well, armed and ready for action, on board. She allowed the pirate to come quite close to her and showed no signs of resistance.

Had her crew waited until Captain Pedro had given the signal to his boarders, nothing could have prevented the capture or destruction of him and his whole crew. Fortunately for these, or for those few, at least, who now survived—by some mistake the merchantman disclosed her real character before the captain's ship had actually thrown her grappling-irons and sent on her boarders. It was too late, indeed, for the vessel to escape, and many of the crew had been killed at the first discharge from the decks of her opponent, but the result had been that which we have seen.

None of those who had been saved with Captain Pedro were seriously hurt, except Philippo, the men who had been badly wounded among the boat's crew having naturally enough been those who had failed to reach the shore. It did not take many words for the captain to tell his tale to the Hermit, who in return informed him of what they had seen at the cave. Pedro stamped in fury upon the ground.

"That vile Ferdinando!" he cried, "would that he stood here before me!"

(To be continued.)

PICTURE PAGE WANTING WORDS (FOR PRIZE STORY.)

THE SEA.

350

THE SEA.

BY THE EDITOR.

OU ask why the sea is so restless,
    Why it changes both colour and form;
Why it sparkles and shines, or looks angry,
    When 'tis grand with the terrors of storm.

"Oh! wee little Nell, my sweet grandchild,
    A marvellous thing is that sea;
Its wonders, its terrors, its changes,
    Strange mysteries ever will be.

"It is deeper than man can e'er fathom,
    It has shores which no ship has e'er found,
In its depths there are wonders untold of,
    With its surface it kisses the ground.

"My Nell must not cower or shudder
    As she looks at the beautiful sea;
Little one, though to some it is cruel,
    'Tis kind both to you and to me.

"Just think how many a voyage
    Grandfather has made in a ship;
Just think of the shells you've discovered,
    And this morning—just think of your dip!

"Then think of the fish and the sea-weed,
    And all the Anemones bright—
Of the sand, and your wonderful castles:
    Love the sea, Nell, that gives you delight.

"Love, Nell, all our Maker's creations,
    Full of beauty the great and the small;
The glorious sea with its wonders,
    Earth's caverns, or mountains so tall!

"And now, little woman, come kiss me,
    Get your hat, and we'll go for our walk;
Hand-in-hand we'll enjoy the sea-breezes,
    And then we'll go on with our talk."

351

PUZZLES.

DIAMOND PUZZLES.

1.

My first's a useful article of which you're all aware.
My second's what you might be, if you were not what you are.
My third's a country for tea-planting, famed afar.
My fourth's a name more fit for slave than king or czar.
If you cannot find my fifth, my second then you are.

2.

One clue I'll give to find my first,
Which is, its exactly the same as my last:
For I'll tell you as much as I durst.
If you don't find it out too fast.
I'll tell you some more if you like.
My second you do when you thirst,
But you don't when you drink too fast:
So I've told you my second and first.
P'haps you don't understand what I've said:
It a fearful muddle you call,
And you can't get it into your head.
Or I've laid my third for you all.
My fourth is a puzzle, but still
For thousands it sometimes may sell.
Of my fifth I've not more to say
Than of my puzzle it forms a part,

Just to help out my rhyme it means vain;
And arrogant--words of that sort.
My sixth is not what it is.--
"How is that?" you declare, like a shot,
As red-hot with anger you fiz--
"How can a thing be what it's not?"
Now if it were what it is,
My Puzzle, I tell you, would stop;
Whereas I've a letter to add,
The same as the one at the top.
At last you have now reached the end,
And, if you're not out of your mind,
Just read it once more, my good friend,
Then, perhaps, 'twill be easy to find.

DOUBLE ACROSTIC.

Read my initials down aright,
A warrior will come to light.
My finals, upwards read, will show
His greatest victory, I trow.

1. A town in the Bay of Biscay.
2. Not suited.
3. A king of Israel.
4. Regular.
5. Impetuosity.
6. Display.
7. Debate.
8. A niche.
9. A pronoun.
10. Mistakes.

Answers to Puzzles on Page 320.

CHARADES.

1. Somerset.
2. Denmark.
3. Samson.
4. Weather-glass.
5. Postman.

DOUBLE ACROSTICS.

1.

1. N arcissu S.
2. O utla W.
3. R y E.
4. W in D.
5. A antelop E.
6. Y ar N.

2.

1. A lderma N.
2. M arbl E.
3. E ndo W.
4. B arel Y.
5. I utagli O.
6. C ourie R.
7. A hnwic K.

WORD SQUARES.

1. Star.
2. Tale.
3. Alas.
4. Rest.

HOODIE.

By Mrs. MOLESWORTH, *Author of "Hermy," "The Cuckoo Clock," &c.*

CHAPTER XII.—HOODIE AWAKES.

" And till we're nice old ladies
We'll love each other so."

HEN Martin joined the two little girls again, her face looked not only grave, but white. Maudie felt frightened, she hardly knew why. Hoodie, in a state of defiance to meet the expected scolding, was so amazed at its not

coming that the surprise kept her quiet. So they all three walked home in silence, though as fast as possible. No lingering by the way to gather flowers, or to watch the ducks in Farmer Girton's pond! Martin held a hand of each little girl, and merely saying now and then, "We must go straight home, my dears," marched steadily on. It was a strange unnatural kind of walk—the children felt something mysterious about it, without knowing

353   A A

what, and poor Martin's heart was terribly sore. She *could not* scold Hoodie, naughty as she had undoubtedly been, for sad fears were picturing themselves before her—what might not be the result of Hoodie's disobedience?

"Supposing," thought poor Martin, who was of a very anxious, as well as affectionate disposition, "supposing this is the last walk we ever have together? oh dear, oh dear— Scarlet fever is an awful thing once it gets into a family, and the kind that is about is a bad kind, they say."

She did not lose her presence of mind however. As soon as ever they reached the house, she sent the two children straight up to Maudie's room, a plainly furnished little room opening out of the day nursery, and told them to wait there till she came to them. Then she went at once to see their mother, and some time passed before she came up to them.

"What's the matter, Martin?" said Maudie, timidly. "Why do you look so sad?"

She did not notice that her mother had followed Martin into the room.

"Martin is rather troubled about something," said her mother, "and you must both try to be very good. And I want to tell you that dear little Hec and Duke are not coming home this evening. They are going to stay a few days at the Rectory."

Maudie gazed up into her mother's face. She saw there were tears in her eyes.

"Mamma!" she exclaimed. Then in a low voice she whispered, "I understand, mamma. I'll try to be good, and I'll pray to God for us not to get the catching illness."

Mrs. Caryll stooped and kissed her.

"I knew you would be good, dear, and try to make Hoodie so too. Poor Hoodie— she does not know what her disobedience may have caused."

The next few days passed slowly and strangely. It was strange and dull to be without the boys, and to Hoodie it was particularly strange that no one scolded her for what she knew she had deserved scolding for. They went out a walk twice a day, by the doctor's orders, who came to see them the morning after the unfortunate visit to the cottage. Every one was very kind, but every one looked grave, and very soon

Hoodie began to find it very dull to have no lessons to do, no Hec and Duke to play and quarrel with, and to have to spend all their time in the two rooms, except of course when they were out with Martin, who never left them for a minute. It was very dull, but worse was to follow. On the morning of the sixth day, Maudie woke with a headache and a bad pain in her throat, and bravely as she tried to bear it, it was plain to be seen that the poor little girl was suffering very much. Martin would not let her get up, and an hour or two after breakfast, Hoodie, sitting alone and very disconsolate in the day-nursery, heard Dr. Reynolds and her mother coming up stairs. She jumped up and ran to meet them.

"Mamma," she said, "Martin won't let me play with Maudie and I've nothing to do. Martin is very cross."

Mrs. Caryll looked gravely at Hoodie.

"Hoodie," she said, "you *must* be obedient."

"And Miss Maudie doesn't want her, ma'am," said Martin, appearing at the door of Maudie's room. "She can't bear the least noise; and any way it's better for Miss Hoodie not to be near her, isn't it, sir?" she asked, turning to the doctor.

He shrugged his shoulders.

"As to infection," he said, "separating them now is a chance the more, that's all one can say. But one must do one's best. And in any case the child is better out of a fevered atmosphere. I would prepare another room for her, I think," he added to Mrs. Caryll, and then they both went into Maudie's room and Hoodie heard no more.

Hoodie sat by herself, drumming her little fat legs on the side of the table.

"I wonder what they mean," she said to herself. "I wonder what the doctor means about affection. That's loving—at least people always put it at the end of their letters whether they're loving or not. I think people tells lots of stories when they'se big—*lotser* than when they'se little. And it's all that horrid Martin that's stoppened my going in to Maudie's room —I don't believe Maudie said she didn't want me."

Just then Martin put her head out at the doorway of the inner room.

"Miss Hoodie," she said, "please ring the bell—there's no bell in here—and when Jane comes up, tell her to send Lucy to speak to me at the other door—the door that opens on to the passage."

Hoodie executed the commission with great alacrity—even having a message to give was better than having nothing at all to do, and ringing the bell had always been greatly after Hoodie's own heart.

Somewhat to her surprise, a few minutes after Jane had gone down again in search of Lucy, Lucy herself came into the nursery.

"You were to go to the *other* door. What a time you've been of coming up," said Hoodie politely.

"I've *been* to the other door, Miss Hoodie, and Martin has told me what she wants me to do," replied Lucy. "Poor Martin, I'm right down sorry for her, and poor little Miss Maudie," said Lucy. "Now, Miss Hoodie, I'm going to take you out into the garden a little, and when we come in I'm going to stay with you in the sewing room."

Lucy's manner had become more decided, and somehow Hoodie did not make any objection. She let Lucy put on her hat and take her into the garden, quietly enough.

"Is Maudie *very* ill, Lucy?" she asked.

"I hope not," said Lucy, "but it's too soon to say much yet."

"Why are you sorry for Martin?" was Hoodie's next inquiry.

"Oh, because it's such a upset, and her that's that fond of you all," said Lucy. "I'm sure if there's anything I can do, I'll be only too glad. I'm very glad I've had the fever."

"Why are you glad? When did you have it, and was it the affection fever like what Maudie's got?" asked Hoodie.

Lucy did not laugh. She was rather a matter-of-fact girl.

"I had it when I was six, and people don't often, almost never, have it twice," she replied. "That's how I'm to take care of you, Miss Hoodie, otherwise they'd have been afraid of my catching it. Your mamma's a very kind lady that way, and it's dreadfully catching—just see how poor Miss Maudie's got it with that one minute in that cottage the other day."

355

Hoodie stared at her.

"Did Maudie catch it that day she ran to tell me to come away from the baby's mother's cottage?" she said.

Lucy stared at her in turn.

"Of course," she said. "Didn't you know that, Miss Hoodie? It can't be helped now, you see, and we must hope Miss Maudie will get better. But it'll be a lesson to you to be obedient another time. Let's go and gather some flowers, Miss Hoodie, and make a little nosegay for you to send in to Miss Maudie."

But Hoodie shook her head, and she had a look in her face which made Lucy wish she had not told her what she had, though never doubting but that the child already knew it.

"Maudie wouldn't care for any flowers from *me*. Nobody will ever love me at all now," she said. "It was me that made Maudie ill. Oh, I do wish God had made me ill instead of Maudie, for everybody loves her, and nobody loves me."

"Miss Hoodie," said Lucy, really startled. "You *mustn't* talk so. Everybody would love you just as they do Miss Maudie if you'd try to be a good and obedient little girl."

Hoodie shook her head again.

"You don't know, Lucy," she said. "I have tried and it isn't any good, so I've left off."

Lucy trembled a little as to what this announcement might be followed up by, in the way of special naughtiness. But her fears were misplaced. Hoodie was perfectly good and gentle all day—almost too much so indeed; Lucy would have liked to see a touch of her old self-will and petulance, for she could not help fearing she was to blame for the strange depression of Hoodie's spirits. She was very kind and good to the little girl, and did her utmost to amuse her, but it was a strange, sad time. The house, lately so cheerful with children's voices and the patter of their restless little feet up and down the passages, was now silent and gloomy, and the servants spoke with hushed voices and went about with anxious looks. Hoodie was not allowed to go near Maudie's room—she only saw her mother and Martin now and then at the end of the passage, or out of the window, for they were both engrossed in nursing Maudie. Every morning Hoodie sent Lucy as soon as she awoke to ask for news of Maudie, and though she said very little, there was a look in her eyes when Lucy brought back the answer—"Not much better yet, Miss Hoodie,"—that went to Lucy's heart.

"I'll never say Miss Hoodie has no feelings again," she said to herself, "never."

After a few days there came a morning when Lucy, who was not very clever at hiding *her* feelings, came back to Hoodie looking graver than usual, and with something very like tears in her eyes.

"Isn't Maudie better *yet*, Lucy?" asked Hoodie with a sad sort of impatience.

"She couldn't be better *yet*, Miss Hoodie," said Lucy, "an illness like that always takes its time."

"But is she *worser* then?" said Hoodie, staring up in Lucy's face.

"I'm afraid she is, rather. Her throat's so sore," said Lucy, turning away.

Hoodie said nothing, but sat down quietly on her little chair, leaning her head on her hands. A few minutes after, Lucy went down to the kitchen with Hoodie's breakfast things—she happened not to shut the door firmly, as the tray was in her hands, and when she came up stairs again, she was surprised to hear some one talking in the room.

"Who can it be?" she said to herself, for Mrs. Caryll had given strict orders that in case of any infection about Hoodie herself, none of the other servants were to be with her. Lucy stopped a minute to listen. The voice was Hoodie's own. She was kneeling in a corner of the room, and the words Lucy overheard were these—

"Maudie is worser," Hoodie was saying, "Maudie is worser, and if she keeps getting worser she'll die. And it wasn't Maudie's fault that she got the affection fever. It was Hoodie's fault. Oh, please, dear God, make Maudie better, and Hoodie won't mind if *she* gets the fever, 'cos it was her fault. Hoodie's been so naughty and poor Maudie's good. And everybody loves Maudie but nobody *can* love Hoodie. So please, dear God, make Maudie

better," and then she ended in her usual fashion—"For Jesus Christ's sake. Amen."

Lucy stood holding her breath at the door. When she saw that Hoodie got up from kneeling and sat quietly down on her chair again, she ventured to enter the room. Hoodie looked at her rather suspiciously.

"Lucy," she said, with a touch of her old imperiousness, "I think you should 'amember to knock at the door."

"Very well, Miss Hoodie," said Lucy meekly, for somehow she could not have helped agreeing with whatever Hoodie chose to say, "I'll not forget again."

Hoodie sat quite quiet, still leaning her head on her hands, doing nothing and seeming to wish for nothing.

"Are you not well to-day, Miss Hoodie?" Lucy asked, at last.

"Yes," said Hoodie, "I'm kite well, and I think Maudie 'll be better to-morrow."

But all day long she continued very, very quiet, and once or twice Lucy wondered if she should let Hoodie's mother or Martin know how strange the child seemed.

"I'll wait till to-morrow any way," she decided. "It seems a shame to trouble them more to-day, for this has been much the worst day with Miss Maudie, I fancy. It's to be hoped it's the turn."

And when to-morrow morning came she was glad she had not troubled them, for Hoodie seemed better and brighter than for some days past. She did not seem impatient for the news of Maudie, not as impatient as Lucy herself, who ran along to tap at Martin's door as soon as she awoke, and came back with a relieved face to tell Hoodie that the news was much better this morning, Maudie seemed really to have got the turn.

"I knew she'd be better to-day," said Hoodie composedly. "Didn't I tell you so, Lucy?"

And when they went out into the garden she carefully gathered a nosegay for Maudie, choosing the prettiest flowers and tying them together with a piece of ribbon she took off one of her dolls.

"Take those to Maudie's room, Lucy," she said, "and tap at the door, and tell Martin they're for Miss Maudie with Miss Hoodie's love, and she's very glad she's better."

"Miss Maudie will be pleased, I'm sure," said Lucy, thinking to herself as she said so how very pretty Miss Hoodie was looking. Her eyes were so bright, and her cheeks so rosy, and on her face there was such a pretty smile while she was arranging the flowers, that Lucy could not resist stooping down to kiss her.

"Never was a sweeter child than she can be when she likes," said Lucy to herself, as she made her way with the nosegay and the message to Maudie's room.

Altogether things were beginning to look much brighter again, and, reassured as to Maudie's being really better, Mrs. Caryll went to bed that night for the first time for a fortnight, with a lighter heart.

"Maudie is much better," she had written that evening to Cousin Magdalen, "and it is not now likely that Hoodie will get the fever, as so many days have passed. Somehow I have never felt very uneasy about Hoodie from the first, though 'by rights,' as the children say, she should have had it and not poor Maudie, as it all came through her disobedience. And even if she had got it, I should not have felt so anxious as about Maudie—Hoodie is so very strong. But I hope now that we need not be anxious about either, and that our troubles are passing over."

Poor Mrs. Caryll would not have written so cheerfully had she known that that very afternoon Lucy's fears about Hoodie had again been aroused. The little girl would not eat anything at tea-time, though she drank eagerly two or three cups of milk. And after tea she said her head ached, and she was so sleepy and tired that Lucy thought it well to put her early to bed.

"Such a pity," thought Lucy, "just when she was looking so bright this morning. I wish I could think she had just caught cold, but the weather's so fine, it's not likely."

All night Hoodie tossed about uneasily. She started and talked in her sleep, and by morning she looked so flushed and strange that Lucy felt that she must at once tell Martin, and that there could be no question of Hoodie's getting

up and being dressed. She wanted to get up, poor little girl, but her head felt so giddy when she raised it from the pillow that she was glad to lay it down again. And before the day was many hours older, there was no doubt that Hoodie had got the fever.

She knew it herself, though nothing was said about it before her, and she had her own thoughts about it in her mind, which she expressed to Lucy when no one else was there.

"I've got the affection fever, Lucy," she said. "I'm sure I have, 'cos I asked God to make Maudie better 'cos it wasn't her fault, and I said I wouldn't mind if I had it, 'cos it was my fault."

And poor Lucy, not knowing what to say, turned away to hide the tears in her eyes.

"I don't think we need be anxious about her," said Mrs. Caryll to the doctor, "she is so much stronger than Maudie?"

But Dr. Reynolds did not reply very heartily; the truth being that he saw from the first that Hoodie was likely to be much more ill than Maudie had been. And Hoodie herself from the first, too, seemed to have a strange, babyish instinct that it was so.

"I'm glad Maudie is better," she said often during the first day or two, to Lucy, "'cos you know it wasn't her fault. I don't mind having the affection fever, but it is rather sore. Everybody loves Maudie so, it's a good thing she's better."

"But everybody loves you too, Miss Hoodie," said Lucy, tenderly, "specially when you're such a good, patient little girl."

Hoodie made a movement as if she would have shaken her head, only the poor little head was too heavy and aching to shake.

"No, Lucy," she said, "not like Maudie, 'cos she's so good, and I'm not. I did try, but I had to leave off. And my bird's dead, you know, though I did ask God to take care of it every time I said my prayers. But I'm glad God's made Maudie better. I 'appose it's 'cos she's good. But I don't mind having the fever —not now my bird's dead, 'cos he did love me, didn't he, Lucy? "

Her mind was beginning to wander, and for many days and nights Hoodie knew nothing of anything that passed about her. Sometimes she seemed in a sort of stupor, at others she would talk incessantly in her little weak childish voice, till it made one's heart ache to hear her. She did not suffer so much from her throat as Maudie had done, though otherwise so much more ill. The fever seemed to have seized her in its strong, cruel arms with so hard a grasp, that often and often it appeared to those about her as if it never again would let her go, but would carry her away out of their sight, without her even being able to bid them good-bye—murmuring ever those sad words which seemed to be burnt into her childish brain, about nobody loving her because she wasn't good like Maudie, about having tried in vain to be good, and that her birdie was dead and God didn't love her either, always ending up that it was a good thing Maudie was better, "wasn't it, Lucy?" Though when poor Lucy choked down her tears to answer cheerfully "Yes, indeed, Miss Hoodie," poor Hoodie could not hear her voice, and began again the same weary murmurings.

It was very sad for them all—most sad of all for Hoodie's mother, whose heart grew sore as she listened to her poor little girl's faint words. It seemed to her that never before had she understood her child, and the great longing for love that had been hidden in her queer-tempered, fanciful nature.

"Oh, Hoodie darling, we do love you—dearly, dearly," she would sometimes say as she bent over her; but the bright eyes, too bright by far, gazed up without seeing, and the weary little head, shorn of its pretty tangle of fuzzy hair, moved restlessly on the pillow, while Hoodie kept talking about her dead bird and nobody loving her, through the slow weary hours while life and death were fighting over her little bed.

"If she dies without knowing us again, it will break my heart," said Hoodie's mother to the doctor; and what could he say, poor man, but shake his head sorrowfully in sympathy?

They tried to prevent Maudie knowing how ill Hoodie was, but it was impossible. When people are ill, or recovering from illness, they seem to guess things in a way that is sometimes quite astonishing, and so it was with Maudie.

She was now much better—she had been half-dressed and lifted on to a sofa in her own room some days ago, but when she found out about Hoodie, she fretted so dreadfully that it threatened to make her ill again.

"Oh, do let me see her?" she cried. "I don't mind if she's too ill to know me. I don't mind if she can't speak to me, but I must see her. Poor Hoodie, dear little Hoodie," she went on, the tears streaming down her face. "Oh, mamma, I don't think I was always very kind to her. I used to tell her we'd be happier without her, but I *do* love her. Oh, do let me see her?"

For unfortunately, through hearing some of the servants talking, Maudie knew some part of what Hoodie had been saying in her unconsciousness, and it was this that was distressing her so greatly.

Oh, children dear, remember this—there is *no* pain so terrible, no suffering so without comfort, as the feeling sorrow *too late* for unkindness or want of tenderness to others—little sharp words which did not seem so bad at the time, careless or selfish neglect of the wishes we could have gratified with just a little trouble—how they all rise up *afterwards* and refuse to be forgotten! Our grief may then exaggerate our past unkindness perhaps, and, as is the way with our weak human nature, things out of our reach seem of double value; the affection we knew to be always at hand we never prized enough till we lost it. But should we not take this as a warning? Avoid the *habit* of small unkindnesses, of sharp, hurting words—even though in your heart you do not mean them. Try, my darlings, every hour and every day, to behave to each other as you would wish to have behaved, were this day to be your last together. Then indeed even the sore parting of death would lose half its bitterness—the kingdom of Heaven would already have begun in your own hearts—the happy kingdom where there is neither sorrow nor bitterness, nor tears—the kingdom over which reigns the beautiful Spirit of Love.

At last there came a day on which the doctor said that without risk Maudie might be taken to see Hoodie—only to see her—there was no thought of her speaking to Hoodie, or

Hoodie to her, for the little girl was lying in a stupor—quite quiet and unconscious, and out of this stupor, though he did not say so, Dr. Reynolds had but little hope of her waking to life again. The fever had let her go at last, had thrown her down, as it were, careless of how she fell, and the poor little shaken worn-out Hoodie that it had left there, white and thin and lifeless, hardly seemed as if it *could* ever rouse up again to live and talk and play—and there was nothing to do but to wait.

So Maudie was carried into the room where this unfamiliar Hoodie was lying, and allowed to look at her poor little face and to cry quietly to herself as she looked. In whose arms, children, do you think she was carried? It was in Magdalen's. When she heard of the trouble that had fallen over her little friends she could not rest till she came to them. She had had the fever long ago, she wrote; she was so strong that nursing never made her ill or tired—she could sit up a whole week of nights without being knocked up. But when she arrived she found that in the way of actual nursing there was little to do. Hoodie lay still and lifeless—all the restlessness gone; for her indeed, it seemed to Magdalen, there would never again be anything to do, no care and tenderness to bestow—and the thought brought burning tears to poor Magdalen's eyes, though she bravely drove them back, and did her best to comfort Maudie and her mother.

"Cousin Magdalen," said Maudie, when they had sat for a few minutes by Hoodie's bed, "Cousin Magdalen, can't we do *anything* to make her better? Oh, dear, dear little Hoodie, oh how I wish I had never been the least bit not kind to her."

Then raising herself in her cousin's arms, she knelt on her lap, and leaning her head on Magdalen's shoulder, she said, while her voice was broken with sobs—

"Oh, dear God, *please* make Hoodie better. We do so love her—and she doesn't know how we love her, because I've been unkind to her sometimes. Oh, dear God, *please* make her better."

And then, her voice changing a little, as if she were afraid that her simple entreaty was hardly solemn enough to be considered

359

"prayer," she added, like Hoodie, "For Jesus Christ's sake. Amen."

A slight movement just then made itself heard in Hoodie's cot; a flutter more than anything else. Magdalen, gently putting Maudie on her chair, started up in alarm. She knew that any change in Hoodie was now most critical. She bent over the child, the better to observe her. A faint smile came fluttering to Hoodie's face, and in another moment, with a little effort, she opened her eyes. But she did not seem to see, or if she saw she did not recognise Magdalen, for the word that she whispered was "Maudie."

Low as it was, Maudie heard it.

"She's speaking to me," she exclaimed.

"Yes, Hoodie dear, what is it?"

Magdalen lifted her on to the bed. She could not refuse, though afraid that perhaps she was not doing right. The two little sisters lay close together.

"Maudie," whispered Hoodie again, in a little, weak, faint voice. "Maudie, I was waking, and I heard you speaking so nice. I heard you say 'Please God make Hoodie better, 'cos we *do* so love her.' I didn't know that, Maudie, I've been so naughty. But if you want me to get better I'll try. God's been very kind except that He let birdie die. But I love you better than birdie, Maudie, and perhaps God 'll make me better too."

She could not say any more, but she smiled again as Maudie put her arms round her and covered her face with loving kisses. Then Martin, whom Magdalen had summoned, gave her the wine the doctor had ordered in case of her awaking; Hoodie took it meekly, and then turning her head on the pillow murmured gently, "I'm very sleepy, but I'll soon get better. The affection fever was very sore, Maudie."

Hoodie was right. From that moment she did begin to get better. They were still very anxious about her—there were many days still to pass before it was quite sure that she was out of danger, and for many more after that she was so weak that it hardly seemed as if a child's usual strength could ever come back to her. But in time all came right, and terribly ill as she had been, the fever left no lasting harm. And the life that began for the two little sisters from this time was a bright and peaceful one—they had learnt to value each other and each other's love as never before, and from the moment that it came home to Hoodie that she really took into her fanciful little heart how dearly she was loved, half her troubles seemed at an end. Day by day she learned new ways in which even she, a little simple child, might help and comfort and cheer those about her—she lost the old sore feeling of being nothing but a trouble and a worry, an "alvays naughty" Hoodie, and never again was any one tempted to say that among the fairies invited to baby Julian's christening, those of sweet temper and unselfishness had been forgotten.

They are grown-up now—much more than grown-up. If you met them in the street, if they came to call on your mother some day, you would not guess they were quiet little Maudie and queer-tempered Hoodie. And as for Hec and Duke!—they could jump you up on their great strong shoulders as easily as the ogres they used to be so fond of making up stories about. There is only one thing which, if you heard it said, as it often is, might remind you of the children I have been telling you about. Men and women as they are, separated sometimes by half the world, it has always been remarked of them how much they love each other—brothers and sisters in deed, as well as in name, friends, tried and true to each other through all the difficulties and sorrows and troubles which have come to them as to everyone else in this world of many colours; of rainy as well as of sunny days—of discouragement and disappointment, but of happiness too —and love through all.

Cousin Magdalen's dark hair is beginning to get white now, but still I feel sure you would think her very pretty. Did she ever write out the story that she promised to tell Hoodie and the others some day? By the bye I must not forget to ask her the next time we meet.

TALKS ABOUT THE MONTHS.

DECEMBER.

By Mrs. GEORGE CUPPLES.

"Chill December brings the sleet,
Blazing fire, and Christmas treat."
* * * * *
"Merrily, cheerily, ring out the chimes!
Christmas-tide is the most blessed of times!
Once more returned to us, Christmas is come,
Bringing sweet joy and peace to every home."

THE flowers, the foliage, and the verdure have all vanished, and the winds howl and are cold and piercing; all the flocks are gathered into sheltered home enclosures, where they may receive from the farmer's provident care the food which the earth now denies them. The labourer is now no longer seen in the fields, but the sound of his busy flail is heard daily in the barn. Birds, insects, reptiles, all seem to be gone, and the squirrels that played their merry antics on the forest-trees have shrunk into the hollows among the branches till the cold winter is past.

The milky way, or milky circle, is aglow in the sky at this season; a radiance caused by the condensation of the light, or innumerable little stars closely contiguous to one another. According to a myth this glorious track is spoken of as

" A path sublime there is in cloudless heaven
Brightly displayed, and by its stream distinct.
The Milky Way 'tis called, by which the gods
Pass to the regal halls and palace gates
Of the great Thunder deity."

The window panes are covered with fairy tracery, and the boys are out having a fine time of it, skating or sliding. Many a shy bird, rarely seen at any other season, now draws near to the houses in search of food, and sly Reynard is stealthily stealing round the farmyards and hen-roosts in the hope that some stupid fowl has stayed beyond hours, or that Mary the henwife has forgotten to lock the door carefully. If she has, the cunning fox will not be long in pouncing upon an unfortunate hen, and in spite of its squeals and shrieks will hurry it off to his den O.

The robin is twitting out his low sweet song in the holly bushes, the red clusters of berries throwing a cheerful warmth around the places in which they grow. Here and there we see the mistletoe sometimes growing on old apple and hawthorn trees and very rarely on the oak. Wherever the Druids selected a grove of oaks for their heathen worship, they always planted apple-trees about the place, so that the mistletoe or *All huel* might be trained around the trunks. The mistletoe was carried in the hands of the Druids during the festival called Yule-tide, and then laid on their altars as an emblem of the life-giving advent of the Messiah.

December, like the three preceding months, derives its name from the place which it held in the old Roman calendar, where the year was divided only into ten months, as its name, which comes from the Latin word *decem*, ten, indicates.

In this month the Romans celebrated their Saturnalia, which were games or holidays in honour of Vesta, their goddess of purity. December was called by the Saxons *Winter-Monat*, or the winter month, and after their conversion to Christianity *Heligh-Monat*, or *holy month*, on account of the Nativity of our Saviour.

The twenty-first of this month is St. Thomas's Day and falls on the winter solstice, the shortest day in the year. In some parts of the country the day is marked by a custom, among poor persons, of *going-a-gooding*, that is to say they call at the houses of their richer neighbours, to beg a supply either of money or provisions to procure *good things*, or the means of enjoying themselves at the approaching festival of Christmas. And in other parts, too, it is customary for children on St. Thomas's Day to go round from house to house to beg for apples, singing—

" Wassail, wassail through the town,
If you've got any apples, throw them down ;
Up with the stocking, and down with the shoe,
If you've got no apples, money will do ;
The jug is white and the ale is brown,
This is the best house in the town."

But of all the days in the year perhaps the one we look forward to with the greatest expectation of happiness is Christmas Day. The day before we are up betimes decking the house with holly and some sprays of mistletoe in every corner, while we know that cook is busy mixing the great pudding in the kitchen below. We are called away from our decorating to help to carry it to the great copper, for of course no pot can be found large enough to take it in. Aunts and uncles and cousins by the dozens are all present to witness the interesting ceremony, the little ones quite envious of Harry and Dick, who have been selected by cook to carry the precious burden. Cook has no fears in her mind as to it turning out the best pudding that ever was made, and so walks along with as serene a face as possible.

And when the pudding has been safely dropped into the copper, and when all the decorations have been completed, and evening has come, how delightful to draw round the blazing fire when the yule-log is burning at a fine rate, and listen to some delightful story; for we all know that people who cannot tell stories at other times can do so very well on Christmas Eve.

" 'Twas Christmas broached the mightiest ale,
'Twas Christmas told the merriest tale;
A Christmas gambol oft could cheer
The poor man's heart through half the year."

The burning of the yule-log is an ancient Christmas ceremony of our Scandinavian ancestors, who at their feast of *Juul* used to kindle large bonfires in honour of their god Thor ; and many animosities and unkind words are forgotten and forgiven round the hearth on this night, for in the face of such a cheery blaze one cannot help remembering it is lighted to welcome the morning on which Christ the Saviour was born.

It is pleasant to think that this night is being kept by almost every one the world round. That no matter where our friends may be, Christmas Eve is being remembered. Perhaps there is no yule-log being burnt, but they think of those that were in their youth, and their hearts are turned homewards, it may be from a vessel in the Arctic regions frozen in, hard and fast ; or it may be from one becalmed in the Tropics. At any rate, whenever and wherever the thoughts of home come on this night, one feels the better for them for many a long day. Therefore let us try to keep up the old customs as much as we can, the best and most harmless of them, for everything that draws our recollections homewards in after years is certain to draw them heavenwards also.

In Germany, Christmas Eve is for children the most joyous night in the year. The Christmas-tree is all in readiness, and the presents that all have been preparing, some of them for many months before, are now spread out and make a goodly show. And as we said before, the poor have not been forgotten, and many a little tree well laden with useful things has found its way from the hands of the children of the rich to those of the poor.

What gay times there used to be in merry old England at Christmas. "What!" you say, "merrier than we have now? Are you forgetting the large pudding that has been boiling away all this time in the pot? and

363

could any one be happier than when it is seen coming in at the dining-room blazing with bright blue flames?" Well, I grant the shouts are loud and merry enough at sight of the pudding, still, for all that, the festivities in the olden times must have been on a very large scale indeed. In a few places the old games connected with Christmas are kept up with much spirit, both indoors and out, such as the mummers or masquers, or *guisers* as they are called in the northern counties, when the boys go out dressed up in all sorts of masquerade dresses acting little plays, appropriate to the occasion, or not appropriate, as the case may be. Then there is the game of snap-dragon ; and what fun it causes when any one who makes a clutch at the raisins in the bowl gets his fingers burnt in the flaming spirits instead.

" Here he comes with flaming bowl,—
Don't he mean to take his toll,
Snip! Snap! Dragon!
With his blue and lapping tongue
Many of you will be stung,
Snip! Snap! Dragon."

In many places sweet voices have been practising the Christmas carols, and of all the ceremonies, perhaps this is the best of all, and when we are awakened by the sweet singing on Christmas morning, our hearts go out in kindly feelings towards our friends, and we forget all the jealousies and strifes that may have risen up between us, and we respond with all our heart,

" Now to the Lord sing praises,
All you within this place,
And with true love and brotherhood,
Each other now embrace ;
This holy tide of Christmas
All others doth deface.
O tidings of comfort and joy !
For Jesus Christ our Saviour
Was born on Christmas Day."

We have thus traced the seasons through their varied changes. We have seen all Nature shrouded in the sleep of Winter—then bursting into life in Spring—then glowing with beauty and sweetness during Summer—and finally, having completed the purposes for which all this life and beauty were called into being, during Autumn—again sinking into repose.

And we have seen that all are beautiful, that all show the care and protecting hand of Almighty wisdom and goodness. That although we now look in vain for those charming objects which have lately delighted us, yet we know that this is only a period of rest, and that all things will soon reappear in the freshness of new-born beauty.

We have learnt too that the changes in the seasons work together for good; let us then in return be grateful to Him who directs them for our benefit and comfort.

> "There's nothing bright above, below,
> From flowers that bloom, to stars that glow,
> But in its light my soul can see
> Some feature of the Deity."
>
> *　　*　　*　　*　　*
>
> "Then let us all rejoice amain
> 　　On Christmas-day, on Christmas Day ;
> Then let us all rejoice amain
> 　　On Christmas Day in the morning."

HARK, HARK, THE DOGS DO BARK!

♪ = 220

Hark ! Hark ! the dogs do bark, the beggars have come to town.

Some in rags and some in tags and some in vel - vet gowns.

HARK, HARK, THE DOGS DO BARK!

JERRY.

JERRY.

BY THE EDITOR.

THINK that all you little folk will agree with me when I say that those people who don't care for dumb animals are almost, if not quite, as disagreeable as those who do not care for children. I cannot bear the people who say they like both children and dogs in their proper places. Children in the nursery, dogs in the kennel, and so forth.

I know I am rather fonder of the society of children and animals than most people, and, to prove this, I will just mention that at the present moment, while I write, I am enjoying the society of my little son, who favours me with a cheerful tune on a particularly loud and discordant trumpet; while two amiable white rats—pets of the same young person—are running about the table, gaily scampering, every minute or two, over my manuscript. Some people might object to this. I do not; for, as I said before, I like children and animals, and do not mind even if they are sometimes out of their proper places.

I do not think that any of my readers who are not fond of animals will glance at this story: the very picture on the opposite page will be disagreeable to them. Now to me it is simply delightful. Darling doggies; so human-looking, so child-like in their hatred of a dose of physic! And the poor fellow on the chair, the unlucky one who is to be dosed this time —But it is of him I have to tell my tale.

One cold cold evening in December—when King Winter was reigning in good earnest, when fingers turned blue and noses red, and people indoors were thinking they wouldn't go out, while those out of doors were thinking how soon they could get in to their warm fire-sides, if they were lucky enough to have any —a poor blind man stood at the corner of a street in London, selling pencils. In one numbed shaking hand he held his little stock in trade, and with the other he held a piece of string, the end of which was attached to a dog's neck. This dog was not handsome, he was of no particular breed, and indeed was uglier than most mongrels. Still, Jerry—that was the dog's name—had as affectionate a heart,

and as good an understanding, as most of his kind, which is saying a great deal. Jerry was of a dull brick-dust colour, with a harsh wiry coat; plain all over, but he had handsome dark eyes, and curious long brown eye-lashes.

The winter's evening was very cold, as I have said, and the blind man, not finding that his trade increased as the hours went on, and feeling, only too acutely, that the cold did so, determined upon wending his way homewards. The corner which he had taken possession of was at some little distance from his home : he had chosen it because it was in the midst of a crowded thoroughfare, and his pencils generally found purchasers amongst the passers-by.

Poor Edward Brown had been struck by lightning ; and had so lost his sight. His children were grown up, and scattered about the world, and he and his old wife were left to live alone. She was a tidy, respectable old Irish woman, who kept their one poor room neat and comfortable, and did such scraps of needlework as she could get to do. But the bread-winner was still the blind man, with his basket of simple wares, which he went out to sell every day, led by his good dog Jerry.

In this bitter weather Jerry's kind old mistress made her husband carry a piece of carpet for the dog to sit upon. "Lest the crayture should get the rheumatics," said she ; "for shure it's agin the nature of a dog to sit without stirring hisself about a bit." Whether the sight of Jerry and his carpet attracted the attention, and softened the hearts of people, I cannot say ; but it is certain that the little basket he held in his mouth was seldom empty. However, on this particular evening people seemed too cold, and too intent upon their own affairs, to take much notice of the dog or his blind master. Accordingly they made their move homewards rather earlier than usual.

The cord by which Jerry's blind master held him was but slight, and a good deal worn, but Jerry did not require that sort of strength to hold him near his master ; the affection in his honest heart did that. However, this winter's night, just as the two friends had started, they were suddenly involved in a dense and excited crowd. Some unfortunate oxen were being driven through the street, and wearied, thirsty, goaded, and bewildered by the lighted shops, the passing carts and carriages, and the general hurry and flurry of the London thoroughfare, two or three of the miserable creatures rushed upon the pavement. In the confusion the blind man was jostled, poor Jerry trodden upon, the basket knocked over, and the cord between Jerry's neck and the blind man's hand was broken.

Jerry was kicked and chased; the oxen butted at him, and nearly trampled him to death. To make a long story short, poor Jerry was lost; by no fault of his own he was separated from his master.

Before I tell you what became of him, I had better say a word about Edward Brown. He was rather knocked about at first, and lost a good many things out of his overturned basket, but the alarm over, people round him seemed suddenly to recover their wits, and seeing he was a blind man, they set to work to help him. Then it was he found that his best friend, his faithful Jerry, was gone; and his trouble was indeed very great. He called and whistled, but all to no purpose: poor Jerry was careering wildly along at that time with his broken string at his neck, many streets away; while several foolish mischievous boys were running after him, calling out "mad dog!" he, poor fellow, in reality the most sane and sensible of them all. Jerry at last rushed into a dark passage, and lay panting in a corner, while the hue and cry passed him. He was safe; but oh, so miserable! for, you may be sure, a feeling of self-reproach gnawed at the honest dog's heart, when he remembered that he had allowed himself, in the dreadful confusion of the moment, to be driven from his blind master. Jerry felt he was lost, and his heart ached when he thought that he should perhaps never see his kind friends again.

After a little while Jerry turned out from his place of refuge, and trotted demurely down the street, determined, this time, to give no foolish person an excuse for saying he was mad. On the contrary, he adopted the most sedate and sensible air he could put on, and

walked solemnly along, sniffing right and left, trying to discover, if possible, the way to his humble but beloved home. Alas for poor Jerry! through many hours of the cold winter's night did he wander about the almost deserted streets, but the longer he wandered the more confused he became, the less he seemed to think he should ever find his way home. Nobody was about who would speak a kind word to the poor lost dog. Now and then he saw a policeman, but then he hid himself as well as he could, for the first one he met had chased him the length of a street with what Jerry felt convinced was no friendly intention towards him. At last, worn out and faint from cold and hunger, our unhappy friend curled himself up in a doorway and slept.

Now in the early morning a man came walking down the street in which poor Jerry lay. He walked with a halting step, as one who was not in his prime, and who was not ignorant of the pangs of rheumatism. The name of this man was Caleb Carely, and he was just such a person as you would expect to see after hearing his footsteps. He was rather below the middle size, with legs bending forward at the knees. He had grey hair, just enough to form a fringe round the back of his head, and a shaven face: Caleb had a good face, kindly and gentle-looking, in spite of its many wrinkles. His profession, or trade, was that of animal doctor; he could not be called a veterinary surgeon; I fear he would be looked upon by such as a quack; but he was quite celebrated for the wonderful cures he effected amongst the brute creation. Many ladies sent their favourites to Caleb, when they would not have trusted them to a regular veterinary surgeon; for Caleb was not only clever, but so wonderfully loving and kind to the animals, that they all loved him in return; and even little sick birds would soon learn to know him and come at his call. Caleb made his own medicines: he was a clever botanist, and had a wonderful knowledge of the medicinal properties of herbs, which he turned to good account for his dog, cat, rabbit, and bird patients. On this cold December morning he was on his way to the house of a friend—a dealer in herbs—in order to purchase one that he wanted for a decoction to be administered to a sick bull-dog.

As Caleb passed the doorway where Jerry lay he stopped, for he detected the dark mass lying motionless upon the cold stone. Stooping down, he touched it, and found a rough hairy substance beneath his fingers—the coat of the hapless Jerry.

"Hullo, my friend," said Caleb, "you've got a hard cold bed this freezing morning." Then lifting the dog up, he saw that poor Jerry was indeed in a bad way: his legs were cramped so that he could not stand, and his usually bright eyes now looked very dim.

"A mongrel, and not handsome!" said Caleb to himself; "however, he's a dog, and I'm partial to all of 'em—I'll see what can be done." So instead of going on to his friend's house, Caleb tucked poor Jerry under his warm coat—warm, though somewhat the worse for wear—and retraced his steps to his home.

I need not describe the good old man's home or its inhabitants: my readers have only to turn to the picture, and there they will see Caleb, surrounded by his patients, and about to administer a restorative dose to our poor friend Jerry, whom we see seated on a chair, looking, as Caleb himself said, "very sadly." The other dogs appear much interested in the proceedings; all but the bull-dog, who has a very sulky expression, and does not seem to care for anything or anybody but himself.

Jerry did not enjoy taking his dose, but afterwards he was grateful to his kind new friend, for he soon felt wonderfully better, and frolicked round Caleb, jumping up and licking his hand. Then, having enjoyed a good breakfast of hot bread and milk, he was quite able to run beside Caleb when he went out again in crder to get the herb he required. Jerry had a vague hope that his new friend might take him near his beloved home, and that he might be able to find his way to it. How our doggie longed for the power of uttering words!—he barked and barked, and talked in his dog language, as well as he could: he was quite beside himself for joy for a few minutes when Caleb stooped down, and patted him, saying: "You're telling me that you're lost: yes, I know it quite well, poor frozen fellow." But

when the old man added, "But why don't you tell me whom you belong to?" Jerry drooped his tail and hung his head in despair.

Caleb called at his friend's, procured his herb, and then turned to go home by another way. It was a bright, clear, frosty morning, and Jerry, refreshed and warmed by rest and food, and comforted by the good old Caleb's kindness, felt quite exhilarated as he trotted along by his side. The sun was out, people walked briskly; many carrying skates; and there was a cheerful appearance about the world in general which had a corresponding effect upon the lost dog. The only drawback to Jerry's enjoyment was his uneasiness and anxiety about his blind master. "What will he do without me?" thought Jerry. And in spite of his sorrow, a certain feeling of pleasure at the thought of his own importance—a weakness which even dogs are not exempt from—rose in his heart.

"Ah!" sighed Jerry, "if I could only see my dear master and mistress, I should be happy indeed!" Scarcely had he uttered these words to himself (in dog-language, of course), when Caleb abruptly turned a corner, and Jerry's wishes were fulfilled. Caleb had come by a way unknown to Jerry, to the very street the faithful dog knew so well. And—joy of joys! there was the blind man standing at his usual corner, with his basket of small wares and a stick; but alone! Regardless of passing carts or carriages, with a short sharp bark of delight, Jerry bounded across the crowded street, and was at his master's feet in a moment. I don't know who rejoiced at this meeting the most—Jerry, the blind man, Caleb, or Mrs. Brown, who found Jerry at his post, when she, in the course of the day, came to see how the old man was getting on without his dog. "And sure," she said afterwards, "whin I found the crayture sitting there beside him as large as life, why, if yer'll belave me, yer moight hev knocked me down wid a feather."

Caleb and the Browns became great friends owing to their introduction by Jerry; and they all had a happy dinner together on Christmas Day at Caleb's abode; his poor patients coming in for a share of good cheer, Jerry was made much of by the whole party.

SWEEP, SWE-E-P!

SWEEP, SWE-E-P.

FOR VE-RY LIT-TLE FOLKS.

POOR lit-tle sweep, with a round red face—
That is, red where the soot does-n't lie—
Stands out in the snow this cold win-ter's
    morn:
Sweep, Swe-e-p! is his con-stant cry.

It's hard to stand in the ear-ly dawn,
    When King Win-ter is hold-ing his own,
Out-side in the cold, when there's com-fort with-in,
    And cry *Sweep, Swe-e-p!* all a-lone.

When you're co-si-ly tuck-ed in your lit-tle warm beds,
    Pray think, lit-tle read-ers dear,
And pi-ty the poor boy co-ver-ed with soot,
    Who is cry-ing *Sweep, Swe-e-p!* so near.

He car-ries the brooms, and helps with the sacks,
    Works hard, and lives on poor fare.
On-ly a boy, with the work of a man,
    He is cry-ing *Sweep, Swe-e-p!* down there.

He earns his own bread, and his mo-ther's too;
    She is sick, as well as so poor:
But her brave lit-tle boy earns e-nough for both.
    He is cry-ing *Sweep, Swe-e-p!* at the door.

Oh, child-ren, whose homes are hap-py and bright,
    Who have all that care can be-stow,
Think how hard is the life of this poor lit-tle lad,
    Who is cry-ing *Sweep, Swe-e-p!* in the snow.

THE HERMIT.

By the Right Hon. E. H. KNATCHBULL-HUGESSEN, M.P., *Author of " Uncle Joe's Stories," &c.*

CHAPTER IV.

T that moment a deep groan broke from Philippo, whom the pirates had placed upon the ground and around whom they were standing whilst the above conversation passed.

" Poor fellow," said the Hermit, " his course is run, I fear : there can be little hope for him with that deep wound in his side."

So saying, he stooped over the wounded man,who at that moment opened his eyes and gazed upon the person whose voice he had heard.

Scarcely had he done so, when he gave a kind of a shriek and fainted away immediately. They dashed water in his face, and one of them gave him a sip of brandy from a flask which he had about him. Presently the man opened his eyes.

372

The Hermit.

"Where is he?" he said, "where is he? where is my dear old master? Surely it was his face I saw. Oh how cruelly I wronged him! I am punished now though. If he would but forgive me before I die: "

The Hermit stepped forward.

"Pietro Manti," he said, and the wretch started again when he heard the tone of the voice which pronounced his real name instead of that by which he had been known among the pirates. "Pietro Manti, I am not one to bear malice against a dying man. Grievous is the wrong you have done me. May Heaven forgive you as I do."

"Ah, Marchese!" groaned the man. "It is but too true that which you say. Yet before I die I can do something to restore to you that of which I helped to rob you. Witness all to what I now say;" he gasped for breath, but recovered himself by a mighty effort, and as Captain Pedro and the surviving pirates stood around, he said, slowly, but very clearly and with great earnestness, "I swear by all sacred things and by all which good men hold to be sacred, that I tell the truth now, when I know I am close to death. The Marchese Cellano here—my kind old master of old days—is as innocent as the babe unborn of anything of which he was charged by the Count Benjamin, and for which he was driven from his regiment. The Count gave me much money, I hid the cards and loaded dice where he told me, I was his slave. He wished, I know not why, to ruin the Marchese, and I, oh wretch that I am, I helped him to do it!"

As the wretched man spoke these words, the pirates looked at each other in astonishment, Captain Pedro being the only one of them who understood what they meant. The Hermit then spoke—

"You hear, my friends," he said, "what this man declares, and it is useless for me any longer to conceal my rank, though I had wished that it, together with much of my past life, might have been forgotten. I am indeed that unhappy Marchese Cellano, who was, years ago, ruined by the machinations and treachery of him whom you have known as Baron Ferdinando. But perchance this is not all ye have to hear, and there may be something more

373

closely affecting yourselves." Then bending over the dying man, he said,

"Pietro Manti, I have already assured you of my forgiveness, but if you would be forgiven elsewhere, make what atonement you can— Have you no more to tell? How came you on board the ship which has just been destroyed? What was your object, and what your intention?"

The man groaned again heavily.

"Ah me," he cried, "I die of thirst, and this pain which racks me through and through. For the love of heaven, water!"

They poured water down his throat again, and once more gave him some brandy, after which he spoke, though still with difficulty.

"The truth of what I have told you may easily be proved," he said. "Sewn tightly within my doublet is a paper which contains a statement which I drew up some time since, intending to extort money from Count Benjamin, if need should be, by placing it in the hands of a friend who should threaten him with exposure. It tells the whole story of the plot against the Marchese, and contains besides some notes from the Count to me, with directions which will help to show the truth, and some private memoranda of his besides with which I made free, in order to have proofs of what I should disclose if it became necessary. They will help my lord to establish his innocency. For me, the villain Count has deceived me with the rest of you—you are all betrayed!"

The pirates started, but at a gesture from Captain Pedro remained silent, whilst, after a gasp which seemed likely to be his last, the unhappy man continued—

"He sent me on board your vessel as a spy, to glean and impart to him all information respecting your proceedings, and the secret of your buried treasure. This last, however, he discovered for the most part without my aid, thanks to the open-heartedness with which you treated him, and which might have softened the heart of a man less base than he is, and turned him from his purpose. That purpose was to get rid of you all, and appropriate your treasure to his own purpose. This was the plan:—

"He was to give information of your being in

this bay to the authorities of the neighbouring country, and counsel them to send a ship, disguised as a merchant ship, but supplied with guns, and having, besides her crew, a number of soldiers sufficient to overwhelm you.

" Confident in the certainty of your destruction, I know he had planned to carry away your treasure yesterday or to-day—about the time at which he thought you would be watching for your supposed prey or actually attacking her. I was to have left you two days since, and he promised to ask the captain that I might go with him for a short time, in order to give me an excuse for leaving the vessel which I had joined by his orders. But he never made the request, but left me on board, unable to get away, doubtless believing and hoping that I should be killed with the rest of you, and thus the man who knew more of his crimes than any other man would be removed from his path for ever."

Here the poor wretch paused and gasped again—again they gave him water, but it was of no avail—he groaned again, then tried to speak once more, and then having raised his head a few inches from the ground, with a sudden convulsive movement fell back, dead.

For a moment the whole party remained silent, their hearts filled with mingled surprise and anger. Then the captain directed that the body of the dead man should be searched, and there indeed was found a packet such as that which he had described, which was immediately handed to the Hermit.

They forthwith deliberated as to what would be their best course to pursue. There they were, fourteen men besides the Hermit, but only the latter and the three who had gone on shore with him had any serviceable weapons except daggers, inasmuch as most of them had thrown away all that they could in their struggle to swim to the shore. It was evident, however, that there was but one chance of that which at this moment they valued almost more than their lives—namely, revenge.

From the account given by the Hermit and his party, and judging by the short time which had elapsed since the Baron Ferdinando had been with Captain Pedro in the cave wherein the Hermit had been carried, it seemed most

probable that the outer cave, which Stefano had visited, had been the first which the robbers had plundered. The question then arose, whether they would have been satisfied with the booty obtained there, or have gone on to empty the other caves also.

Pedro strongly inclined to the latter belief, and if so, it was scarcely possible that they could have accomplished their object within so short a period. He therefore determined that they should all go at once to the cave which they knew to have been plundered, and thence track the footsteps of the robbers, in order to find out which direction the latter had taken.

Accordingly, they advanced without delay upon the cave in question, and of course found things as the Hermit's party had told them. They found, however, something more. A good many articles of clothing had been among the concealed property, and these came in exceedingly well to supply the pirates with dry garments in place of those they wore, which had been thoroughly drenched in their involuntary swimming-match. There was a better find still in store.

The robbers, having secured what they considered the most valuable part of their prey, had not searched every hole and corner, and had chanced to overlook a recess in which Captain Pedro had concealed a quantity of arms. This was the very thing they wanted, and when in addition to this, they found a certain quantity of dried provisions which had not been removed from the place where they were hidden, they really began to feel quite cheerful again. Their captain gave them a few minutes for refreshment, and then, every man being armed and ready, they set out in pursuit of the robbers.

It did not require the sagacity of Red Indians to follow the trail, which lay before them without any attempt at concealment. The plunderers of the cave, whoever they were, had evidently loaded several mules with their booty, and had pushed on through places where the brushwood allowed them to do so, for some forty or fifty yards, until they had come into an old and almost disused track, along which they had turned and could be traced for several hundred yards further.

Here the tracks became somewhat confusing, but after a short investigation they came to the conclusion that the party must have separated, and Captain Pedro was not long in guessing what had happened.

"Those tracks," he said, "lead out of the forest, and in all probability the villain who has plundered our cave has sent some of his party with the beasts laden with the spoil, to carry it off, safe from our pursuit. But this smaller pathway, up which we can see that some of the fellows have gone, leads to another of our caves, and in all likelihood they have had it in their minds to go there and perform the same feat. They can hardly have had time to get away, and we shall catch them red-handed ; we will therefore follow at once."

So saying, the captain led the way, and the fifteen men advanced upon the track of the robbers. Ere long they arrived at the entrance of another of their hiding-places, but this appeared to have been entirely undisturbed, which puzzled the captain for a moment. Presently, however, he exclaimed, addressing the Hermit—

"I think I know what is the meaning of this. I do not think that I ever told that rascal of this cave, and I remember very well telling him that most of our treasures were hid in the cave near the sea and in that to which I first took you. This shows me that it must certainly be by him that this robbery has been committed, although indeed we had little cause to doubt it after what Philippo has said. He has probably gone on to the further cave, thinking that he would make a clean sweep of all our goods while he was about it."

Captain Pedro gnashed his teeth as he spoke, and again they pushed forward. In a little while they arrived at the very spot at which the captain, the Hermit, and the old woman had come out from the cave into the forest. The Hermit recognised it at once by the huge blocks of stone and rock already mentioned, and perceived from the time they had been walking that they had come by a somewhat roundabout way from the shore.

The party now began to advance very cautiously, for Captain Pedro knew that as no animals such as horses or mules could be taken into the cave on account of the narrowness of the passage, the party before them could not be far off, unless indeed they had passed by the cave altogether. Presently he directed the party to stop, and creeping forward with the greatest care, proceeded to investigate the matter alone.

Almost immediately he returned with triumph upon his countenance. Some twenty yards from the mouth of the cave, where the trees and brushwood became thicker, and the passage of a beast of burden almost impossible, he found three mules tethered to a tree, and apparently left alone. From this the captain came at once to the conclusion that the robbers, whosoever they might be, were few in number and could therefore be the more easily overpowered. Had they been numerous, he said, they would most likely have left one of their party with the mules, and also to act as a scout. As it was, he judged that they had all entered the cave, in order to bring out the valuables therein as soon as they could, and start at once upon the homeward track.

There was but one opinion as to the course to be pursued. The passage must be entered and the matter followed up at once. They might of course have waited until the robbers re-appeared with their booty, and have attacked them as they emerged from the cave, but the impatience of the pirates was too great, and these men, who had acquired the whole of their treasure by plundering other people, were just as indignant at being made the victims of a similar process as if it had all been gained by honest labour.

Each prepared himself for a struggle, and it was evident that there would be little mercy shown if they overcame the spoilers. Captain Pedro himself first entered the passage, but stumbled immediately over something which lay at the entrance. It was the body of old mother Breenwole, with a red handkerchief twisted round her venerable neck, which plainly denoted the method of her death. Not particularly lovely in life, the old woman's countenance was very much the reverse in her present state, and her features were distorted by the last agony. She had evidently been only killed a short time, for she was still warm, and the captain had no doubt that she must either have met the robbers accidentally, or perchance had been in league with Count Benjamin or Ferdinando, had helped to guide the party to the mouth of the cave, and had then and there met the due reward of her perfidy at the hands of the very people who were about to profit thereby.

Speculation upon the matter was idle, however, for it was evident that the hour for action had arrived. Having laid the body of the old woman aside, the pirates followed their captain, and one by one entered the narrow passage. Very quietly they crept along, stepping noiselessly over the rough stones, and taking every precaution that their approach might not be discovered by those they sought. After some little time they came very near the cave, and distinctly heard voices speaking in a low tone.

Captain Pedro looked round to see that his men were all following, crept on and on until he got to the rock round which the cave was entered, and then suddenly rushed forward. In an instant the state of things was apparent.

Five men were employed in rifling the contents of the cave. Four of these were engaged in pulling from their hiding-places the various articles of value which formed the treasure of the pirates, whilst the fifth was receiving them from the hands of his companions and arranging them on the table in such manner as to enable them to be the more easily carried away.

The first mentioned individuals were all unknown to the Hermit, and appeared to be of an inferior grade, but in the fifth he instantly recognised his enemy, the treacherous Count Benjamim. The robbers leaped to their feet as soon as they found they were discovered, and seized their arms. But Captain Pedro shouted in a voice of thunder—

"Back, dogs, ye are taken like rats in a trap, but your lives shall be spared if ye surrender—all but one."

As he spoke, his followers came rushing after him into the cave, and the robbers saw at once that resistance was useless. Count Benjamin, however, knowing well enough that for him the game was up, determined to make an effort. Ever crafty, his cunning did not desert him

even at this critical moment, and he resolved to play a desperate card. He addressed the pirates as coolly as if he were in command of a victorious force and they his captives, instead of the position being exactly the reverse.

"My men," he said, "your lives are all forfeit to the state. I, whom you see before you, can alone save you. I desire to do so. Do not be deceived: to take my life could help none of you, but aid me, and I not only promise you a free pardon, which my interest can obtain for you, but also an amount of riches greater than all that you have in this cave. I vow it on the honour of a gentleman."

He spoke boldly, and even the pirates who had been most incensed against him, were struck by the calmness of his bearing in that hour of danger. But Pedro left no time for hesitation.

"Friends!" he cried, "you hear a traitor's voice. Who sold us to the ship of war? Who has lost to us our own vessel? Who has plundered our caves? Is a traitor ever to be trusted? Believe this villain, and you put your necks in a halter."

The manner in which the pirates received these words at once showed the Count that he had nothing to expect from them. A glance at his companions told the same tale. They had already laid down their arms at the command of Pedro, seeing at once that this was their only chance for life. One hope only remained.

The ascent by way of the ladder through the tree was close behind the spot where the Count stood; he took his resolution immediately; with a rapid movement he overset the lamp, and at the same instant darted to the ladder. If, in the darkness, he could manage to accomplish the ascent, he might yet escape from his enemies. The result of his attempt threw the occupants of the cave into the greatest possible confusion. No one at first seemed to understand the position of affairs, and everybody ran here and there, stumbling over everybody else, and not knowing what had really happened.

Count Benjamin, however, never lost sight of his object, and made straight for the short passage behind him which led to the ladder—this once gained, and he felt that it would be like a new life given to him. He had no difficulty in finding the passage, having kept his eye on it as he threw over the lamp: he entered it, and cautiously, though as quickly as he could, crept up to the ladder: three more seconds and he would be safe! But at the very instant that he placed his foot upon the lowest round of the ladder, a powerful hand was laid upon his shoulder, and a deep voice thundered in his ear—

"Turn, traitor, and face Carlo Cellano!"

The unhappy wretch collapsed as if struck by a thunderbolt. His teeth chattered in his head; he trembled in every limb like one with the palsy, and with a groan of despair and horror, sank in a heap upon the ground.

The pirates after a short interval obtained a light, and were able to ascertain more exactly the position of affairs. As the robbers had been interrupted before they had been able to carry off any of the booty within the cave, and as this was the largest depository of their treasures, they were rather pleased than otherwise.

Matters might have fared much worse with them but for the avaricious nature of Count Benjamin, who, fearful of having too many associates to share the spoils with him, and relying upon the absence of Pedro's band and their probable destruction, had only taken with him seven companions in all, and had sent away three of them with the mules bearing the treasure captured in the first cave. Had he had the seven all with him in the last cave, they might have given some trouble to the pirates, and had he taken a larger body of men, and posted scouts outside, the position of Captain Pedro's party might have been awkward. As it was, however, all had turned out as the latter could have wished, save in the matter of the plunder of the smaller cave.

It now remained to be determined what should be done with the prisoners. The four men captured with the Count had been promised their lives by Captain Pedro, and although some of the pirates were rather inclined to grumble at this, yet they held, even in their rough life, that the word so given was sacred. Moreover, their chief reason for destroying these men would have been their knowledge of the secret of the caves, and the captain pointed out to

them that now they had lost their vessel, the latter would no longer be of the same service to them. So they agreed to spare the men's lives, and only bargained for being permitted to give them a sound flogging, which was duly administered under the superintendence of old Stefano, and was not soon forgotten by those who underwent it.

There remained Count Benjamin, alias Baron Ferdinando, to be dealt with. The Hermit, whom we may as well call by his real name, the Marchese Carlo Cellano, declared his desire that the wretch should be given up to the authorities, so that his own fair fame might be cleared before the world, and a punishment inflicted upon his enemy according to the due forms of law. But to this Captain Pedro stoutly demurred.

In the first place, he said, law was so uncertain, and lawyers such curious customers, that this Count or Baron, being rich and influential, might get off altogether. In the next place, although it might suit the Marchese to have the trial conducted before a court of justice, neither the captain nor his followers particularly desired to appear as witnesses in a place where inconvenient remarks might be made about themselves, and, added to these reasons was the fact that they had a very substantial grievance of their own against the prisoner, with whom they were resolved to deal upon their own account.

The request of the Marchese, therefore, was of no avail, and all that Captain Pedro would grant was that the accused should have a fair trial then and there. Confronted with his accusers, the miserable man lost all the former courage of his bearing. A ghastly pallor overspread his countenance, and he trembled in every limb.

Captain Pedro acted as judge, and directed twelve of his men to serve as the jury, whilst old Stefano and the Hermit stated their several charges against the prisoner. The four robbers who had been taken with him, and who scarcely felt themselves safe yet, willingly gave evidence as to his having hired them to assist him in plundering the caves, to which he had shown them the way.

He attempted no defence, and indeed

appeared paralysed with affright, and utterly unable to speak. The jury took but a very short time to consider, having resolved to find the poor wretch guilty before they had heard half that was to be brought against him. Then it became the duty of the judge to pass sentence, about which his only doubt was whether to yield to the loudly-expressed wish of some of the pirates that the prisoner having committed such crimes of treachery as to constitute him a worse criminal than was often found, should be put to death with such tortures as would aggravate the punishment to the greatest degree.

Here, however, the entreaties of the Hermit prevailed, and the wretched man was quietly strangled with the same handkerchief as that with which he had put an end to old mother Breenwole.

The pirates then prepared to quit the cave, carrying with them such of their valuables as they deemed it best to remove.

As the events of the last few days had changed the whole current of our friend the Hermit's thoughts, he desired them to accompany him out of the forest, and promised that, if they would give up the trade of piracy (to which respectable people had considerable objections), he would use his influence to obtain for them a free pardon, and such suitable employment as they might desire.

As they had lost their vessel, and the greater part of their comrades, the men, after some consultation, resolved to accept the offer. They accordingly conducted the Hermit out of the forest, accompanied him to the chief city of the country, and acted under his advice.

Everything turned out as well as could possibly have been expected. As soon as it had been found out who the Hermit was, and what had been his story, people could not make too much of him.

Not only were his friends the pirates pardoned, but people of position and consequence vied with each other in procuring employment for them. Captain Pedro was appointed to the command of one of the finest men-of-war in the service, and old Stefano became head butler to an affluent nobleman.

The Marchese Carlo Cellano became the rage.

His innocency having been completely established by the documents found on Philippo and by the latter's dying confession, everybody at once discovered that they had always believed him innocent, and it was astonishing to think that he could ever have been deemed otherwise by anybody. But although he found himself able to re-occupy his estates, and again enjoy his title and the privileges of his rank, he never attempted to re-enter his regiment, or mingle with those who, say what they would, had treated him as if they thought him guilty.

He held aloof to a great extent from all society, and clung with faithful tenacity to that pipe which had so comforted him in his solitude. Seated beneath a shady tree upon the lawn of his beautiful villa, or upon a couch at the window which commanded the most magnificent view over the surrounding country, he would smoke as if it was his greatest pleasure, and dream over the past with a feeling curiously commingled of joy and sorrow.

He had conquered in the struggle—but at what a terrible cost. His enemy had indeed fallen, but together with him had fled the hope of his own youth, the dear ones who had made that youth so happy—above all, the affianced bride whom he had so long and so faithfully mourned. She, indeed, lived, but, immured within the convent wall in which she had taken refuge from the base Count Benjamin, she seemed as much lost to him as if the grave had actually closed over her.

One day as he was musing over this, the one sorrow of his life which time seemed unable to alleviate or remove, a note was put into his hand, which he read, carelessly at first, but afterwards with more interest. It was couched in these words:—

"One who knew the Marchese Carlo Cellano in earlier and happier days would fain congratulate him on his return to life and fame. If the Marchese is in the orange grove of the Celli gardens at sunset to-morrow he may see the writer."

Our friend laid down the note and pondered upon the question — not whether he should accept the invitation, for to that he made up his mind at once, but as to who the writer could possibly be. Having no clue whatever, he soon came to the wise conclusion that he had better not guess when he should probably know without doing so in a few hours.

Accordingly, having fretted himself meanwhile as little as he could, he was at the appointed place at sunset on the following day. Several persons passed and repassed him, without speaking or taking any notice of him, until at last he observed that two figures, much concealed by long black veils, had done so more than once, and still did not seem to leave the place. He fixed his eyes upon them as they approached again, and as they came close to him, he saw the one grasp the arm of the other and distinctly heard the words—"It is he!"

The Marchese took off his hat, and bowing to the ladies, for such they evidently were, asked if they were expecting any one.

"Yes," replied the one who had not yet spoken. "We await a very old and very dear friend—but fear he has forgotten us."

At the sound of that voice the Marchese started as if he had been shot.

"That voice!" he cried—"Bianca? Is it indeed you?"

The lady threw back her veil and disclosed the features of his former betrothed.

"It is I, indeed, Carlo," she replied, "I who have never ceased to think of you, but who am, alas! forgotten."

"Forgotten," exclaimed he. "Never, dearest lady; but are you not a nun, whom it were a crime to think of? So I was told, and deemed that my misfortunes had separated us for ever."

"No action of mine has done so," replied the lady. "I have vowed no vow and taken no veil. I took refuge in the convent, as you know, and there have I stayed for these long years, but never whilst I believed you to be alive would I become a nun. The unhappy man who is dead spread reports of your death after his recovery from a wound which he said he had received whilst defending the convent from some robbers who were about to attack it. He was found upon the ground, run through the body with a grievous wound, and was long in recovering. But I never believed those reports, and I am as I was when I entered the convent."

This was not strictly true, as the lady must have been several years older, but it was sufficiently near the truth to satisfy our friend, especially when the story was confirmed by the lady's companion, who turned out to be none other than his own sister.

The rest of the story may be told in a very few words. The Marchese Carlo Cellano and Bianca were married as soon as the wedding clothes could be made and proper arrangements carried out. They lived very happily all their lives, and had strong sons and beautiful daughters to cheer their declining years. And for the good of all married ladies I may record it as a true and undoubted fact, that Bianca never once interfered with her husband's smoking. Now and then, it is true (but not often), she said that it kept him up a little too late at night, but on the other hand its soothing influences were very great, and during the whole course of their long and happy life as a married couple, Bianca always declared that, in her solemn judgment and opinion, a pipe of good tobacco was as desirable a thing for a Marchese as for a Hermit.

WINTER.

COLD, and chill, and drear,
    Is Winter.
Dull the closing year:
    Sad Winter!
All the world shines white
    In Winter.
Nearly always night:
    Dark Winter!

Huddling sheep, all cold,
    Dread Winter.
Alas! the year is old
    In Winter;
But though dark and chill
    The days of Winter,
" Peace on earth, Good Will "—
    Was sung in Winter.

Answers to Puzzles on Page 352.

DIAMOND PUZZLES.

1.
```
      A
    A S S
  A S S A M
    S A M
      M
```

2.
```
      D
    S I P
  S N A R E
D I A M O N D
  P R O U D
    E N D
      D
```

DOUBLE ACROSTIC.

Biarritz.
Unfit.
Omri.
Normal.
Ardour.

Parade.
Argument.
Recess.
Thou.
Errata.